Political Campaign Communication

Inside and Out

Second Edition

LARRY **POWELL**

The University of Alabama at Birmingham

JOSEPH **COWART**

PEARSON

Boston   Columbus   Indianapolis   New York   San Francisco   Upper Saddle River   Amsterdam
Cape Town   Dubai   London   Madrid   Milan   Munich   Paris   Montreal   Toronto   Delhi
Mexico City   São Paulo   Sydney   Hong Kong   Seoul   Singapore   Taipei   Tokyo

Editor-in-Chief, Communication: Karon Bowers
Assistant Editor: Stephanie Chaisson
Editorial Assistant: Megan Sweeney
Production Project Manager: Clara Bartunek
**Project Coordination, Text Design, and Electronic
   Page Makeup:** Integra Software Services, Pvt. Ltd.
Marketing Manager: Blair Tuckman
Manager Central Design: Jayne Conte
Cover Designer: Karen Noferi
Cover Photo: newscom

Credits and acknowledgments borrowed from other sources and reproduced, with permission, in this textbook appear on the appropriate page within text.

Library of Congress Cataloging-in-Publication Data
Powell, Larry.
  Political campaign communication : inside and out / Larry Powell, Joseph Cowart.—2nd ed.
    p. cm.
  Includes bibliographical references and index.
  ISBN-13: 978-0-205-00609-0 (alk. paper)
  ISBN-10: 0-205-00609-4 (alk. paper)
  1. Campaign management—United States.   2. Political campaigns—United States.
  3. Communication in politics—United States.   I. Cowart, Joseph, 1944–   II. Title.
  JK2281.P68 2013
  324.7'30973—dc23
                                                                    2011042908

1 2 3 4 5 6 7 8 9 10—CRW—16 15 14 13 12

PEARSON

ISBN-10:   0-205-00609-4
ISBN-13: 978-0-205-00609-0

CONTENTS

PREFACE

Both of the authors grew up in political environments, among families who assumed that political involvement was both a right and a responsibility of American citizens. The importance of politics was drilled into each of us well before we reached high school.

At the age of eight, Joseph Cowart worked in a precinct handing out literature for Wallace "Wah-Wah" Jones, a candidate for sheriff in Fayette County, Kentucky. By the time he was sixteen, Cowart was a precinct captain despite the fact he was not yet old enough to vote. By the age of twenty, he was a veteran political organizer and eventually became a full-time political consultant.

Larry Powell was a relatively late bloomer. His first campaign activity came at age thirteen, distributing literature during his father's run for a state legislature seat. As a junior in high school, he ran for student body president and won. His actual tenure in office was less successful—a lesson he interpreted as meaning he was more successful at understanding the campaign process than at governing.

For Cowart, politics was a family business. They made no money from this activity, but it was, as his mother said, "Our contribution to make our community a better place to live." She instilled a respect of, and duty to, democracy. Her lessons remained with him after years of representing veteran politicians, managing multimillion dollar campaigns, editing television spots late into the night, and shmoozing at length by telephone with reporters. His resulting philosophy of campaign leadership is simple. Don't make the candidate something he or she is not. Never lie. Always tell the objective truth and never "settle" for the technical truth. Don't ever mistake the candidate's accomplishments for your own accomplishments.

As a campaign professional, Cowart's contribution to these ideals has been to keep them foremost in his mind and in his planning while applying the latest technology, tactics, and strategy to the political landscape. His goal has remained the completion of campaigns in which candidates have the opportunity to express their ideas to an audience receptive enough to elect them to public office.

Larry Powell's father was a political activist. Harold Powell was a news junkie decades before CNN, Fox News, and other news networks went on the air. Evenings at home began with watching *NBC Nightly News*, the only network broadcast available at the Powells' rural home. Sunday mornings meant rising early enough to watch *Meet the Press* before heading to church. This all seemed normal at the time; Larry Powell didn't learn until he studied the Nielsen ratings at Auburn University that fewer than 3 percent of U.S. households tuned into the show.

Both authors realize that others may not share our desire to understand the intricacies and controversies of our chosen field of study. We do hope, however, that students will share our trust in the democratic process and that this book will help them better understand that process. We believe that by looking at campaigns from both an inside and outside perspective, each reader can become a more critical observer of the political communication process.

NEW TO THIS EDITION

Since the release of the first edition, political campaigns have adapted to a changing world. Thus, this edition includes several features not available in the first edition. Here is a brief overview of some of the most important changes in political campaign communication found within the second edition:

- Updated discussions to reflect the new research and knowledge in the field of political campaign communication are included throughout the text.
- A brand new chapter devoted to the Internet in political campaigns (Chapter 10).
- Newly added discussion on the role of media in political campaigns, including the "spiral of silence" and the "third-person" (Chapter 5).
- Updated discussion on campaign ethics include the ever-increasing number of ways in which candidates and campaigns can get into trouble (Chapter 16).
- Newly added discussion on the technique of embedding reporters into news events, a discussion on media bias, and a new section on the relationship between politics and entertainment media (Chapter 7).
- Updated and expanded discussion on the twenty-first-century development of two new strategies—Republican efforts to develop a "permanent majority" and Democratic strategies aimed at appealing to the "political brain" of voters (Chapter 3).
- Expanded discussion on new techniques developed in Internet polling and robo-polls (Chapter 11).
- New discussion on the major advancement of Internet protocols to contact voters via phones.

ORGANIZATION

What has not changed is our "inside and out" approach to learning about political communication. That approach has been continued and is similar to that of participant-observation research. We hope to provide analytical information useful to the outside observer, along with a campaign perspective that will contribute to an understanding of strategic decision making.

One of us is a professional outsider, a member of the academic community, who studies campaigns as an observer. The other is a professional insider, a campaign consultant whose career is that of a campaign participant. In this text, each chapter approaches its topic from both perspectives, although the seesaw of which view gets more attention will vary by topic. Interviews and campaign case studies further illuminate the insider perspective.

Organizationally, the book is divided into three sections. The first part provides an overview of political communication issues. Chapter 1, an introduction, identifies some of the distinctive elements of political campaign communication. Chapter 2 looks at academic research related to the development of political attitudes. This topic is sometimes omitted from campaign-related books, but we feel it is important for understanding the different perspectives that voters bring to any political campaign. Campaign professionals who overlook the socialization process are dooming themselves to defeats, and outside observers who do not consider it will typically oversimplify the causes of any particular electoral victory or defeat. Chapter 3 provides both an overview of campaign strategies and the book's first in-depth look at the inside of campaigns. This information provides the reader with some understanding of the processes involved in developing a campaign strategy and of the factors that can influence that strategy. Chapter 4 looks at the images of political candidates, an area that has drawn a great deal of attention from both the academic and consulting communities. It is also one in which the two communities seem to be converging toward a common approach of defining and understanding how electorates develop, maintain, and constantly re-evaluate their image of a candidate.

Chapter 5 examines media theory, with a heavy focus on the academic perspectives regarding the media and their influence on campaigns—including the Bullet Theory, Limited Effects Model, Agenda Setting, Uses-Gratification, and the Spiral of Silence.

The second part of the book provides more insight into the insider view by looking at the campaign team. Chapter 6 starts by looking at the team itself—the campaign organization. This chapter identifies and describes some of the roles and functions that an effective campaign organization must perform. Chapter 7 focuses more closely on campaign communication in the mass media. This chapter is the "inside" complement to Chapter 5, which looked at media from the "outside" perspective. The focus here is on the mechanics of developing, distributing, and assessing the effects of campaign media. Chapter 8 examines an often overlooked aspect of campaign communication: direct voter contact. There was a time when this was the major form of campaigning for many candidates—a time when winning an election meant seeing as many people as possible, shaking hands, kissing babies, and connecting with more voters than the opposition. The rise of television diminished this role, but it has never disappeared. Chapter 9 discusses the role of political speeches in campaigns. Our focus will be on distinguishing political speeches from other forms of speech making. An understanding of those differences helps the reader to understand how the construction and delivery of any other political message is related to the campaign process. Chapter 10 is a new chapter for the second edition. It looks at the ever-expanding role of online communications in the campaign process. This chapter examines social media, the Internet as a means of direct voter contact, and the Internet as a form of mass communication. Chapter 11, the last chapter in this section, looks at political polling—one of the mathematical components of any political campaign. We hope to demystify this process by explaining how a political poll is developed, implemented, analyzed, and used in a campaign.

The third and final section looks at five specific campaign concerns. Chapter 12 addresses press coverage and media relations, a topic that has practical implications for campaigns and creates serious philosophical issues for the academic community. The focus is on understanding the symbiotic relationship between the press and a campaign. We hope such an understanding will provide insight into why some issues are covered and others dismissed, and why some candidates are treated as legitimate contenders by the press while others receive little coverage. Chapter 13 looks at the role of political money in campaigns. One of the biggest differences between the academic and consulting views of campaigns may revolve around the role of campaign finances. Our goal here is both to help the reader understand the rules of the game as they apply to campaign finances and to focus on the rhetorical impact that money can have on campaigns. Chapter 14 focuses on the role of interpersonal influence. This topic has received a great deal of research from the academic community. As a result, communication scholars have gathered a great deal of insight into the way that voters converse with each other on political topics. A related topic, interpersonal communication among political elites, has received less attention. We take a look at the factors involved here, including lobbying and legislative cue-giving. Chapter 15 discusses critical event analysis—a topic of equal interest to both the academic and consulting communities. Many times, the public's response to any political candidate is based on the events associated with that candidate. An intern disappears from her Washington, D.C. apartment and a California congressman loses reelection. Terrorists fly planes into the World Trade Center and the Pentagon, and campaigns alter their schedules, cancel fund-raising events, and increase their use of patriotic appeals in campaign messages.

Finally, we end with Chapter 16 and a consideration of ethical questions in political communication. This second edition includes a new discussion on the increasing problem of resume inflation and a broader discussion of negative campaigning. We don't propose to offer many answers, but we do hope the reader will give ethical concerns more thought.

To consider these ethical issues fully, the readers should also realize that the two authors come from different ideological backgrounds. Joe Cowart's family roots are those of lifelong liberals. He has continued their tradition by working entirely for Democratic efforts and their allies (labor unions, for example). Larry Powell comes from a conservative political family. He grew up in an Alabama environment in which conservative Democrats became the first generation of Republicans in the South.

Our ideological differences have never been a problem. Neither of us believes that either party has a monopoly on the truth. We are both skeptical of any person—regardless of his or her political orientation—who argues otherwise.

We both believe in the value of the two-party system, but we both also believe this system was more effective when the disagreement between parties were about issues rather than personalities. Perhaps this book will make a small contribution toward redirecting the focus toward issues.

If so, we will consider ourselves successful.

GIVE YOUR STUDENTS CHOICES

In addition to the traditional printed text, *Political Campaign Communication: Inside and Out, 2nd Edition,* is available in the following format to give you and your students more choices—and more ways to save.

The **CourseSmart eTextbook** offers the same content as the printed text in a convenient online format—with highlighting, online search, and printing capabilities. Visit **www.coursesmart.com** to learn more.

MySearchLab® WITH PEARSON eTEXT

MySearchLab is an interactive website that features an eText, access to the EBSCO ContentSelect database and multimedia, and step-by-step tutorials which offer complete overviews of the entire writing and research process. MySearchLab is designed to amplify a traditional course in numerous ways or to administer a course online. Additionally, MySearchLab offers course specific tools to enrich learning and help students succeed.

- **eText:** Identical in content and design to the printed text, the Pearson eText provides access to the book wherever and whenever it is needed. Students can take notes and highlight, just like a traditional book. The Pearson eText also is available on the iPad for all registered users of MySearchLab.
- **Flashcards:** These review important terms and concepts from each chapter online. Students can search by chapters or within a glossary and also access drills to help them prepare for quizzes and exams. Flashcards can be printed or exported to your mobile devices.
- **Chapter-specific Content:** Each chapter contains Learning Objectives, Quizzes, and Flashcards. These can be used to enhance comprehension, help students review key terms, prepare for tests, and retain what they have learned.

Learn more at www.mysearchlab.com

ACKNOWLEDGMENTS

Larry Powell wishes to acknowledge the contributions that several others made toward the completion of this book. His wife Clarine gets first nod, for her love, patience, and tolerance during his writing of this book. His father, Harold Powell, planted the seeds for this work decades ago when he instilled an appreciation of politics. Political pollster James T. Kitchens has been a colleague, friend, and coworker since their days together at the University of Florida; many of the ideas in this book are the result of conversations with him. Senator Richard and Dr. Annette Shelby gave a young assistant professor his first chance to work in a real campaign. Editor-in-Chief Karon Bowers and co-author Joseph Cowart deserve special thanks for always working to improve the final version, and thanks to Dr. Mark Hickson for encouraging its completion.

Joseph Cowart acknowledges his wife, Marthena, for her understanding, encouragement, suggestions, and love over the nearly four years of this undertaking. Deep appreciation also goes to U.S. Senator Zell Miller, for giving him a beginning in the business and an early appreciation of the intellectual underpinnings of campaigns aimed at governance, and to Larry Powell, a co-author of infinite patience who built and maintained the structure and substance of this work.

We would also like to thank the reviewers of this text for their valuable comments and suggestions: Vanessa Beasley, Texas A&M University; Hal Fulmer, Georgia Southern University; John Gastil, University of Washington; James L. Hutter, Iowa State University; Thomas Marshall, University of Texas at Arlington; Steven Livingston, George Washington University; James McDaniel, Northern Illinois University; John Murphy, University of Georgia; Robert Sahr, Oregon State University; and Robert Terrill, Indiana University.

LARRY POWELL
JOSEPH COWART

An Overview of Political Communication Issues

Forgive those of us in academia for our insistence on organization, but there is a reason for our obsessiveness. Organized information is easier to learn and easier to teach. With that in mind, *Political Campaign Communication: Inside and Out* is organized into three major sections.

The first part is an overview of political communication issues. Chapter 1 begins at a basic level—defining the concept. As elementary as that seems, it is a crucial beginning point. Discussion of all subsequent issues will depend on a common understanding of "political communication." Agreement on something as simple as a definition is not always easy. In fact, a key aspect of this chapter will be understanding how political communication is defined differently by the academic and consulting communities. Further looks at the topic will reveal that definitions of the topic vary, even within the academic community. Sometimes "political communication" is defined so broadly that it can encompass almost any form of interaction between groups or individuals. Sometimes it is defined so narrowly that it fits within only one area of study. We will define it so that its primary focus is on communication related to political campaigns. That does not mean we will look only at campaign communications, since many of the messages offered by politicians and candidates during nonelection periods are also campaign related.

Chapter 2 focuses on political socialization—how people form, develop, and maintain their political attitudes. Some books that focus on campaign communication omit this topic. After all, the socialization process begins at an early age, before most people are even old enough to vote. As such, some might argue, it has little direct relationship to any specific election campaign. We disagree. This topic is approached early because the formation of partisan attitudes influences most subsequent elements of the campaign process. People who are lifelong Democrats or Republicans are often resistant to persuasive efforts from the other side. Understanding why they are so resistant is important to understanding political campaign communication, and new research on the topic has provided an updated view of the topic.

Chapter 3 looks at campaign strategies. After completing a list of readings on campaign strategies, a graduate student approached one of the authors and described herself as "naive." "I always assumed that candidates simply put themselves on the ballot, presented their ideas to the public, and the public selected the one they preferred," she said. Hardly. Most successful campaigns are organized around well-defined campaign strategies that provide guidelines for the selection of campaign messages, the timing of campaign activities, and the choice of tactics employed. Strategies are generally campaign specific—a new one is devised for each particular campaign. But some general strategic models have been developed, and they are presented in this chapter. In addition, this second edition provides an update of the twenty-first-century strategies, that is, those used in the 2000, 2004, and 2008 elections. The techniques used to develop such strategies are also described.

Chapter 4 looks at the images of political candidates. This chapter offers both an academic and a consulting view of the topic. In the past, some academic studies of candidate images have focused on breaking the concept down into its component parts. A number of different approaches have been suggested for that, and several of these are discussed. Other academic viewpoints assume that the candidate's image is a holistic concept that can be hard to dissect. The consulting community generally agrees with this approach. As a part of the campaign's persuasive efforts, consultants try to identify what factors contribute to an overall positive or negative opinion of a candidate or politician. Pragmatically, the goal is to identify those elements that can enhance the image of your candidate or detract from the image of the opposition. Despite these two divergent goals, though, both fields have a great deal in common on this topic.

Chapter 5 provides an overview of media theory as it relates to political communication. This chapter is heavily oriented toward the academic view of political communication, so much so that some campaign-based books leave this subject out. Some academic books on political communication will focus entirely on this topic. We believe this chapter is essential to a broad understanding of campaign communication. Modern media theories such as Agenda Setting, Uses-Gratifications, and the Limited Effects model have direct campaign implications. This edition also adds discussions of the Third Person Effect and the Hostile Media Effect. Consultants often make use of the ideas developed by the theories, even if those same consultants can't name the specific theory behind their tactics. We believe an understanding of these concepts will make the reader a more informed and objective observer of the political campaign process. That is, after all, the major purpose of this book.

Political Communication: An Introduction

The 2008 U.S. presidential election was one of the most exciting in the history of the nation. After eight years of Republican leadership in the White House, Democrat Barack Obama won the presidency and became the first African American president. The election was historic for other reasons too. Both parties pioneered the use of digital technology to aid in fund-raising, voter turnout, and grassroots organization. The result was a watershed year, one in which new media was seen as playing a major role in the new presidency (Hendricks & Denton, 2009). The field of political communication, it seems, was facing some of the most dramatic changes that the profession had ever seen.

And that was just the beginning. The dust had barely settled on the election before the U.S. Supreme Court issued a ruling on campaign finance regulations that changed the playing field for corporate involvement in politics (Smith et al., 2010). The decision signaled a new round of moves and countermoves for financial contributors. Corporations, which had faced strict regulations and limits on contributions in the past, would now be able to expand their involvement in politics. What changes would that trigger for academicians and consultants who study and work in political communication?

The term "political communication" evokes images of candidates and campaigns, debates and issues, propaganda and persuasion. As a subject, it is both simple and complex. It is simple because it focuses on such a narrow and specific topic. It is complex because it incorporates so many diverse disciplines and addresses a mass audience. Consultants and other political practitioners often come from diverse educational backgrounds and yet work together in a specialized environment. Scholars who study the topic find themselves following tangential lines of research that lead through the fields of mass communication, political science, law, advertising, marketing, and rhetoric.

Political communication is the study of those communication processes that contribute to the exchange of ideas in the democratic political process. That simple definition covers a lot of academic territory, thus emphasizing the complexity of the subject matter and the broadness of its application. An important facet of this definition is that it is not merely limited to political campaigns. That broad view is intentional. The reality of political communication today is that it is a constant, on-going activity that extends well beyond those few months immediately preceding an election. Most major politicians have consultants available at all times, a factor that caused Democratic consultant Shrum (2007) to label himself as a "serial campaigner" (p. 1). One of Shrum's most active times as a consultant, in fact, was in a nonelection environment—working with President Bill Clinton during the Monica Lewinsky controversy.

Consultants are involved in all facets of the communication process (including lobbying), with some developing reputations among the public at large (Nagourney, 2007). If their presence becomes too apparent, however, they can detract from the process by becoming the target of criticism that does little to progress discussion of an issue (Leibovich, 2009). Candidates and parties are constantly looking for ways to reduce consulting costs, but they rarely succeed (Drew, 2007). The problem is that most professionally run campaigns work under an eighteen-month span; planning starts in midyear prior to the next November election, a benchmark poll is conducted fourteen months out, and the consulting activities increase after that as the election draws nearer. For a congressional incumbent, that means that the "nonelection" time is limited to only about six–eight months out of every two-year span. Ignoring that factor would distort the consultant's view of the process.

In a democracy, political campaigns are at the center of this collection of processes. They are the beginning and ending points for political communication. Ideas flow into a campaign and flow out as messages. As the messages are presented within the campaign context, some are accepted or rejected by the voters, who make their decision known by the candidates they support. As messages become refined, they are transformed from time to time as legislative proposals. Those proposals are offered by elected officials who consider their actions in the context of and as a rationalization of both their past campaign and their next campaign. Meanwhile, an ongoing community often exists in the background—a community composed of newspaper editors, special interests, public interests, lobbyists, and others. As the campaign debate continues, their input results in the emergence of other proposals for legislative action.

As the proposal passes through the legislative process, it becomes a factor in the next campaign. If it becomes law, it proceeds to an implementation phase where special interests and public interests and others attempt to reshape it within legislative parameters. The proposal then returns to the political campaign as an accomplishment, something a candidate can tout as an achievement that merits reelection. If it fails in the legislative process, and if interest remains, it becomes fodder for a new campaign message, something the candidate can use as a message regarding a problem that still needs to be addressed. And the process begins anew.

Tying down this concept merely emphasizes its complexity. One colleague tried to explain it to a student by saying that political communication was a combination of persuasion and organizational communication. His explanation was correct but insufficient. Without understanding the path it follows—into, through, and after political campaigns—comprehending political communication will be difficult, if not impossible.

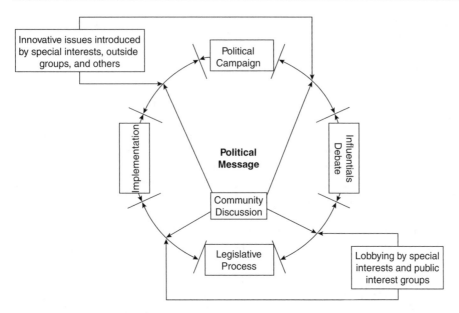

FIGURE 1.1
The Flow of Campaign Messages

To offer useful insights and an understanding of this complex system, our discussion will include (1) the U.S. political system, (2) the actors within that system—particularly the consultants, and (3) those communication processes that focus primarily on the campaign and legislative processes. A number of valuable political communication studies have been done on systems outside the United States; we will refer to these when their results have some relevancy to the American political system. We will focus heavily on the roles of the actors within the system, particularly the role of political consultants. We believe that a better understanding of these roles and the communication behaviors associated with them will provide a better understanding of the political campaign process.

Most of the discussion will focus on the political campaign process. Campaign activities often offer valuable insights into effective political communication. Hart (2000) argues that campaigns are essential to the function of a democracy; they inform us about issues, sensitize us to the concerns of others, and increase our awareness of the political world. Campaigns are the focal point for most political communication activities. Campaigns are the source of much of our information about political issues. Campaigns are obviously the route by which many politicians attain public office. Once elected, they become part of a perpetual, even permanent, campaign in which they must constantly work toward reelection (Blumenthal, 1982). If they choose not to run again, the campaign communication continues anyway as both parties maneuver to enhance the chances for their chosen candidates. Because of this, legislatures (both state and federal) have become increasingly concerned over the ballot-box implications of their decisions. For that reason, we will also look at political communication at the legislative level, particularly as it applies to political campaigns. Both political parties maintain year-round strategy-planning teams whose purpose is to evaluate and respond to current events in terms of their long-term electoral implications. Even at the local level, zoning and other decisions are often influenced by electoral implications (Staley, 2001).

Our major goals will be twofold. First, we hope to broaden the reader's perspective on the role of political consultants. These campaign professionals sometimes appear to have split personalities; sometimes they are viewed as kingmakers by the press and the public and sometimes they are maligned as unethical campaign practitioners. We will examine their role by analyzing what they do in campaigns and by providing insights from the consultants themselves. We invite the reader into that discussion by examining their role at various levels within a campaign.

Second, we hope to shed light on the relationship between the consultants and the academic community that studies political campaigns. In the past there was often an arms-length relationship between the two. That boundary seems to be shrinking as more university professors serve as independent campaign consultants, while an increasing number of consultants serve as university lecturers. If that gap is closed even more, we believe that both groups can benefit. The consulting community could benefit from the constant expansion of ideas among the academic community for communicating with the public. The academic community's ability to objectively observe campaigns could benefit if they have a better understanding of the role of campaign consultants. Neither will reach full productivity until they understand each other.

ACADEMIC OBSERVERS vs. PROFESSIONAL PRACTITIONERS

Political communication is both an area of academic study and a professional activity. The differences between the two communities are enough that they do not even use the term "political communication" in the same way. Academicians speak of political *communication,* in the singular. Consultants are more likely to use the phrase political communication*s*, adding an *s* to speak of the concept in the plural. The plural form is rarely used in the academic community, and the different forms of expression reflect one of the philosophical differences between the academic and the consulting communities. Academicians view political "communication" (singular form) as a collective noun describing a single academic discipline; when more specificity is needed, it is used (still in its singular form) to represent a holistic process, an abstraction that captures all the variables and factors related to the discipline. For consultants, political "communications" (plural form) refers to the messages used by candidates and their campaign to communicate with the voting public. Any particular political communication (singular form) is a singular noun referring to a specific message. Thus, when the academic and consulting communities sit down to discuss the topic, they frequently do so with different semantic meanings attached to the term. Unless both are aware of those differences, they may find themselves talking about different things.

Philosophically, academicians are more likely to approach the topic from an outside perspective with the intent of describing the process so it can be understood better and making suggestions to improve the process. Political professionals (candidates and consultants) are more likely to approach the topic from an internal and personal perspective with the intent to (1) improve their ability to communicate with their target audience, (2) increase their chances of promoting their political agenda, (3) make a profit, and (4) improve their reputations for future marketing purposes.

The academic community often view political consulting as, largely, a profession that no decent person would undertake, an impression that media consultant Raymond Strother (1999) argues "is taken from movies and stories attributed to a group of bottom-feeders..." (p. xiii). There is some legitimacy to the image. Even among the ranks of professional consultants, there are complaints about the lack of professionalism that exists with some of those in the field. As Mark McKinnon, a media consultant to former president George W. Bush once said, "The problem with political consulting is you don't need a license or a degree. Anyone can just show up with a camcorder. It is the ultimate in hackery" (quoted by Nagourney, 2007, p. WK1).

Political consultants often dismiss the academic criticisms as irrelevant to their task of assisting in the election of their clients. Academics find that political consultants and their recommendations are directly connected to the dysfunctions they detect in their study of campaigns and resulting government programs and services. Political consultants say they advise their clients in a way that assists them in ducking and weaving through a process complicated by legally mandated financial restrictions, governmental regulation of advertising, survey research, message development, and the creation of TV ads, radio ads, print ads, telephone banks, direct mail, and collateral print pieces. As such, consultants often take an amoral perspective on their campaigns. As Lippmann (1955) noted, "the power of the expert depends upon separating himself from those who make decisions, upon not caring...what decision is made" (p. 241). This view can alienate an idealistic academician, but it is crucial to the consultant's role.

An outgrowth of academic study is the development of recommendations on how to improve the electoral process. Such recommendations usually bring little reaction from political consultants. Instead, they are more interested in using the existing rules of the game to their client's advantage. They coach the tactics of political counterpunching, using their skills to recognize when such tactics are necessary.

The Outside View of Academics

The field of political communication attracts academic interest from a number of areas. Speech communication professionals often study the process in terms of public speaking, campaign strategies, and media usage. Journalism classes will examine campaigns and issues in terms of news coverage. Political scientists are interested in how the campaign process can influence and affect government institutions. Psychologists study the attitudinal factors related to voting decisions. Sociologists examine the broader implications of political trends on society. Regardless of the academic discipline, academicians tend to approach the topic as skeptical, outside observers. Lippmann (1955) once argued that campaigns often "…substitute misleading fictions for workable ideas" (p. 49). Edelman (1964) was skeptical of politicians and their ability to lead public opinion in a new direction. He argued, instead, that much public opinion formation is a strategic process in which opinion leaders try to persuade the public to think about issues along particular lines, to activate existing values, prejudices, and ideas. Similarly, consultants have been the target of constant complaints about their eagerness to use stereotypes—particularly racial stereotypes—in their campaign communications (Miller & Gordon, 2005).

Some academicians are also skeptical about the role of the media in the political process. After reviewing media coverage of the 1968 presidential campaign, Graber (1971) concluded, "The public received an image of the ideal president based primarily on personal qualities, with little information provided on [a] candidate's political philosophy or executive ability." Two separate studies on the 1980 and 1984 presidential elections found that most news coverage of the elections was about competition and controversy rather than issues (Patterson, 1980; Patterson & Davis, 1985). Robinson and Sheehan (1983) reported that a majority of the news coverage in 1980 failed to contain even one issue-related sentence.

Academicians are also skeptical about the ability of a relatively uninformed public to make rational decisions, based primarily on what Caplan (2007) describes as "the problem of voter ignorance" (p. 6). Typical of this view is that advocated by Nimmo (1974), who argued for the need of the public to become "politically self-competent persons" who are capable of better and more rational decisions. Nimmo's goal is representative of the "rational man" concept in classic democratic theory, a tendency to view ideal voting behavior as being motivated by an issue orientation.

And, as noted earlier, academicians are sometimes skeptical about the role of political consultants in the electoral process. Typical of this view is Nimmo's (1970) assertion that the consultants' "orientation toward business and technology threatens the very bases of the new politics." Furthermore, he added, when "a candidate uses opinion surveys and image advertising to give the appearance of being the leader of a popular movement, he is captive not only of the movement but of the technicians as well. He becomes a manufactured, contrived "personality" (p. 197).

Novak (1974) argued that just the opposite more frequently happens, with the voters selecting candidates who reflect their own self-image rather than those with the strongest stand on policy issues. Research has also consistently shown high levels of voter apathy and low levels of voter knowledge on most issues—factors that make it difficult for an electorate to make rational decisions (Neuman, 1986). Hofstader (1967) went further, arguing that most political rhetoric was based on a paranoid style that targets paranoid public (see also, Sanders & Newman, 1971; Smith, 1977). Such data consistently reflect academic skepticism with the naive idealism of public opinion in the United States.

Such attitudes are understandable. The academic community is, after all, an arbiter and guardian of democratic values and principles. Academicians are, in a way, the caretakers of the tools of democracy, protecting us from unrestrained pragmatism on the part of the consultants. Academicians serve as watchful critics who provide checks and balances on professional politicians by instructing the media how and when to put the brakes on consultants. In that sense, the academic community plays a role in holding campaign communication accountable for what is said and done. One goal of this book, indeed, is to increase the number of such "watchdogs" by enhancing the critical skills of the average citizen in making an informed voting decision.

The Inside View of Political Professionals

Today's campaigns are run by professional consultants who provide services related to media, polling, and other forms of communication. The average voter often has only a cursory understanding of how they do their job; more often, as Medvic (2000) noted, their activities "...are shrouded in mystery" (p. 91). Johnson (2000) divided what they do into three broad categories: strategists, who develop campaign messages; specialists, who provide essential services such as fund-raising, opposition research, and speech writing; and vendors, who supply campaign products and services. Major campaigns will use all three types, with varying degrees of success.

Despite the modern emphasis on consultants, their role is nothing new. Nimmo (1970, p. 36) argued that the consulting industry is a direct descendant of the public relations profession that matured in the 1920s as the nation became increasingly influenced by mass media. In 1933, Clem Whitaker and Leone Baxter used basic consulting principles to help defeat a referendum question in California, and their success sparked the formation of their consulting firm, Campaign, Inc. (Friedenberg, 1997). During the mid-1940s, Murray Chotiner was a consultant to a number of Republican senatorial and congressional campaigns; one candidate under his tutelage was a neophyte California congressional candidate named Richard Nixon. During the 1950s, Stephen Shadegg started providing consulting services to Barry Goldwater. By then, the industry was visible enough to attract the attention of academic investigators (Bernays, 1947; Pitchell, 1958). The dean of the modern consulting industry, Matt Reese, first opened his office in Washington, D.C. in the early 1960s. Today, the field is so specialized that some consultants focus on working in one state, or on one issue, or both (McKinley, 2009). By the early 1980s, the growth in the use of campaign consultants prompted Sabato (1981) to write, "There is no more significant change in the conduct of campaigns than the consultant's recent rise to prominence, if not preeminence, during the election season" (p. 3).

When experts discuss the controversial growth of the consulting industry, one aspect that is often overlooked is what role the consultants replaced—that of the political bosses (Perlmutter, 1999, p. 1). Before the advent of national media, many elections were often decided by a handful of individuals who made their decisions in backroom deals. While remnants of that system still exist in isolated areas, much of it has faded away. As Herrnson (2000) noted, "Campaign professionals have replaced local party organizations as the intermediaries between candidates and voters" (p. 88). The increasing role of the media, and of consultants, has essentially killed that system because the use of the mass media provides a way for candidates to communicate with the voters directly while bypassing the political bosses.

Consultants bring a blend of experience and expertise to the political arena—expertise in the fields of communication technology, strategy development, and experience in the campaign process. Their presence in a campaign can affect an election, but not necessarily decide it. As Herrnson (2000) noted, "Campaign professionals cannot eliminate the advantages of incumbency, nor can they turn an incompetent politician into one of presidential timber" (p. 88).

They do, however, bring an expertise to a campaign that can make a difference in many elections. They may lack, though, an academic background for their professional expertise. As Franzen (1999) wrote, "Although several universities now have programs in campaign strategy and management, most consultants have no academic training in the profession, and many would scoff at the notion that it could be learned in school" (p. 295). Perhaps because of that attitude, the academic community has sometimes targeted the role of consultants in campaigns. Bloom (1973), for example, argued that political consultants are a bane on the process, creating a "crisis in democracy." Consultants themselves paint a more pleasant picture. Allyn (1999) argued that consultants serve a positive role, simplifying complex issues so that they can be comprehended by average voters. Today's consultants, he argued, "make democracy...work on an everyman level, a valuable leveling service to the system" (p. 306).

Regardless of whichever impression is the more accurate, consultants are a part of the reality of modern politics. Major political campaigns are dominated by political professionals, and that may include both the candidate and the consultant. Their task is to identify a message and find a means of communicating that message to the people who have decisional power (the voters). Thus, for political professionals, the goal of any specific campaign is a pragmatic one of finding the best combination of tactics and strategies that will provide the best chance of winning over the most voters to their side.

Any one campaign is only part of the overall picture. Apart from any specific campaign, political consultants also run businesses (Johnson, 2000). They have ongoing expenses that include personnel, office space, travel expenses, and general office overhead. This overhead requires sufficient revenues to maintain operations. So, while they take a pragmatic approach to aiding a candidate, they also take a pragmatic approach to the day-to-day activities of running their business. Idealism is nice, they might agree, but it doesn't pay the bills. As Denton and Woodward (1985) noted, "Today's professional politicians are politicians only insofar as they earn their living working for political candidates and campaigns. They are professionals in the sense that they possess unique skills and knowledge relevant to human motivation and mass communication technology. They are experts and specialists first, and political in the traditional use of the word second" (p. 52).

Professional consultants are sometimes skeptical toward academic approaches to campaigns. Most would not attempt to develop their own theory of political communication; even if they did, they would likely abandon it by the next election as new situations dictated new strategic moves. Moreover, most consultants maintain that it is impossible to adequately understand the political environment unless issues suggested by funding, moving public opinion targets, and variations in campaign communication skills are considered.

One element that the consultants and academicians have in common is an emphasis on their professional reputations. While an academic reputation adds to a professor's credibility, a consulting reputation is valued primarily because it can add to the consultant's bank account. As Perlmutter and Wu (1999) noted, consultants "are only as reputable as their last election performance" (p. 332). Thus, from a consultant's view, winning an election is a positive goal, because it demonstrates success at working with a particular client. Even more important, victories enhance the consultant's reputation and serve as a marketing tool for future sales efforts. Upset wins, in which a long-shot candidate beats a heavily favored opponent, are particularly important. They become reference points that can anchor a consultant's entire marketing effort for the next election cycle.

AREAS OF RESEARCH RELATED TO POLITICAL CAMPAIGN COMMUNICATION

Political campaign communication is related to a number of other disciplines, and yet is also distinctly different from each.

Persuasion

Mutz, Sniderman, and Brody (1996) noted that "Politics, at its core, is about persuasion" (p. 1). The persuasive elements of political communication are one feature that attracts students in fields such as marketing and public relations. Political communication, though, is a very specific form of persuasion. Its persuasive intent differs from those who do professional marketing and commercial advertising in very distinct forms. In politics, the idea, issue, or candidate is sold to a self-qualifying public on election day, using modified mainstream principles.

Organizational Communication

Political campaigns are often the product of an organization that uses paid personnel, volunteers, and subcontractors to achieve its goal. Indeed, many techniques learned from organizational communication can make a campaign organization more productive. Still, a campaign is not a typical organization. Frequently, the campaign organization more closely resembles Berne's (1963) definition of a "crowd" (a differentiated but unstructured collection of people) rather than a "group" or an "organization." While a small group of individuals form the core of the campaign organization, effective implementation of the campaign often relies upon loosely formed coalitions of supporters and volunteers who may be unknown to the candidates themselves.

Another difference between political communication and organizational communication is what's known as the "famous-versus-rich" question: If you had your choice, would you rather be famous or rich? In a business organization, the answer is "rich"; the goal of most business organizations is to make a profit. In political campaign communication, the answer is "famous"; politicians have to be well known to be successful. That difference shows up in a number

The Conflict Between Academics and Consultants

James T. ("Jim") Kitchens is one of the few people who have viewed political communication as both an academician and a consultant. Before becoming a full-time political pollster, Kitchens served as an assistant professor of communication at Texas Christian University; some of the research he conducted during his academic tenure is cited elsewhere in this book. His consulting credentials include work for a number of statewide and congressional candidates, including former Speaker of the U.S. House of Representatives Jim Wright (Dem.-Texas), Congressional leader Martin Frost (Dem.-Texas), Alabama Governor Fob James, Kentucky Attorney General Ben Chandler, and dozens of congressional candidates.

Q: How would you describe the general view that consultants have of academics?

A: I think most consultants believe academicians are out of touch with the reality of political campaigns. Academicians work in such a theoretical environment that they often have no idea of how campaigns function.

Q: Why do you think that?

A: Because of the way they write about campaigns. There are two things that you notice. First, there's an incredible focus in the academic community on presidential campaigns, using conclusions from those to generalize to political campaigning in general.
But presidential campaigns are so unique, so different from everything else, and academicians seem to often overlook that. Second, academicians often don't recognize the pragmatic reality behind many campaigns. They write about what each campaign should be doing, in an ideal world, without considering the fact that most campaigns have to make their decisions with limited resources and a finite amount of money. Most campaigns are always struggling for money, and they make decisions that are cost efficient, not ideal.

Q: What's the other side, how do academicians view consultants?

A: Probably as charlatans, people who will sell any idea to anybody and who really don't believe in anything. They think of consultants as people who will work for other people, whether they believe in them or not. If academicians decide to work in a campaign, they prefer to think they would only work for somebody they believe in.

Q: Where does that image of consultants as charlatans come from?

A: They see that kind of consultant on television. They see the kind of consultant who talks about how they manipulate people, or how they trick the voters into supporting their candidate. There are a limited number of consultants like that, but the exposure they get creates an image for all political consultants. I also think there's a general lack of communication between the consulting community and the academic community. I know the AAPC [American Association of Political Consultants] is working on a program to create more joint communication between the two communities, but not a lot has been done yet.

Q: But consultants do have a basic ethical code. For one thing, most work only for one political party.

A: I think that's more of a pragmatic business move than an ethical code. Candidates don't trust consultants who work for both parties. Most consultants get into the business through one party or the other, and they stick to that party for their careers. Dick Morris is the only person I know of who has been able to work for both Democrats and Republicans over a long period of time.

Q: There seems to be a basic difference in goals. Academicians aim for a democratic process in which the truth will prevail. They sometimes believe consultants are only interested in winning, not the truth.

A: The truth doesn't always emerge at all. Both sides of a political campaign will argue their case, but their positions on any issues have gotten so extreme. Messages become extreme because extreme messages are effective. That's what the electorate wants and responds to. In some ways, you could say the electorate gets the type of political campaign that it wants and deserves.

Q: Where do the consultants fit in this search for the truth?

A: Consultants are not on a search for the truth. Consultants are effects oriented. Consultants are paid to win. We're like football coaches—if we don't win, we don't work. That means that the candidate is the moral conscience of the campaign. Ultimately, it is up to the candidate to say they do or do not want to use some particular technique or some particular argument.

Q: Does that mean that positions on issues are irrelevant?

A: The consultant is not on a search for the truth about any particular issue. I'm not in the business of government; I'm in the business of politics.

Q: What's the difference?

A: Government is concerned with policy, and a policy needs time to emerge. Most public policies cannot be judged on a short-term basis, and that includes the few months' duration of a campaign. It takes time to see how policies work. In politics, the voters look for general answers; government looks for specific details. The battle of a campaign is a battle of ideas and messages about where we want to go. Government is the process of working out the details of that. You can't do that in thirty-second TV ads. You can't do it in a thirty-minute program or a nationally televised debate either, because not enough people watch either of those. You have to do campaigns with general messages about where we want to go. The specifics is the job of government.

Q: What do consultants see as the major benefit of the academic community?

A: I don't know that other consultants think a lot about academics. I do, because I come from that background, but most don't even think about academics. They should, because I've seen how valuable it can be. A lot of our strategic recommendations are based on theories of communication. We take the theory and apply it to a specific situation. And some academic research is very valuable. Most consultants don't know that, though, because they never read an academic journal. That's the way that political mythologies develop. "You never mention your opponent's name." That's a political mythology. There's no theory behind that. There are plenty of instances in which you had better mention your opponent's name. Another one you often get is, "That approach doesn't work here." That's just not true. We know that the principles of communication theory are general principles that work regardless of the area of the nation where that particular campaign is held. The "that-doesn't-work" mentality usually means that the last person who used it lost the election, but they could have lost it for a dozen other reasons. The technique may still be effective there, if there's a theoretical justification for using it.

(Continued)

(Continued)

Q: What can the academic community learn from consultants?

A: First, they can learn some pragmatic things about the way campaigns work and how decisions are made with limited resources. Second, they can learn more about the persuasive process if they'd look down the ballot. A lot of the early studies were done on presidential campaigns, and that's not the place to be looking for media effects.

Q: What do you see as the major weakness of consultants, as viewed from an academic perspective?

A: The biggest problem is that there is no licensing procedure within the profession. Anybody who wants to do so can call themselves a political consultant. There is no requirement that they have the academic or educational credentials to do so. That creates a situation in which we have a relatively naive consumer group—candidates—who have no means of evaluating consultants. All they have to go on is whether the consultant has worked for winners, even if the consultant had little impact on those winning campaigns. It's hard to imagine that we've turned over our democratic process to a group of people who don't have to prove they know what they're doing, but that's what happened. The candidates, at least, need some criteria for evaluating consultants. I'd like to see some minimum educational requirements established, but I don't think we'll ever see it. ■

Source: Reprinted by permission of James T. Kitchens.

of subtle ways, including speeches. Politicians make speeches to enhance their credibility, while businessmen make speeches to increase the profit margin for their organization.

Advertising

Students from the field of advertising are often attracted to political communication. After all, modern politics is an exercise in advertising. Politicians communicate their ideas to the voters by way of the mass media while using a variety of advertising techniques. Yet, people whose training is limited to advertising are often ineffective as political consultants. There is an intensity to a political campaign that is totally different from that of most campaigns for a commercial product. Success is based on a much higher standard: The politician must get a majority of the target audience, not just a significant market share. Also, most advertising campaigns are designed for ongoing sales; few advertisers are used to handling the concept of a one-day, one-time sale (election day).

Marketing

When students from the field of marketing look at political communication, they see an area in which they can provide insight; at the same time they can learn something new about their profession. As with many related fields, political communication encompasses some elements taken from the field of marketing, but makes adjustments for what is still an unusual marketing situation. One element that political communication experts have learned from the marketing profession is the concept of demographic targeting. Candidates don't try to persuade all of the voters to support them, just a majority. This can often be done by identifying subgroups of voters who can be united to form that necessary majority. Still, such demographic targeting is usually ineffective by itself, producing the "I-should-have-won" postelection response. Furthermore, the targets of political communication and marketing tend to differ dramatically. A successful political coalition, for example, might include support from both older voters and low-income voters, two groups that are seldom targeted by commercial marketing firms (Harwood, 1998; Jamieson, 1984).

Group Communication

Students of group communication find a number of interesting factors that may attract them to political communication. Political interest groups are a key component of the political communication process. Campaign activities and decisions are typically made as a result of group discussions and group decision making. Special interest groups form to advocate special issues or to serve as a focal point for ideological views. Social movements develop around groups as the public and the press look to them as representatives of ideas. Activated group members may lobby politicians on behalf of their causes. Coalitions are formed as the campaign group solicits support from a number of other groups, encouraging them to focus their efforts on a common goal.

Religious groups, in particular, have been active in the political arena. Separation of church and state may be a key element of the constitution, but there is no clause that mandates a separation of church and politics. The two elements are often linked in today's political arena. The most obvious linkage is an ideological one. The Religious Right has become an active participant in state and local politics, using the political arena to advocate its positions on issues of morals and values. But the ties go back much further. Martin Luther King, Jr. launched his civil rights protests from the pulpit of the Dexter Street Baptist Church in Montgomery, Alabama. The church provided King with (1) a platform to articulate his ideas, (2) a ready-made organization to implement them, and (3) moral justification for his actions (Selby, 2001). King's success in the public arena can also be traced back to his religious background, particularly his training as a speaker. Political candidates often seek from voters the same type of passionate devotion to a cause that a preacher seeks from his parishioners.

Political Science

Political scientists have an obvious interest in political communication, particularly as it relates to political campaigns. The campaign process can influence and affect government institutions in dramatic ways by influencing leadership decisions and legislative actions. Still, the two concepts are not synonymous. The field of political science is primarily interested in government; political communication is studied in terms of how it affects that broader concept. For students of political communication, government is the secondary concept; it is studied in terms of its relationship to the communication process. That relationship has grown closer over the years. As a result, a number of incumbent activities and decisions—factors that were once the domain of government—are now being increasingly evaluated in terms of their campaign implications (Blumenthal, 1982).

THE DISTINCTIVE NATURE OF POLITICAL COMMUNICATION

Whether a campaign is for a public office or for a referendum, the candidate or the issue requires a specialized form of marketing. Such marketing is characterized by outcome planning for a maximum positive result for the particular day that voters go to the polls. As a result, despite its relationship to several other forms of communication, political communication retains a very distinctive flavor. As Jamieson and Campbell (1997) noted, a political campaign is more short-lived and intense than a campaign for a commercial product. Denton and Woodward (1985, pp. 8–12) identified five general characteristics of political communication: (1) short-term goals, (2) communication based on objectives, (3) importance of the mass media, (4) short-term orientation, and (5) the importance of considering audiences.

Perhaps the most distinctive feature of the campaign process is the one-day sale idea. Most election campaigns are based on audience response during a relatively short span of time (often just a single day). Even with the development of mail-in elections and the growth of early and absentee voting in many states, the time span in which the "sale" must be made is relatively short compared to the continuous sales of many consumer products. While public opinion polls may show who is ahead at any interval leading up to the election, the ultimate decision is based only on the total responses received by one specified date. The entire campaign process is targeted toward maximizing responses on election day.

That day can be critical. In 1968, Democratic candidate Hubert Humphrey staged a major comeback late in the presidential campaign, nearly finishing in a dead heat with Republican Richard Nixon. Some pundits believe Humphrey might have won the election if it had been held three or four days later. Such might-have-beens make for interesting speculation, but are ultimately irrelevant to the process. What is important is who is ahead on election day, not three days before or after.

Commercial advertisers have to take an entirely different perspective. If they're selling soap, they want to sell it every day—not just once every four years. Their persuasive campaigns have to be oriented toward that approach. Furthermore, they have to be concerned with point-of-sale displays, packaging, ongoing promotions, and even factors such as seasonal impact. Soap can be easily purchased, picked up at any number of stores that stock it on their shelves. Not so for the political candidate. The motivation of their target audience is different. Most voters participate in elections out of a sense of "duty and a responsibility as citizens of a democracy" (Becker et al., 2009, p. 38). Voting also requires a level of effort and participation that commercial products seldom encounter. A voter has to go to one specific polling place to cast a vote. Making that trip is nearly always an interruption to the individual's normal routine. Voting is not an easy activity, particularly when compared to the ease with which commercial products can be purchased. For a vote to count, the voter must cast a ballot in a specific manner, one that is consistent with state and local laws. In the 2000 presidential election, for example, some 20,000 votes in Florida—most of which were probably intended for Al Gore—were disqualified because they had been double-punched for two presidential candidates (Gore and Independent Pat Buchanan).

Despite the added difficulty of the process, political professionals are judged by a stronger standard than commercial advertisers. As Jamieson and Campbell (1997) noted, commercial advertisers can often be quite content with a relatively small share of the market. If a product consistently garners 20 percent of the market, for example, it can be highly successful and profitable. A political candidate who gets only 20 percent of the vote, however, has typically lost by a landslide. Typically, success is measured by the ability to get at least 50 percent-plus-one of the vote. Granted, there are some exceptions to that trend. The winner of some primaries is based on a simple plurality of the votes, rather than a majority. Some states are using extended absentee voting periods while others are opening voting to a several-week or longer period. But even in those instances, the size of the market that must be captured and the limited time available to advance ideas is daunting by consumer-based standards. Political consultants also have a harder job when it comes to image development. As Jamieson (1984) noted, the politician brings a documentable past to the political arena. All campaign messages have to either use those elements of the candidate's record or to be ready to defend them.

One factor is common to both domains. Like most other forms of communication, political communication assumes that the audience can function as an agent for change. Still, political communication has its own distinctive spin to this concept. Sometimes, change can occur very quickly with little impetus from individual participants. The vote of a single person can contribute to the majority decision that ousts one set of leaders and replaces them with another. That gives the political communication process distinct advantages over other systems, some of which lead to the deaths of the ousted leaders.

Finally, the financial aspects of political communication make it distinctly different from many other forms of communication. While most of the attention on a campaign focuses on the campaign itself, another campaign is being run behind the scenes. At the same time candidates *spend* money to communicate with the voters, they must simultaneously *raise* money to fund the process. This dual spend–raise role is not unique to campaigns; many charities operate on a similar basis. It is a process that makes it distinctively different from most other forms of commercial advertising.

DEFINING POLITICAL COMMUNICATION

Given the diverse fields that affect political communication, it should not be surprising that academicians often disagree about its most basic concept: how to define it. Conceptualizations vary widely, from scholars who discuss international politics to those who equate it with power plays within an organization. Who has not heard the complaint, for example, that an unqualified employee got a company promotion only because he or she knew how to "play politics" within the organization (Kennedy, 1980)? While that approach goes beyond the scope of this book, it does serve to emphasize the broad range of definitions that academicians, professionals, and voters have regarding the concept.

Others view the concept of political communication as being inherently unethical. Corcoran (1979, p. xv), for example, argues that politicians typically use communication "…not to convey information, but to conceal or distort it…, (bearing) no relationship to the organization, coherency and clarification of information and ideas." Many others might agree with George Orwell's (1949, p. 363) assessment that "political speech and writing are largely the defense of the indefensible." But such approaches are not really definitions so much as judgments about the process. In essence, as Denton and Woodward (1985) noted, such descriptions leave political communication "deficient by definition" (p. 13). More can be learned about the process by approaching political communication from an objective viewpoint rather than a judgmental one.

Others have more benign views of political communication. Hart (2001) views political campaign communication as a three-way conversation among political elites, the press, and the public. The exchange of information in that conversation becomes a source of information about issues, the views of other people, and the processes that contribute to political outcomes. Denton and Woodward define political communication as "public discussion about the allocation of resources…, official authority…, and official sanctions" (p. 15). This approach emphasizes three major factors related to politics—money, power, and sanctions; but even this approach has its limitations. Specifically, the focus on "public discussion" overlooks the role of lobbying, a critical factor in many legislative efforts.

Perloff (1998) corrects that problem by defining political communication as "the process by which a nation's leadership, media, and citizenry exchange and confer meaning upon messages that relate to the conduct of public policy" (p. 8). These authors like Perloff's broader view of the field, which is similar to our own. For the purposes of this book, political communication will be defined as *the study of the communication processes that contribute to the exchange of ideas in the democratic political process.* This definition reflects both the simplicity of the concept and the broadness of its application. An important facet of this definition is that it is not merely limited to political campaigns. Legal hearings, FCC regulations, and a variety of forms of popular culture could fall within the realm of that definition. Unfortunately, all of the various manifestations of political communication cannot be adequately encompassed within a single book. This book will narrow that view somewhat by focusing primarily on political communication in its most observable form: the political campaign.

Still, even though this book is campaign oriented, it is important to remember that political campaign communication today is a constant, ongoing activity that extends well beyond those few months immediately preceding an election. Most major politicians have consultants available at all times, and the consultation process is involved in all facets of the communication process (including lobbying). Furthermore, most professionally run campaigns work within an eighteen-month time frame; planning starts in the middle of the year before the next November election; a benchmark poll is conducted fourteen months beforehand; and the consulting activities increase after that as the election draws nearer. For a congressional incumbent, that means that the "nonelection" time is limited to only about the first six–eight months out of every twenty-four. Ignoring that fact would be to not recognize the consultant's view of the process.

Political communication is a form of strategic communication, whether it be a discussion between two individuals in the halls of Congress, a television commercial broadcast over the airwaves during a campaign, or an employee jockeying for a raise from her company. That element of strategic communication is critical and represents a common factor on which the academician and the consultant agree. Overlooking that element will lead to mistakes, causing the consultant to lose a campaign and preventing the academician from furthering his understanding of the process.

We shall focus on the inner workings of both sides to improve the general understanding of their work product, goals, and objectives (how voters think, how to develop a strategy based on that understanding, and considerations regarding the impact of the media). We will start with political socialization, since the formation of partisan attitudes influences most subsequent elements of the campaign process. From there, we shall work through the strategic considerations and the campaign elements, followed by postelection considerations, and finish with a chapter on campaign ethics. Arguably, the discussion of ethics should come first, since it should be—ideally—a value system that guides decisions at each step of the process. We considered this option, but put it last anyway, reasoning that the discussion would be more fruitful if the participants had a more thorough understanding of the process first than if they entered that discussion as neophytes. Ethical discussions about campaign communications are most valuable when they are founded on solid information. This is another of the few issues on which both the academic and consulting communities agree.

We hope this book will provide insights to both perspectives, and thereby make that discussion more useful to both sides of the debate.

SUMMARY

Political communication is defined as the study of the communication process that contributes to the exchange of ideas in the democratic process. This concept is often viewed differently by the academic and consulting communities. Academicians view political "communication" as a collective noun that describes an academic discipline. For consultants, political "communications" refers to the messages used by candidates and their campaigns to communicate with the voting public. Philosophically, academicians are more likely to approach the topic from the perspective of an outside observer, while consultants view the process as inside participants.

This book defines political communication in terms of campaign communications, an approach that encompasses those messages offered by politicians and candidates during nonelection periods that are also campaign related. Political communication includes several distinctive elements: (1) short-term goals, (2) communication based on objectives, (3) a reliance on the mass media, (4) a short-term orientation, and (5) an importance placed on audiences. Its more distinctive characteristic is its frequent reliance upon the one-day sale idea—the stated objective is based on an audience response in a relatively short span of time.

Campaigns are the process by which politicians attain public office. Once elected, they become part of a perpetual campaign in which they must constantly work toward reelection. Thus, the process of political communication is often a continuous one in which political messages become part of the legislative process, and vice versa.

QUESTIONS FOR DISCUSSION

1. What is the role of consultants in campaigns? Do they contribute to or inhibit the democratic process?

2. What is the role of the academic community? How could that role(s) contribute to or inhibit the democratic process?

3. When asked if positions on issues were irrelevant in campaigns, pollster Jim Kitchens said, "The consultant is not on a search for the truth about any particular issue. I'm not in the business of government; I'm in the business of politics." What, in your opinion, did he mean about the differences between the "business of government" and the "business of politics"?

Political Socialization: The Development of Political Attitudes

Lamar County, Alabama, looked like fertile ground for Republicans during the 2000 elections. The rural area in west Alabama fit the stereotype of a conservative, Bible-Belt area that might be receptive to the Republican messages of tax cuts and family values. Polling data indicated the attitudes and values of most of the county's voters were in line with those of the Republican Party. When the election was over, though, the Alabama Republican Party viewed the results with mixed emotions. Their presidential candidate, George W. Bush, had done well there, as had several statewide candidates, but participation in the local Republican primaries was disappointingly low. Why? One local resident had a simple explanation: "We may be conservative," he said, "but we've always been Democrats."

That statement explains their partisan attitudes, but why do people vote? According to Becker et al. (2009), the answer is simple: They vote because they view "it as a duty and a responsibility as citizens of a democracy" (p. 38). But, if so, how do they develop that perception? And how does that sense of duty translate into partisanship, that is, why do some become Democrats, some Republicans, and some prefer independent or third-party candidates?

Such attitudes illustrate the importance of understanding political socialization in modern campaigns. Political socialization plays an essential, if sometimes overlooked, role in the development of political attitudes. Academicians sometimes disregard political socialization as a campaign variable because it has little direct impact on any single election, or those factors that do have an impact occurred years before the event under study. The lifestyles and socialization patterns of baby boomers, for example, may have directly influenced voting behavior during the 1990s. Still, such analyses are more likely to be made on a post-mortem basis, rather than studied in advance of any particular election campaign.

Consultants take a different perspective, although their initial response is similar to that of the academic community. Generally, consultants will disregard the theoretical aspects of political socialization, viewing it as an abstraction that has little impact on any particular campaign in which they are engaged. Still, they pay close attention to the impact of socialization on voting behavior. A distinguishing feature of political consulting is the need to target specific audiences so as to create a distinctive strategy and to deliver a persuasive message. No campaign can expect to win a hundred percent of the vote. Attempting to do so is one of the most common mistakes made by campaign amateurs. Instead, the goal of the campaign is to gain enough votes to win the election or force a runoff.

To do that, the campaign typically divides the electorate into three categories: (1) support for the candidate, (2) support for the opposition, and (3) swing voters. The crucial element of this division is the identification of the opposition's support—voters who are unlikely to support your candidate regardless of what happens during the campaign. Those subgroups are eliminated from campaign targeting, thus reducing the cost of voter communication. Almost equally important is your candidate's own core support, voters who will stick with the candidate regardless of campaign events. In most cases, core support for or against a candidate is based on partisan allegiances. Party identification is more stable than any other political attitude (Abramson & Ostrom, 1991; Green & Palmquist, 1994). Further, candidates who focus on issues important to their party have an advantage at the polls (Benoit, 2007).

What makes it such a stable anchor of political preferences? The answers are found in the years of political socialization leading up to any particular campaign. Some voters grow up as Democrats and remain Democrats for most of their lives. Others are steadfast Republicans who rarely shift to the Democratic side. In both cases, the individuals are exhibiting behavior based on lifelong partisan attitudes, and those attitudes have an impact on the campaign process.

Those hard-core attitudes and values serve as the bedrock for establishing legislative districts and as the starting point for developing a campaign strategy. Understanding the fault lines between audiences means understanding how voters arrive at their decisions in the context of a political campaign. For the consultant, the question becomes: What is it that makes the voter a Republican or Democrat or Reform or Libertarian and/or conservative and/or liberal, and so forth? For the academic community, the question posed by those who research the process of political socialization is: How do voters develop their political attitudes?

The attempts at answering both questions fall within that realm of academic study known as "political socialization." Political socialization is defined as "the study of the developmental processes by which children and adolescents acquire political cognition, attitudes, and behaviors." Still, the implications of the research are hardly limited to childhood. Quite the contrary, Cook and Scioli (1972) reported that political orientations acquired in childhood have important influences on adult behavior. In other words, the political attitudes developed by children strongly influence which candidates they will support when they become adults.

Since major studies of the socialization process require in-depth analysis over a period of years, many of the current research conclusions are rather tentative in nature and have come from a number of theoretical approaches. Scholars who work in this area frequently debate the relative validity of the different approaches to political socialization. Such a debate is beyond the scope of this book, but it is important to realize that there is more than one perspective. The goal of the academic community is to resolve the discrepancies in those various perspectives while working toward a unified theoretical approach. Consultants are more likely to either ignore the theories, focusing on the common societal impact that they attempt to describe, or to look for insights within each one that might be useful to them.

Atkin (1975) identified three distinctive conceptual frameworks used by political socialization researchers: (1) Systems Theory, (2) a Structural-Functional Approach, and (3) Individual Analysis. The Systems Theory approach views the political system as one that operates under a continuous process of demands (output) and support (input). In this view, the continuous political socialization of incoming members of the society becomes a major means of support. The Structural-Functional Approach assumes that conformity is a key element in maintaining the cultural system, resulting in the inculcation of youth with a desire to fulfill role expectations concerning normative political behavior. Individual Analysis focuses on those agents or factors that have an influence on the political socialization process.

Despite the variety of approaches, some conclusions have been drawn. Generally, it is believed that most political attitudes develop through a two-step process that begins during the elementary school years (or earlier). At this time, children typically develop abstract emotional attachments and identification with political figures and institutions. This is then supplemented with specific knowledge gained during adolescence (Greenstein, 1968).

MAJOR SOCIALIZATION AGENTS

Those who study socialization from the perspective of the individual as the primary unit of analysis have generally sought to identify those agents that are most likely to influence a child's political orientations. Those agents generally viewed as having the strongest influence are the family, the news media, and political parties.

Family

The standard conclusion of most research is that the family is the single most important influence in the development of a child's political orientations, particularly for preschool children. Research consistently shows a relationship between the political values of parents and their children (Glass, Bengston, & Dunham, 1986). One reason is simply time; before a child reaches school age, they are usually in the company of their parents more than any other source of influence. After the age of six, other factors come into play, including the school system, mass media, and peers. But the family impact remains important. Like most academic inquiries, though, this topic has generated its share of controversy and alternative explanations.

The Simple Transmission Model   The most basic model for parental influence can be described as the simple transmission model, which is to say, parents pass along their political orientations to their children (Jennings & Niemi, 1968). Thus, children who grow up in Republican homes are likely to vote Republican when they become adults. Conversely, children who grow up in Democratic households are likely to be loyal Democrats when they reach adulthood. While this model has some appeal, based purely on its simplicity, critics of the approach argue that it is overrated. While it may have some validity, it is not always fully supported by the data. There is indeed a positive relationship between the parents' political orientations and those of their children, but the strength of the relationship is often unimpressive. Thus, children tend to have similar, but not identical, political values as their parents.

Alternative Explanations   At least two alternative explanations have been offered to explain this phenomenon. One approach argues that the relationship is a by-product of common experiences. Connell (1972), for example, argues that political attitude formation is shaped by common experiences, not the processes within the family. In essence, this approach argues that older and younger generations may develop their political orientations at the same time, in a parallel developmental process, rather than in a serial form, which is passed from parents to children. Support for this view comes from Berinsky's (2009) analysis of wartime rhetoric. His major conclusion was that public opinion was influenced more by the rhetoric of war than by war itself, but the finding that the rhetorical influence impact spanned generations supports the common-experience explanation. Similarly, Sigel (1970) argued that shared social status may account for much parent-child correspondence. Political orientations often correlate closely with social status, with high-income groups generally adopting Republican positions, while low-income voters are often strong Democrats.

Media

According to Becker, McCombs, and McLeod (1975), the media serve as an information-giving function to adolescents and younger children, although the permanency of these effects is not certain. The media's impact on children appears to be stronger than it is on adults. Some studies, for example, have found that adults sometimes demonstrate high resistance to media influence, but those studies have not been able to replicate similar results for children. Quite the contrary, children often believe and are influenced by what they see on television and in other media. Furthermore, children have considerable exposure to politically relevant information, especially among older age groups. That exposure is typically in place during the elementary school years, when they begin watching news programs with their parents. After that, exposure increases with age, with political interest often nurtured through exposure to both broadcast, print, and online media.

That exposure does not necessarily translate into political attitudes, but it does have an impact on political knowledge. Chaffee, Ward, and Tipton (1970) reported that the mass media are the single most important source of political knowledge for children. Generally, children consider newspapers to be their best source for information, but they rarely seek it out. Instead, television serves as the heaviest source for most of their political information, particularly for highly "visible" aspects of politics such as the presidency. For example, during 1998 and early 1999, even young children were aware of the possible impeachment of President Clinton, a by-product of their heavy TV viewing habits.

Generally, young people recognize this impact themselves. They perceive that the media have an important influence on their opinions about political issues. Furthermore, the media also have an effect on the public's attitudes toward political institutions. Television entertainment content, in particular, may affect orientations toward such elements of the political system as police and trust in the justice system. The impact of television is even stronger for low-income families. Children from low-income homes, particularly boys, are more reliant on television for their knowledge and less dependent on their parents than are children from middle-income homes.

More recent research has found that entertainment programming has a socialization effect on viewers. Holbert (2005) has been a leader in calling for research regarding the relationship of entertainment and politics, but others have followed a similar theme. Riegert (2007), for example, argues that viewers develop attitudes about politics based on how political life is represented on television dramas, comedies, and reality shows. Trueth (2005) offered a similar analysis devoted entirely to comedy shows, while Giglio (2005) argued the popular films had a similar socialization effect in terms of politics. Dargis and Scott (2009) even argued that the cumulative effect of a series of movies with positive depictions of black men (e.g., *Guess Who's Coming to Dinner, Driving Miss Daisy, I Am Legend, Training Day, In the Heat of the Night*) contributed to the public's readiness in 2008 to elect Barack Obama as the nation's first black president.

When entertainment crosses into the realm of politics, the impact is often on specific issues and trends. Thus, researchers have argued that crime dramas influence attitudes on gun control and capital punishment (Holbert, Shah & Kwak, 2004), other dramas can influence attitudes on environmental issues (Holbert, Kwak, & Shah, 2003), and both comedies and dramas can influence attitudes about women's rights (Holbert, Shaw & Kwak, 2003). Other studies looked specifically at the drama *The West Wing* in terms of its potential framing of ideological issues for viewers (Parry-Giles & Parry-Giles, 2006; Holbert et al., 2003).

Still, despite all the evidence for media influence, there is no clear evidence that mass media affect overt political activity. They affect political knowledge, and can have an impact on opinions about specific political issues. But there is no clear indication that the media either increase or decrease voter turnout among young people, or that they directly affect their political party affiliations. The media's impact is often affective in nature, rather than as a stimulus for behavior.

Political Parties

Political junkies tend to get involved in the process early, often with specific party identifications. Former U.S. Senator Max Cleland, for example, first became interested in politics when he was ten years old. He watched the 1952 Democratic National Convention on television, decided to campaign for Adlai Stevenson, created signs on cardboard, and remained a lifelong Democrat (Cleland & Raines, 2009).

Political parties play dual roles in the political socialization process, sometimes serving as a causal factor influencing the socialization process and often displaying the effects that result from years of socialization. The result is a cyclical process in which new members to the political process identify with one of the parties and then contribute to the socialization process of younger citizens. Modern scholars, however, may continue to debate the nature of that reciprocal process. To what extent do parties contribute to political socialization, and to what extent are they merely a reflection of past socialization trends?

For years, most scholars would have argued that the parties were a major socialization agent, noting that party identification played a powerful role in perceptions and judgments about candidates and issues (Campbell et al., 1960). The Democrat party, for example, dominated elections in the southern United States for decades (Key, 1949). Furthermore, while other parts of the nation lacked the single-party focus that dominated much of the South, that didn't decrease the impact of partisanship nationwide. In general, during the late 1940s and early 1950s, significant numbers of the nation's voters exhibited strong partisan identifications (Key, 1952). Sometime afterward, though, signs of weaker party identifications started appearing. Some observers point to the 1964 presidential election as a key indicator, one in which many white southern Democrats voted heavily for Republican Barry Goldwater (Miller & Shanks, 1996, p. 153). Four years later in the 1968 Nixon–Humphrey election, a definite antiparty trend was apparent among many voters (Jennings & Markus, 1984). By 1976, those same antiparty voters had contributed to a growing decline in party identification (Miller & Shanks, 1982).

The 1990s saw changes in partisan allegiances among American voters, although descriptions and explanations for those changes have varied. An eight-year study (1992–1999) of 13,651 adults by the Scripps Howard Foundation and Ohio University found that the fastest-growing political groups in America are "other" and people who said they were undecided. Fewer than one third of those voters identified themselves as strong partisans for either political party, while 58 percent said they were politically independent. During the time frame of the study, Democrats dropped to their lowest level in 1994 and 1995, when only 14 percent described themselves as strong Democrats; those dates corresponded to the time that Republicans took control of both the U.S. Senate and the House of Representatives. Republicans hit their lowest level in 1998 during efforts to impeach President Clinton when only 10 percent identified themselves as strong Republicans. Arterton (2000) attributes the decline in partisan influence to technology and modern campaign practices. One of the major benefits of party organizations, he argued, was to provide a link between candidates and voters, but, he adds, "Modern politics have eviscerated these networks, replacing them with polling and mass communication. In the process, the individual voter has become a cipher, a statistical construct rather than a living, breathing person" (p. 22).

Although partisanship decreased during the 1990s, there was no corresponding drop in ideological independence. Ninety-three percent could identify themselves as either liberal, conservative, or middle of the road, compared to 92 percent in 1992. Others, however, have argued that partisan identification has actually increased, particularly if a longer period of time is examined. Abramowitz and Saunders (1998), using data from the 1976–1994 American National Election Studies, concluded that the 1994 and 1996 elections reflected an increased polarization of partisan identification. They pointed to the Reagan and post-Reagan years as the source of the increased polarization, noting that during that time "clearer differences between the parties' ideological positions made it easier for voters to choose party identification based on their policy preferences" (p. 634).

Generally, academicians have argued for the positive benefits of partisanship in debates of political issues, based on the idea that debate between the two positions produces more effective solutions (e.g., Swartz, 2005). However, during the mid-1990s and in the first decade of the twenty-first century, partisan polarity had become a major problem. Baker (2008) traces the problem back to Republican efforts to impeach Bill Clinton over the Monica Lewinsky controversy. Gormley (2010) goes a little further back, tracing the start of partisan bickering to the animosity that developed with Robert Bork's nomination to the Supreme Court, the subsequent Clarence Thomas–Anita Hill controversy, and reaching full force in Kenneth Starr's investigation of President Bill Clinton. Regardless of the cause, the result was an atmosphere that one observer labeled "political poison" (Baker, 2008) that has made it harder for Congress and the Senate to reach legislative accords (Hulse, 2010).

Some scholars point to 1976 as a watershed year in partisan participation. In that year, both parties (particularly the Democrats) instituted a number of reform rules that changed the state laws regarding delegate selection to the parties' national conventions. As Trent and Friedenberg (2000) noted, "the change in rules and the proliferation of primaries have weakened political parties, the traditional vehicle for building coalitions and forging consensus" (p. 6). But other factors may also be involved. Fiorina (1981) argued that party identification can be influenced by retrospective evaluations of party performance. Subsequent research has indicated that policy preference can be a key factor (Franklin, 1992), particularly when a party takes a strong partisan position that is not supported by the voter. Miller and Shanks (1996) conducted an in-depth study of partisan attitudes over four presidential elections and concluded that long-term party identification was the single strongest predictor of voting choice.

Political parties play a major role in modern campaigns, providing fund-raising, organizational, and rhetorical support to their candidates and the issues they support. Still, such roles are largely dependent upon the parties' ability to attract large numbers of members. Those members provide the party with volunteers who work on campaigns, provide financial assistance, and ensure a core voting bloc from which to expand an electoral base. The question remains, though, as to what extent partisan identification is a result of partisan activities, and how much results from the influence of media or families or from simple partisan shifts that occur over time.

Critics also argue that political parties can have a negative impact on socialization by the demographic groups they choose to target. This argument is most frequently made in terms of racial or ethnic groups. Southern blacks, for example, have supported Democrats at a rate of around 90 percent ever since they gained voting rights via the Civil Rights Act of 1964. Much of that party allegiance is due to the role of President Lyndon Johnson and the Democratic Party in pushing that legislation, but some of that Democratic loyalty might also be due to the opposition at the time from Republicans. Columnist Eugene Robinson (2010) argues that

Republicans have failed to make major in-roads in the African American vote since then because of party policies that "let black voters drift away from the GOP, and even encouraging them to stay away" (p. 7A).

OTHER SOCIALIZATION AGENTS

The family, media, and political parties are generally considered the three biggest influences on a child's political orientations, but two other factors—peers and the educational system—are also known to have an influence.

Peers

Beginning in the early teenage years, one's peers tend to gain more influence on a child's social maturation. Peer pressure becomes more intense, and children become increasingly sensitive to what their friends think of them. Becoming "one of the crowd" is a high-priority goal, one that defines social success for many teens. Surprisingly, though, this stage has relatively little effect on the child's political socialization. There is little indication that friends or peers have a major impact on political development during middle school or high school. The socialization impact of friends and peers during the high school years seems to be more geared to social activities than political orientations. There is some evidence, however, that friends play a significant role in the political attitudes of college students. When that occurs, those orientations can produce long-term effects that influence an individual's political behavior for years.

Schools

Of the major socialization agents, research has generally indicated that education has the least impact on political attitudes. Still, schools do play a significant role in teaching concepts, beliefs, and attitudes about the operation of the political system, particularly for younger children. The schools also impart detailed information about political processes. Teachers are particularly important as sources of information about some of the less visible aspects of government. Typically, for example, children learn more about the Supreme Court, and concepts such as the separation of powers, from school than they do from the media.

The impact of the educational system is largely limited to information. Attempts to use the schools for propaganda purposes (teaching anticommunism courses, for example) have generally been unsuccessful, and social studies or civics classes at the secondary level has little effect. Not surprisingly, then, the educational systems typically have little identifiable impact on the attitudes and values that young people take into the political arena when they become voters. Although explanations for this effect vary, one factor appears to be constant. The impact of the educational system itself is overridden by the effect of the schools as a site of social interaction. Specifically, interaction with peers at school (particularly at college) can have an impact on attitudes that exceed the impact of the educational system itself. Thus the school, at least, serves as a socialization agent by providing a location in which peers can influence one another. But that influence appears to be, at best, an indirect one. Similarly, despite popular perceptions that college professors influence their students to hold liberal views (Jenson & Denker, 2009), that doesn't seem to be a factor. The latest research indicates that university professors have no impact on the political ideology or views of their students (Fritschler, 2008).

POLITICAL SOCIALIZATION STYLES

Sigel (1970), in an analysis of parental influence on political socialization, argued that the content of parental communication may be less important than the manner in which their political values are transmitted. What may be more important is whether parents encourage their children to engage in self-expression and political controversy. Subsequent research in this area has identified two general approaches to politics, a socio-orientation and a concept orientation. Socio-orientation is a people-based perspective that stresses the importance of maintaining harmonious personal relations, avoiding controversy, and repressing personal feelings. Concept orientation is an ideological or issue perspective that stresses the importance for the child of expressing his or her own ideas, using conversation to discuss controversy, and challenging positions taken by parents and others. Parents can stress either, neither, or both of these styles, resulting in four categories of behavior that can be labeled political socialization styles. Table 2.1 illustrates these categories.

Families that stress neither a concept nor a socio-orientation are called laissez-faire. In these families, children are not prohibited from challenging their parents' views, but neither are they encouraged to do so. Children in such families are given few directions on the use of interpersonal communications. Laissez-faire families have children who spend little time on homework and earn moderate grades in school. They spend little time in political activity, and are moderately knowledgeable about politics. They watch moderate amounts of violence on television.

Families that stress social relations are protective. The children are encouraged to get along with others, taught not to be confrontive or to express dissent, and are given little chance to encounter discrepant information. These children are taught to use interpersonal communication to maintain peace. Protective children spend little time with school work at home and earn low grades in high school. They spend little time in extracurricular political activities and have a moderate amount of political knowledge. Children in protective homes generally watch high amounts of violence on television.

TABLE 2.1

Types of Political Orientations

Socio-Orientation

		Low	High
Concept Orientation	Low	Laissez-faire	Protective
	High	Pluralistic	Consensual

Pluralistic families are those that emphasize concept-oriented communication. The children are taught that ideas are important and they are encouraged to form opinions and discuss them openly. Children from pluralistic homes have been found to be more knowledgeable about public affairs, earn better grades in school, are more active in school and politics, and want to be more like their parents. They watch very little violence on television.

Consensual families place an emphasis on both socio-orientation and concept orientation. The children are told to both maintain social harmony through communication and introduce diverse points of view into conversations. Thus, consensual children are taught to keep the peace while expressing strong opinions. Consensual children have little political knowledge, spend lots of time on homework but get only moderate grades, and are only moderately active in political matters. They generally watch high amounts of violence on television.

Wheeless and Schrodt (2001) expanded the assumptions behind concept orientation by examining the impact of partisan socialization on information processing. They argued that those voters who had developed rigid views about politics would be both apprehensive about listening to information that was not supportive of their views and more inflexible in responding to that information. Their early research on the subject has supported that concept. Generally, conservatives are more apprehensive about listening to new information than moderates or liberals, and they are more likely to be inflexible when listening to such information. Still, while the differences are statistically significant, they are not always big.

It appears that several other socialization factors (as yet unidentified) also affect how political partisans respond to and process political information.

Another group of researchers have argued for an entirely different approach—one based on the relationship of the individual citizen to the political arena. Along this line, Holbert and Benoit (2009) argued for what they called the study of *political connectedness*. Their work was an extension of earlier research by Neuman (1986) on political sophistication, a term he defined as "a generalized propensity to participate in political activities, that is, an inclination to respond to political stimuli" (p. 103). Neuman proposed a three-dimensional structure of sophistication that includes political knowledge, salience, and conceptualization. He used these concepts to develop what he called a theory of three publics. One group (about 20 percent of the population) are a political and have little involvement in political activities. A second group of political elites have high levels of political sophistication and play an active role in the political process. However, Neuman argued that the success of democracy depends on the behavior of the third group, the mass public. Holbert and Benoit's work was essentially an attempt to provide a better understanding of those in the third group who were relatively involved in the political arena.

THE INVISIBLE YOUTH VOTE

Despite the amount of study devoted to both politics and political socialization, one general conclusion is that the United States, as a whole, has been rather ineffective at instilling its political values into its youth. In the early 1980s, researchers noticed a gradual downward trend in U.S. voter participation (Abramson & Aldrich, 1982), a trend that continued into the 1990s (Teixeira, 1992). In 1997, the Swedish-based International Institute for Democracy and Electoral Assistance reported that voter participation rates in the United States were the lowest of any advanced democracy and lower than most fledgling democracies (Patterson, 1999), with the United States ranking number 139 out of 163 countries. The 1996 presidential election was the first national contest in modern times in which a majority of adults of eligible voting age stayed home. In the 1998 election, only 36 percent of the voters went to the polls.

Some scholars point to a general rise in political apathy as the cause. DeLuca (1995) attributes the rise in apathy to two factors: alienation created by systemic problems in which elites control the process, and individuals who give up their personal responsibility for participating in government. Dionne (1991) blames modern campaign techniques, arguing that "Election campaigns generate less excitement than ever and are dominated by television commercials, direct mail, polling, and other approaches that treat individual voters...as mere collections of impulses to be stroked and soothed" (p. 10). Delli Carpini and Keeter (1996) attribute it to a decline in political knowledge, noting that "Compared to what people ought to know..., the public is ignorant about much of the details of government and politics" (p. 17).

Much of the low turnout can be attributed to a general decline in voting by younger voters. Generally, American youth have been neither knowledgeable nor interested in politics. In 1979, a Gallup Poll survey of 1,012 teenagers found that teens overwhelmingly failed a five-question quiz about American government. Only six out of ten could name the vice president of the United States. Most (52 percent) could not answer two questions correctly, and only three percent correctly answered all five. Such numbers reflected a growing trend of political ignorance that was of concern to scholars (Bennett, 1988). Gallup also found a correlation between several demographic variables and knowledge scores. Those teens from white-collar families and those whose parents had attended college tended to do well, while those from blue-collar families and whose parents did not attend college did not do well. Those findings added support to the theory that political socialization is influenced by shared social status of younger and older voters.

Later data are even more discouraging. An analysis of the 1998 election indicated that more younger voters are dropping out of the democratic process. That study, which examined the youth vote from 1972 to 1998, showed a continuous drop in turnout among eighteen–twenty-four-year-old voters (Patterson, 1999). In the 1972 presidential election, when Richard Nixon defeated George McGovern, almost 50 percent of voters aged eighteen to twenty-four went to the polls. In 1996, when Bill Clinton faced Robert Dole, the number had dropped to 36 percent. In the November 1998 off-year elections, the number dropped to 20 percent—an all-time low.

The latest study added further support to the social status theory (Didion, 2001). There was a double-digit gap in voter turnout between college-educated (41 percent) and non-college educated youth (25 percent). The study also added another variable to the socialization process—religion. Young people who attended religious services every week were more likely to vote in 1998 (43 percent) than those who never attended (25 percent).

Why such low political involvement? Some researchers argue that placing blame on a single cause is impractical (Cassell & Luskin, 1988). Still, many do blame the parents, since most young people (nearly 80 percent) live in homes where politics is rarely mentioned. Others blame the schools for not preparing young people to vote. At the very least, research indicates that the schools can play a vital role in confirming the importance of exercising one's vote (Miller & Shanks, 1996, p. 52). Didion (2001) attributes this low rate of participation to citizens who feel left out of the process, noting that nonvoters have less education, less money, and a lesser feeling of having a stake in the political process than do voters.

Others, however, argue that such pessimistic assessments of the socialization process are unnecessarily negative. Popkin (1991), for example, argued that voters do not need a lot of detailed information to make valid voting decisions. "There is much that voters *do* know about government, and many ways in which they manage to consider issues without high levels of information" (p. 42). All that is needed, he argued, is that the voters know something about the state of the economy or proposed legislative measures that could affect them or their values.

The dawn of the twenty-first century spurred scholars to look at the impact of young voters in the 2004 election (e.g., Bystrom & Dimitrova, 2007; Chicksand & Carrigan, 2006; McIlwain, 2007). Later studies saw some signs of improvement. McKinley and Banwart (2005) reported that a "Rock the Vote" debate dialogue developed with CNN "encouraged greater identification between young citizens and the candidates, contributing to a heightened level of political efficacy among young voters" (p. 153). A 2007 study by Jasperson and Yun (2007) was more optimistic, despite finding large levels of cynicism among young voters. One conclusion of the study was that youth participation could increase if there were greater exposure to political information. Further, that greater exposure to political information has been occurring. Young voters have a heavy reliance on the Internet as a source of information, and one by-product of that behavior has been greater exposure to political information (Wells & Dudash, 2007). Much of that exposure has come via political blogs (Sweetser-Trammell, 2007). As a result, in 2008 Barack Obama was able to use the Internet to communicate with and activate a significant number of young voters (Hendricks & Denton, 2010). That initially seemed to bode well for Democrats and long-term commitment to liberal ideas, with some observers suggesting that Republicans risked "losing a generation" of young voters (Connelly, 2009, p. WK3). That trend seemed to stall, though, in 2010. By then, young voters largely retained the liberal social ideals that made them Obama supporters, but they became economic conservatives as they were increasingly unable to find jobs in an economic recession and a weak job market. As a result, self-identification of young Democrats had declined, compared to 2008 (Johnson, 2010).

THE SOCIAL COST OF VOTING

While a teenager, one of the authors volunteered in a voter turnout program aimed at getting rural voters to the polls. After driving to one man's house to provide him with transportation to the polling place, he was surprised when the elderly farmer politely refused the ride, saying, "There's not that much difference between any of them." Later in the day, the real explanation for the elderly gent's response was given by someone who knew him well. He couldn't read, something most of his neighbors did not know. For him, voting would have required assistance that he was too proud to accept.

That story is but one example of the social cost of voting. Many active politicians often overlook the fact that the social cost of voting can create a barrier for some who would otherwise participate in the political process. Such citizens get a "free ride" from the governmental process—accepting government services from elected leaders while not participating in the selection of those leaders (Olson, 1971). Voting requires making time to register, visiting a bureaucratic office, filling out forms, and possibly taking off time from work. While active voters take such factors casually, accepting them as part of the system, newcomers will have a different perspective. Sometimes, those who are new to the process feel uncomfortable in engaging in any of these activities and often fear ridicule if their lack of knowledge of the process were revealed. Add to that a social environment in which those around them do not vote, and there will be little social incentive to behave otherwise (Straits, 1990). Tyson (1999) refers to this phenomenon as "intimidation factors associated with voting," noting that "infrequent voters often lack not only a rationale for voting but also knowledge of the process itself" (p. 131). Faced with both a lack of knowledge and uncertainty about the process, becoming part of that process can be psychologically intimidating. For these voters, tuning out is easier than tuning in.

The social cost of voting can be countered. During the 1960s, massive voter registration drives in the South added thousands of new African American voters to the voter rolls. The desire for recognition of their civil rights was stronger than their inhibitions about the process, and the organizers of the drives recognized the need to educate new voters about the process. Still, it can be difficult to do. Efforts to expand the voter pool must recognize and deal with the uncertainties and fears that inhibit participation.

PARTISAN ORIENTATIONS AND THE POLITICAL CONSULTANT

For the political consultant, the pragmatic impact of political socialization is that of partisanship. Generally, the consultants accept the conclusion reached by Miller and Shanks (1996): "As a long-term stable predisposition, party identification is not only a point of departure for electoral analysis; it is the most important of several predispositions that provide continuity across electoral epochs" (p. 512). Most voters, including those who describe themselves as Independents, exhibit a strong degree of loyalty to one or another political party (Keith et al., 1988). That loyalty can often be described with demographic data, as some demographic groups (low-income voters, for example) tend to lean toward Democratic candidates, while others (high-income groups, for example) tend to be more Republican in their political orientation.

Consultants make assumptions about voters based on such demographic factors and use those assumptions to aid the development of campaign strategies and message targeting. For example, Republicans frequently target upper-income, suburban voters as critical elements in their campaign strategy and Democrats often target older voters, a group often assumed to be sympathetic to issues promoted by the Democratic Party.

In general, consultants tend to view such demographic targets as relatively immutable groups, a view that is consistent with findings from socialization research. Political orientations that have been developed through a lifetime of experiences are often difficult to change. Rather than attempting to change them, consultants more frequently recommend working within those constraints according to the maxim of "Work your strengths." Instead of attempting to "cross the fault line," those demographic groups perceived as being in the opposition's corner are simply eliminated from the campaign's target list.

Most such decisions are based on financial concerns. A political campaign with a relatively small budget is unlikely to make major inroads toward changing long-held beliefs. In such cases, political consultants use this information to exclude certain groups from their campaign plans. Miller and Shanks (1996) identified three major venues for change in party identification: racial, regional, and religious. Most consultants would agree with those categories for targeting purposes, but they would also add other social factors, such as income, to their possible target list. Republicans generally do not target black voters, low-income voters, or voters who live in strong "Democratic" regions; Democrats similarly do not target religious evangelicals, upper-income white voters, or voters who live in districts with a history of supporting Republican candidates.

Still, changes in political orientations do occur. As Miller and Shanks (1996) noted, "Partisan identifications are demonstrably not immune to change after their initial values have been shaped by childhood and early adult experience" (p. 495). After all, the 1960s reflected a time in which young people who joined the political process tended to have liberal views, a political outlook that was more consistent with that of the Democratic Party. By the 1980s, the electorate as a whole had become more conservative, with young voters demonstrating more affinity for the Republican Party.

What triggers such changes? One explanation is that it is a natural cyclical process, one that tends to occur over about twenty years of development, or for a new generation. That approach would predict that the current conservative trend, one that corresponded with the election of Ronald Reagan as president, is approaching an end. Sometime within the next ten years, this approach would argue, the pendulum is likely to swing in the other direction and the U.S. electorate will become more liberal. Winogard and Hais (2008) predicted such a shift led by a new generation of voters they called "Millenials." Support for this idea was found in the 2010 elections, which identified a generational gap between conservative "Tea Party" voters, who were primarily older voters, and young voters (Bai, 2010).

Another factor that influences such shifts is the presence of a charismatic leader, particularly at the presidential level. Voters sometimes, in fact, define their partisan leanings in terms of their presidential vote choice (Markus & Converse, 1979).

Democratic strengths during the 1960s corresponded with the election of John F. Kennedy, a highly charismatic speaker, as U.S. president. Similarly, Republican swings during the 1980s were associated with the election of a popular and persuasive Republican president, Ronald Reagan (Abramowitz & Saunders, 1998). Similarly, the election of Democrat Barack Obama sparked speculation that he might be the leader of a new generation of Democrats (Harwood, 2009). But the impact of presidential preferences is not limited to popular presidents. As Miller and Shanks (1996) noted, retrospective evaluations of presidential performance often has an impact on partisan preferences: "Most explanations of presidential elections involve some component in which voters may cast their ballots against the incumbent party if they disapprove of the way the president is handling his job" (p. 500).

A charismatic leader rarely accounts for all of the partisan shift, however. Instead, it may only increase ticket-splitting behavior, particularly at first, in that the popular leader is a person who generates personal support. Still, support for the leader may not be translated into partisan shifts for other candidates. Such across-the-board shifts are more likely to be influenced by either dramatic issues or some watershed event. Miller and Shanks (1996, p. 497) described this effect as "the electoral consequences of controversies"; the controversy surrounding a watershed event helps individual citizens define their views of appropriate goals and priorities for government. Thus, while John F. Kennedy may have been a symbol of the Democratic Party, a full shift to Democratic partisanship might not have occurred had not other issues (such as the Vietnam War) also affected political attitudes. Similarly, the civil rights movement of the 1960s played a crucial role in defining party allegiance for a number of people (Carmines & Stimson, 1989), particularly new African American voters who were getting their first chance to participate in the electoral process. And while Ronald Reagan may have been personally popular, the popularity of the Republican Party as a whole was not increased until conservative economic policies became popular.

Interestingly, issues or controversies that may have the most impact on altering partisan predispositions may have little impact on any one specific election, while issues that have a dramatic impact on an election may have little or no impact on partisan shifts (Page & Brody, 1972; Page & Jones, 1979). Instead, many times such shifts are based on contemporary, short-term forces that can quickly change (Miller & Shanks, 1996, p. 207). For example, voters' perceptions of the economy was the issue that had the greatest impact on Bill Clinton's 1992 presidential win, but that issue had little impact on partisan identification among the voters; conversely, that same year, the abortion issue sharply divided individual voters along partisan lines, with some individuals shifting their partisan identification because of it. Still, abortion had little impact on the outcome of the election (Miller & Shanks, 1996, p. 504).

Political orientations can shift over time (Beck & Jennings, 1991), even among political elites. Ronald Reagan began his political career as a liberal Democrat, but was elected president as a conservative Republican. Alabama Republican Senator Richard Shelby began his career as a liberal Democrat in the Alabama state legislature. Former Texas Senator Phil Gramm—known as one of the most conservative members in Congress—also began his political career as a Democrat. As the lifestyles of voters change, so too can their political orientations. Some liberal

Democrats who devote their lives to education may become Republicans once they become part of the free-market economy. Some conservative Republicans may become Democrats if their lifestyles shift out of the marketplace and into other areas of life.

Voters of all ages are constantly acquiring new information, leading to a resulting adjustment of their political orientations (Delli Carpini, 1989). Partisan loyalties may shift, with the advantage of any one party changing slightly, from election to election. But such changes tend to be made gradually, in small increments. As Miller and Shanks (1996, p. 495) wrote, "...partisan identifications respond very slowly to voters' impression of current party leaders, their policies, and their success or failure in handling government." Also, campaign communications can alter some assumptions about political orientations. For example, for years the South was viewed as an area that was off-limits to most Republican candidates. The "Solid South" was a Democratic stronghold that Republicans dare not challenge for fear of wasting time and money. That view changed, however, when Ronald Reagan appealed to blue-collar and rural voters in the South with a message about conservative values that was targeted to them (Dallek, 1999; Dallek, 2000; Greffenius, 2001). The "Reagan Democrats" allowed the Republican Party to make major gains in the Southern states.

Such an effect might indicate that political orientations are more malleable than many researchers have expected. At the very least, the decade-long decline in partisan allegiances means that consultants have a larger target audience of potential party switchers than existed during the 1980s. If a candidate can target a message that appeals to a particular group of voters, then they might be receptive to those ideas regardless of its partisan source. If so, then the future of political communication might find considerably more flexibility among those voters than in the past. That possibility could be intriguing for both the academic and consulting communities.

SUMMARY

Political socialization, which is how people develop their political orientations, is an important topic for both academics and consultants. For the academic community, studies of political socialization help to explain shifts in political behavior while identifying those agents (media, family, party, peers, friends, schools) that can affect political attitudes. Such information is critical for understanding the modern political process, but the information gleaned from such studies goes far beyond politics and reaches into a broad realm of socialization into modern culture. How we develop our political attitudes is closely tied to how we develop our self-concept and how we learn the roles that guide our lives in modern society.

For consultants, an understanding of how people develop core partisan attitudes helps to influence their basic decisions on targeting and messages. The concept is expressed in a basic consulting tenet: "Work your strengths, not your weaknesses." Naive candidates often forget that maxim and try to appeal to everybody in the constituency. The very nature of political socialization, though, is that such efforts are doomed to failure. Any attempt to appeal to all the voters faces the continuous resistance from voters who have spent a lifetime developing attitudes and values that are in direct opposition to some things that the candidate will be advocating. As a result, more experienced consultants merely write off some voters and concentrate on communicating with those who will be more likely to be receptive to their message. A combination of polling data, demographic data, and past voting data will be used to assess and identify those voters, but the ultimate concept will be a simple one. A lifetime of developing political attitudes will make some voters more receptive to your message, while others will be less receptive. Understanding that concept can be crucial to the chances of campaign success.

QUESTIONS FOR DISCUSSION

1. A woman legislator favors a "woman's right to choose" and is opposing a measure that would require a twenty-four-hour waiting period and counseling before receiving an abortion. To whom should she target her position statement? What are the benefits of such targeting? Should she attempt to convince her opponents that they are wrong? Are there any groups she should exclude from her efforts? What socialization factors would be relevant to her decision.

2. The largest newspaper in the state is attacking a candidate for state senate for his pro-gun views. What socialization factors might influence his constituency's views on this topic? How would those factors influence his response to the newspaper?

3. Your parents oppose construction of a new mall on the edge of your neighborhood. You enjoy hanging out at the mall. What socialization factors might explain the differences in your attitudes? What issue or issues will likely be the biggest source of disagreement on this topic? Why?

4. Examine the sources of your own political beliefs. To what extent were you influenced by your parents? By the media? By your friends? By your education? By political parties? Which of these had an influence on your political ideology? Which had an influence on your level of interest (or lack of interest) in politics?

5. The study of political socialization assumes that political orientations obtained in childhood affect adult behavior. To what extent, though, should political socialization be viewed as a lifelong process through which adults also acquire new information and adjust their political orientations?

Campaign Strategies

How important is a campaign strategy? That depends on the experience of the candidates and the type of office they seek. Political amateurs often qualify to run for an office based purely on the hope that they might win or that they can out-hustle the other candidate. Although such campaigns succeed frequently enough to give new candidates hope, particularly at the local level of politics, most are doomed to failure (Thomas, 1999). Furthermore, while a local candidate might have a chance of winning without a plan, one running for federal office will not. For major campaigns, a candidate who enters a political campaign in the twenty-first century without a comprehensive strategy is doomed to failure. A campaign strategy is the controlling authority for the campaign budget, dictating targeting, staffing, fund-raising, scheduling, and nearly every other function of the campaign. It identifies the target groups, thus dictating budget allocations for TV and radio ads, direct mail, and phone banks. It provides a guide for both the on-site staff and consultants who are needed to carry out the campaign plan. These factors, in turn, provide an indication of the cost of the campaign, which leads to the fund-raising targets necessary to be successful.

Some historians point to the 1828 election of Andrew Jackson as the beginning of modern campaign politics (Parsons, 2011), but most modern professional political practitioners began to emerge in 1930s California during the Merriam–Sinclair gubernatorial campaign. America found an increasing use for professional political consultants (Mitchell, 1992) after World War II. One such example came in 1946 when a group of California Republicans, the Committee of 100, pooled their resources to defeat an incumbent Democrat they abhorred (Costello, 1960). After raising funds, the group hired Murray Chotiner, a veteran politico already known for his ability to guide winning Republican campaigns, on a part-time basis to guide their campaign.

Their first obstacle was fundamental—they had no candidate. Democratic representative Jerry Voorhis, the hated incumbent, was believed to be far too strong for conventional Republicans to risk the race. The group undertook a very unconventional recruiting method: they placed an "announcement" in the newspapers of the congressional district. Applications were invited from "any young man, resident of the district, preferably a veteran, with a fair education, no political strings or obligations, and possessed of a few ideas for [the] betterment of the country at large" (Costello, 1960).

The result yielded wide-ranging historical and political consequences. A young naval officer who was finishing his World War II military duty found out about the announcement and responded. The young seaman's name? Richard Nixon. The committee had one main question for him. Was he a Republican? "I guess I am. I voted for Dewey," Nixon reportedly said. The resulting campaign against Voorhis became the beginning of a political career for Nixon that included terms in the U.S. House of Representatives, the U.S. Senate, the vice presidency, and the presidency.

The Voorhis–Nixon campaign, however, was also remarkable for another of its features—the use of a "hired gun" consultant to run a congressional campaign using a pretested campaign strategy. The strategy developed by Chotiner for that campaign pulled together tactics he had previously developed, tried, and refined in a number of other electoral campaigns. Chotiner advised Nixon to attack Voorhis as a Communist sympathizer. In a time when attacks were often ignored by incumbents, Nixon triumphed. Voorhis, by ignoring the attacks, betrayed his lack of understanding that an attack by a well-funded opponent can be extremely effective.

After the Nixon victory, campaigners learned to take a holistic view of the campaign process. This approach led to the development of a comprehensive campaign model instead of a focus on individual campaign messages. Any specific message is useful only to the extent that it contributes to the overall campaign strategy, as expressed in the strategic model. Thus, for consultants, strategic models—including demographics, voter history, public opinion, the means of communication, potential funding, and others—serve a decisional function: decisions are made in terms of whether an action will contribute to the overall campaign strategy. For academicians, strategic models can serve as a descriptive framework that can be used to analyze a campaign, providing a better understanding of why a campaign was or was not successful.

STRATEGY ANALYSIS

Before developing a campaign strategy, consultants first evaluate the factors that are likely to affect the outcome of the campaign. The specific process for making this evaluation varies, and several different approaches have been developed for this purpose.

SWOT Analysis

SWOT is an acronym for "Strengths, Weaknesses, Opportunities, and Threats." As the name implies, SWOT analysis forces the campaign to evaluate itself by these four categories.

Strengths are defined as assets of the candidate and the campaign. This includes positive attributes of the candidate, any major voting blocs committed to the candidate, and financial resources. Factors that contribute to the credibility of the candidate, either with the news media or with the voting public, would be listed and discussed in this category. This includes the candidate's record, the ability to attract eminent supporters, and the ability to raise funds, to mention a few.

Weaknesses are the flip side of the coin and include negative aspects of the candidate's record, the inability to attract eminent supporters, and the inability to raise funds. Pollsters Bill Hamilton and Dave Beattie refer to these elements as "sponsor roadblocks." "Whether a first-time candidate or a long-term public servant, every candidate has voted for, said, implied, or done something that will upset some group," they note (Hamilton & Beattie, 1999, p. 99).

Opportunities are factors outside the campaign that could provide a positive benefit to the candidate. These might include the state of the economy, partisan trends that favor the candidate, the general mood of the electorate, or the presence of a major campaign issue on which the candidate has a potentially popular record. The analysis of opportunities requires both the art and craft of political practitioners. The goal is to develop a list of possible events that can be used for your candidate's benefit.

Threats are external factors that could adversely affect the campaign. These may include negative moods among the electorate, partisan trends that negatively affect the candidate, and campaign issues that work against the candidate. It also includes institutional and cultural barriers to the candidate's success. The goal for this part of the analysis is to anticipate problems and to limit their negative impact on the campaign.

All four factors of SWOT provide the candidate and his or her consultants with an all-encompassing view of the campaign. While not all events will be anticipated, many can be. As a result, such an analysis can be useful in preparing an overall campaign strategy.

Who'll Say What

Another approach to strategy analysis, and one that can be used in conjunction with SWOT, is to divide anticipated campaign rhetoric into a four-box matrix defined by two categories: "What our candidate will say" vs. "What their candidate will say," and "What will be said about our candidate" vs. "What will be said about their candidate." The result is a four-box matrix, as shown in Figure 3.1.

The result is a chart of anticipated campaign messages, both by your side and by that of the opposition. This chart can then be used for polling purposes (to test the strengths and weaknesses of all messages) and for planning campaign strategies.

What Will Be Said About . . .

	Our Candidate	*Their Candidate*
What Our Candidate Will Say	. . . About himself	. . . About the other candidate
What Their Candidate Will Say	. . . About our candidate	. . . About themselves

FIGURE 3.1
"Who'll Say What" Matrix

CAT Analysis

CAT analysis (Powell & Kitchens, 1986) focuses on identifying the contingencies, assumptions, and tactics of a campaign. Contingencies are those threshold conditions that must be present for the candidate to have a chance to win and for a campaign strategy to be effective. Thus, contingencies are "if-type" statements, such as, "If Condition X is present, then Strategy Y can be effective."

Assumptions are those elements in a campaign that serve as the premises for campaign communications, or the rationales behind campaign decisions. Assumptions, in effect, are predictive statements about the reactions of political communication elements. For example, predictions about how an opponent might respond to a campaign message would fall into this category. So would predictions about a change in the voters' perception of a candidate during a campaign

Tactics are the specific maneuvers in a campaign that take advantage of the contingent conditions and/or operationally define the assumptions of the campaign. Frequently, in major campaigns, tactics are the implementation efforts suggested by the campaign consultants. Implementation is often based on polling data, which test the contingent conditions and assumptions of the campaign. This process allows for conclusions about the rhetorical circumstances of a campaign, the campaigners' perceptions of themselves, and the candidates' perceptions of the voters. The results of CAT analysis provide a schematic description of the elements needed for successful communication in a particular political situation and can be useful in determining why particular political communication attempts are successful.

Different strategies require different tactics. For example, Trent and Friedenberg (2000) categorize campaign styles into incumbent styles and challenger styles and identify specific activities that are associated with each style. Tactics associated with incumbent campaigning include the following (p. 82):

1. Creating pseudoevents to attract and control media attention.
2. Making appointments to state and federal jobs, state and national party committees.
3. Creating governmental task forces to investigate issues of public concern.
4. Appropriating federal funds and/or grants.
5. Consulting or negotiating with world leaders.
6. Manipulating the economy or other important domestic issues.
7. Endorsements by party and other important leaders.
8. Emphasizing accomplishments.
9. Creating and maintaining an "above-the-fray" posture.
10. Depending on surrogates for the campaign trail.
11. Interpreting and intensifying a foreign policy problem so that it becomes an international crisis.

Most of these tactics can be subdivided into a few basic tactics. In most cases, they revolve around the incumbent's use of his or her office to influence media attention upon them as individuals, influence the issue agenda of the press and the public, articulate and discuss those factors that have been a benefit to the voters, and increase support among elite opinion leaders.

Some of these tactics are available to nonincumbents, particularly those running for an open seat. Emphasizing accomplishments, such as lauding the amount of federal money brought home to a district, is a common tactic for incumbents, challengers, and open-seat candidates alike. Nearly all candidates for major offices also rely on surrogate campaigners, with family members or friends making appearances on their behalf. Such a tactic is essential given the time constraints on an individual candidate.

Tactics associated with challenger campaigns include the following (p. 94):

1. Attacking the record of opponents.
2. Taking the offensive position on issues.
3. Calling for a change.
4. Emphasizing optimism for the future.
5. Speaking to traditional values instead of calling for value changes.
6. Appearing to represent the philosophical center of the political party.
7. Delegating personal or harsh attacks in an effort to control demagogic rhetoric.

Trent and Friedenberg generally treat this list as strategy options. Consultants, though, are more likely to regard them as tactical options, that is, as specific moves that may be employed as part of a broader strategic plan. As we will see later, one common strategy for challenging an incumbent—The In Man–Out Man strategy—often uses two of these tactics ("Attacking the record of the opponent" and "delegating harsh attacks") plus one not mentioned by Trent and Friedenberg ("inoculation").

Situational Analysis

Agranoff (1976) discussed the effect of situations on campaign strategies and argued that campaigns can and should be planned, organized, and executed on the basis of a systematic strategy. As a guideline for situational analysis, Agranoff offered the following "Checklist for Strategic Assessment":

1. *Campaign resources.* All campaigns must confront the problems of how to most effectively deploy scarce resources. There is only so much time, so much money, and so much candidate energy that can be expended before election day.
2. *Campaign setting.* All campaigns operate within the confines of a given campaign setting, and that setting includes several factors that are relatively immutable (the campaign will not change) and several factors that are mutable (the campaign can change). The campaign should identify which factors can be changed, and direct their efforts at controlling them.
3. *Strategic assessment.* A crucial element in the overall strategic assessment is to meet three functions of campaigns: conversion (persuading voters to support a candidate), reinforcement (solidifying the commitment of supporters), and activation (getting out the vote). The campaign must draw strategic inferences from its possibilities, knowing that reinforcement and activation are much more likely than conversion.

4. *Planning.* The planning of campaign strategy depends on information and research. The campaign must know as much as possible about the constituency, the candidate, the opposition, and other crucial factors in the race. Campaign information includes both scientific data and political experience and judgment.

5. *Systematic strategy.* All of the above considerations must be integrated into a single, comprehensive, overall strategy. Once the elements of the strategy have been set, the remainder of the campaign should simply unfold according to the dictates of the master plan. The small, day-to-day decisions should be guided by the larger strategic plan.

Jackson (1977) noted that Agranoff sets up an "ideal type" for campaign management, but recognizes that even the best-managed campaigns will fall short of the ideal. He also views the campaign as an ongoing process that does not end with the election. This has evoked criticism, particularly as it applies to the U.S. Congress. Mayhew (1974) argues that congressional effectiveness is limited because the members of Congress are "single-minded seekers of re-election," a mind-set that results in a lack of concern for the programmatic impact of the legislative process. In its extreme form, Mayhew argues that every behavior—every speech, every press release, every roll call vote, every pork-barrel project—is undertaken primarily for the purpose of influencing voters with only an incidental concern for effective public policy or programs. Among the more serious consequences of this behavior are delays in legislation, the shaping of political deals, and efforts to develop symbolic but unproductive legislative acts and resolutions.

Still, for better or worse, it is clear that the political process does continue after elections if for no other reason than a public servant's actions in office become campaign fodder for the next election, as suggested by every analytical model discussed in this chapter. Also, it is the very nature of democracy for the electorate to vote out of office those who do not represent them adequately.

TWO STRATEGIC MODELS

The In Man–Out Man Strategy

The In Man–Out Man strategy (Kitchens & Stiteler, 1979; Powell, 1974), initially developed by Murray Chotiner, is designed for use against an incumbent. The campaign is based on the development of bipolar images for the incumbent (In Man) and the challenger (Out Man). From a CAT analysis perspective, the In Man–Out Man strategy is limited by one contingent condition: It only works when there are only two major contenders, the incumbent and the challenger. It is an ineffective strategy in multicandidate primaries or in general elections that have a serious third-party candidate. Its basic technique of developing bipolar images is effective only when the voters have an either/or choice; a multicandidate race allows a voter to vote against the incumbent without voting for the challenger using the strategy. Former Alabama lieutenant governor Bill Baxley got his start in politics by using the strategy to defeat an incumbent attorney general, an upset victory that was the impetus for a long political career. "People ask me when

I knew that I had it won," he has said. "I knew that we had it won on the last day of qualifying when I was the only one to qualify against him, because I knew that we would then be able to implement our strategy."

One major assumption of the In Man–Out Man strategy is the role of negative voting. The primary emphasis of the strategy is to get the electorate to vote *against* the incumbent. As Chotiner said in describing the strategy, "if you do not deflate the opposition candidate before your own candidate gets started, the odds are that you are going to be doomed to defeat." Thus, the negative campaign against the incumbent is crucial to demonstrating differences between the challenger and the incumbent.

A second assumption of the In Man–Out Man strategy is the need for the challenger to be perceived as a viable alternative. Research has consistently demonstrated the presence of a proincumbent inertia among the electorate, particularly during good economic times. Thus, a negative campaign against an incumbent is usually not, by itself, enough to defeat an incumbent. In the absence of a positive alternative, the probability increases that the voters will either support the incumbent or simply not vote at all. In either scenario, the challenger is likely to lose the election.

A third element of the strategy is the need to inoculate voters from counterattacks on the challenger. If an incumbent discovers that support is diminishing because of attacks from the challenger, the incumbent is likely to counterattack in an effort to stop the challenger's momentum. Inoculation would arrest the challenger's growing support.

The two reported analyses (Kitchens & Stiteler, 1979; Powell, 1974) of the In Man– Out Man strategy have both implemented the strategy in a three-stage developmental pattern, although the specifics of some stages varied slightly. In both studies, the first stage is an attack stage, but the source of the attack differed. One campaign (Powell, 1974) used attack messages delivered directly by the candidate, while the other (Kitchens & Stiteler, 1979) engaged the incumbent with third-party attacks, reducing the probability (or effectiveness) of a "mud-slinging" charge directed toward the challenger.

The second stage, positive image building, revolves around efforts to get the public to vote for the challenger (Assumption 2). Powell reported an implementation of this stage based on Social Judgment theory, that the campaign assumed that the voters lacked strong commitments to the incumbent. The positive messages for the challenger were designed to attract hard-to-reach voters. Kitchens and Stiteler reported using a media event (a 100-mile walk) to build the positive image.

The third stage, inoculation, was consistent in both reports. Both studies reported the use of McGuire's "threat-motivation" form of inoculation (McGuire & Papageorgis, 1961). The challenger's supporters were alerted to the potential use of counter-persuasion techniques by the incumbent, identifying the possible source and type of the messages, and a reason for the attack. The latter served as a counterattitudinal response, which was designed to limit the effectiveness of the counterattack. In 1992, Eugene Reese, a young lawyer, ran for the Montgomery, Alabama, circuit court judgeship and combined all three elements into a single campaign motto: "The Best Judge Money Can't Buy!"

Assumed Incumbency Strategy

The Assumed Incumbency strategy (Powell & Shelby, 1981) recognizes the value of incumbency in some political campaigns. Incumbency provides automatic legitimacy, increases fund-raising potential, and usually results in the incumbent being considered the front-runner, or likely winner, early in a campaign (Trent & Friedenberg, 2000, pp. 79–82). The Assumed Incumbency strategy seeks to gain those same advantages by generating the perception that Candidate A is the natural choice to replace Incumbent B. The Assumed Incumbency strategy can be effective if three conditions are met: (1) the incumbent is not running for reelection, (2) the incumbent was popular, and (3) some link or argument can be established that Candidate A is the natural choice.

If those conditions are met, then the strategy assumes that direct confrontation between the candidate and the opposition should not occur, since such confrontation would bestow legitimacy on the opponent. Thus, the Assumed Incumbency model works from a candidate-to-issue confrontation, rather than a candidate-to-candidate perspective. The strategy also assumes that past voting behavior for the actual incumbent can serve as a base for establishing vote expectations (and targeting goals) for the assumed incumbent. And finally, the strategy dictates which media should be employed at what times to achieve these effects. Since the strategy progresses through the stages of legitimacy, identification, and reinforcement (discussed in the following paragraphs), the media associated with these primary functions should be used at each stage of the strategy. Press coverage is the primary medium used during the legitimacy stage, because of the status-conferral ability of the press to bestow legitimacy on a candidate (Lazarsfeld & Morton, 1960). Billboards and signs are the primary medium for the identification stage because of their ability to increase name recognition. Finally, broadcast media were used in the reinforcement stage because of the need to communicate a message that needed reinforcement.

As a set of tactics, the Assumed Incumbency strategy is implemented through a three-stage developmental process—legitimacy, identification, and reinforcement. The legitimacy stage is initially directed to opinion leaders, including the press. This select audience is presumed to already have some acquaintanceship with the candidate and is in a position to disseminate whatever message it receives. If a sufficient level of name recognition does not yet exist, preliminary identification work may be necessary, since voters are unlikely to bestow legitimacy on an unknown candidate. The goal of the legitimacy stage is to generate expectations of the candidate as the front-runner, or likely winner. This goal is achieved with a rhetorical stance that identifies the candidate as the heir apparent or the natural choice for the position. This stage is comparable to Trent's (1978) "surfacing" stage in presidential politics, and its intent is to establish the candidate's qualifications for the office with the press. Legitimacy is a threshold that any campaign must reach before it has a chance of being successful. Jimmy Carter, for example, after winning the 1976 presidential election, mentioned several problems that he had had to overcome—being from the South, not being from Washington, a lack of campaign funds, and a weak campaign organization. Still, despite this list of problems, Carter noted that "The biggest problem I had... was substantiality of campaign efforts in the minds of the people. Nobody thought I should be taken seriously" (quoted in Schram, 1976, p. 7).

The successful completion of the legitimacy stage will provide an impetus for the second stage—identification. A by-product of status conferral from the press is increased public visibility and wider name recognition for the candidate. The candidate becomes a political celebrity and name recognition increases. Tactics shift to handle the change in goals; press coverage shifts from a focus on establishing legitimacy to one of maintaining one's name before the public. Press releases used during this phase typically announce activities that keep the candidate's name in the media (e.g., serving as a guest speaker, receiving political honors, or working on current legislation or political problems). Those political media used primarily to increase name exposure, such as billboards, bumper stickers, signs, and posters, are introduced during this phase.

Increased name recognition leads to the third stage—reinforcement. If the initial stages of legitimacy and identification are successful, then a set of expectations about the candidate are generated. In the reinforcement stage, the campaign must reaffirm the candidate's legitimacy by meeting those expectations. The premise of legitimacy implies that a candidate is competent to hold a position and understands the problems to be faced. The rhetorical stance in this stage, then, is characterized by competency coupled with empathy.

These three stages—legitimacy, identification, and reinforcement—serve as rhetorical guidelines as well as the messages themselves. The value of the messages associated with these stages is supported by Fenno's (1978) analysis of elements essential to building positive voter response—qualification, identification, and empathy. In the Assumed Incumbency model, legitimacy is the initial goal that provides the impetus for communicating these concepts. In 1991, Richard Ieyoub was a candidate for attorney general of Louisiana running in a crowded field to replace a retiring, well-known, and well-liked incumbent. He adopted the motto, "The Only Prosecutor in the Race," and progressed through all three phases.

THREE TRADITIONAL MODELS

While new strategic models seemingly arise with each new election, three traditional models for campaign strategies have been around for years: (1) the Easy Decision strategy developed by Stephen Shadegg, (2) the Ticket-Splitting strategy developed by DeVries and Tarrance, and (3) Joseph Napolitan's Least Objectionable Candidate. These three models are important because each makes different assumptions about subgroups of the electorate, particularly in terms of what types of voters make up the critical "swing groups" who decide elections and how those voters are reached with campaign messages.

The Easy Decision

Stephen Shadegg (1972) advocated a multipurpose campaign strategy aimed at making the voting decision an easy one. According to Shadegg, the voting public consists of three distinct subgroups—the "committed," the "undecides," and the "indifferents." The committed voters are those "strongly prejudiced toward one party or another," and few campaign messages are targeted toward them. Undecided voters, he argues, are "frequently those who are truly best informed. They recognize that sometimes only slight shades of gray separate two candidates... (and) they frequently find it difficult to make a decision." The crucial swing voters, he argues, are the indifferents, "those who don't vote at all, or vote only in response to an emotional appeal or as the result of some carefully planned campaign technique [that] makes it easy for them to reach a decision." Their votes are based more on emotion than reason, he added. "Political decisions are made by the indifferents," he wrote, "that segment of the body politic [that] really couldn't care less."

To reach these voters, Shadegg recommends strategies that sharpen the differences between candidates. "These differences may have no real bearing upon the candidate's competence. But if they can be displayed in such a fashion as to be easily recognizable, the indifferents will show their gratitude for this assistance by voting." Shadegg admits that such decisional factors may have little direct reference to the issues of the campaign. "Political campaigns generate and fatten on a certain type of hysteria...," he wrote. "In contests where it is sometimes difficult to find a truly major difference between competing candidates, the voter is almost forced to rest his decision upon some relatively unimportant difference."

Ticket-Splitting

DeVries and Tarrance (1972) take an entirely different perspective, arguing that the crucial swing votes in elections are ticket splitters, those voters who vote for both Democratic and Republican candidates in the same election cycle. Furthermore, their perception of this swing vote differs from that of Shadegg's indifferent voter. DeVries and Tarrance describe the ticket splitter as "slightly younger, somewhat more educated, somewhat more white collar, and more suburban than the typical middle-class voter." In addition, the ticket splitter tends to consume more media output about politics and is more politically active than the straight Democrat (but less so than straight Republicans). As described by DeVries and Tarrance, the ticket splitter is not a one-issue voter and cannot be easily reached by highly emotional approaches. Instead, this swing voter is viewed as a complex voter, knowledgeable about campaign issues, and oriented toward problem solving by candidates instead of by political parties.

The implementation of the ticket-splitting strategy reflects the importance placed on these assumptions about the profile of the ticket-splitting voter. Media buys are based on the probability of ticket-splitting behavior (based on voting analysis from past elections). For example, the ticket-splitting broadcast media strategy may focus heavily on newscasts and sporting events, since ticket splitters watch more of those kinds of shows than the average voter. Campaign messages are designed to reflect the issue-oriented, problem-solving emphasis preferred by the ticket splitter. The focus is on providing the voter with information. DeVries and Tarrance even suggest a format for the ideal ad aimed at a ticket splitter: "Present the problem, demonstrate an understanding and ability to handle that problem, and end with a soft-sell editorial."

Ticket-splitting behavior can be easily identified by using both polling and analyses of past voting behavior. As a result, ticket-splitting analysis has become a standard procedure in many campaigns. Still, questions have been raised about the accuracy of DeVries and Tarrance's profile of this voter, such as, Were the data that formed the basis of their conclusion campaign specific or could they be expanded to other campaigns? Initially, DeVries and Tarrance assumed that the profile was highly accurate for most campaigns. That supposition seemed to be supported when they ran subsequent campaigns that identified similar profiles for these swing voters.

Doubt was raised in the mid-1970s, however, when Mississippi Republican Gil Carmichael ran a U.S. Senate campaign. Although Carmichael lost to Democratic incumbent James Eastland, Carmichael was successful in getting a significant number of ticket-splitting votes from Mississippi's rural areas—an outcome that went against the traditional profile (Powell & Flick, 1982). Further doubts were cast on the traditional profile when Ronald Reagan ran for president, getting significant support from rural Democrats in the South. More recently, an examination of ticket-splitting behavior in Florida (Kitchens & Powell, 1994) added more data to the doubts, concluding that ticket-splitting was a by-product of campaign communication rather than a trait representative of any particular type of voter. That conclusion assumes that the profile of the so-called typical ticket splitter is likely to change with every election, depending on which groups are targeted for campaign communication.

These instances have been sufficient to cast doubt on the ticket-splitting strategy, particularly among academicians. Still, while the academic community has largely given up on this approach, it still has a major impact on campaigns. Both parties regularly conduct studies on the phenomenon, particularly at the state level. In some places (Florida, for example), the studies have broadened the base of knowledge on ticket-splitting down to the precinct, carrier route, and voting box level. Thus, ticket-splitting is one of those rare academic areas in which the consultants have more detailed information than do most academicians. Unfortunately for the academic community, though, this information is closely guarded and used for strategic purposes.

The Least Objectionable Candidate

Shadegg, DeVries, and Tarrance are all Republicans, and their campaign strategies reflect their Republican heritage of looking for an edge that will increase the chances for their candidates. Although there are differences in the campaigns, they assume the need for defining a distinct image for their candidate, one that makes their candidate appear to be the best choice for the voters. Democratic consultant Joseph Napolitan (1972) offered a different approach, arguing that voters do not support their ideal "best" candidate, but merely choose the one who is "the least objectionable." Candidates win, he believes, not because they appeal to the most voters, but because they offend the fewest.

Adherents to this strategy believe that elections are decided by moderates, a group of voters who are neither extremely conservative nor extremely liberal. Any candidate who is identified too strongly on either side of the ideological perspective is likely to lose. Operationally, this leads to campaigns that use generalized messages, overladen with equivocations. Messages are created that can be interpreted by the voter in a manner consistent with the voter's own position. It can also lead to bland campaigns in which the candidate is accused of not taking a firm position on issues. But, if the candidate has still offended only a few, Napolitan would argue that they are in a position to win the election.

TWO STRATEGIES FOR THE TWENTY-FIRST CENTURY
Partisan Politics and "The Permanent Majority"

For much of the twentieth century, the maxim among political pundits was that candidates should appeal to their partisan base in the primaries, but move to the middle for the general election (e.g., Shadegg, 1972). That concept was particularly important to Republicans; for much of the 1900s, Democrats outnumbered Republicans in many states and across the nation as a whole. One by-product of this registration gap is that Republicans developed more sophisticated campaign strategies to offset the Democratic advantage in numbers.

The election of President Ronald Reagan in 1980 signaled an increase in Republican identification nationwide that triggered a steady increase in the number of voters who identified with the Republican Party. That trend developed into full-blown partisanship with the Republican impeachment of President Clinton in the 1990s (Baker, 2008). By 2000, Republican strategist Karl Rove had examined polling data on national trends and concluded that Republicans had enough support that they could win a presidential election by abandoning the middle and appealing only to the partisan base. The former "middle" voters, he and others concluded, really shared political ideology with the GOP.

Support for his argument could also be found in a two-decade decline in support for Democratic ideology. Starting in the 1980s, the Democratic Party had adopted an increasing number of positions that appealed to specific interest groups within the party, but that put them at odds with a majority of Americans. These included unpopular positions on gun control (viewed as anti-Second Amendment by many), pro-abortion, pro-gay rights, and antireligion. The Republican Party, meanwhile, positioned itself on the opposite side of these issues, using them as "wedge" messages to drive swing voters away from the Democratic side of the ideological fence.

By 2000, the Republicans had done an excellent job of mobilizing the "religious right" to turn out such voters for their cause. Rove believed that the wedge issues were strong enough to give the party national control—particularly in a presidential campaign. Thus, George W. Bush, who had worked across party lines as Governor of Texas, became a partisan campaigner for President in 2000. His partisan appeals were not unusual during the primary, but he kept up the approach in the general election. That, in itself, was a major shift in campaign strategy.

The Republicans' math was actually a little off. Democrat Al Gore won the popular vote in the 2000 election, but Bush won after a ballot controversy in Florida. Once Bush was in office, Rove (2010) joined the White House staff and started openly working on what he called a "Permanent Majority," that is, developing a plan to appeal to white, middle-class voters, plus a growing Hispanic minority, that would lead to partisan numbers that would ensure the election of Republican candidates for years to come.

The plan didn't work. Bush successfully won reelection in 2004, but only after third-party ads falsely accused Democrat John Kerry of not earning his medals from the Vietnam War. The "permanent majority" started disintegrating over immigration issues, as many Republican voters refused to follow the party line on a lenient immigration policy that would solidify the Hispanic vote for the GOP. By 2006, the Democrats made major gains in the Congress and the Senate. As one reporter wrote of Rove's plan, "Hailed as the genius behind Mr. Bush's presidential victories and the Republican gains in 2000 and 2004, Mr. Rove now carries the burden of a 2006 election that cost his party control of Congress and called into question the political theories that are his stock in trade" (p. WK4).

In 2008, Democrat Barack Obama won the presidential election and threw a major wrench in the machinery of the permanent majority (Heilemann & Halperin, 2010; Plouffe, 2010). Republicans made a major comeback in the 2010 congressional elections, but by then the idea of a permanent majority had been abandoned. Regardless, the decade from 2000 to 2010 had established the format of a new kind of campaign strategy—one based on appealing to a large partisan base rather than seeking votes from moderate positions.

At this writing, many candidates of both parties continue to use this strategy, particularly at the state or district level. Republicans use it in strong Republican districts, while Democrats use it in areas with strong Democratic support. It can still be effective, if the following assumptions are present:

1. Identification with the candidate's party significantly outpaces that with the opponent's party, particularly if that partisan identification exceeds a majority.
2. Partisanship becomes the primary anchor for the voters' decisions. In some areas, a local issue (e.g., weak economy) may override partisan concerns.
3. The candidate has a record of strong identification to the party. Generally, newcomers to either party have a tougher time employing this approach.

Academic research has documented the success of this approach. Developed Issue Ownership Theory based on a 1980 case study. The theory argues that candidates who emphasized the issues identified with their political party had an electoral advantage. Benoit (2007) later tested and supported that theory in an analysis of candidates' television ads.

There are those who raise ethical questions about this approach. Typical of these critics is the work of Hacker and Pierson (2010), who call it "winner-take-all" politics (p. 3). Hacker and Pierson argue that both parties are at fault. They would agree with Baker, who noted that after the Republicans went after Clinton in a partisan-based impeachment effort, "It definitely poisoned the well on both sides. Without getting into the merits of anything, there's no doubt there were Democrats waiting from the day George Bush took office to even the score for Bill Clinton. And Republicans are the same today with Barack Obama and the Rod Blagojevich scandal"

(p. WK1). The problem is that partisan campaigns extend beyond the boundaries of the campaign itself, making it harder for legislators to reach consensus on legislation (Hulse, 2010).

THE POLITICAL BRAIN

Republican success at the polls prompted some Democrats to reevaluate their traditional strategies. Among the most influential of these works was a book by Drew Westen (2007), titled *The Political Brain*. Westen argued that Democrats had been losing because the party had based its electoral arguments on logic, that is, appealing to the rational part of the voters' minds and disregarding the impact of emotion on voting behavior. Westen, a professor of psychology at Emory, argued that the Democratic Party should focus on emotions rather than issues, policies, and facts. He wrote that "With the exception of the Clinton era, Democratic strategists for the last three decades… clung tenaciously to the dispassionate view of the mind and to the campaign strategy that logically follows from it" (p. 13). **Westen further described this approach as an "irrational emotional commitment to rationality" (p. 13).** He argued that Democrats should recognize the role of the voters' emotion, even if those voters did not always recognize those reactions themselves. They don't know it. This was a particular problem for Democrats, he argued, because "Democrats run from every issue where there's passion involved. If you don't say anything, you are giving them the right to define the public's feeling."

Westen cited psychological research that included brain scans of voters who viewed photos containing contradictory information about their candidates. The scans showed that neurons in the brains lit up for supporters of both parties, but both sets of supporters found psychological means for denying any significant contradictions. The conclusion: Democratic attempts to identify illogical arguments by Republicans were doomed to failure, because the voters' biases would ensure that they minimize or rationalize the information. Subsequent research indicates that voters show a similar partisan bias in evaluating candidates' debate performance (Holbert, LaMarre, & Landreville, 2009). It was a situation that Caplan (2007) called the "myth of the rational voter" (p. ix).

Westen's ideas were reinforced two years later by a work by another psychologist, George Lakoff (2008). Lakoff argued that Republicans won more elections because they were more effective at manipulating voters. He recommended that Democrats use the same approach, arguing that "Democracy is too important to leave the shaping of the brains of Americans to authoritarians." Much of the specific recommendations of this approach involves the use of word selection and value articulation. In terms of words, for example, the political brain approach recommends that Democrats talk about "the middle class" instead of "the poor." Candidates are also encouraged to embrace their religious faith (Weiss, 2010). Barack Obama's 2008 presidential campaign epitomizes this approach, including his use of "hope" as an inspirational term (Obama, 2006) and his willingness to acknowledge his religious faith, despite attending a church with a controversial pastor.

If all of this sounds familiar, that's because it is a twenty-first-century version of Shadegg's Theory of the Indifferent Voter from the 1960s. His strategy, the Easy

Decision Model, assumed that campaign messages must touch emotional buttons that make the voting choice an easy one for voters. Thus, Shadegg's approach to campaign strategy recognized the importance of emotion in influencing voter behavior and did it decades before the works of Westsn (2007), Caplan (2007), and Lakoff (2008).

POSITIONAL STRATEGIES

One approach to strategy development relies on positional rhetoric to distinguish the candidate from the opposition. While each can have its own distinctive elements, most of these approaches are variations of Shadegg's Easy Decision model. In each case, the purpose of the positional strategy is to define a position that will make it easy for the voters to make a decision that favors the candidate. The variations of this approach are too numerous for all of them to be included, but three variations can serve as examples: the "Only Alternative," "Role Definition," and "Triangulation Strategies."

The Only Alternative, or the "Anybody But Them" approach, attempts to position the candidate as the only viable alternative to an unpopular opponent. When there are only two candidates in the campaign, this approach usually becomes a negative campaign, which is similar to the In Man–Out Man approach. What typically makes it different is the absence of any comparative messages. The messages focus instead on negative factors related to the opponent, with little or no positive messages about the candidate provided. Strategically, that can be a risky gamble; a lack of positive information about candidates can keep voters away from the polls, rather than attract them toward the only alternative.

Another scenario for this approach occurs during the primary nomination process. Although several candidates may officially be on the ballot, one candidate will sometimes campaign on the basis of being the only "viable alternative" for defeating the nominee of the other party. In this instance, the focus of the campaign messages is on the legitimacy or credibility factors of the campaign, rather than the issues. The argument becomes, "Vote for me, because I can defeat the other guy," rather than "Vote for me because I represent your issues."

The Role Definition strategy attempts to gain an advantage with the voters by defining the candidate as an "ideal candidate" (Nimmo & Savage, 1976) for the office being sought. For example, if polling data reveal that the voters' ideal candidate is one who is a problem solver, then the Role Definition strategy would try to develop an image of the candidate as either the "only" problem solver among the contenders, or at least the "best" problem solver in the race. The specific nature of the ideal role can vary with each campaign or position, but the overall goal remains the same—the candidate whose image comes closest to the ideal has the best chance of winning the election. The 1990 campaign for attorney general of Alabama is the prototype for the Role Definition strategy. In that campaign, three different candidates were running for the position, but only one of them had experience as a prosecutor. That candidate ran a campaign based on "the-only-one-who-has-prosecuted-criminals" argument and won the election.

When the candidate of a political party finds that winning a political campaign—or even advancing significantly—will be extremely difficult for social, cultural, or even more abstract reasons, he or she may resort to a strategy of triangulation. This approach creates a distraction, which can reduce the number of votes cast for an opponent. Typically, these votes may be deflected to a third candidate or be dissuaded from being cast at all. Perhaps a burning issue may be raised that engenders support from groups that change their customary voting habits. In the days before campaign finance disclosure, straw candidates were recruited by some major candidates to siphon votes away from their opposition. Although this probably happened less than charged, there is no doubting its effectiveness. The emergence of effective third-party candidates (especially H. Ross Perot) replicates the straw candidate effect in recent years.

The strategy can be used, however, without the presence of a third candidate, if an issue or message can be identified that separates the candidate from traditional ties and allows them to siphon votes from demographic targets that were previously hard to reach. In 1985, for example, Virginia State Senator Douglas Wilder was running against Marshall Coleman for the governorship. As a liberal African American in a state with less than 20 percent of the electorate also African American, Wilder had little chance of winning without attracting the support of white voters who typically held moderate or conservative views. Wilder handled the problem by challenging Coleman on the issue of abortion and making it the focus of his campaign. Most of Wilder's television advertising budget was expended on the topic. Republican women voters, particularly in populous northern Virginia, deserted Coleman in sufficient numbers to secure Wilder his victory.

Most famously, following recommendations from political consultant Dick Morris, triangulation became a major buzzword for the presidential campaigns of Bill Clinton. In 1992, Clinton attempted to demonstrate his independence from Jesse Jackson. Before a meeting with Jackson, Clinton criticized a rap singer, Sister Souljah, for being an irresponsible leader of African American youth. White voters took this as a signal that Clinton would be his own man, not beholden to any group, unlike their sense of his Democratic opponents, and helped him beat Jackson and his other rivals for the nomination.

SUMMARY

The study of campaign strategy often seems to have a dual personality, with academicians looking at it objectively and practitioners searching for strategic advantages. Even within the campaign, such dual viewpoints will occur. Hershey (1974) noted that candidates and their campaign managers often view the campaign differently. Part of those different perceptions is due to the differences in role specification, and part from the greater amount of ego involvement demonstrated by the candidate. Still, that dual personality often makes it harder to pin down the specifics of a campaign strategy.

From inside the campaign, the development of a campaign strategy is a precampaign activity. Candidates, their staff, and their consultants develop the campaign plan in advance, using it as a road map for organizing and executing campaign tactics. For academicians, analysis of campaign strategies are more often postelection activities. Unless the particular academic researcher was personally involved in a campaign, they may lack the information necessary to view the strategy as a precampaign activity. And, even if they did have such information, most scholars would wait until after the election to report their conclusions about the strategy. Either way, the dual nature of campaign strategies persists. For consultants, strategies are early campaign decisions. For academicians, strategies are postcampaign analyses.

Furthermore, communication scholars have only recently begun to examine the persuasive implications of some political campaign strategies. Campaign consultants, meanwhile, use specific, if less formalized, strategies to guide their own activities. Although not always developed to a theoretical level, strategies function both as comprehensive plans and decisional models for campaigns. By suggesting an overall framework for a campaign, political communication strategies provide a means of plotting campaign development. As decisional models, they offer a basis for adaptive decision making in responding to events as they occur during a campaign.

Discussing all possible strategies is a task that goes beyond the scope of this book, but those discussed here provide a foundation of basic models. In real life, consultants develop their own hybrid strategy for each campaign, but most of those hybrids are combinations of those mentioned in this chapter. Thus, there are thousands of possible strategies, although most are only minor variations of the archetypes presented here. Most start with some form of strategic analysis, such as the "Who'll Say What" or SWOT analysis, which serves as a framework for helping the consultant develop the strategy. Understanding those approaches and how they are used by consultants can also serve to help academicians analyze campaign strategies.

QUESTIONS FOR DISCUSSION

1. Consider a recent local election in your area. What was the campaign strategy of the winner? Of the loser? Was one candidate slated to win regardless of strategy, or did the strategic moves of the campaign make the difference between winning and losing?

2. What is the difference between strategy and tactics? What is the first step in developing either?

3. Why is it advantageous for a political campaign to have a strategy?

4. A U.S. senator who is finishing his first term is the target of a grand jury investigation, but has already raised enough money to run a viable campaign. Design a strategy for this candidate to follow. What would be a good strategy for the opponent to follow?

5. Some strategists and communicators consider ticket splitters to be the key group in finding support among persuadable voters. Why? What strategic notion might appeal to a ticket splitter?

6. What is the relationship between the elements of strategy and the various stages of communications?

The Image of the Political Candidate

In the presidential election of 1948, President Harry Truman was the leader of a splintered Democratic party and faced primary opposition from both a progressive candidate (Henry Wallace) and the "Dixiecrats," represented by Strom Thurmond. After bargaining to retain the party's nomination, he then faced strong Republican opposition from Thomas E. Dewey. Most observers—and most polls at the time—were confident that Dewey would easily defeat the besieged Truman.

Rather than combat that image, Truman took advantage of it. He openly ran as the underdog, telling audiences, "My name's Harry Truman, I work for the government, and I'm trying to keep my job." The approach redefined his image in terms of humility, toughness, and identification with the common person. Dewey, meanwhile, was increasingly seen as slick and urban, "the little man on the top of the wedding cake," as Alice Roosevelt Longworth described him (Combs, 1980, p. 151). Facing those sharp contrasts in images, the voters sided with Truman in an upset victory, one that helped illustrate the impact that candidate images can have on electoral results (Klapp, 1964).

A candidate's image is often the focus of the campaign message as it is amplified for television ads, phone banks, and direct mail. But some observers criticize consultant-based campaigns for focusing on images and relegating issues to the electoral woodshed. The consequence, their argument goes, is that voter decisions are inevitably based on shallow and emotional impressions rather than a rational understanding of candidates and their positions on issues. Consultants often maintain that image-based campaigns appeal to real voter concerns. Moreover, many consultants say that without meeting such image thresholds, voters will not give weight to issue-oriented discussions, since issues and images are often interlinked. Additionally, many consultants believe that unless a candidate can establish a strong personality in a campaign context, voters will not believe that he or she has the tools needed to perform as a political leader in a pluralistic democracy.

The very nature of the controversy has led to extensive academic investigations into the nature of political images. One classic work, by Nimmo and Savage (1976), examined and summarized much of that research up to the mid-1970s. Their work, in turn, spurred other academicians to investigate the concept further. The resulting data are sometimes confusing, given that individual researchers have approached the field with their own code-specific terminology. Understanding that research requires a synthesization of results by looking at studies that have identified similar concepts, although perhaps using different terminology. Most research studies on political images can be divided into one of four general research questions:

1. What is the nature of candidate images?
2. How are such images developed?
3. What influence does the campaign have on the candidates' images? and
4. What influence does the candidate's image have on electoral decisions?

THE NATURE OF CANDIDATE IMAGES

Nimmo and Savage (1976) defined an image as "a human construct imposed on an array of perceived attributes projected by an object, event, or person" (p. 8). This definition views candidate images as multifaceted phenomena with several key dimensions and identifiable modes of orientation. That description implies that the very nature of political images is a complex psychological element that could potentially be described in any number of ways, depending on the viewpoint of the observer. Not surprisingly, that is what has happened in the academic community, as different researchers have described the nature of images in different ways.

Some scholars view the political candidate as an orator whose utterances can be analyzed with theories that go back to the work of Aristotle. From that perspective, the key components of an image are the trustworthiness of the candidates, their authoritativeness on the issues of the day, and the extent to which their rhetoric indicates good intentions toward the audience. That approach was easily adaptable to public debate within the early days of American democracy. Subsequently, several researchers have attempted to describe the nature of public images in an era of mass communication. McCroskey, Jensen, and Todd (1972) recommended a five-factor breakdown for images of public figures: character, competence, sociability, composure, and extroversion. The first two—character and competence—conformed to two of Aristotle's original factors (trustworthiness and authoritativeness), but the other three assume that images conveyed by way of mass media can be multifaceted.

Another approach that considers the interplay between the mass media and images is the concept of the television personality (Lang & Lang, 1968). This approach identifies the political image as a three-factor design composed of television performance, political role, and personal image. A similar perspective is the view that the candidate as a political actor is concerned with two basic dimensions, a political role and a stylistic role (Graber, 1972). Campbell (1966) preferred to eliminate the stylistic role and discuss the image as a composite of four characteristics: background and experience, leadership ability, personal qualifications, and policy stands.

The American Institute for Political Communication, or AIPC (1970), offered a five-dimensional approach: leadership ability, political philosophy, speaking ability, intelligence, and honesty. Its unique contribution to the image is perhaps the third dimension, a recognition that communication skills play an important role in image formation. The nature of television has amplified the importance of one's speaking ability because of the intimate and instant nature of communications in today's world.

The approach used most often by consultants was offered decades ago by Trenaman and McQuail (1961). They viewed the political image as composed of three major components: leadership strength; judgment as a person (having enough humility and integrity); and disposition toward voters (having empathy). This appears to be the approach that comes closest to the consultants on images. Although the terminology used is slightly different, most consultants view the ideal candidate as a strong leader who will lead the voters, a person of integrity who will be honest with the voters, and an empathic person who understands the voters. In fact, it is hard to imagine a successful candidate who did not exemplify these attributes. In particular, academic research on presidential candidates has focused heavily on leadership (Barber, 1964) and character (Barber, 1972), with the ethical controversies of the Clinton administration focusing attention on both elements.

Furthermore, this three-dimensional approach has been somewhat supported by academic research. Researchers into ideal images have identified a hierarchical image type of the ideal public official as political hero (Trenaman & McQuail, 1961, pp. 163–164). The ideal political hero was identified as being first, a strong leader; second, a person of integrity; and third, an empathic person who was perceived as understanding the voters. The only discrepancy from the consultants' three-dimensional approach was that this research also identified a fourth dimension that sometimes came into play—the candidate as a hard worker. Most political consultants agree with this fourth dimension; they find it hard to imagine voters choosing a candidate who projected an image of being something other than "hard working."

This approach is also consistent with some traditional approaches to rhetorical theory. Garver (1994), in his examination of Aristotle's rhetorical theories, noted the importance of a speaker integrating logic and character. He emphasized the applications of Aristotle's classic work to modern situations in which an effective speaker understands the importance of both practical reason and virtue in presenting a case to the public. While the terminology may be different, the concept is similar. Modern politicians should be honest with the voters and work to implement reasonable ideas as public policy. The public wants, Garver might argue, a person of character who does the job well.

An alternative view of ideal images suggests that a voter's perception of an ideal candidate will differ in accord with the partisanship and other predispositions of individual voters. Miller and Shanks (1996, p. 501) argued that "...the very large bivariate relationships between personal evaluations and vote choice can be traced primarily to the impact on both variables of partisan identification and other predispositions and performances, rather than to the impact on the vote of the candidates' personal qualities per se." Elsewhere they note, this approach does not necessarily "minimize the evidence of consequences of a campaign so much as it recasts the role of the campaign. The selling of a president may still be possible, but the creation of an appealing image would seem to be necessarily based on relatively enduring pre-existing predispositions" (p. 506).

The ideal candidate for one voter may not be the same for another. Research on this matter has identified four distinct and different ideal types (Nimmo & Savage, 1976, p. 68). These four ideal types—the decision maker, the empathic leader, the moral exemplar, and the partisan advocate—are frequently identified in terms of a particular emphasis on one of the four characteristics identified earlier. The decision maker focuses on the candidate's leadership skills and decision-making activities. The empathic leader understands the voters, putting the public ahead of partisan politics. The moral exemplar is a leader of integrity and conviction, a person of reason who articulates his or her convictions. The only ideal type that does not fit the three-dimensional ideal image is that of the partisan advocate. The ideal partisan advocate is honest, but not necessarily empathic; furthermore, such types often reject the idealism of the moral exemplar, particularly if the candidate's ideals are extreme.

THE DEVELOPMENT OF CANDIDATE IMAGES

Questions about the nature of candidate images inevitably lead to additional questions about how voters develop these images? That question has inspired a number of studies into the psychology of image formation, which, in turn, has led to a multitude of possible theories. In fact, nearly any psychological theory related to attitude development or impression formation can be applied to image.

Attribution theory (Heider, 1958; Kelley, 1967; Shaver, 1983) would ascribe image formation to the attributions that voters attach to candidates whom they support and oppose. In such instances, factors such as partisanship and ideology become dimensional antecedents that influence those attributions. Thus, conservatives are likely to attribute conservative ideologies to the candidates of their choice, while labeling the opposition as liberal. Perceptual Balance theory argues that images are developed as voters process information about candidates and their position on issues in relationship to the individual voter's own position on such issues. Again, partisanship and ideology are factors used in the psychological synthesis to attain an image that is perceptually balanced for the individual. This leads to voters perceiving in candidates what is favorable to themselves while distorting or ignoring that which is unfavorable. Similarly, advocates of dissonance theory argue that images are a form of psychological rationalization, a process that helps the voter justify a behavioral decision to vote for or against a particular candidate.

Image formation can also be applied to Social Judgment theory. In this approach, the various issue positions and ideological views taken by a candidate are evaluated by the voter in terms of whether those stances were acceptable or unacceptable to the voter. A perception that the candidate's position was similar to that of the voter would trigger a process of assimilation, with the voter forming a positive perceptual image of the candidate. In that case, the voter's image of the candidate would likely include distortions of the candidate's actual position on issues, perceiving the candidate's views to be more similar to their own than they actually are. Conversely, if a candidate's ideological position was at odds with those of the voter, then that candidate would be viewed as unacceptable and an image formed viewed the candidate as more extreme and further away from the ideal of that particular voter.

Political Chaos theory posits that the image of public theory can be dramatically influenced by outside events, particularly if those events are difficult to control. Karl Rove (2010) and others argued that Hurricane Katrina, which severely damaged New Orleans in 2005, had a negative impact on the image of then president George W. Bush. Others suggested that the BP oil spill had a similar negative impact on the image of President Barack Obama (Bai, 2010; Rich, 2010a). Even positive events can have a negative impact on an official's image. After Barack Obama won the Nobel Peace Prize in 2009, he became the object of ridicule by late-night comics (Leibovich, 2009).

But regardless of which theory is advocated, some elements remain consistent, including the interrelationship of information about the candidates and the voters' interpretations of those data. As Nimmo and Savage (1976) noted, "…a candidate's image is as much a function of what people project to him as of his efforts to project to them" (p. 10). Thus, candidates' images consist of how they are perceived by voters, based on both the subjective knowledge possessed by voters and the messages projected by the candidate. The voters use information and perceptions about the candidate to form affective (positive–negative) evaluations that may affect their electoral behavior. Cognition, evaluation, and behavioral manifestations are the factors that outline the essential elements of the image process.

Cognition

Nimmo and Savage (1976) noted that all images have a cognitive element that reflects those portions of a candidate's image that are treated as facts by the voter. These elements are the ones that voters regard as true or false. For example, former president George H. W. Bush is a Republican who fought in World War II as a fighter pilot, served as head of the CIA, and was vice president under Ronald Reagan. Such facts are what a typical voter could know about Bush, but what any given voter knows may vary significantly from what another voter knows. Some voters might remember that he was vice president, for example, but not remember his association with the CIA. Other voters might know other facts about Bush that are even more extensive than what the first group knows (for example, knowing that he played baseball at Yale). All such cognitions—whether accurate or inaccurate—would contribute to a person's total image of George H. W. Bush.

Evaluations

Based on the information (both accurate and inaccurate) that the voter has about a candidate, the voters are then in a position to form an evaluative, positive-or-negative, opinion about that candidate. Describing that process depends upon which of the earlier-mentioned psychological theories you follow, but some elements seem to be common to all theories. The voters apply what they know, understand, and believe about candidates to form inferences about the candidates' ideological, partisan, and moral values. Those perceptions are then compared to a voter's own beliefs. To the extent that a state of homophily (McCroskey, Richmond, & Daly, 1975), or similarity exists, then the voter is likely to form a positive opinion of that candidate. To the extent that there is a difference between the perceived values of the candidate and those of the voter, then a state of hetereophily (nonsimilarity) exists, and the voter is likely to form a negative opinion. This evaluative dimension is the easiest for pollsters to gauge during a campaign, with polls that ascertain favorability ratings or some other form of positive or negative responses that measure both the direction and strength of the voters' affective evaluations of the candidate.

Behavioral Manifestations

The ultimate goal of a political campaign is to have an image with the voters that will result in at least one positive behavioral manifestation (voting). In some cases, a voter's behavioral manifestation may be stronger than an affective image; voters may choose a candidate they do not know or have any opinion about, for a variety of reasons (party orientation, positive response to the person's name, a "favorite son" connection, a common ethnic background, and so forth). Still, in most major campaigns, voting behavior is a result of evaluative images, with the voter more likely to cast a vote for that candidate for whom they have the highest positive rating, or the least negative rating.

Voting, though, is not the only behavioral manifestation associated with a candidate's image. The images of some candidates can trigger a variety of behaviors, ranging from volunteer work on behalf of the campaign or a candidate's cause to an attempt to assassinate the candidate. Some candidates (perhaps with the assistance of their political consultants) seem to be more adept at image manipulation than others, motivating their impassioned followers to donate time, effort, and money to the cause. Others are content to convey milder images to attract a mass following of voters.

What is not fully known, however, is the extent to which behavioral manifestations are a result of candidate image development, and how much is a by-product of the personality of the candidate's followers. During the 1992 presidential election, for example, Reform candidate H. Ross Perot spurred millions of voters to volunteer for his campaign, distribute literature on his behalf, and actively campaign across the nation. The question remains, however, as to how many of these people were actually inspired just by Perot's rhetoric. Did they engage in such activity because they were swayed by Perot's arguments, or did Perot's image attract a personality type that was more likely to engage in political activity? An example might be drawn by comparing political supporters to audiences at musical concerts. The crowd at a rock concert behaves in a manner that is different from an audience at an opera. But, are the differences in audience behavior a result of the kind of music being played, or does the different kind of music attract a different kind of audience member. The answer is likely to be some combination of both factors, but the nature of that interrelationship needs further analysis.

IMAGE INFLUENCES ON ELECTION DECISIONS

Research has consistently reported that candidates' images play a crucial role in voting behavior. Voters respond to candidates on the basis of the images they have of them. Voters are more likely to vote for a candidate for whom they have a positive image, than one for whom they have a negative image. In essence, voters prefer to vote for somebody they like, and that "liking" dimension is heavily influenced by the image they hold of that candidate. It's not always an easy decision, though. Sometimes dissonance exists because the voter has a positive image of all of the candidates, or a negative image of them all; in those cases, relative evaluations come into play, with the voter generally opting for the most positive or least negative option.

Attempting to influence voting decisions without affecting a candidate's image is relatively futile. If a positive image component can be established with a majority of the voters, then vote intention is likely to follow; if not, it can be enhanced by a variety of get-out-the-vote efforts. But such voter turnout programs are doomed to failure if a positive image dimension has not been established.

Consultants assume that the campaign can have an impact on a candidate's image. Furthermore, the academic community tends to agree with this conclusion. Granted, some academicians believe the mass media do not directly contribute to changes in voting intentions. Most of them, however, do not attempt to extend that argument to the images of those candidates. Regardless of its ultimate impact on behavior, the mass media affect what people know about candidates, how they perceive candidates, and how they feel about them. For example, McClure and Patterson (1974) found that televised network news had little impact, but exposure to political advertising had a direct impact on voters' beliefs about the candidates.

The impact of a negative opinion is particularly important, for two reasons. First, a negative feeling toward the candidate of the voter's preferred party can override the impact of partisanship among moderate partisans. Second, negative images tend to be more precisely defined by the voters than are positive ones. Powell (1977) found that most voters could identify only one or two positive dimensions (usually a holistic "good guy" label) about candidates they supported, but they could provide multiple reasons for the candidate they voted against. Clearly, this may be the intended outcome for a campaign that projects a negative image about its opponent both directly and indirectly. A campaign may brag, for example, that its candidate is "The best judge money can't buy."

Finally, the nature of the impact that the campaign has on an image may depend on the type of media employed and/or the nature of the candidate's personal qualities. After the 1952 election, some analysts suggested that television improved Dwight Eisenhower's image, but did little for his opponent, Adlai Stevenson; conversely, Stevenson seemed to benefit by radio coverage of the campaign. Others have made similar arguments about the 1960 Kennedy–Nixon debates, where Kennedy was perceived as having done better among television audiences, while Nixon was perceived as the winner by radio audiences. Similarly, studies on the 2008 election indicate that Barack Obama had an image edge among online users, perhaps because his campaign was adept at using social networks as a means of communicating with voters (Denton, 2010; Hendricks & Denton, 2010). For that reason, consultants may alter image-related messages on the basis of the nature of the campaign, the candidate, and the opponent.

CAMPAIGN INFLUENCES ON IMAGES

The impact of candidate images on campaigns is widely accepted and sometimes hotly debated. Sometimes overlooked, however, is the opposite phenomenon—the impact of the campaign on the candidates' images. The possibility, even probability, that the campaign can have such an influence justifies the existence of political consultants. Consultants work within the campaign environment, working with verbal and visual messages, in an attempt to enhance the image of their candidate. At the same time, the opposition's campaign is engaged in similar activity on behalf of its candidate.

Many of the campaign factors that contribute to the candidate's image, however, are outside the control of both the candidates and their consultants. A candidate has little control over the campaign messages of the opponent, much of which could be negative information that could adversely affect an image. An opponent's campaign, however, can be forced to expend scarce resources to preserve its own image, thereby limiting its ability to project that image. Also, neither the candidate nor the consultants can, in the end, affect news coverage of the campaign. While all consultants seek favorable coverage of their candidate, the ultimate decisions regarding coverage of both issues and candidates belong to the press itself (Ryan & Wentworth, 1999, p. 80). Those decisions about who, what, and how the press will cover the campaign will ultimately affect the candidates' images (O'Sullivan & Gieger, 1995).

In addition to the news media, the nature of the campaign activates a number of other factors that affect a candidate's image. Topping this list is the partisanship factor. Images are strongly related to the partisanship of the voters, but partisanship by itself does not account for all aspects of a candidate's image. Still, political parties and their candidates exhibit an interrelationship and mutual influence that affect the images of both the candidates and their parties. At the beginning of a general election campaign, that mutual influence appears to affect candidates more than the parties. Partisans more positively evaluate candidates after they become their party's nominee (Raven & Gallo, 1965). When contenders are nominated—particularly in presidential campaigns—and thus become the party's representative, partisanship has a strong influence on voters' images of the candidates. The partisan impact on images not only influences the image of the candidate, but also those of the political parties. As the campaign progresses, the events surrounding the campaign can transfer elements of the candidate's image back to the party. Therefore, if a presidential candidate is viewed as the "champion of the middle class," that image is more likely to be associated with other members of the same party by the time the campaign is over, even if those other candidates are running for positions that are not related to the federal government.

The ultimate impact of the campaign on images may be demonstrated by the very act of winning or losing the election itself, particularly winners who move into positions of authority or losers hoping to live to campaign for another office in the future. Nimmo and Savage referred to these phenomena as "Congratulations Effects" and "Condolences Effects." Key (1961, pp. 478–479) noted that those candidates who support the loser often accept defeat graciously (congratulations) or console themselves with the conclusion that the outcome will probably have little impact on history (condolence). Either way, the images of both the winner and the loser are likely to be altered by the outcome. Two significant effects have been identified: The image of winning candidates is positively enhanced by the victory, and perceptions of different image traits are altered for both the winning and losing candidates.

First, some who voted for losers shift to the winner, reporting that they voted for the winner when they actually did not (Key, 1961). Even if such a dramatic shift does not occur, there is a general tendency for voters to develop more favorable feelings toward the winner (Paul, 1956) as both supporters and opponents accept the victory and react to the winner as a public official instead of as a candidate. The images of the two candidates—the winner and the loser—often become more similar after the election, with both being perceived more favorably (Stricker, 1964). Raven and Gallo (1965) found that phenomenon occurring regardless of whether partisans were rating their own candidate or that of the opposing political party.

Second, perceptions of different image traits are altered. The winner's perception as a person of influence immediately increases, while the loser's decreases. The loss can potentially benefit the loser's image, though, if voters view him or her more positively; the loss reduces the loser's views as a political threat, which decreases the polarization of the political environment. Furthermore, sympathy for the loser can shift the public's focus to stylistic elements of the loser's image. The result could be that the loser becomes less of a political threat but more likable. Thus, while Bob Dole lacked enough popular support to win the 1996 presidential election, his image was still enhanced so much after his loss that he became a popular television spokesman for a commercial product (Visa Check Card), a soft drink (Pepsi), and a medical issue (erectile dysfunction).

In the final analysis, the prime objective of political campaigns is to win. Furthermore, there are campaigns where image is the desirable vehicle to ride to victory. In 1974, former Georgia governor Lester Maddox was being challenged by State House majority leader George Busbee in a three-week runoff election for governor. Maddox was then lieutenant governor and presiding officer of the state senate, but enjoyed attention achieved through stunts like riding the streets around the Capitol on his bicycle—backward! He enjoyed a certain notoriety as a segregationist, if not as an all-out racist, for preventing African Americans from entering his restaurant during the 1950s and 1960s.

Busbee was personally pleasant but not completely comfortable with the rigors of public discourse. An attorney, his political experience was primarily twenty-plus years as a backroom operative. The news media felt a responsibility to provide "socially acceptable" coverage. A serious discussion of issues was generally considered to be an invitation to Maddox to raise race as an issue in an effort to motivate a greater turnout among more conservative voters, who were regarded to be less likely to vote in the nonpresidential year. Busbee chose to mount a campaign around the motto, "A Work Horse, Not a Show Horse." Consequently, the news media challenged Maddox to prove he was a serious governmental manager, but issues in the traditional sense were never raised. Quickly, the race became a contest of who knew more about the "controls" of government, and Busbee was elected.

THE ROLE OF GENDER

Hillary Rodham Clinton's election as New York's senator drew a great deal of media attention during the 2000 election, but Ms. Clinton's campaign was but one of many in which women sought elective office. Even though such political bastions as the U.S. Senate are still dominated by males, an increasing number of women have been entering the political arena over the past three decades. Before 1970, few women held major public office at either the state or city level (Mandel, 1981). By 1999, women held more than 20 percent of state legislative offices and were governors of three states. Long gone are the days when Lurleen Wallace campaigned for the governor's seat in Alabama as a surrogate for her husband George, who was prohibited by law from seeking an additional term. Today's women candidates campaign on their own merits and on their own issues.

Still, because of gender stereotypes, women have a number of image problems to overcome that a comparable male candidate might not face (Edwards, 2009; Kahn, 1993, 1994; Norris, 1996; Robertson, 2001). They are often viewed as less competent and unable to handle the tough negotiations associated with politics (Eagly, Makhijani, & Klonsky, 1992). They are expected to be less assertive and aggressive in their speaking styles, a demeanor more appropriate for traditional female stereotypes (Haas, 1979; Newcombe & Arnkoff, 1976). In the past, if they tried to assume a leadership position traditionally held by a man, or use leadership behaviors typically associated with men, women candidates got negative reactions from the voters (Eagly, Makhijani, & Klonsky, 1992). Overall, Falk (2010) found that press coverage of women candidates has been consistently biased, up to and including Hillary Clinton's 2008 presidential campaign.

To overcome such problems, successful women candidates must typically use highly explicit messages, giving precise statements about their position on issues—a demand voters don't generally make of male candidates (Bernstein, 2000). Male candidates may campaign on platitudes about the need for improving education ("We must return the concept of learning to our schools"). On a similar issue, Bernstein argued that women candidates must be more specific in their campaign messages ("We've got to lower the number of students in each classroom, while increasing teacher salaries by ten percent"). Except for the explicitness require-ment, most women candidates have adapted to the modern political arena and have adopted many of the same techniques and tactics that have been used by male candidates in the past (Bystrom & Miller, 1999). Female candidates run just as many negative ads as men (Dabelko & Hernson, 1997), but audience expecta-tions on these ads may be different from those of male candidates (Swain, 2001). Typically, women candidates attack their opponents' position on issues (Benze & Declercq, 1985; Kahn, 1993) rather than on personal matters.

Part of the problem may be the male dominance that is still maintained in many other areas of politics. In television entertainment programming, the role of women has expanded dramatically. TV shows such as *The West Wing* showcase independent women who are heavily involved in and sometimes at the center of political issues. Police dramas such as *Police Woman* and *Cagney and Lacy* have depicted women as crime fighters on a par with male detectives. A range of action-adventure serials (*Xena: Warrior Princess, Relic Hunter, Sheena*) have portrayed women as heroes of epic legends.

Such attitudes, however, have not yet fully made their way into the political arena. The identified trend of women adopting the same techniques as male candidates may be merely an artifact of a gender difference because male consultants continue to outnumber female consultants. Men also make up the majority of news anchors and reporters (Paletz, 2002, p. 137) and far outnumber women as makers and sources of political news (Holland, 1987). Often when women do appear in news stories, they are presented as passive respondents to public events rather than as participants in those events (Rakow & Kranich, 1991).

Despite these problems, women continue to make progress in the political arena. In the 2008 election, Hillary Clinton was a viable candidate for the Democratic presidential nomination (Gutgold, 2009; Sheckels, 2009). The image problems faced by women candidates have been worked through a transitional stage that has resulted in increased numbers of women seeking and winning public office. More changes are likely to occur in the future, as both the academic and consulting communities learn more about the impact of elections on the images of women candidates.

SUMMARY

In some respects the juxtaposition of "image versus issues" is a false one. The political commercials that evoke strong reactions from academicians (flag waving, shallow, and so forth), are often criticized equally by consultants for their lack of a specific message. Consultants believe any communications opportunity that does not "move" votes is an opportunity lost, and messages that focus on images often lack the specifics that consultants are seeking.

Academicians must sometimes define such a dichotomy, one that separates issues and images, in order to evaluate images in their research. Such a dichotomy, though, often does not exist in the consultant's world. Images are conveyed through issues, and issues are discussed in terms of the candidate's image. The complex nature of political images will continue to evoke in-depth research on the part of academicians. Meanwhile, consultants continue to simplify the process, at least during the duration of the campaign itself. Working with a limited number of image dimensions—leadership, integrity, and empathy—they continue to work with those cognitive elements that can affect the evaluative dimension of a candidate's image. This work, ultimately, can lead to the voting behavior they seek.

Despite the complexity, some factors have emerged. The image of a political candidate is often a multifaceted impression that includes information about the candidate, personal evaluations of the candidate, and attitudes that affect voting behavior related to the candidate. Voters often seek an ideal candidate, with all candidates falling short of their expectations. Still, they are more likely to vote for the candidate whose image is closest to that ideal.

The complexity of the subject, though, means that the function is never really complete. Candidate images can and will be altered by the campaign itself, and on those events that might precede the next election. Even death will not necessarily end the process; after all, academicians continue to discuss the images of such past political figures as Andrew Jackson, Abraham Lincoln, Franklin Roosevelt, and John F. Kennedy. The candidate may die, but the image lives on.

Media Theory and Political Communication

During the 1957 gubernatorial campaign in New Jersey, Democrat Robert Meyner faced Republican Malcolm Forbes in a campaign in which only one television station reached most of the residents in the state (Schram, 1976). Airtime on Channel 13 was a valuable commodity sought by both candidates, particularly the then popular block programming format in which thirty-minute or hour-long blocks of time were purchased so the candidates could address the voters directly. To make one last appeal to the electorate, Democrat Meyner purchased such an hour-long block from 10:00 to 11:00 P.M. on the night before the election. When Republican Forbes learned of the purchase, he countered by buying the following hour—11:00 P.M. to midnight—so he could get in the last word before voters went to the polls.

True to form, Meyner's program came on the air at 10:00 P.M. But after only fifty-five minutes of speaking, Meyner signed off with a thanks to the voter. That was followed by the playing of the "Star Spangled Banner," and the remainder of Meyner's five minutes was spent showing the station's test pattern. Most viewers, assuming the station had gone off the air for the night, turned off their sets and never heard Forbes's rebuttal. The angry Forbes cried foul, but there was little he could do; the voters never knew of the complaint until after the election. Meyner's program had its maximum media impact, while Forbes was unable to communicate with the voters.

The incident was an early example of the power and prestige that candidates place on the media's ability to communicate with voters. The struggle to prevail in a contest of ideas requires presenting those ideas to targeted publics in a persuasive manner. In modern political terms this means competing candidates must present themselves through advertising, direct mail, telephone banks, printed material, and other techniques. To be successful, the means of communicating must deliver a believable message. Historically, that means of communication has been some form of mass media. Consequently, media scholars have devoted much research to developing and testing media theories. Different scholars have proposed differing frameworks for understanding the cultural and attitudinal impacts of the media. Over time, the focus of these studies have often shifted perspectives, ranging from manipulative approaches to propaganda to audience-based research on media use. The theme that pervades all, though, is that an understanding of media and its impact is important to an understanding of the contemporary climate of political campaigns.

During most of the twentieth century, the academic community often monitored the impact of mass media. Some of its members sometimes expressed surprise and concern at the ability of mass communication to influence the mass public—surprised by the occasional magnitude of media impact and concerned about the potential for its misuse. Other members have scoffed at such issues, sometimes viewing the mass media as an environmental element that has little impact on the lives of people. A third group of members have sought to isolate potential effects in an effort to isolate and identify what impact the media have and what they cannot do.

The result of such studies has led to the development of several theories regarding media impact. The early studies were naively simple by modern standards, alternately viewing media impact as either an uncontrollable monster or a toy soldier with no weapon. Over time, though, more sophisticated theories developed. The consultants, meanwhile, were picking up lessons from each new approach and applying them to the campaign environment.

The growth of modern media theory can be traced to the 1930s when U.S. academicians watched in astonishment as Adolf Hitler rose to power in Germany, a power attained and maintained through the dictator's effective use of propaganda and persuasion. Through his public speeches and public relations campaigns, Hitler developed a solid base of national support for his radical ideas. Observers from other nations looked on with both fear and curiosity, trying to identify and study the persuasive techniques that seemed to be so effective for the German dictator. The result was some of the first serious investigations into the impact of mass media.

THE BULLET THEORY (HYPODERMIC MODEL)

One of the first observations made about Hitler's persuasion efforts were their almost infallible effectiveness. Apparently, if Hitler presented a well-constructed and well-delivered message to the German populace, it was almost invariably effective with most of the populace. This conclusion led observers to make assumptions that came to be considered the first classic model of mass media effects, a theory alternately referred to as either the "bullet" theory or "hypodermic" model (Bineham, 1988). Both terms were based on the same concept, which was that the media had direct and discernible persuasive effects (Hovland, Lumsdaine, & Sheffield, 1949; Werrett, 1933). Audiences were viewed as passive, almost gullible, recipients of the message, particularly if that message was delivered in an effective manner. Thus, mass persuasion was assumed to be effective, if properly used. Research was designed to identify those elements of motivational and persuasion research that increased the effectiveness of the message.

Propaganda Techniques

Much of the early research in this area focused on the propagandists' tricks of rhetoric in explaining the effects of the message. The results were the identification and investigation of several propaganda techniques, including name calling, stacking the deck, and bandwagon effects (a complete list is provided in the box on page 65). Academicians typically decry such propaganda techniques as an unethical form of persuasion that does not encourage a full debate of ideas. Brydon and Scott (1994), for example, describe propaganda

▶ PROPAGANDA TECHNIQUES

The following techniques were those identified by the Institute for Propaganda Analysis in the 1930s.

Name Calling. A labeling technique used when a person, group, or issue is characterized by a negative term. The propagandist's intent is to evoke a negative emotional reaction. Thus, a proposal might be labeled "liberal," "ultraconservative," or "radical" to describe it in a negative way.

Glittering Generality. A phrase that sounds good but has no inherent meaning. Many have been used so often that they have become clichés, particularly in the political sense, including such statements as "We must do what's right," "A better tomorrow," and "Representing the people."

Transfer. A technique in which candidates link themselves with an idea or object that has a positive connotation, or in which they link their opponent to an object that has a negative connotation. A candidate who wants to be perceived as strong on national defense, for example, might be depicted with military hardware.

Testimonials. The endorsement of a candidate by someone else. Usually, the person offering the endorsement has high credibility, and the intent of the testimonial is to transfer some of the endorser's credibility to the candidate. When a testimonial comes from a relatively unknown person, it is usually intended to create a referent transfer with the group that the endorser represents. Thus, an endorsement from an elderly woman might be used to appeal to elderly voters.

Plain Folks. An attempt to convey that the candidate is just like the people who vote for him. This sometimes emerges as a "good ole boy" argument.

Stacking the Deck. The presentation of a one-sided argument that ignores the arguments of the opposition. This approach is frequently used in political literature and advertisements with the intent to imply that the opposition has no legitimate argument.

The Bandwagon Effect. A manifestation of the "Everybody is doing it" argument. This is frequently seen in political campaigns, often with the "Polls show I'm ahead" argument or the use of multiple endorsements in an attempt to increase credibility ("Every newspaper in the district has endorsed me").

Sources: Ellul, J. (1965). Propaganda. Trans. by K. Kellen & J. Lerner. New York: Knopf.
Jowett, G. S., & O'Donnell, V. (1986). *Propaganda and Persuasion.* Beverly Hills, CA: Sage.

techniques as "devices that bypass reasoning altogether in an attempt to persuade the listener at any cost" (p. 417). One exception is Jacques Ellul (1962/1965), who argued that propaganda is an inevitable and desirable tool for stabilizing culture in a modern society. Ellul views propaganda as the dissemination of cultural mores, rather than a deliberate lie. From a pragmatic point of view, most political campaigns generally adopt Ellul's thesis, even if the candidates or consultants involved have never heard of him. Jowett and O'Donnell (1986) describe propaganda as "a form of communication that is different from persuasion because it attempts to achieve a response that furthers the desired intent of the propagandist" (p. 13). That pretty well sums up the candidate's goal in a political campaign, and propaganda prospers as a result.

Still, as the early studies progressed, the researchers gradually came to the conclusion that mass propaganda was not always effective, particularly with all audiences. At that point, the research tended to branch into subunits as researchers tried to identify which "bullets" were most effective with which "targets" (audiences). Generally, though, the early research had trouble duplicating Hitler's broad persuasive impact, particularly on political issues. Much of Hitler's success was due to his ability to so totally control the media that his message was the only one heard by the German people. In fact, his attempts at similar propaganda techniques to audiences in other countries were generally ineffective (Jowett & O'Donnell, 1986, pp. 137–142). Hitler's propaganda, it turned out, worked only when the population was hearing one side of an issue. In the presence of alternative messages, the effectiveness of many of these propaganda techniques is diminished. In addition, Villa and Rodgers (1999) concluded that the success of the most extreme element of Hitler's rhetoric, the Nazis' "Final Solution" campaign, was not totally due to Hitler's propaganda. Many of the ideas of the Nazi party existed before Hitler came to power, they noted; the Nazi ideology intensified those "views through the use of propaganda, but did not create them" (p. 24).

THE LIMITED EFFECTS MODEL

While the bullet theory dominated studies of the mass media for a few years, some researchers eventually started to note problems with the model, particularly in the United States. American voters, it turned out, were not nearly as malleable as the German population appeared to be. In fact, they sometimes appeared highly resistant to persuasion, particularly through the mass media. The first serious blows to the bullet theory grew out of studies at Columbia University and the University of Michigan. The first of these was the 1940 Erie County study conducted by Lazarsfeld, Berelson, and Gaudet (1948). This longitudinal study followed voters from May 1940 until the general election in November of that year. The results showed that nearly half of the November voters already knew five to six months before how they would vote. Another 25 percent had decided during the parties' national conventions, when the final nominees were chosen. Only 25 percent actually made their voting decision during the campaign. Of these, only 8 percent actually changed their voting intention, once a decision had been made.

Furthermore, the study concluded that the issues of the campaign were relatively unimportant to the voting decision. Rather than monitoring the media for information to help them make a decision, voters used such information to support vote decisions that were based on social predispositions. In essence, most voters would have made the same vote decision without the media. They merely used the media to seek reinforcement of that decision, not new information.

The results of that study were essentially replicated by Berelson, Lazarsfeld, and McPhee (1954) in a similar study in Elmira, New York, during the 1948 campaign. This time, 67 percent of the voters had made their decision by June. Fifteen percent more decided in August, and another 11 percent soon afterward. Only 10 percent made their voting decision during the actual campaign span of the final month.

The results were again interpreted as showing that the media had only limited effects on voters' decisions, with most votes cast on the basis of social predispositions. Subsequent research by Campbell and Kahn (1952) and Campbell, Gurin, and Miller (1954) identified the influence of party affiliation as one such predisposition, but the basic premises of the limited effects model had been established.

This approach was summarized by Klapper (1960) as the "Rule of Minimal Effects." Under this approach, audience processing of media information was considered to be highly selective, conditioned by partisan predispositions, and subordinate to interpersonal influence (the two-step flow, which is discussed later). In essence, this approach assumed that political campaigns could make only minor dents on attitudes and were more likely to reinforce an existing cognitive state. Instead, the model assumed that the public generally responds to the media in a selective manner. The overall effect, for most people, is that the media only succeed in reinforcing existing public opinion, instead of contributing to changes to the public opinion development process. Mass persuasion becomes subordinate to interpersonal influence.

Two theoretical explanations were developed as a result of this study: the selectivity hypothesis and the two-step flow. The selectivity hypothesis grew out of the argument that voters selectively used the media to support vote conclusions that were based on their predispositions; in other words, they were seeking reinforcement rather than information. As a result, four separate levels of selectivity were postulated: selective exposure, selective reception, selective perception, and selective retention.

Selective exposure refers to the idea that people tend to choose from the communication experiences available to them, selecting those messages that are more likely to support their existing beliefs and attitudes. In political campaigns, this is frequently exhibited in partisan exposure to campaign messages, which suggests that Republicans will tend to expose themselves to messages from Republicans, and Democrats are more likely to seek out messages about Democrats (Klapper, 1960, p. 20). Although the growth of thirty-second television ads may have watered down this effect somewhat, the concept still has some validity in today's campaign environment.

Selective attention refers to the assumption that audiences are more likely to pay attention to those messages that support their existing beliefs and attitudes.

Information theorists note that the eye can process about 5 million bits of data per second, but the brain is capable of processing only about 500 bits during the same time. Given that disparity, only a portion of the available data is actually processed by an individual into any long-term memory bank (Egeth, 1967). In that situation, the selectivity hypothesis argues that the respondent is more likely to process information that is supportive of their current lifestyle, including their current political attitudes.

But what if the voter is both exposed to the message of the opposition, and pays attention to it. That message can still be distorted through the process of selective perception. A person's past experiences, attitudes, and expectations will influence their view of that message. Finally, even if the message is perceived in a manner similar to what was intended, there is no guarantee that it will be remembered for any extended period of time. The principle of selective retention states that a person more accurately remembers messages that are favorable to one's self-image than messages that are unfavorable (Levine & Murphy, 1943). The overall impact of the selection process, therefore, is to limit the impact of any message that reaches voters through the media.

The two-step flow hypothesized that media effects were mediated by the presence of opinion leaders. In this approach, the media had little direct effect because the ultimate interpretation of information reached the public only after it had passed through interpersonal channels. In essence, local opinion leaders interpreted the media in light of the social predispositions of their community, with the result that the media reinforced attitudes instead of having changed them. This hypothesis will be discussed more thoroughly in the chapter on opinion leadership.

Criticisms

Over the years, scholars have identified a number of theoretical problems with the limited effects model. The most obvious of these is that the so-called limited effects are not all that limited. In the classical studies on the topics, the limited effects were typically measured in numbers that ranged from 10 percent to 25 percent. While such percentages may be small in comparison to the entire population, they are more than enough to make a dramatic impact on an election. Presidential elections are rarely decided by more than 20 percentage points; thus a swing by 10–20 percent of the voters would be enough to change the outcome of an election.

Second, the classic studies in the limited effects model were all conducted before the widespread use of television as a mass medium, but the conclusions were subsequently generalized to the television's effects. While many of the effects do hold for television, the swing vote is still sufficiently large to have a major impact on elections.

Third, the classic studies focused only on presidential elections, elections that are highly visible and highly partisan. The size of the undecided vote is frequently larger in less visible races, creating a situation in which the impact of the media increases.

Fourth, the nature of the campaigns that were studied for the limited effects model also cast doubts about their conclusions. The 1940 election revolved around the reelection of Franklin Roosevelt, a highly popular president generally credited by the voters with helping them to recover from the Great Depression of the 1930s. It should not be surprising that so many voters knew, in advance of the election, that they planned to vote for him in November, even though it was a tradition-breaking run for a third term.

And, finally, while academicians were reporting the limited effects in Elmira, New York, President Harry Truman was using the 1948 presidential campaign to pull off one of the major upsets in U.S. presidential history. Despite almost universal expectations that Republican Thomas Dewey would win that election, Truman won with an energetic whistle-stop campaign that was reported nationwide by the media. The effects of the media may have been limited, but they were enough for Truman to win.

Campaign Implications

Despite the limitations of the limited effects model, the research did provide insight into voting behavior that has proven to be beneficial to campaign professionals. The first lesson was the importance of attitudinal reinforcement. In terms of campaigns, that lesson was simple: Work your base first. It's easier to motivate your own supporters to vote than to persuade someone who is against you to change his or her mind; in other words, to alter the voting intentions of an opponent's supporter.

Another assumption of the limited effects model was that mass persuasion was subordinate to interpersonal influence. From a campaign perspective, the importance of this view was the influence of opinion leadership and interpersonal communication. It emphasized the need to identify and persuade opinion leaders. Some campaigns, including George McGovern's 1972 primary campaigns, placed a major emphasis on interpersonal communication programs (Devlin, 1973).

AGENDA SETTING

The limited effects model dominated mass media theory up until the early 1960s. Eventually, though, researchers became intrigued by the obvious disparity between the theory and the eagerness of politicians and mass marketers to use the media to advance their ideas and sell their products. Furthermore, even if the impact of the media was small, it could still be a significant factor in a campaign. Sometimes only small differences separate winners from losers (Jeffries, 1986, p. 259). At this point, McCombs and Shaw (1972) suggested that media theory should look at a different variable. Instead of persuasion, they suggested, the major role of the mass media was issue definition. In other words, "The mass media may not be successful in telling us what to think, but they are stunningly successful in telling us what to think about." Indeed, the media can play a critical role in defining what is and what is not a public issue. A decade before McCombs and Shaw outlined the basics of agenda setting, Cohen (1963) argued that the media could play a critical role in focusing public attention on an issue. As Tuchman (1982, p. 184) wrote, "News does not mirror society. It helps to constitute it as a shared social phenomenon, for in the process of describing an event, news defines and shapes the event."

Roberts (1992) goes further, suggesting that agenda setting might be a two-step process in which acceptance of the media's issue priorities can ultimately affect voter behavior. In other words, by influencing what we think about, the media may also be influencing what actions we take.

Part of the impact is due to the pure omnipresence of the media. Woodward (1997) reported that the average adult American spends almost 1,500 hours a year watching television, and information on television becomes topics for public discussion. Not all of that exposure is on news and public issues, but that makes little difference. Even entertainment programs can have an impact on public perceptions (Gerbner et al., 1990). The result is public issues as mediated reality—events and people are known only through the media.

Generally, the public opinion process (as it relates to any specific issue) begins when the media focus on an issue. Once the media define an issue, it becomes part of the public opinion agenda. Typically, three distinct stages of public response occur. First, the media raise awareness of the issue. Second, diffusion of information about the issue occurs, as the media and political elites disseminate their views. And third, discussion of the issue, by the public, proceeds. At that point, a cyclical process between the public and the media may be established, that is, as the public discussion increases, the media feed new information about it to the public.

Agenda setting asserts that audiences take note of the saliences of the news media and incorporate a similar set of weights into their personal agenda, which means the media's priorities become the voters' priorities. Lippman (1922) first asserted the idea in his classic book, *Public Opinion*. McCombs and Shaw (1972) tested the hypothesis during the 1968 election, finding a correlation between issues emphasized by the news and what voters regarded as key issues of the campaign. That conclusion was supported by an interpretation of some data from Berelson, Lazarsfeld, and McPhee's study of the 1948 election, which indicated that voters with minimal interpersonal contact were more in line with news coverage of the campaign. Support for the hypothesis has subsequently been relatively strong, with most research indicating that when the public sees news stories about a particular problem on television, they tend to regard the issue as more important and report having stronger feelings about it (Iyengar & Kinder, 1987).

Agenda-Setting Models

Researchers continue to refine the agenda-setting model. Typically, three different models have been investigated: the awareness model, the priorities model, and the salience model (McCombs, 1976; Shaw & McCombs, 1980).

The Awareness Model The awareness model of agenda setting is based on the assumption that awareness of an issue depends on media coverage of that issue. It essentially measures whether voters are aware of or ignorant of the issue itself. The awareness model suffers from the unique theoretical fault of being too accurate to have much theoretical importance. If an issue is not covered by the media, most people are not aware of it, making the two terms almost theoretically synonymous.

As a result, most research in this area has turned to the gatekeeping function of the media. Media sources employ gatekeepers, who select the stories to be included in the broadcast or in the newspaper. Larson (1995) argues that gatekeepers hold significant power in determining what the public thinks about, and their gate-keeping decisions have "ripple effects." Larson cited sexual abuse as an example of the agenda-setting function. In the mid-1980s, one gatekeeper featured a story about a child care center in California where evidence of sexual abuse had surfaced. After the initial report, other stories appeared in other cities; newsweeklies and family magazines carried stories about sexual abuse in day care centers.

Gatekeepers function with two kinds of inherent bias: ideological, where stories are chosen to fit in with a certain philosophical viewpoint; and structural, where stories are chosen because they fit the media's format. While ideological bias has received the most criticism, structural bias is predominant. Larson notes that stories that are dramatic and can be squeezed into a twenty- to thirty-second news bite are likely to be considered. Other factors considered are the presence of photographs, "official voices," and issues that affect the local community.

An aspect of gatekeeping that has received more focus recently is that of news priming. News priming refers to the ability of the media to set expectations for viewers (Kenski, 1996). For example, if the news media predict that an election will be close, and then someone wins by a sizable margin, a person in favor of the winning candidate will be more satisfied than if the media had predicted a clear victory. One example of the influence of news priming is the behavior of presidential candidates and their campaigns before televised debates. A candidate's predebate rhetoric is a delicate balancing act that has to simultaneously demonstrate confidence in his or her skills without creating expectations that are too high to be met by his or her actual performance.

The Priorities Model   The basic assumption behind the priorities model is that media audiences will adopt the same agenda, in the same rank order, as do the media. In simple terms, this approach hypothesizes that media audiences will judge as important what the media judge as important. This, of course, is the most radical approach and does not take into consideration individual differences. Still, despite the extreme nature of the hypothesis, it tends to have the best fit for many situations.

The Salience Model   The salience model is an intermediate explanation that falls somewhere in between the basic explanation of the awareness model and the extreme fit of the priorities model. The salience model assumes that heavy media emphasis on a topic can move it into the top rank of what is important to the audience. However, it predicts that this movement will occur for only a few issues that are constantly being emphasized in the media. Furthermore, the audience discriminates only in terms of high and low importance. Thus, the exact priorities of the media are not reproduced.

Research Considerations

Agenda setting, as an independent variable, has been operationalized in two ways: the total amount of coverage devoted to an issue (column inches or number of minutes) and by the priority of coverage an issue is given (front page or lead story). Benton (1976) broke agenda setting into three different categories. The first level involved merely the identification of broad issues. At the second level, voters were able to identify subissues, specific problems, causes, and proposed solutions. At the third level, they could identify specific information about subissues, including pro and con arguments. Generally, this line of research has indicated that newspapers have more influence than television does at agenda setting at the upper two levels.

Generally, two different approaches have been used to measure agenda-setting effects. The intrapersonal approach measures those issues that an individual personally considers to be important; in other words, what they think about. The interpersonal approach measures those issues that are most frequently discussed with others; in other words, what they talk about. Generally, the salience model has the best fit on the intrapersonal approach, while the priorities model does well under the interpersonal approach.

Contingent Conditions McCombs (1992) noted that, after the first set of tests of the agenda-setting hypothesis, research quickly turned to exploring those contingent conditions that contributed to the phenomenon (McCombs & Weaver, 1973). McCombs (1976) identified four such conditions:

> *High exposure to the mass media.* The media's issue agenda has little effect on those who do not expose themselves to the media.
> A *need for orientation.* Agenda setting is more likely to occur among those voters who have an inherent curiosity about their surrounding environment. The media satisfy that curiosity (Weaver, 1980).
> *Frequency of interpersonal discussion.* This line of research has tried to expand the two-step flow hypothesis to agenda setting and has done so with mixed results. Frequently, the conflicting results of this research are often a by-product of different definitions of agenda setting, such as the intrapersonal vs. interpersonal approaches. Wanta and Wu (1992) reported that interpersonal communication enhanced agenda-setting effects for issues that receive extensive media coverage, but inhibited the effects for little-publicized issues by providing salience cues that conflict with media messages. They also found that frequency of discussions is the strongest predictor of issue salience.

Weaver, Zhu, and Willnat (1992) found that interpersonal communication served a bridging function by influencing and linking personal and social perceptions on the salience of drug abuse. Neither personal experience nor exposure to newspaper coverage was significantly correlated with these perceptions. In effect, the media's agenda on drug abuse had been passed along through interpersonal communication to audiences who were not exposed to it by the media.

Low Motivation

Agenda-setting effects appear to be most pronounced on voters who are not highly involved in the election. Highly involved individuals develop a comparative framework for evaluating political information. When news events and information are reported in the media, they can compare that information with their earlier beliefs, attitudes, and values. Voters who are not highly involved frequently lack such frameworks or prior information to make such evaluations. Consequently, they are more susceptible to media influence.

Campaign Implications The agenda-setting function of the press was reflected in a number of significant campaign techniques. First, it recognized the value of news coverage as an important campaign factor. This is sometimes described in terms of the "30–30 Rule": Thirty seconds on the nightly news has more impact than thirty minutes of paid advertisement. The basis of the rule is an assumption by the campaigns that the news media are seen by the voters as a relatively unbiased source of information (as compared to the candidates themselves). Voter responses to any campaign ad can be tempered by cynicism; after all, the candidates are unlikely to say anything bad about themselves or good about their opponent. Thus, campaigns are elated when their candidate receives news coverage from the media, and particularly if that coverage focuses on the major theme or issue of the candidate's campaign. The result of that mentality has been an increased attempt on the part of the campaigns to influence favorable news coverage through press releases, free video segments, and staged events. News priming also comes into play, as campaigns work to develop scenarios that will put their candidate's performance in the best possible light.

The second major impact on campaigns was through the selection of campaign issues. Agenda setting emphasized the need for campaigns to devote much of their efforts to issues that the audience considered important. Campaign polling techniques put more emphasis on questions that could help define that agenda, with strategies being developed that in turn reflected the audience's priorities. When the campaign heats up, particularly during the last two weeks, those issue decisions become critical. Typically, the candidate who is able to control the agenda of the media is the candidate who will most likely win the election.

A candidate often has little or no control over the media's agenda, and that could adversely affect the campaign. In 1980, for example, Jimmy Carter ran for reelection as president while the nation was embroiled in the Iranian hostage crisis (Conover & Sigelman, 1982). In 1979, Iranian activists attacked and captured the U.S. embassy in Iran, holding its employees hostage. Those U.S. citizens were still being held hostage during the 1980 presidential campaign, and the one-year anniversary of the event fell on the same day as the election in 1980. News coverage of the crisis represented an issue that was detrimental to the campaign and likely contributed to Carter's defeat.

Furthermore, despite the media's strength at setting agendas, its capacity to do so is limited. Zhu (1992) argued that this limitation makes agenda setting a zero-sum game in which any issue that garners more attention from the media does so only at the expense of other issues, which lose attention or are dropped completely by the public's attention meter. In essence, only a small number of issues can maintain public interest at the same time, meaning that increased coverage of any one issue will result in decreased coverage of others. Hertog, Finnegan, and Kahn (1994) found little support for that notion and argued that the displacement effect is not as powerful as once assumed. While that notion has been disputed, particularly on medical-related issues (Hertog, Finnegan, & Kahn, 1994), candidates and consultants generally work under such an assumption. Getting a new issue some attention can be difficult.

Research on agenda setting has been so consistent that the focus on the topic has shifted to looking at the topic from new viewpoints (McCombs, 1992), including the exploration of candidate images and political interest as alternative agendas, and studying agenda setting as a dependent variable instead of as an independent variable ("Who sets the news agenda?"). Both of these areas of study have direct implications for campaigns, particularly in terms of candidate images and agenda sources. The indirect impact of agenda setting on candidate images has been an assumption made by most consultants for years, providing part of the impetus for concerted public relations programs. Also, campaigns have similarly worked on tacit programs to identify those who have the most impact on the news agenda of the press, and targeting those individuals with specific information about their candidate and issues.

USES-GRATIFICATION

The bullet theory and limited effects model were both message oriented, focusing on the impact of the message on the audience. The agenda-setting model was channel oriented, focusing on the priorities of the media. One theory that deviates from both of these approaches—focusing upon the audience instead—is the uses-gratification model. This approach assumes that audiences use the media to gratify personal needs related to the political campaign, a concept often summarized by saying, "What people do with media is more important than what media do to people." Thus, uses-gratification research represents a movement from concerns over attitudinal and behavioral change to a focus on perceptual and cognitive changes.

By focusing on audiences instead of media messages or the source of those messages, this approach has much to offer communication students. Such an approach, however, also has inherent difficulties. The most obvious problem is that it's not really a media theory, but could more accurately be characterized as a descriptive approach to studying media. The internal motivations that drive audiences to use media are difficult to test, thus making uses-gratifications a hard theory to verify or dismiss. As a result, it often raises as many questions about media use as it answers. Still, it makes an important contribution to understanding the media by providing a valuable audience-based perspective.

Why People Seek Out the Media   An early study by Blumer and McQuail (1969) identified five possible gratifications that people might seek from the political content of media: vote guidance, reinforcement, surveillance, excitement, and interpersonal utility. One other, personal identity, has been suggested.

Vote guidance refers to the use of the media for assistance in making voting decisions. Swanson (1976) labeled this function "decisional utility" and reported that it had the strongest relationship to exposure to the mass media. This led him to conclude that "the bases of political information acquisition are not rooted in partisan attitude protection or validation, but rather are formed in the individual perceiver's desire to understand his world and act towards it confidently with predictable consequences."

Reinforcement is a need that urges people to seek out political media messages that reinforce their existing attitudes. This is, in essence, a continuation of the selectivity hypothesis as an explanation for media gratification.

Surveillance refers to a receiver's desire to keep up with what's going on in the world, or to keep in touch with events in the world. An audience that wants to stay informed tends to engage in a lot of scanning behavior, without seeking a detailed knowledge of events. Generally, surveillance appears to lead to superficial political activity.

Excitement needs refer to those who listen to political messages for the sheer fun of it. They may view politics as a sporting event, with them as the spectators, while others are fascinated by the competitive nature of the allegorical battle. In essence, the campaign becomes political drama (Combs, 1980).

Interpersonal utility refers to our need to have information to use when talking with others. Thus, the media become a source of information, providing knowledge for future discussions or arguments with others. Several subcategories have been identified, including information seeking, informal discussion needs, and opinion leadership needs (gathering information so that we can offer opinions on an issue). Swanson divided it into three subcategories: political discussions with friends, offering advice to others, and asking others for advice.

Larson (1995) argued that some people seek out messages for personal identity needs. This need is based on the idea that we learn to identify who we are by what we view, read, and listen to. Larson argues that self-confident people meet identity needs through reading; those who are not as self-assured rely more on viewing messages. In many ways, this is an application of the "political relationship" theory to uses-gratification. The political relationship theory is discussed in the next section.

Why People Avoid Media   Just as some people use the media to satisfy personal goals, some people avoid political media for the same reason. At least four factors have been identified as contributing to this effect.

Alienation   Many voters feel powerless and left out of the political process, thus seeing no need to seek political information. This "my-vote-doesn't-matter" syndrome means that the voter has no incentive to seek political information, and therefore, rarely does. The result is a low level of political activity.

Partisanship   Highly partisan voters avoid the media for a different reason—they are highly involved in the election, but their voting decisions have already been made. As a result, they have no particular need to gather additional information on the candidates. This behavior does not extend to partisan elites, of course. They continue to seek out information that can be used for interpersonal arguments.

Relaxation Although many people enjoy the excitement of a political campaign, many others do not. For them, political information provides little of the sought-after diversion that they need. Rather than listening to political information, they would rather engage in an activity that offers them pleasure and relaxation. Such people use television for escape gratification (Canary & Spitzberg, 1993). Political information from the media is shuffled to the back of their minds, or perhaps disregarded entirely.

Instrumental vs. Ritualistic Uses Rubin (1983, 1984) proposed that media usage by individuals fell into two distinct categories, instrumental uses and ritualistic uses. Individuals with an instrumental orientation toward television search for what they want to watch and regard television as a tool that serves a distinct purpose (to entertain, inform, excite, and so forth). These individuals choose programs that fulfill these desires, and remain highly involved with those shows to fulfill those goals (Rubin, 1984; Rubin & Perse, 1987). In contrast, people with ritualistic television motives do not regard television as a tool but as a way to satisfy more emotional and relational needs. Some ritualistic viewers watch television for companionship, or escape (Dobos & Dimmick, 1988). Others watch out of habit or when they are bored, perhaps because more fulfilling relationship opportunities are not available.

Much of the research in this area has focused on identifying gender differences in media usage, extending research that indicates that men and women use television differently (Comstock, 1989). Men are more likely to be purposeful and goal-directed in their television watching. They plan what they will watch (Morley, 1986, 1988) and use remote controls (Walker & Bellamy, 1991) to more easily achieve these objectives (for example, to acquire information or to be entertained). Nathanson, Perse, and Ferguson (1997) described this as an instrumental viewing style, with goal-directed reasons for watching.

Women are more likely to use television to satisfy relationship (Lull, 1980; Rubin & Rubin, 1982) or ritualistic needs (Nathanson, Perse, & Ferguson, 1997). Their overall viewing patterns are less active, with justifications including using television watching to feel less lonely or because there was nobody to talk to. Thus, they are more likely to regard television as a social vehicle to spend time with others; television becomes a secondary activity around which interpersonal or emotional objectives are sought (Morley, 1988).

Men are more likely to control television watching, using the remote control to frequently change channels in search of greater variety and stimulation (Perse & Ferguson, 1993). They are also more likely than women to select programs during group viewing (Heeter, 1988) and to use the remote control to try to annoy others (Walker & Bellamy, 1991). Program loyalty, or watching programs regularly, decreases for female heads-of-households when they watch with male adults (Webster & Wakshlag, 1982). Fathers usually have the most influence in program selection and are least likely to ask others' permission before changing channels (Lull, 1982). Women are more likely to report that someone else changed the channel even though they wished they hadn't (Heeter, 1988).

Even when alone, however, women may not use television purposefully. Because of domestic responsibilities (Hochschild, 1989), distracted television viewing may be an accompaniment to other activities (Perse & Ferguson, 1993).

The concept of distracted viewing has led to research on active and passive television watching. People who are active in general tend to watch cable channels (Ferguson & Melkote, 1997), supporting the theory that people who are active in general, or have more leisure time, have larger (perhaps "more active") channel repertoires. Webster and Lichty (1991) argued that program choice and media exposure are based on both media factors (availability of channels to watch) and the general leisure time of the audience. Blumler (1979) argued that such viewer activity is not an either–or condition, but is based on a number of factors. That argument may have even more weight today, given the potential of the Internet to change the way that people obtain political information (Graber, 2001).

Criticisms of Uses-Gratifications Uses-gratification theory has its critics, and the most basic problem is that of measurement of needs. The theory assumes the presence of an underlying need that can only be measured as expressed behavior (usually self-report questionnaires). Thus, critics can argue that many findings under the uses-gratification model could be adequately explained by some other theoretical perspective. Littlejohn (1996), for example, points out that the theory does not focus on how the media can have negative cultural effects on the audience. Littlejohn also argues that it does an inadequate job of explaining the media's unconscious or ritualistic effects on the audience.

Campaign Implications Despite the criticisms of the approach, uses-gratification has made some major contributions to practical campaign behavior. First, research in this area has consistently identified television as the medium that serves as the most universal needs gratifier. This finding is reflected in the heavy use of television by campaigns today. Second, uses-gratification research has consistently found that the gratification model tends to apply more to older voters than to younger voters, that is, older voters are more likely to use the media for their own purposes. Conversely, younger voters, who seem to be less goal-directed in their consumption of media, appear to be more influenced by media messages. This factor has generally led to an assumption in campaigns that younger voters are a bellwether group. In other words, if a television ad is effective, it will first show up in increased support among younger voters. Third, the model has had a major effect on making campaigns focus on the needs of the audience. The assumption of the uses-gratification approach is that the impact that campaign media have on voters depends to a large extent on the motivations of the voters to follow the campaign. Interest in the campaign determines, to a large extent, the attitude change among voters related to the campaign. Thus, to be successful, the campaign must aim to provide optimum gratification to the voters. Although media may not change any attitudes directly, failure to provide gratification could result in a loss of support.

RELATIONAL THEORIES

Another approach to media impact falls into the category of relational theories of media impact. These approaches assumed that the major impact of the media is the psychological relationships developed between the viewers and the persona in the media.

The Friendship Theory

Surlin's (1978) friendship theory argues that viewers consider television characters to be "significant others," or surrogate friends. This decision results from viewers' perception of cognitive similarity between themselves and the character. The result of this identification leads to watching the program that features the character more often. Once the surrogate friendship has been established, the viewers accept the point of view presented by the character (Surlin, 1974; Tate & Surlin, 1976; Vidmar & Rokeach, 1974), adopting the perspective of the character who serves as the significant other. The result is gratification, which in turn serves as a basis for watching that show more often.

The theory becomes relevant to politicians whenever the significant character addresses a political issue. Powell and Anderson (1984), for example, found that viewers who identified with a character from *Carter Country* tended to shift their attitudes toward homosexuality as the character underwent a similar attitude change on the show. In essence, a character who becomes a significant other can serve as an attitudinal anchor for political issues. This possibility was emphasized again in 1992 when controversy erupted when Vice President Dan Quayle complained about Candace Bergen's character on the sitcom *Murphy Brown*. Quayle criticized the show for portraying the character as an unwed mother, arguing that it was not a suitable role model for family audiences. While he may not have articulated it directly, Quayle's criticism is based on the assumption that there is some validity to the friendship theory.

Political Relationships

Seymour-Ure (1974) took the relationship approach to media effects in a different direction, focusing entirely on the political arena. Although his data were based entirely on the British political system, some parallels can still be seen in American politics. Seymour-Ure argued that the major effect of media on politics was the establishment of political relationships, either at the individual, institutional, or systemic level. As an example of how the media can affect an individual relationship, he noted that the media defined an Enoch Powell speech on nonwhite immigration as a threat to Conservative party leader Edward Heath, leading to Heath's firing of Powell from his shadow cabinet position. At the institutional level, Seymour-Ure argued, the mass media's treatment of the British monarchy (an institution) made the nation's (a system) legitimacy partly dependent on that of the monarchy.

Seymour-Ure's analysis has at least two important implications for American politics. First, his argument about relationship development implies that the media made the existence of national campaigns possible (and, perhaps, inevitable).

Second, and this is also a problem with his approach, he assumes that the major political action is among political elites. His most carefully documented media effects are upon elite individuals, implying that the media operate to make it more difficult for nonelites to find a way to participate in the political process. While this is frequently the case, there are numerous instances in American political history where nonelites (civil rights protesters, for example) have driven public opinion to a point where they have had some impact on public policy.

INFLUENCE GAPS

Zaller (1996) argues that people are influenced by mass communication in proportion to their exposure to messages and their knowledge of candidates. Studies that report limited effects, he argues, have been limited by methodological problems. They frequently look only at presidential campaigns, where effects tend to be smaller than in other campaigns. Such intensive campaigns create cross-cutting changes that cannot be detected when using the general linear models that most research studies use. Such models are typically applied to only a single case of mass persuasion at a time, Zaller says, processes that "virtually guarantee systematic underestimation of media impacts" (p. 37).

Zaller views each campaign as a holistic message that either reaches the voter or it does not. In a two-candidate race, that assumption generates four potential campaign scenarios: Voters may be influenced by both campaigns, neither campaign, by Candidate A but not by Candidate B, or by Candidate B but not by Candidate A. In the first two cases, in which the voter is reached by both or neither of the campaigns, the impact of the media should be negligible, creating situations in which minimal effects will be observed. However, if either candidate is able to dominate the media (scenarios 3 and 4) to the disadvantage of the opponent, the probability of media impact is high.

Zaller also argues that the media's impact will vary, based on the extent to which voters are receptors of mass media information (particularly news), a phenomenon he refers to as a "reception gap." Voters who are moderate news watchers, he argues, are those who are most likely to be converts and switch parties to vote for an incumbent, particularly if the incumbent dominates the media. The incumbent's media advantage fills in the reception gap for such voters; as they learn more about the incumbent, the likelihood of their supporting the incumbent increases. Conversely, if both the incumbent and the challenger have intense campaigns, some habitual viewers will switch to the challenger as they learn new information about that person.

Zaller is not alone in raising questions about the information gap that exists among voters. Several studies have noted that voters are often ill-informed on issues, and the media may be partly to blame for that situation. Studies have often found that news coverage on presidential elections focuses on competition and controversy rather than providing information on issues (Patterson, 1980; Patterson & Davis, 1985). Similarly, Robinson and Sheehan (1983) reported that a majority of the news coverage in 1980 failed to contain even one issue-related sentence. Such results triggered calls for more responsible coverage of campaigns by the media.

OTHER ISSUES

The Spiral of Silence.   Elisabeth Noelle-Neumann (1973, 1977, 1991, 1993) posits a theory of political media called the Spiral of Silence, that is, the tendency for people in the minority to conceal their real attitudes about politicians and political issues. As she wrote, "Individuals who...notice that their own personal opinion is spreading and is taken over by others, will voice this opinion self-confidently in public. On the other hand, individuals who notice that their own opinions are losing ground, will be inclined to adopt a more reserved attitude" (p. 139). Thus, the theory is essentially a theory of public opinion, as distinguished from personal attitudes. From this perspective, public opinion is defined as "Attitudes one can express without running the danger of isolating oneself" (Noelle-Neumann, 1993, pp. 70–71). Griffin (2006) described it as "the increasing pressure people feel to conceal their views when they think they are in the minority" (p. 408). Further, the theory argues that voters are rather adept at identifying when their own views differ from those of the public. Thus, the spiral of silence theorizes a three-step process in individuals' decisions to articulate their political attitudes: (1) They have the ability to gauge trends in public opinion, (2) they have a justifiable fear of social isolation if they express unpopular opinions, and (3) that leads to an understandable reluctance to express minority opinions.

The theory is the foundation for several theories that can be empirically tested (Griffin, 2006). These include three predictions in which the amount of "talk" about political issues is the dependent variable (Scheufele, Shanahan, & Lee, 2001).

1. Voters with majority opinions are more likely to express their opinions than those with minority views.
2. Voters with minority opinions are more likely to express those opinions with a friend than a stranger, since there is less fear of isolation from a friend.
3. Voters in some subgroups are more likely to express their opinions than others. These include men, young adults, and people in the middle and upper class. Women, older adults, and lower-income voters will be more likely to remain silent.

At first glance, the spiral of silence appears to be a sociological phenomenon, but Noelle-Neumann (1991) argues that voters pick up their ideas about majority opinions from the media. "I have never found a spiral of silence that goes against the tenor of the media," she wrote, "for the willingness to speak out depends in part upon sensing that there is support and legitimation from the media" (p. 276). Thus, the media has an impact not only on voters but also on the electoral process (Noelle-Neumann, 1983).

Noelle-Neumann (1993) also argues that the public quickly picks up shifts in political momentum by monitoring the media. As she wrote, "when a swing in the climate occurs for or against a party, a person, or a particular idea, it seems to be sensed everywhere at almost exactly the same time, by [everybody]" (p. 19). Thus, according to this theory, voters are adept at monitoring the media to (a) identify current majority opinions and (b) to make predictions about future trends based on assessments of momentum changes. The media, meanwhile, is perceived as having an intrusive role in the political process.

Empirical research has generally supported the spiral of silence (Scheufele & Moy, 2000). Glynn and McLeod (1984) found support for the theory in a post-hoc analysis of the 1980 election between incumbent Jimmy Carter and challenger Ronald Reagan. Reagan won that election in a landslide after public opinion polls predicted a tight race. Moy, Domke, and Stamm (2001) also identified a silence effect in the public discussion of the issue of affirmative action.

There are, of course, critics of the theory. Perhaps the most obvious point of criticism is the assumption regarding fear of isolation as the cause of the spiral of silence (Griffin, 2006). There are plenty of instances in which people with minority views are quite willing to express their opinions. Further, rather than fearing social isolation, many people glorify it. During George W. Bush's presidential administration, for example, Republicans dominated in terms of public support and most states were identified as "red" Republican states. Regardless, many ideological Democrats proclaimed their minority status with bumper stickers identifying themselves as a "Blue Dot in a Red Sea."

Noelle-Neumann (1979) deflects this argument by arguing that such behavior is a necessary aberration to the spiral of silence. "The chance to change or mold public opinion is reserved to those who are not afraid of being isolated. By saying and doing the unpopular, by shocking, they...can carry their ideas to supremacy" (p. 155). Thus, she adds, progress comes from artists, intellectuals, reformers, and noncon-formists who are not afraid of isolation and willingly express minority opinions.

Hostile Media Effect   The modern history of media-based victimage can be traced back to the 1970s and President Richard Nixon. Nixon, in his on-going disagreement with the press (Liebovich, 2003), carefully pursued a strategy that involved changing references to the journalistic profession from "the press" to "the media," under the assumption that the latter phrase was devoid of connotations regarding the objectivity of "the press." Nixon's efforts at this change were so effective that "media" is more commonly used as a description of journalism than is "the press" (Nolan, 2005). Nixon and his aides also compiled an enemies list of hostile reporters and often appealed for sympathy from the public by portraying himself as a victim of media that he claimed were too liberal (Liebovich, 2003).

The Nixon administration's attacks on the press included assistance from his Vice President Spiro Agnew and his infamous "nattering nabobs of negativism" description of the media (Barone, 1996; Hart, 1994). Agnew's use of semantics as a divisive strategy eventually was referred to in some circles as "The Spiro Strategy" (Fineman, 1995, p. 28).

This antagonistic relationship to the press has led to a line of research on hostile media effect, that is, the perception that the media are biased against one's candidate. Some research has found that the perception of a hostile media exceeds that of reality (e.g., Kyun & Yogo, 2007), but other studies have occasionally found some bias present on some networks/channels (Coe et al., 2008). Further, many of the perceptions of hostility reflect the partisan views of the audience

(Coe et al., 2008; Schmitt, Gunther, & Liebhart, 2004), while Elder and Greene (2003) reported that gender was a factor, with women more likely than men to view the media as hostile to the candidate they favored. Such findings led Matheson and Durson (2001) to conclude that the hostile media effect was largely a perception that reflected a form of in-group bias.

Other research points to the possibility that the hostile media effect is a by-product of rhetorical discussion of the topic. Stadler (2009), for example, reported that perceptions of a hostile media were based more on what respondents "heard" about the media rather than what they had actually seen in the media themselves. Similarly, Choi, Yang, and Chang (2009) reported that evaluations of a hostile media effect were based heavily on the perceptions and values of the respondents. Further, the presence of a potential hostile media effect engenders additional rhetorical discussion on the topic. Hwang, Pan, and Sun (2008) found that indignation of a perceived hostile media resulted in voters being more willing to discuss the issues reported by the media. Those discussions were also more likely to be with other individuals who shared their political ideology (Eveland & Shah, 2003). Further, the impact of Nixon's antagonism toward the press continues today. Specifically, Republicans, more so than Democrats, continue to view the media as hostile toward their candidates (Stadler, 2009).

Third-Person Effect The third-person effect refers to the tendency of media audiences to believe that media have a stronger impact on other people than on themselves. For example, when someone sees a media report that is at odds with their own beliefs or values, they don't believe that depiction will have any effect on them. However, they do believe that other, more gullible, individuals will be susceptible to the story's influence. The concept was initially developed by Davison (1983) and triggered a number of other studies. Price and Li-Ning (1997) described this as the "belief that the greatest media impact will be on them rather than me or you" (p. 525). Perloff (1993) defined it as "the notion that individuals assume that communications exert a stronger influence on others than on the self" (p. 167); Jie and Gonzenbach (2008) described it as an "overestimation of the influence of mass media on people" (p. 375); and Atwood (1994) called it an "illusion of media power" (p. 269). This effect is the stimulus for a variety of attacks on the media, including calls for censorship of pornography and criticisms of violence in the media (e.g., Chia, Kerr-Hsin, & McLeod, 2004; Hoffner & Buchanan, 2002), or what Rojas, Shah, and Faber (1996) called "for the good of others" (p. 163). In political communication, it is related to the Hostile Media Effect in that when voters see an adverse story in the press, they believe that the story will influence "vulnerable" voters and cost support for their candidate (Rucincki & Salmon, 1990, p. 345). This effect is particularly strong among voters who are ego-involved with a candidate, issue, or party (Perloff, 1989) and can vary depending upon group identification (Gardikiotis, 2008). The effect also has a partisan difference, with Republicans more likely to exhibit the third-person effect than Democrats (Banning, 2006), while religiosity is a factor on moral topics (Golan, 2002).

Research typically focuses on the impact of news coverage, poll results, endorsements, and television ads. Voters generally view celebrity endorsements of candidates as having no impact on themselves, but they do believe they can influence other voters (Brubaker, 2008). There is no across-the-board third-person effect regarding poll results (Lee, 2010), but those with negative attitudes toward polls often believe pollsters report their results in an attempt to influence vulnerable voters (Price, 2006). In terms of television ads, the effect appears more pronounced with negative ads (Hong & Riff, 2008; Ran & Ven-Hwei, 2007).

Does the third-person effect have an influence on campaigns? Apparently so. It seems to have a direct impact on strategic voting, that is, voting for a particular party to counter the perceived effect of hostile media coverage toward that party (Cohen & Tsfati, 2009). Thus, while there is a perception that the media affects others, the third-person effect can have a real behavioral influence on the first-person themselves (Golan, Banning, & Lundy, 2008; Golan & Day, 2008).

More recent research has looked at the third-person effect and the Internet. Initial research indicates that the third-person effect operates with the Internet in a manner similar to traditional media, assuming, of course, that the voter has sufficient computer skills and Internet access (Xigen, 2008). Further, the effect is consistent whether the media source is a newspaper, online news, or blogs (Banning & Sweetser, 2007).

SUMMARY

The impact of media on political behavior is a complex and ever-changing subject. The sheer volume of media exposure in modern society argues for some type of potential impact, but quantifying and specifying the exact nature of the media–audience relationship is complex. As researchers try to learn something about today's media, another theory is being developed that may invalidate many of their conclusions. Thus, academicians continue to chase the elusive answers. Still, the academic community has addressed a number of critical issues. In some instances, mass media can be used for propaganda purposes; an understanding of such techniques will make a person less susceptible to undue influence. Various scholars have debated whether political impact has a little impact or a massive impact on voters, but the answer seems to fall somewhere in between. The media can have a major impact on some voters, and a little one on others. It can influence the public's agenda on some issues, but not on others. What impact that does exist is likely mediated by interpersonal influence and the individual motivations of the voters. Still, despite all of these mitigating factors, the media are still the primary means of communication between candidates and voters. As such, it continues to play a vital role in the campaign process.

That's why consultants continue to assume that media can and do have a direct impact on electoral results. Much of the campaign budget and campaign time is devoted to media communications. Furthermore—as we will see in a later chapter—those media campaigns can often make a difference in determining which candidate wins an election. To help in that process, consultants rely upon some of the ideas developed by the academic community, and they continue to use any such idea until it doesn't work anymore, keeping in mind that the technologies of modern media are constantly changing.

QUESTIONS FOR DISCUSSION

1. What is the difference between a theory and a model? Is the uses-gratifications approach to media a theory or a model? What about agenda setting?

2. Your environmental group is attempting to build public opposition to genetically altered food grains. With only a few exceptions, you have been met with scant interest from opinion makers in the news media. Why have you had a difficult time presenting your point of view? Based on either the awareness, priorities, or salience models, how could you create a program that would improve your chances of getting news coverage?

3. Although crime has not been an issue in your candidate's campaign for state senator, recent polling suggests that voters are concerned that she has not taken a vigorous position against it. Although they still support her, that support has grown perilously thin. Is there an explanation for the voter response within the uses-gratification model? Does the model suggest a solution? Are there threshold issues about which candidates must reassure the electorate in order to be successful?

4. In polling provided to the campaign, your candidate for attorney general is running a close but weak second in an open primary, a very unusual circumstance for a Democrat. Four other Democrats are in the race. The lone Republican is ahead. Your candidate is clearly the most experienced and toughest on crime. Even the Republican president of the United States is shown making generous comments about your candidate in your television ads. What changes can your campaign make to move ahead?

The Campaign Team

Modern political campaigns are team activities. When an individual decides to run for public office, a team is assembled that includes professionals, family members, friends, and volunteers. The structure of the team will vary with each campaign, as will the nature of the team members. A number of specific functions are typically fulfilled by some team members regardless of the particular organization's structure. Part Two will examine those functions and the tasks associated with each.

Chapter 6 opens this part with a discussion of the campaign organization. At first glance, the day-to-day operations of a campaign look similar to that of any other organization. Beneath the surface, though, are distinct differences that are so unique to the area that an entire subfield of consulting has emerged. The modern campaign manager must form a temporary campaign organization that meshes the talents of the candidate, the candidate's family, volunteers, and professional consultants. The campaign manager is the "general" who keeps each team member focused on an assigned task. This second edition has also added the role of "online director," a recognition of the growing importance of the Internet in modern campaigns.

Chapter 7 looks at campaign communication in the mass media. The key team member for this section is the media consultant, the "guru" who advises the campaign on messages, produces the media advertisements, and directs the placement of those ads in the appropriate media outlets. When a war analogy is invoked, media consultants are often compared to the air force—that member of the team who provides air cover for other campaign activities. Media consultants often work in multiple formats—television, radio, and newspapers, for example—while maintaining a consistent theme and strategic approach. This chapter examines their role and how they function within the campaign.

Chapter 8 looks at the role of direct voter contact, an activity that is less visible than mass media ads but no less important in many campaigns. If the media consultant represents the air force, then the direct voter contact team members represent the ground forces of a campaign. Telephone banks contact voters individually to identify supporters, increase voter turnout, and to communicate messages in support of or opposition to some candidates. This second edition updates that section by adding a discussion of "robo-calls." Direct mail consultants offer services to mail letters and brochures to individual voters who have been targeted on the basis of specific demographic and attitudinal bases.

Chapter 9 addresses the role of political speeches and the people who write them. Political speeches are the way in which the candidate personally articulates the campaign's messages and themes. The speechwriters are the communication specialists who must find a way to express the candidate's ideas in a way that communicates with the voters and maintains a message that is consistent with the overall campaign theme.

Chapter 10 is a new chapter added for the second edition. This addition represents the increasingly important role that the Internet played in campaigns during the first decade of the twenty-first century. The Internet has increased the potential of direct voter contact by allowing campaigns to use e-mail and Web sites to exchange information with supporters. Campaigns increasingly used YouTube and other sites to reach voters via video media. Further, the 2008 campaign of Barack Obama demonstrated the potential impact that social media could have on campaigns.

Finally, Chapter 11 examines the role of polling in political campaigns. The pollster is the intelligence unit of the team, the person who provides the team with information used to make campaign decisions. The pollster's function is really much broader than just that of conducting public opinion surveys. Most polling firms also provide other forms of communication research services, particularly focus groups. By using a variety of research approaches, the research portion of the team can provide both descriptive and qualitative information that can contribute to campaign decisions. When they've done that, the team is ready to go to work.

Campaign Organization

In 1996, Missourians for Riverboat Gambling wanted to add slot machines to the list of legalized gambling options in the state's riverboat casinos, a change that required a referendum for an amendment to the state's constitution. Polling data indicated that the issue had enough public support to pass a referendum, but there were organizational problems.

State law was specific. Any group that wanted an amendment on the ballot was required to get a substantial number of petition signatures from at least six of Missouri's eight congressional districts. Consulting firms that specialized in petition gathering had been hired early, but they had met with only partial success. With only twenty-three days left before the deadline, about half of the state had not been reached. No signatures had been obtained from most of western Missouri, including Kansas City.

Faced with failure, the committee hired a team of political consultants to organize the process. Want ads were placed to hire workers to gather the signatures. Training materials were developed; training sessions implemented; and a centrally located headquarters established and equipped with telephones, fax machines, computers, and minimal office furniture. Finally, a payroll system was implemented to ensure that the new workers were paid on a timely basis.

Signature gatherers were provided with briefing materials that encouraged voters to sign the petition—not because they necessarily supported slot machines, but "to give the voters of Missouri the right to decide the issue." To avoid antagonizing the opposition, there was no attempt to publicize or advertise the signature campaign itself. Instead, all activities were kept at an organizational level.

In the end, a thousand petition gatherers were hired, trained, and paid to obtain a goal of 62,000 valid signatures. A core staff of twenty, working sixteen hours a day, managed the effort. The result: 147,000 signatures were gathered and the amendment went on the ballot and easily passed at the subsequent election.

This example represents the dramatic impact that the campaign organization can have on elections. While such organizational aspects are relatively invisible to the voting public, the campaign organization still plays an important role. A great campaign organization will not ensure victory, but a poor one can contribute to defeat. A better campaign organization—particularly one composed of professional campaign workers—has a better chance of winning. Or, as Medvic (2001) noted, "the more types of consultants hired to assist with various aspects of the campaign, the better candidates will do at election time" (p. 104).

The day-to-day management of the campaign organization is different from most other professional organizations (Steinberg, 1976a, 1976b). Several elements make the campaign organization distinctive. First, it is generally temporary in nature: a group of individuals—some professionals and some volunteers—who are brought together for a relatively short amount of time with the goal of completing a task that will lead to the dissolution of their jobs within a few weeks or months. Second, that situation is fertile ground for conflict between the various consultants, the paid vs. volunteer workers, the idealists, and the "win-at-all-costs" advisers. Third, the managers of the campaign organization have remarkably little control or legitimate authority over the others in the organization. The manager can advise the candidate, but ultimate decisions for campaign activities are those of the candidate. The manager can issue orders to others in the organization, but many of those are other consultants (who are more used to giving orders than taking them) or volunteers who can walk away from the job with little or no penalty. Fourth, volunteers are often outside the normal channels of communication within the organization (Lewis, 1999), a situation that requires the development of communication channels created precisely for them. And fifth, the campaign organization has to have constant performance reviews; an annual performance review is simply not timely enough for an effective campaign.

As campaigns have become more complex, the role of the campaign organization has also evolved—particularly at the presidential level. That organizational expansion has raised eyebrows among some critics. Several observers have complained that modern campaigns are controlled too much by political professionals (Polsby & Wildavsky, 1968; Thurber & Nelson, 2000). The role of the consultant often continues well after the campaign, providing continued influence on government even after the election is over. Consultant Dick Morris (1999), for example, continued to provide advice and consultation to the White House during most of Bill Clinton's administration.

The result, Blumenthal (1982) argued, is that campaigns have become too organized, resulting in the political environment becoming increasingly dominated by the campaign organization. Staff members from the campaign take a position on the staff of the newly elected official or remain active on the sidelines as consultants to the candidates. That action has led to a situation that Blumenthal calls the "Permanent Campaign": after a candidate achieves election, the campaign organization stays intact to help the newly elected official make policy decisions. As a result, Woodward (1997) noted, "A concern for public opinion remains the central focus of any campaign" (p. 125). Positions on issues and legislative votes are decided on the basis of political impact. Nor is that effect limited to the primary campaign organization; all sorts of volunteer organizations that participated in the campaign can have an impact. Polsby and Wildavsky (1968) noted that, particularly at the presidential level, there is a danger that "the volunteer organizations will take on lives of their own and attempt to dictate strategy and policy to the candidates" (p. 180).

Others have argued that the role of the campaign organization has been diminished over the years. As a result of the growing influence of consultants, the professional organization has become a more dominant force in campaigns while the organizational influence of political parties has diminished (Thurber & Nelson, 2000). Campaigns of the 1940s and 1950s used the campaign organization for the latter purpose (Cass, 1962). "A veteran organizer," Key (1949) wrote, "can by his personal influence gather to the fold political cronies that he has used and who have used him in previous years" (p. 403). The consultants of the 1940s were frequently organizational experts whose expertise was who they knew rather than what they knew. "The special asset of these men is not their organizing ability or their political acumen alone," Key (1949) wrote in describing the 1940s system, "it is their intimate acquaintance with county politics and county politicians."

That focus on county politics highlights another change in campaign organizations. The increased role of the media in campaigns has altered the organizational structure of campaigns. During the 1940s and 1950s, statewide campaigns were typically organized by geography, with a state organization structured to communicate with district or county organizations (Cass, 1962; Key, 1949, pp. 403–405). Today's campaigns are more frequently organized by function, in terms of what roles or media outlets are necessary to reach the voters. Furthermore, those roles are often handled by campaign consultants, individuals who will not be directly involved in the administration of the elected official's duties.

ORGANIZATIONAL ROLES

The Candidate   At the top of a campaign organization's organization chart is the candidate. Some candidates are self-starters, individuals who chose to run for office for personal reasons; others are recruits, candidates who seek an office at the urging of friends, neighbors, or interested third parties (Nimmo, 1970, p. 42; Seligman, 1961).

Although the campaign manager is responsible for the smooth day-to-day operation, it is the candidate who is ultimately responsible for the campaign. All information is fed to the candidate through the filter of their handpicked experts and managers. The candidate is responsible for approving his or her campaign message through speeches, letters, op-ed pieces, and through statements at news conferences. Additional political communication can be inferred through the candidate's schedule. Other information about the campaign can be inferred through the candidate's personality, clothing, haircut, eyeglasses (or lack thereof), marriage (or lack thereof), religiosity (or lack thereof), and myriad other minor factors.

Candidates also set the tone for their campaigns in terms of both organizational style and temperament. Some candidates insist on micromanaging their campaigns, while others remain aloof from the day-to-day operation. Energetic candidates inspire their campaign workers to engage in a similar work ethic, while laid-back candidates might generate a comfortable and relaxed work environment. In either case, there are no models that guarantee success.

A major factor often overlooked by campaigns is the need to keep the candidate fresh. Campaigning can be a tiring activity, and candidate fatigue can trigger any number of mistakes that could cost the candidate any chance of winning. Some observers attribute a fatigued candidate for Edmund Muskies' crying on camera before the 1972 New Hampshire primary and, more recently, Howard Dean's "scream" speech after the 2004 Iowa caucuses (Leibovich, 2008).

The Campaign Manager Overly elaborate organizations that consume large amounts of money without contributing to a persuasive message can contribute to failure. For example, a campaign that leases an airplane—seldom a cost-effective practice—may be at a competitive disadvantage. Thus enters the campaign manager. The campaign manager must be a master of cost-benefit analysis as well as the political arts. His or her job is different from that of standard business management. They are in charge of an organization that will cease operating at a known time. Even if fully successful, it will stop.

Early in the campaign, a decision must be made as to how much authority the campaign manager will have (Nimmo, 1970, p. 45). When the candidate takes a strong role in management, often the manager is weak. When the candidate takes a weak role in management, the campaign manager is strong. Either way it is up to the effective manager of the campaign to implement the campaign strategy (Kelley, 1956). This task requires the manager to negotiate the best prices for the products the campaign consumes—printing, advertising and its production, travel, and so forth. Every amount more than the minimum resources can result in a less persuasive campaign. As a result, the campaign manager will plan "minute details" for some campaign events in an effort to achieve maximum impact (Nimmo, 1970, p. 120).

The campaign manager must also motivate the staff to their best efforts during long hours with little financial reward. While many staff members may imagine themselves as members of the candidate's future staff, it is generally illegal for the candidate to promise something of value in a future public office for current labors. Generally, the staff cannot be fired, and separations can result in "sour grapes" news media reports—something no campaign seeks.

Political staffs are difficult to motivate. Some staff members are local political junkies who are drawn to the "action" of political campaigns. Others are transient to politics. Some are simply devoted to the candidate. Unless the campaign managers can convince each that he or she will learn something or that the manager has the best interests of the candidate at heart, the manager will fail.

The campaign manager must also deal with the consultants. Consultants look at the manager as someone who will get their checks mailed on time. After that, consultants hope the campaign manager will not "poison the water," causing the candidate to lose confidence. If a consultant does not start with confidence in the campaign manager, they may simply undermine the candidate's confidence.

Campaign managers who begin the process as a "best friend" of the candidate usually will not have this problem. On the other hand, "best friends" often lack the skills needed to run an effective campaign. The requisite knowledge, from effective mailing techniques to the nomenclature for advertising, is know-how the average layperson does not have. Also, a less politically knowledgeable person may not have the skills needed to assist in the interpretation of survey research.

A professional campaign manager is more likely to have these and other skills, but not have the full confidence of the candidate. The average candidate fears many things about the campaign environment, not the least of which is the potential abandonment by a cynical outsider. In the final analysis, the best campaign managers run these cobbled-together organizations well only when real confidence can be instilled. Campaign managers can accomplish this with impressive resumes, lengthy hours on the job, doing a good job, and by being a good manager.

The Political Director   The political director is charged with arranging alliances with other politicians, special interest groups, civic associations, political clubs, labor unions, environmental groups, business groups, and other groups. Political campaigns will work to consolidate natural constituencies through their political operation. For example, Republicans might attempt to ally themselves with Chambers of Commerce while Democrats do the same with labor unions. Although there are no hard-and-fast rules, these alliances are often a cost-effective means of communicating with voters. The leaders of the various groups serve as elite opinion leaders who can pass on the campaign message to larger numbers of voters. Also, the very fact of such alliances reinforces the campaign messages and counter-messages. Often during campaigns, a candidate will advertise their "endorsers" for just such a purpose.

The Field Director   The field director is responsible for organizing activities that identify supporters and harness their energy to pass the persuasive message to others and maximize the turnout of voters friendly to the campaign on election day (Pohl, 1971, pp. 140–141). Typically, a field director will use existing political activists to find others by direct contact with voter groups by the candidate. As the campaign matures, activities begin to focus on voter identification and turnout. By creating programs, the field organization will contact voters and ask them whom they support. Lists of friendly voters are developed in this way. Beginning a few days before election day, friendly voters are contacted and urged to vote. Efforts can range from highly elaborate organizations with the creation of county and city committees with campaign representatives appointed down to the precinct, or even street levels, to merely the appearance of a field organization. The "work your base" maxim comes into play here. Many campaigns will highly organize areas where they are very strong, with little or no organization in other areas.

The Finance Director   Most candidates have to ask others for money (Thomas, 1999, p. 68), and the finance director helps them do that. The finance director has responsibility for raising funds through direct contact by the candidate, fund-raisers, or through a finance committee. For that reason, the finance director is often a well-known (or at least well connected) member of the community "whose knowledge of the responsive sources of funds has been acquired through long observation or experience" (Key, 1949, p. 401). The finance director oversees a campaign finance committee whose members may be either a collection of the candidate's closest friends and/or supporters who have provided the larger contributors to the campaign. The main task of the finance committee is to cast an ever-wider net for fund-raising purposes.

The campaign organization is an engine that manufactures and distributes the campaign message. The fuel that feeds this machine is money, for which the campaign also has the responsibility for raising (Pohl, 1971, pp. 39–45). Some campaigns require high-test and many will run on regular. Others run dry before they cross the finish line. Without money, no campaign organization can achieve its potential, much less win its election. No amount of money can necessarily keep a campaign from losing a campaign. The campaign organization requires computers, printers, office furniture, brochures, palm cards, a letterhead, postage, posters (lawn signs), larger signs, radio commercials, television commercials, automobiles, telephones, air charters, air fares, motel rooms, personnel, and paid expert consultants, just to mention a few items. Tiny campaigns need fewer items. Huge statewide campaigns need vast resources. This function of the campaign is discussed in more detail in a later chapter.

The Press Secretary   The first job of the press secretary is to promote the campaign message to the news media. No employee of the campaign has a greater responsibility for knowing and implementing the message on a day-by-day basis. It is virtually impossible for a campaign to be successful without a solid relationship with the news media. The press secretary is responsible for the campaign's relationship with the news media and for carrying the message to editors and reporters. It is often true that so-called free media are insufficient to elect a candidate. It is equally true that news reports that do not support the campaign message can defeat a campaign. If the press secretary is successful at his or her day-to-day job, then newspapers, magazines, television news programs, radio news programs, and the Internet will deliver the message to voters. The press secretary will often travel with the candidate to facilitate interviews on the campaign trail. The role requires the ability to write press releases and the ability to influence observers. In some campaigns, the press person also writes speeches for the candidate.

The Research Director   There are two kinds of research in modern politics, issues research and opposition research. Issues research is the data required to support the candidate's position on a given issue. Such data can be received from recognized experts on a topic (university professors, for example), special interest group supporters, libraries, Internet research services, and other sources.

Opposition research falls into three categories: research on the opponent, research on the campaign's own candidate, and research on the voters. Opposition research is often controversial because it rather emphatically suggests that the campaign will attack its opponent (or that it expects the opponent to attack them). Such data can be as simple as a public records search for such information as tax compliance, divorce decrees, lawsuits, property holdings, education, and family. However, those can be remarkably revealing at times. One of the authors was involved in a local campaign for tax collector where a simple search of the public records revealed that one of the candidates had not paid his property or business taxes; that fact became a focal point of the campaign and led to that candidate's defeat.

Opposition research can also include hiring private detectives or professional opposition research consultants. The advantage of professionals is that they tend to know where to look for information, are more discreet in their searches, and offer better protection to the campaign. Also, their work product tends to be in a form that can more easily be used by campaign media consultants. For incumbents, the research focuses on their political record (particularly the voting record of legislators), but other issues also come into play. The authors have been involved in campaigns in which opposition research uncovered such facts as:

- A wealthy candidate who was claiming an agricultural exemption on his home as a means of reducing property taxes;
- An incumbent legislator with a criminal record, including one arrest for indecent exposure;
- Another incumbent who had written a letter to the parole board in support of the release of a convicted rapist who was the son of a major campaign donor.

Major campaigns also hire professional opposition research consultants to investigate themselves. Such a practice allows candidates to understand how their public record can be interpreted by their opponent and thus allows them to anticipate potential attacks. That information is then used to prepare defensive responses that explain those sensitive portions of the record from the candidate's point of view.

Research on the voters is typically done with polls or focus groups (but is not limited to those techniques) and is discussed in another chapter. All campaigns, regardless of their budget, can engage in such basic voter analyses as investigation of voting patterns, past voting turnout, and demographic correlates that might affect the campaign (Denton & Woodward, 1985).

The Campaign Attorney   Modern campaigns are often regulated by state and local or federal authorities with a maze of rules ranging from campaign contributions and expenditure limits to the details of when and how to make campaign reports. Also, the campaign interacts with a variety of electronic advertising media that are, in turn, also regulated by a litany of legal requirements. Campaigns, from time to time, will work to get an opponent's negative ads off the air by either threatening a lawsuit or actually suing the opposition campaign. A campaign attorney will facilitate these undertakings.

The Campaign Office Manager   An office manager is the day-to-day boss of the campaign staff. This person is essential to controlling the routine expenses of the campaign from day to day and keeping records suitable for expenditure reports, including the payroll. This person is not necessarily somebody who is politically savvy or overly involved in political activities. However, he or she must be someone with excellent organizational and management skills, the same skills that would be essential to the day-to-day management of any business or organization.

The office manager also has the task of coordinating office functions with a staff that is often composed mostly of "professionally committed party regulars and citizen volunteers" (Denton & Woodward, 1985, pp. 55–56). Those volunteers are often women, young people, and older adults—a subset that works remarkably well together in the political environment, perhaps because they tend to be so focused on telephone sociability goals (O'Keefe & Sulanowski, 1995). Volunteer workers bring their own motivation to the job, but maintaining that motivation for the duration of the campaign can be a challenging task, one that is much harder than that of a typical office manager. If they so choose, those volunteers don't have to come to work when they don't want to.

The Campaign Scheduler A major campaign asset is the ability of the candidate to communicate through speeches, presentations, and interviews and to demonstrate the campaign message symbolically through the nature of a campaign appearance. Good campaign schedulers have a knowledge of the campaign message and the resources available to demonstrate that message. The authors have illustrative experiences:

- A candidate holding a news conference on the banks of the Mississippi River, in the shadows of a grossly polluting chemical plant to demonstrate his commitment to environmental ideals.
- A candidate speaking to striking union workers to demonstrate his commitment to safe working conditions.
- A candidate visiting a school to demonstrate her commitment to higher education.

To maximize the candidate's time, a scheduler is necessary. The scheduler represents the point of contact with the candidate for those outside the campaign. The scheduler makes all travel and logistical arrangements to accommodate events. Among the second-tier positions in the campaign, this is one of the most difficult and most stressful of all roles. It requires somebody with the organizational skills of a CEO and the political tact of a diplomat. The candidate's time will become a major commodity, and the scheduler is responsible for ensuring that time is spent in productive ways. That frequently means turning down invitations from friends, supporters, and financial backers; those refusals have to be made in a tactful manner.

The Campaign Treasurer Most campaign authorities require the appointment of an individual who is responsible for keeping the campaign's financial records. The treasurer is often also responsible for maintaining the official records of the campaign and complying with the relevant campaign finance laws. A treasurer will often act as campaign controller, as well by being the authorizing signature on major expenditure checks for the purchase of advertising time, printing, and so forth.

Online director Modern campaigns use the Internet to communicate with supporters, to reach out to undecided voters, and to raise money for the campaign. The online director oversees these activities by maintaining the campaign's Web sites and updating its presence on social networks.

The role starts with establishing the campaign's Web site. That job requires obtaining a Web site address that is appropriate for the campaign. That may sound like an easy task, but it can often be difficult—particularly if the opposition buys up all the relevant names before your campaign starts to work. Once established, pages must be developed that provide the candidate's biography, position on key issues, photos, and establishes the campaign's message. The site can also be used to post copies of the campaign's communications—media ads, brochures, and samples of the mail campaign.

Maintaining the campaign's presence on social networks such as Facebook and Twitter requires daily (sometimes hourly) updating of the sites. Supporters are eager for new information and comments from the candidate and/or other members of the campaign team. In conjunction with this, the campaign must maintain e-mail lists for all supporters. A key component of the e-mail list is the zip codes of the supporters. This allows for targeted messages that apply to geographic areas, for example, telling supporters when the candidate will be campaigning in their area. They may also coordinate activities with the fund-raising team by using the Internet for small-donor contributions. This function will be discussed in more detail in a later chapter.

While using online communication is useful to the campaign, the online director must always be aware of its potential danger to the campaign. The most active monitors of the campaign's online activities will be the press and the opposition. Any mistake that's posted or sent via e-mail will become fodder for the press and opponents to criticize the candidate—even if the candidate was not involved in the posting.

Consultants and Peer Advisers   The final category of campaign organization are the consultants. In major campaigns, the consultants are part of an "inner circle" (Thomas, 1999, p. 22)—one that may also include friends and peers of the candidate—who are involved in major campaign decisions. Most of the consultant roles are discussed individually elsewhere. These people often deal directly with the candidate but depend on other members of the organization for information and logistical support. Much of the work product of the campaign organization filters upward to these consultants. They frequently get a great deal of internal recognition and financial rewards, while internal campaign workers may work for little or nothing.

This is a typical, though not the only, campaign organization. Smaller campaigns, particularly those at the local level (Thomas, 1999), adapt by having one person fill two or three of the functions, or they do not fill the slot at all. In some campaigns, the candidate is also the campaign manager, or the office manager is called campaign manager. Larger campaigns often add elaborate staffing to functions. Presidential campaigns will have all of this, and will have campaigns in each of the fifty states that will be a smaller version of the national campaign staff.

Winning campaign organizations often inspire candidates to continue their successful efforts in office. Such efforts rarely work. After the 1992 presidential campaign, the Clinton–Gore administration announced it would continue the intensity of the campaign, using the same people in their management of the White House. Within a brief period of time, it became clear that the needs of public administration were not amenable to the emotional, intense styles that typify political campaigns.

POLITICAL PARTIES

Will Rogers used to tell audiences that he was not a member of any organized political party—he was a Democrat. Some scholars agree; Mayer and Polsby (1991) argued that Democrats have more trouble maintaining party unity than Republicans. Others, however, have noted that the organizational influence of both parties has declined with the introduction of reform rules that increased the importance of primaries in selecting party nominees (Polsby, 1983). As the importance of primary campaigns has increased, the role of the party has decreased. This may be a natural evolution of the increased complexity of campaigning. Kolodny, for example, (2000) argued that "modern campaigns demand specialized, technical services that are simply beyond the political parties' institutional capacity to deliver" (p. 110). Consultants have filled that void.

Still, political parties conduct the function of political campaign organizations during periods when the candidates are not active, that is, between elections. The political parties have political directors, field directors, press secretaries, finance directors, and so forth and so on. During campaign seasons, political parties fade into the background, or in the case of presidential campaigns, become an appendage.

The relationship between the candidates and the parties is sometimes adversarial in nature, because their goals are not always synonymous. The candidate's goal is usually to gain a personal victory through the electoral process by gaining popular support; the party's goal is to push an ideological agenda through the attainment of political power. Those different goals sometimes create conflicts between the ideological purity of some party loyalists and the pragmatic goal of the individual candidates. As Safire (2000, February 14) noted, sometimes a "...clubby set of single-issue power brokers prefers to float out to sea in a Viking's funeral than to present a candidate who can appeal across party lines and energize swing voters."

SUMMARY

The campaign organization serves as the vehicle by which the candidate communicates with voters, both through the mass media and on a one-to-one basis. The organization may be a close-knit small circle of friends and advisers, an informal collection of volunteers committed to a candidate, or a nationwide hierarchy that includes volunteers and political professionals. Large or small, professional or amateur, that organization becomes the public interface for the candidate's message.

Successful campaign organizations fulfill multiple functions that include financial, legal, and communication elements. Large campaigns may involve a number of individuals with well-defined roles, each one handling a key function. In smaller campaigns, functions may overlap, with a single person handling multiple duties. Either way, the functions must be fulfilled. If not, the campaign will fail to communicate its ideas to the voters. In a democracy, the candidate with the best ideas should ideally win; realistically, that doesn't happen unless those ideas are communicated to the voters. That responsibility rests with the campaign organization, particularly the candidate and the campaign manager.

Although their role has changed, political parties still play a major role in campaign organizations. They are the major organizational source during non-election periods. The increased use of primaries as a means of selecting party candidates has led to an increased use of candidate-based organizations. Still, once the primaries are over, some members of the various candidates' organizations may be incorporated into the party's organization. Meanwhile, the party itself gears up to provide organizational support to the nominees of its party.

Either way, though, the organizational principle remains. The campaign organization represents the candidate. How well it represents that candidate can affect the election outcome.

QUESTIONS FOR DISCUSSION

1. What type of person would prefer to be a campaign manager rather than a candidate? What type would prefer to be the candidate? Why?

2. One trend during the 1990s and in 2000 was the development of political and campaign shows as a genre of popular entertainment. Television shows such as *Spin City* and *The West Wing* offered a glimpse into the inner workings of a political organization. Why are such programs entertaining? What is interesting about campaign organizations?

3. What happens if a candidate serves as his or her own campaign manager? Are both roles compatible, or does success at one inhibit success at the other?

4. Your best friend is running for lieutenant governor, and he asks you to run the campaign for him. As campaign manager, which of the following is your first task? Why?

   a. Create a finance committee and schedule a meeting.
   b. Create a campaign plan and campaign organization chart.
   c. Send a news release announcing formation of the campaign.
   d. Write a stump speech for the candidate.
   e. Hire the staff.

5. The two primary functions of a political campaign are communications and fund-raising. How are they related? How do they influence other campaign activities such as scheduling, record keeping, polling, and press relations?

6. Political campaigns are different from most other kinds of organizations. What are those differences, and why do they exist?

Campaign Communications in the Mass Media

In 1934, Upton Sinclair surprised the political establishment by running a strong campaign for governor of California. Before the campaign, Sinclair was primarily known as a muckraking author whose targets were often the big businesses of the day. Politically, he was an avowed socialist, an ideology that also scared California capitalists. But his antiestablishment attitudes set well with an electorate looking for someone to lead them out of the Great Depression, and his EPIC ("End Poverty In California") program offered hope.

Alarmed by Sinclair's growing public support, his opponents united to launch a massive public relations campaign against him. The players included some revered names in politics (Earl Warren), advertising (Albert Lasker), and political consulting (consulting pioneers Clem Whitaker and Leone Baxter and Nixon consultant Murray Chotiner). Also joining the fray were some of Hollywood's biggest names, including Cecil B. DeMille and Louis B. Mayer.

Hollywood provided film shorts, the consultants provided strategy and tactics, and the politicians served as the "mouthpieces" against the Sinclair campaign. Business interests supplied as much as ten million dollars to the effort in what was called the first "public relations blitzkrieg" in campaign history. When the dust settled, Sinclair had lost the election to Frank Merriam. Sinclair's attempts to mount a political comeback in 1936 ended with a second, resounding defeat, but his legacy on political campaigning endures. As Mitchell (1992) noted, "The 1934 governor's race in California showed candidates the way from the smoke-filled room to Madison Avenue" (p. xii).

In 1948, media ads were only a minor part of Harry Truman's successful reelection campaign (Diamond & Bates, 1988). By 1952, though, the Dwight Eisenhower campaign found several uses for television (Kaid & Johnson, 2001). Many of their ads were based on an "Eisenhower Answers America" theme, with Eisenhower answering a question presented to him by the public. Today, all major political campaigns are media campaigns, dominated by media consultants who serve as an advertising agency for the political campaign. Candidates for federal office often spend more on broadcast advertising than any other campaign activity (Fritz & Morris, 1992), and most political campaigns spend 70 percent of their budget on television advertising. By definition, therefore, the media consultant is responsible for more than two-thirds of the entire budget and virtually all of the direct communications of a campaign.

THE EFFECTIVENESS OF THE PROCESS

One issue that dogged media consultants for years was whether media campaigns had any effect on elections. The entire approach of the limited effects model argued that the media had little, if any, effect on elections. According to this approach, most voters have either partisan attitudes that will guide their voting decisions regardless of what political ads might be aired. Although most limited effects models can be traced to the 1940s and 1950s, this approach was still considered viable by some observers into the 1970s. In an analysis of the 1972 presidential election, for example, Patterson and McClure (1976) argued that the candidates' ads had little effect, influencing only 3 percent of the total electorate. They did, however, argue that early ads might be important because it reaches the voters before they have made voting decisions.

Cundy (1986) was slightly more optimistic, reporting that ads can influence viewer perceptions of candidates, underscoring the significance of early advertisements to enhance a candidate's image and to act as an inertia factor, diminishing the impact of subsequent propaganda efforts. Still, this approach considers ads to be more effective for inducing resistance to persuasion than actually achieving real attitude change.

Another significant body of literature supports the idea that voters seek information from television ads. Walker (1987) surveyed voters regarding all channels of communication and found that television received the most exposure and received the highest credibility marks for both issues and candidate images. Chaffee and Kanihan (1997) compared the ways individuals gain information in order to make political decisions and concluded that television use far surpassed newspapers as a source of political decision making. Martinelli and Chaffee (1995) surveyed new citizens to determine how they sought information for voting; recall of television ads had the greatest predictive strength. Furthermore, most voters consider campaign advertisements to be more informative than newspapers and television news programs (Kern, 1989; Patterson & McClure, 1976). Also, advertisements typically convey more information than do candidate debates (Just, Crigler, & Wallace, 1990).

Both candidates and consultants work under a pragmatic assumption that the media do indeed influence voters. Consultant Dane Strother (1999) calls television commercials "the B-52s of a political campaign. They can virtually carpet bomb a community or state; the political landscape is inexorably altered in their wake" (p. 186). Strother's argument overstates the case, since sometimes the number of voters influenced by television may be small. Still, they are a significant subgroup. In many elections, that small number of only 3 percent (reported by Patterson and McClure) is still enough to swing an election.

Subsequent research has supported this assumption, reporting that political ads are clearly important for late-deciding or previously uninterested voters. Devlin (1986), for example, reported that ads were crucial to the 10–20 percent of the electorate who are typically reached only through television during the last stages of the campaign. The impact of advertising was succinctly summarized by Jamieson (1984), who noted, "Advertising remains less substantive than most would wish and less powerful than many fear. Nonetheless, it continues to provide an important channel of communication for candidates and a source of information for voters" (p. xxvi).

SCHOOLS OF CONSULTING

Kern reported that political media consultants tend to be dominated by one of two schools of thought, an informational school and an emotional school, or by a combination of the two, which is called dovetailing. For the informational school, the primary purpose of political advertising is to provide the voters with information about the candidates and the issues. The emotional school, which is more influenced by commercial advertising techniques, relies on simple, repeated ideas to create a psychological image of the candidate for the voters.

The dovetailing theory argues that ads are most effective if the issue and the image side of their overall message are complementary. This dovetailing concept goes beyond the verbal messages of the ads and is considered most effective if visual and linguistic elements of the ad also reinforce each other (Kern, 1989, p. 24). Today, most practicing political consultants seem to subscribe to this dovetailing concept, and research has consistently supported that school of thought. Indeed, it is often difficult to distinguish between issues and images within a political ad.

Research has consistently reported that viewers learn about issues from political ads, but the persuasive impact of those messages goes beyond the learning of information. Joslyn (1986) argued that issues are selected for ads primarily for the purpose of building character and image. That conclusion is consistent with other research that found that the purpose of ads that stress issues content can in fact be that of building an image of the candidate (Bennett, 1977; Rudd, 1986). Ads based on this dovetailing approach typically contain three components: an entertainment device designed to arouse and hold the viewer's attention; a message, frequently about the character of the candidate and an issue; and, an attempt to provoke a reaction, surprise, excitement, recognition, affect, or an action message (Kern, 1989, p. 1).

Achieving that reaction may occur in a number of ways, but one of the most common is through the use of a referent. Referential spots use a symbol believed to have affective meaning for the viewer in a fashion that transfers or refers that meaning to the candidate or the opponent (Williamson, 1984). Thus, for candidates who wish to be identified as a champion of the elderly, their ads are likely to depict them in a variety of scenes with older voters. Similarly, "education candidates" are often depicted in school settings.

A more complex approach to creating affective reactions is based on an advertising technique called the "Wheel of Emotion" originally developed in 1984 by commercial advertiser Stuart J. Agres. Kern (1989, p. 31) applied this model for political ads in terms of a traditional problem–solution format ("Buy me and you will overcome the anxieties I have just reminded you about"). The wheel identifies seven negative emotions that can be aroused by political ads, along with a corresponding list of seven positive emotions. The seven bipolar emotions are: anxious–determined, fearful–satisfied, ashamed–proud, sad–hopeful, frustrated–relieved, bored–joyful, and serious–excited. The successful ad is divided into two parts. First, a negative emotion is aroused early in the spot. Second, the candidate is offered as a solution to the problem by identification with the positive emotion, which alleviates the first. Thus, to be effective, the positive emotion evoked by the ad must be the correct one to alleviate the negative emotion raised earlier in the spot.

THE TASKS OF THE CONSULTANT

Regardless of the philosophical school to which a particular consultant may subscribe, the primary tasks of a media consultant include development of the message, scriptwriting, cinematography and videography, editing, and spot buying. The secondary tasks include acting as a clearinghouse for campaign information involving polling, news media feedback, effectiveness assessment, and coordination of all communications to support campaign advertising.

Message Development

The optimum message is constructed when the media consultant works hand-in-glove with the campaign pollster. Both parties must cooperate in the production of a questionnaire that will throw light on those issues that can produce votes for the candidate and deprive the opponent of votes. The media consultant is generally the dominant partner because of the degree to which campaign resources are devoted to his or her activities. For many campaigns, however, the pollster acts as a check-and-balance mechanism, assuring that the media consultant focuses the effort accurately. The media consultant will involve key personnel from the campaign, including the candidate, the campaign manager, the press secretary, and others, as needed. Involvement can be formalized through poll briefings, daily conference calls, and regular planning meetings. Message development continues throughout the campaign. Most campaigns plan for a "message adjustment phase" of the campaign in the form of a second or third round of survey research and focus groups to determine the effectiveness of the initial ads and the development of new and/or different advertising approaches.

Scriptwriting

The script is the first step in the production process, which will result in a finished television or radio advertisement (spot). In early phases of the campaign, scripts will be developed to introduce the candidate or issue and lay a foundation for the delivery of the campaign message. The script conceptualizes the "look" of the spot, the type of narrator, the scenes needed to support the message, and initial suggestions for music and sound effects.

Types of Political Spots We will assume a typology based on five categories: biographical spots, issue spots, attack spots, comparative spots, and inoculation spots. Biographical spots introduce the candidate to the voters; they may include elements of early childhood, education, family, community involvement, political and nonpolitical achievements, logotypes, and campaign slogans. Issue introductory spots serve to acquaint the voters with the facts of an issue, to put it into play, and to remind the voter of the problem. Attack spots are primarily negative messages about the opponent or the opponent's record. Comparative spots present a positive image of the candidate contrasted with a negative image of the opponent. An ad produced by George Stevens for John McCain's 2000 presidential campaign illustrates this type of ad. The spot, called "New Low," argued that Bush had reached a "new all-time low" in attacking McCain's record on assisting veterans. The goal of the ad, one reporter noted, was to create a "contrast between one man who should be president and another who should be spanked" (Bennet, 2000, p. 52). Inoculation spots act to protect the candidate or issue from a potential weakness resulting from some past action, either private or public. Such ads usually are run after polling information reveals the weakness. They can be highly effective in protecting the candidate from future attacks. Pfau and Burgoon (1988) reported that inoculation messages that raise a candidate's liabilities early in the campaign deflect the persuasiveness of subsequent political attacks.

Cinematography and Videography

The first draft of spots are sent to the candidate and key campaign advisers for the correction of facts and approval of the concept. After some give and take, approval is given and the next phase is undertaken. The media consultant draws up a production budget that includes a cinematographer, assistant cameraperson, sound person, a gaffer (electrician), and a grip. Also included are the costs of renting a camera, lights, and other items needed to film on location. Travel expenses, including meals, accommodations, and transportation, are also factored into the budget. The campaign approves the budget and pays all or a portion of it before the beginning of the shoot.

Next, a shot list is prepared. The shot list is a list of items and scenes needed to complete the scripted spots. The production phase may also include assorted miscellaneous shots for use in a later phase of the campaign. The candidate is usually the main subject of these shots, with many showing him or her in germane locations in an office or at home. To assure the best use of expensive resources, advance work on the production phase is critical and many details must be handled. These include considerations about the locations of the production in terms of lighting, electrical facilities, permits and permissions, parking, meals, and overnight accommodations.

Editing

This phase is also called postproduction, and here the spots are actually produced. The first step in the process is the creation of a "select reel." The raw footage (whether film or video) is viewed and usable scenes are tabbed for the select reel. All others are put aside. The spots are then assembled according to, or as closely as possible to, the previously approved script. Spots are literally built, melding scene to scene, adding graphics, logos, superimpositions, layering special effects, and adding music, sound effects, and announcer tracks. All decisions are based on strategic targeting, some more precise than others, including the music and the announcer. During the 2000 Arizona presidential primary, for example, George W. Bush used a Spanish-language announcer in ads that targeted Hispanics, with the voice-over read in Spanish (Leavitt, January 27, 2000).

When the spot is completed, copies or dupes (duplicates) are made, with one copy forwarded to the campaign for final approval. If approved, copies are then sent directly to the television stations (either through a delivery service or by e-mail). In the past, postproduction services have been both time-consuming and expensive, with consultants renting studio time to finalize the edits. Some of that has been changed, however, by developments in computer technology. Media consultants are increasingly using facilities in their own offices as computer capabilities have soared and prices have plummeted.

Time Buying

Concurrently to building the spot, the media consultant is supervising the purchasing of time from the relevant television stations and cable TV systems in the target markets. Polling data will have provided information on the nature of the persuadable voters, and the time buyers design a buy based on programming that appeals to the target audience. The first decision is identification of the media market or markets that will be used. Hutchins (1999, p. 123) defines media markets as "the geographical definition of the combined viewership for an area's TV stations and the combined listenership for an area's radio stations." Media rating services often report media markets as ADIs—Areas of Dominant Influence. Although viewer ratings are assembled for all age groups, media consultants generally purchase time for viewers who are older than twenty-five. Younger voters have historically not voted in great numbers, and targeting only the twenty-five-plus age group increases the cost-efficiency of the buy.

Gross Rating Points The media consultant's task is a combination of science and art, mingled with constant attention to detail surrounding the campaign environment. On the science side, the buying plan is often based on numerical calculations of gross rating points (often called "GRPs," or "points"). Gross Rating Points are an estimation of how many people are reached by a given spot; they are computed as the numerical summation (the total) of the ratings for all programs for which the campaign has placed (or purchased) a spot (Beville, 1988).

"Frequency" is the number of times that a typical voter is exposed to a campaign advertisement. The simplest estimation of frequency is to divide the total GRPs by 100. Thus, a total of 100 points would indicate that the average viewer would see the spot one time. Working under the assumption that the ad must be seen five-to-seven times to be effective, then a total buy of at least 500–750 points is needed for the campaign to have any expectation of the ad having any impact. More points—perhaps up to 1,000—may be needed to reach "penetration," that is, a level in which nearly the entire audience has seen the spot.

Gross Rating Points, however, may not always provide an accurate assessment of audience frequency. Instead, the concept of audience *reach* must be considered. If the campaign buys ten spots on a show with a rating of 10, it will have purchased 100 points of broadcast time. However, not every voter will see it even once. Instead, 10 percent of the audience will see it ten times, while 90 percent will never see it at all. Thus, a more accurate assessment of frequency is to divide points by reach, that is, the viewership as defined by the audience of a particular program or schedule of programs.

As noted earlier, most consultants work under the assumption that a single spot must be seen at least five times (or 500 points) before it has any effect. The first time an ad is seen, it is merely noticed by the viewer ("I haven't seen this one before") but its message is rarely assimilated. On the second airing, there is a recognition response from the voter ("I've seen this ad before"), and some information may be assimilated. By the third time, the information may be fully assimilated ("This is the ad about X"). Still, at this level, the voter has merely assimilated the information; any decisional response to it may require additional exposures (Webster, 1998).

Thus, any ad must have a minimum of 500 points of exposure before it has any chance of having an impact, but even this may not be enough. Traditionally, most media consultants have assumed that a minimum of 750 points are needed for the spot to have maximum impact. More recently, many have been increasing that number to 700 points, because of the dilution and diffusion of the media that has resulted from the proliferation of cable channels (Ferguson & Melkote, 1997; Heeter & Greenberg, 1988), remote controls (Walker & Bellamy, 1991, 1993), and VCR usage. Hutchins (1999), for example, argues that "six to seven exposures weekly are required to ensure that a campaign's messages are being retained" in an "uncluttered" environment (p. 125). When the airwaves are "cluttered" with an avalanche of ads, Hutchins places the minimum number of exposures at ten to twelve, or between 1,000 and 1,200 Gross Rating Points.

Any campaign that plans to do television advertising should plan on purchasing at least 500 points worth of time for each message. Any expenditure less than this would be a waste of money. Highly visible campaigns will spend even more. Congressional campaigns typically assume that they need at least 2,500 points to be effective, enough for three or four different spots. Statewide campaigns for governor or senator will use even more, with 4,000 points often considered a minimum and 8,000 points not uncommon.

Decisional Strategies for Time Buying

Given the high cost of running a campaign, the media consultant cannot afford to waste money by spending it indiscriminately. Typically, buying decisions are made using some specific criteria. Two of the most common criteria are the cost-per-point method, and the roadblock strategy.

The Cost-per-Point Method The cost-per-point method tries to keep costs down by constantly calculating the cost efficiency of a particular campaign program. It does this by dividing the cost of the spot by the rating it receives for the campaign's target audience. Suppose, for example, that a spot on Program A was available for $250, while one on Program B cost $400. Which program is the better buy for the campaign? It depends on the rating that each receives for the target audience. If Program A receives a rating of 5, then its cost per point is $50 ($250 divided by 5). If program B receives a rating of 10, then its cost per point is $40 ($400 divided by 10). Program B is the more cost efficient of the two for this campaign, even though its total cost is higher. Thus, with this approach, the media buyer constantly evaluates each potential placement in terms of cost and rating, looking for the combination that reaches the target voter most efficiently.

The Roadblock An alternative buying strategy, the "roadblock," focuses on ensuring that the campaign's ads reach as many different voters as possible. It does this by picking specific times of high viewership and buying an ad on every available network at that time. Thus, if the target audience was composed primarily of daytime viewers, then the media buyer would purchase at least one daytime spot on every station in the market at the same time. For example, the buyer could choose a time (the 3:00–4:00 P.M. time slot, for example) and purchase one spot during that time on every network in the market (ABC, CBS, NBC, Fox, WB, CNN, and so forth). Or, if the target audience was primarily composed of people who watch news programs, the buyer could purchase a spot on the Six O'Clock News on every station in the market. The result of such a strategy is that everyone watching television during that hour would see the spot at least once. Of course, to be effective, the roadblock must be repeated several times (three to seven), to ensure that the audience sees the spot often enough for it to register.

The Theory of Critical Mass As mentioned earlier, media buying is a combination of science and art. The scientific approach says a television spot will have its maximum impact at some point that ranges from 300 to 700 points of exposure. In reality, pinpointing exactly when that occurs is difficult, and sometimes even 700 points is not enough. National consultants such as Republican George Stevens often want their ads seen ten to twelve times to ensure that it is absorbed by the voters (Bennet, February 27, 2000). One approach to identifying the maximum impact of a spot is called the "theory of critical mass." It can be used by those campaigns that use daily tracking polls to follow voter response to the candidate or issue. Specifically, the daily polling numbers are compared to the buy schedule, and the results are monitored for effectiveness. Typically, the spot will have no recognizable impact on voter response when exposure is less than 300 points. However, at some level of exposure beyond 300 points, the spot is likely to reach a "critical mass" in which all of its information has been assimilated by many of the voters. When this occurs, the tracking polls typically indicate a small (2 or 3 percentage points) but significant shift in favor of the candidate.

Once that first shift starts, it frequently continues for two to four days, as the ad is assimilated by more and more voters. Once the shift levels off, then maximum impact has been achieved, and it is time to change to another spot. The advantage of tracking polls in this situation is that they can help the campaign identify at which point a spot has achieved critical mass. Other than deciding that at least 300 points are needed at a minimum, it is difficult to predict at exactly what point that may occur. An ad that is both dramatic in style and simple in content may reach critical mass soon after it reaches 300 points. A more complex or subtle ad may require a full 700 points or even more to reach such a level. Regardless of the true number of points needed, tracking polls provide a means of constantly monitoring the impact of a spot, thus helping to determine changes in media strategy that may need to be made.

Traffic

Traffic is that department within the broadcast station that schedules the time at which the spot will actually air. In most broadcast stations, the traffic department operates independently of the sales department. Thus, the time buyer is responsible for communicating with the traffic department to ensure that the proper ad is running at the proper time. This is most frequently done in written form, by way of fax or e-mail.

The specific instructions will vary, depending on the strategy of the campaign, but most follow a similar format: an identification of the spot by name and number, and instructions regarding its relative importance in the rotation. A simple one- or two-word name for the spot, along with a production number, is provided by the production company when the spot is sent to the station. The buyer uses this label as a referent for the traffic department, providing rotation information usually expressed as percentages or fractions. Thus, if the campaign had only one spot that it wanted to run, the instructions might read: "Run spot 'INTEGRITY' (#01) 100 percent." If two spots were in the rotation, the instructions might read, "Run spots 'INTEGRITY' (#01) and 'ISSUES' (#02) 50 percent each," or "Run spot 'INTEGRITY' (#01) two-thirds and spot 'ISSUES' (#02) one-third."

OTHER CAMPAIGN MEDIA

Newspaper Ads

Given the importance that news coverage plays in most political campaigns, it often surprises outside observers that newspaper ads typically play such a minor role in most major campaigns. Presidential campaigns, gubernatorial campaigns, and U.S.

senatorial campaigns rarely use them, opting instead for increased spending on television and radio. The broadcast media have an advantage for such campaigns in that they can reach more people, including passive audience members who will later become active voters.

Newspapers are highly popular among consumer advertisers. Baran (1999, p. 109) noted that more advertising dollars find their way to newspapers than to any other medium, spurred by research that indicates the newspaper is the medium most often used by consumers when making a specific purchasing decision. Turow (1996, p. 137) noted that newspapers have an advantage over direct mail and other forms of print media in that many people see the newspaper with its ads as useful, while they consider bundles of direct mail to be junk.

Given such positive demographic attributes, why is it that newspapers are not widely used by state and local campaigns? There are several reasons. First, newspaper ads are generally viewed as an ineffective communication device. DeVries (1975) ranked newspaper ads last among print media in terms of impact on votes, placing them in a position comparable to campaign brochures. This low rating occurs because political ads are often overwhelmed by the mass of consumer advertising in most newspapers. Approximately 60 percent or more of daily newspaper space is devoted to advertising, with most of that devoted to local retail advertising (Baran, 1999; Turow, 1996). Political ads can easily get lost in the shuffle of pages. Furthermore, most campaigns assume that those newspaper readers who are persuadable are more likely to be influenced by newspaper coverage than by newspaper ads, an assumption supported by DeVries's research.

Second, newspaper ads are expensive. The cost per thousand of reaching voters through the broadcast media is often considerably cheaper than trying to reach a statewide audience through newspaper ads. Fairly large spaces are required (sold in terms of cost per column inches) for high visibility, and multiple ads are required. As a result, running a schedule of several ads requires a large budget, one that many campaigns can't afford.

A final disadvantage is a relatively long lead time required by virtually all newspapers. Most papers require submission of ads anywhere from three days to a week for the purpose of review by the management and for advance layout. Unlike television and radio advertising, in which stations are required by law to carry most ads, newspaper management may object to an advertisement and refuse to run it. Or, they may require specific changes as a condition of running the advertisement.

But newspapers do have advantages that appeal to some candidates. The biggest advantage, perhaps, is that newspapers are primarily a local medium. Schultz, Martin, and Brown (1988, p. 360) noted that, with only a few exceptions such as *USA Today* and the *Wall Street Journal,* most newspapers are published and printed locally and the medium is evaluated as a local medium. This attribute is a disadvantage to statewide and national campaigns, but it makes the newspaper particularly important for local candidates. Newspaper ads rise in importance for local candidates, particularly in rural areas where weekly newspapers have a wide distribution. A single weekly newspaper, for example, will remain in the household for days, receiving multiple readings, before the next edition arrives.

That provides the politician with a chance to reach a single household several times with a single ad.

Furthermore, statewide candidates for down-ballot races (secretary of state, or various statewide commissioners, for example) will often find that their races will receive little newspaper coverage. To get their name and message into the newspaper, they will need to purchase advertising. Some of these candidates focus on multiple uses of small names to reinforce name identification. Others prefer larger ads, used less frequently, which allow them to address more issues at one time. Furthermore, purchasing such a campaign ad will sometimes generate additional coverage by the media. News outlets, including newspapers, frequently cover political ads, making the ads themselves a campaign issue and thereby expanding coverage for the ad (Kaid et al., 1993).

Still, for most campaigns, newspapers are not a high priority. The disadvantage of newspaper ads for major campaigns comes from a major asset of newspapers for other purposes. Reading a newspaper requires active involvement on the part of the reader; as a result, total newspaper readership is considerably less than viewership for the television networks. Newspaper penetration in a local market is usually extensive, reaching 50 percent or more of the local households. Those households tend to skew toward higher income and older adults (thirty-five and older) who have some degree of advanced education. Those demographics also tend to have high levels of interest and information about political issues and more likely to be active participants in the political process. As such, information obtained from advertising may play only a small role in their voting decisions.

The campaign also has little, if any, control over where in the newspaper the ad will appear. This affects the demographic makeup of potential readers. Whereas campaigns can choose to advertise on a television sports program to achieve a high probability they will communicate with men of a certain age, no such guarantee is typically made by newspapers.

Occasionally, a statewide or national candidate will use newspapers, either to target a specific geographic area or to make a dramatic statement. One popular form of newspaper advertising is the insert, which is a free-standing piece of printed matter and is often distributed by candidates through newspaper deliveries. The cost of distributing the piece in this manner is sometimes less expensive than using direct mail, and the piece has the advantage of riding on the coattails of the credibility of the newspaper.

Newspaper ads, though, can sometimes cause problems for candidates (Kantrow, 1999). The 1995 full-page newspaper advertisements run by the Republican National Committee (RNC) created a financial and legal tangle for the Republican Party after they offered, in the ad, to give $1 million to the first person who could prove the GOP spending plan that year would not balance the budget or would not increase federal Medicare spending 50 percent by 2002. The ad appeared in *USA Today* and a Capitol Hill newspaper and pictured RNC Chairman Haley Barbour holding an oversized, signed check for $1 million, next to the words: "Heard the one about Republicans 'cutting' Medicare? The fact is Republicans are increasing Medicare spending by more than half. I'm Haley

Barbour, and I'm so sure of the fact, I'm willing to give you this check for a million dollars if you can prove me wrong." The ad included a contest title ("Million Dollar Medicare Challenge"), an entry coupon, an address to send it to, and a deadline—December 20, 1995. The Republican National Committee later labeled the offer a "parody," but not before dozens of people responded, applying for the money. One congressional aide took the Republican Party to court when the RNC refused to pay him.

Outdoor Advertising

Outdoor advertising by political candidates proliferates during campaign season. The public is besieged by billboards, ads on buses, political signs, and bumper stickers touting support for various candidates. Because of their high visibility, outdoor advertising generates a great deal of discussion among political observers, with many debating the merits of various color tones, placement in high visibility areas, and the damage to the campaign because of vandalism from the opponents. The reality for most campaigns, though, is that outdoor advertising doesn't accomplish much, since such signage does not convey the campaign message.

The primary communication function of outdoor advertising is that of improving name recognition. It works remarkably well as a tool for increasing the recognizability of a candidate. And, for some campaigns, that is enough to ensure a victory—particularly for down-ballot races. Once in the voting booth, those voters who are not tied to partisan choices often vote for those candidates whose name they recognize, often not knowing that candidate's position on issues. However, if an opponent to such a campaign ups the ante by using sufficient broadcast advertising, continued reliance on signage will virtually assure a lost campaign.

In more visible campaigns (congressional, senatorial, gubernatorial, presidential), outdoor advertising has minimal utility. Its communication capability often stops at name recognition or sloganeering (Archibald, 1975, p. 230). DeVries (1975, p. 69) ranked billboards near the bottom of the factors that influence vote decisions, ranking them above only the entertainment-oriented media of movies, stage plays, and music. They are particularly useless in runoff elections; by the time a runoff campaign arrives, both candidates have already achieved a sufficient level of name recognition. Billboards can do little to increase it even more during a runoff.

Furthermore, what little impact outdoor advertising has tends to be brief. Billboards and posters are noticed when they first appear and for a week or two afterward; after that, they tend to blend into the environment as other signs and posters appear. For that reason, long-time Republican consultant Steven Shadegg (1972) recommended that all posters and bumper stickers be held back from distribution until some specific time in the campaign that called for a boost in name recognition. If billboards were already being used (they have to typically be purchased for at least one month at a time), he recommended adding a strip of new color or a slogan to them to reinvigorate their impact.

Despite the relative ineffectiveness of outdoor advertising as a communication tool, it still has some organizational and fund-raising value, particularly as a way to maintain enthusiasm among core supporters and potential contributors. Putting up signs provides volunteers with an important campaign function, triggering more enthusiasm for the candidate. Consultant Sean Reilly (1999, p. 153) calls this the "name in lights" effect: "...we think of people whose names are biggest as the 'stars.'" Bumper stickers provide supporters with a convenient means of expressing their support to others, and thereby increase their commitment to the candidate. The increased visibility resulting from both can be a significant aid to fund-raising. But observers should not be misled into thinking that the preponderance of bumper stickers or yard signs for any one candidate is an indication of overall vote support. Some campaigns conduct surveys of bumper stickers, checking to see which candidate is ahead; that technique is highly unreliable as a predictive technique for projecting winners. Bumper sticker distribution tends to be a measure of organizational strength, not public opinion.

Outdoor advertising can also be used for targeting geographical areas. Sometimes the targeting can be remarkably precise. In 1999, for example, in preparation for the 2000 presidential campaign, the Republican National Committee placed a billboard across the street from Democrat Al Gore's presidential campaign headquarters in Nashville. The first ad depicted President Clinton hugging Gore and also offered a quote from Gore: "One of our greatest presidents." Republican officials said the intent of the billboard was to graphically demonstrate the association between Gore and Clinton, despite the vice president's rhetorical efforts to separate himself from the president (Seelye, 1999).

Furthermore, the high visibility generated by billboards give them the potential for some persuasive impact, particularly early in campaigns. In his 1983 rematch with incumbent Louisiana governor Dave Treen, former governor Edwin Edwards began a billboard campaign a year before the election. Drawing on a public perception that times were not good for the state, Edwards's statewide billboard campaign read, "Hang on, Louisiana, Edwin's coming" (Reilly, 1999). Similarly, in a 2000 mayoral campaign in Selma, Alabama, challenger James Perkins Jr. used a sign touting "Joe's Gotta Go" as the cornerstone of his campaign to defeat thirty-six-year incumbent Joe Smitherman.

Books

The 2000 presidential campaign saw the release of a number of books by and about the candidates who were seeking the presidency, including works by George W. Bush (*A Charge to Keep*), Al Gore (*Earth in the Balance*), John McCain (*Faith of Our Fathers*), Bill Bradley (*Time Present, Time Past*), and Steve Forbes (*A New Birth of Freedom*). But such literary pennings are nothing new in politics. Their tradition goes back to 1824 and the release of *The Life of Andrew Jackson*. Numerous others have followed, most of them intent on conveying the idea that the putative author ought to be president. In 1975, Jimmy Carter's *Why Not the Best?* contributed to Carter's image as an honest and open politician. Similarly,

Barack Obama's presidential campaign in 2008 was marked by the 2006 release of his book, *The Audacity of Hope* (Obama, 2006). His opponent, John McCain, tried to match that with a book of his own, one that followed the same theme of Kennedy's *Profiles in Courage*. McCain's version was titled *Hard Call: Great Decisions and the Extraordinary People Who Made Them* (McCain & Salter, 2008). Such success led historian Douglas Brinkley to say that "books can have a huge impact for candidates" by defining their image prior to the election (quoted by Memmott, 2007, p. 1D).

Nor are such books limited to those that promote a candidate's agenda. Books that attack the opposition also have a long history in politics. The 1964 presidential campaign saw two books attacking Lyndon Johnson, *A Texan Looks at Lyndon* and *None Dare Call It Treason*. More recently, Republican Peggy Noonan (2000) took a critical look at Hillary Rodham Clinton's candidacy for a New York senate seat in *The Case against Hillary Clinton,* which was only one of more than thirty books attacking the former First Lady (Arnold, April 27, 2000). One (Sheehy, 1999) even argued that she was addicted to her husband, former president Bill Clinton. Clinton himself has similarly been the target of several attack books. Democrats are not the only targets for such missives, though. Molly Ivins and Lou Dubose (2000) aimed their literary guns at George W. Bush (*Shrub: The Short but Happy Political Life of George W. Bush*) during the 2000 presidential campaign. Books have also been used in statewide elections, although not always successfully. Sandra Baxley Taylor's biography of former Alabama governor Fob James (*Fob*) was released in 1990 to coincide with James's comeback attempt in Alabama politics. Although he lost that campaign, he ran again in 1994 (this time without the book) and won. Similarly, Mississippi businessman Mike Sturdivant ran for governor in 1983, despite a lack of experience in any other elective office. Part of his campaign effort was a book (*Mississippi on the Move*) that articulated his major campaign positions.

The Ongoing Process

The media consultant must pay constant attention to details surrounding the campaign environment. As the buy is made, information is gathered about the opponent's media plan. Television stations are required to maintain a public file about the details of all political advertising, and make it available for public inspection during normal business hours. By analyzing the opponent's advertising buy for targets, duration, and weight (the amount of advertising in a week), the media consultant can draw conclusions about the objectives of their advertising strategy. Such information adds to the general understanding of the campaign and the campaign environment.

During this whole process, it is the buyer's responsibility to send funds, traffic instructions, and duplicates of the spots to the television stations. In recent years, consultants have attempted to apply new technologies to the process. The use of satellites to transmit the spots directly to the stations has been utilized since the early- to mid-1980s. In the mid-1990s, computer compression technology made it possible to transmit spots through a modem.

More changes are likely to come. During the 1998 campaigns, some spots were delivered to stations by way of the Internet. Such capabilities mean that technology is shortening the time frame that separates conceptualization of the spot and the time of its first broadcast on television or radio.

SUMMARY

The media consultants play a major role in political campaigns. While some argue that the impact of their media spots is minimal (sometimes only 3 percent), such small percentages often make the difference between winning and losing an election. Philosophically, media consultants fall into one of two schools: informational consultants (those who concentrate on communicating issue-based messages) and emotional consultants (those who seek to touch a responsive emotional chord among the voters). These two approaches are sometimes integrated into a single media message, a concept known as dovetailing.

The primary tasks of a media consultant include development of the message, scriptwriting, cinematography and videography, editing, and spot buying. The secondary tasks include acting as a clearinghouse for campaign information involving polling, news media feedback, effectiveness assessment, and coordination of all communications to support campaign advertising.

Television and radio represent the biggest advertising expenditure of many campaigns. Other mass media that have also been used include newspaper ads, outdoor advertising, and books. Newspaper ads are rarely used in presidential campaigns, but often play a major role in local elections. Outdoor advertising can be a quick means of increasing name recognition for a candidate. Books are rarely used to communicate directly with voters, but can be used to enhance a candidate's credibility with the press and political elites. Regardless, the television-and-radio campaign must coordinate messages with the other forms of mass media used by the campaign. Logos and slogans used in television ads must be consistent with those used on billboards or in newspaper ads. Message themes articulated in the ads must be consistent with previous articulations by the candidate, including ideas expressed in books or other print media. Coordinating such communication activities becomes the single biggest task of the campaign.

Media consultants are first and foremost businesses (Johnson, 2000). The profession derives its roots from advertising agencies, which have traditionally derived their income from commissions paid by various advertising media. To offer an incentive to professional advertising agencies, advertising outlets have paid 15 percent of their total advertising expenditure to the agency. That is true of newspapers, television stations, and radio stations. In the past decade, savvy political campaigns have taken advantage of the increasingly competitive business of media consulting to negotiate lower commission rates. As Franzen (1999, pp. 300–301) noted, "...that fifteen percent differential isn't written in stone, and high dollar campaigns can persuade the consultant to reduce his commission." These competitive rates often range between 8 percent and 11 percent, with the campaign keeping what is left over to use for other expenditures (often, more television time). The actual cost of executing a buy is generally conceded to be between 3 percent and

4 percent of the total buy. Such costs include buy design and the administrative cost, office overhead, and personnel costs related to the function.

Media consultants also charge an up-front fee. Such fees can be as much as $60,000–$100,000 for a major statewide or congressional campaign. Local campaigns typically have a smaller fee structure. The rationale for the fees is that not all campaigns that begin the election process come to fruition, or to the point where actual advertising is purchased. Media consultants have ongoing expenses that include personnel, office space, travel expenses, and general office overhead. This overhead requires sufficient revenues to maintain operation. Up-front fees help cover that overhead.

QUESTIONS FOR DISCUSSION

1. What is the objective of TV advertising? What if a campaign found a less expensive way to inform voters about its candidate?

2. What is the most important element in TV advertising: content, production values (how it looks and sounds), cost of the time to buy the spots, the number of spots over a given period of time, or all of it equally?

3. If a political campaign has a budget of $1,000,000, how much is the fee of the media consultant likely to be?

4. Your opponent has put up a TV commercial accusing your candidate of being for sale to the highest bidder in the political fund-raising wars. The irony is that the opponent holds every known record for fund-raising. What should your campaign do:

   a. Make a TV ad attacking your opponent as being a hypocrite;
   b. Make a TV ad that says your opponent is making false claims about you as a smoke-screen for his poor record on the issues that matter to people;
   c. Attack your opponent for having a poor record on the issues that matter to people using a series of news conferences;
   d. Ignore your opponent's attacks?

5. In your state, the television stations in the largest media market have decided they will not sell advertising time to candidates below lieutenant governor. Normally, your candidate would spend 40 percent of his media budget in this one market. Would you use your budget to place ads in newspapers and on billboards? If yes, how would you allocate those funds? What would be the characteristics of the newspaper ads and the billboard ads?

6. Halfway through the campaign, the television stations relented. How much of your remaining media budget would you reallocate to television? Why?

Campaign Communications: Direct Voter Contact

In 1978, even as the "Reagan Revolution" was gathering to bring conservatives to power in the 1980s, an assault on organized labor was under way in Missouri. Right-to-work advocates had put an initiative on the ballot to outlaw "closed shop" contracts in the state. Polling made it clear that labor was decisively losing the battle by as much as two to one. The polls also indicated that, in a toe-to-toe, traditional mass-media campaign confrontation, the United Labor Committees of Missouri stood to lose by an even greater margin. The more voters heard of the traditional arguments by each side, the more they broke in favor of the antilabor view.

With only ninety days left before the election, labor hired Matt Reese, a pioneer of direct voter contact methods (direct mail and telephone banks), to guide the campaign. After reviewing the polling data, Reese concluded that the only chance of winning was to run a low-profile campaign while lulling the opposition into a sense of overconfidence. Reese immediately took steps to turn down the public rhetoric and the public campaign efforts by the labor campaign. He replaced that effort with a carefully targeted effort to register new voters in traditional labor families and to target prolabor households with direct voter contact messages using direct mail. Reese permitted television advertising only in the final week of the campaign, using relatively bland spots that were viewed as not particularly effective by the antilabor side. During the last week of the campaign, most observers assumed that the right-to-work referendum was unbeatable.

They were wrong. Reese's plan worked to perfection, with the prolabor side winning by a two-to-one margin. The campaign remains an example of winning by preaching to the choir: focusing on organizational targeting rather than trying to persuade undecided voters. That model is still used in many modern campaigns. While the bulk of most campaign budgets is devoted to electronic media (principally television), most campaigns also at least supplement that with other communication channels. Furthermore, some political campaigns involve situations in which electronic communication is either too expensive or impractical. Campaigns for city council districts, for example, often cover geographical areas that are too small to make a television campaign practical. Similarly, some congressional districts located in major urban areas may not use television campaigns at all. The problem is that purchasing the advertising time on television requires purchasing the entire market covered by the station, while the voting district itself covers only a small portion of that area. In those instances, the campaign will use other communication channels to reach the voters.

These direct voter contact channels tend to fall into three categories: phone banks, direct mail, and the Internet.

PHONE BANKS (POLITICAL TELEMARKETING)

Unlike broadcasting, which reaches large numbers of unregistered voters, telephone banks give political campaigns the ability to target voters who will be participating in the election. Moreover, telephone bank targeting can be further refined through the use of computer-enhanced lists that may include such information as party registration, age, income, education, race, and voter history. Consequently, it is possible to effectively and quietly communicate a carefully crafted message that is aimed at a specific target group of voters. The callers may be a single person or several hundred people. They may be volunteers using borrowed phones or the campaign headquarters phones after hours, or professional phone banks of hired callers working under the supervision of experienced political telemarketers. In their most effective form, the phone bank is centered in one location under unified supervision with a specific goal.

Technology from a burgeoning telecommunications industry has created an extremely dynamic environment for political telephone banks. Computer dialing can detect the presence of a live voter, and connect a telephone worker to the line. If an answering machine is detected, a prerecorded message can be left. Predictive phone banks can completely automate the process to the point of using several different scripts at the same time, vastly increasing the productivity and economic viability of very large phone banks.

The Functions of Phone Banks

Armed with a list of voters and their telephone numbers, a telephone bank can make calls to target voters, to persuade voters, to "get out the vote" (GOTV), to influence early and absentee voters, or to influence legislation.

Targeting   Targeting is typically achieved through a process known as "Voter ID." The phone bank calls voters within the district, asking a series of questions about their voter registration, likelihood of voting, and candidate preference. To the uninitiated, the question format sounds similar to that of a short poll or survey, and many respondents mistake it for such. However, there is no sampling process involved. Instead, the purpose of the calls is to reach as many people within a designated area as possible. Furthermore, the information is used differently from that of a poll or survey. Based on their responses to the questions, voters are categorized into one of three categories: supporters, undecideds, and opposition. In most campaigns, the data on the opposition are discarded or ignored. But voters who are identified as supporters and undecideds become targets for later communication, either from other phone calls or mail.

Persuasion A persuasive phone bank can have three potential goals: to maintain loyalty among those voters who support your candidate, to persuade undecided voters to vote for your candidate, and to dislodge voters who plan to vote for the opponent. Maintaining current support typically uses a reinforcement message; this may involve thanking the voter for the support, acknowledging the importance of that support, and providing that voter with information that might be useful to them in political discussions. Persuading undecided voters requires a strong positive message (one typically developed on the basis of polling data) that provides the voter with a reason for supporting the candidate. Dislodging supporters of the opposition typically uses a negative phone message, one that provides the voters with a reason to vote against the other candidate. Negative phone banks are extremely difficult to counter; because of their lack of visibility, the opposition is often slow to realize their existence and is thus slow to respond to them.

Voter Turnout (GOTV) Telephone banks are highly effective at persuading supporters to turn out to vote. Usually, a concise compilation of attack and positive information is developed to remind the voter why they support the candidate, and then to remind them of where and when to vote. Often the message is tailored to specific demographic or attitudinal descriptions of the targeted voters (Burgess et al., 2000). In effect, GOTV campaigns target the marginal voter. If no special effort is undertaken, these voters typically will stay at home, and their turnout can be critical in close campaigns and campaigns against incumbents.

Early Voting Early voting refers to those votes that are cast before the actual election date. Historically, most early voting has occurred through the use of absentee ballots, but that changed in the late 1980s when some states liberalized their early voting provisions to encourage more early, in-person voting. Typical of these were the changes in the Texas election regulations that provided for early in-person voting by any registered voter during a two-week period before an election. The first major test of the early voting process came in a 1989 special election in Texas's twelfth Congressional District, and phone banks were used extensively by the Democratic candidate Pete Geren to maximize support among early voters in the runoff campaign (Tyson, 1990).

Based on demographic data and voting trends, the Geren campaign selected 9,000 voters over the age of sixty-five for targeted phone bank calls. If they were identified as Geren supporters, they were reminded of the runoff and urged to take advantage of the early voting times and the location of the early voting boxes. The phone bank also identified voters who needed rides to early voting locations and provided those rides. That service, in effect, served as a means of setting up appointments to vote.

Geren won the election by only 1,620 votes, and the early voting totals made the difference. He won those by 3,022 votes. Similar programs have since been conducted in other states with early voting provisions, for a number of reasons. First, in highly competitive campaigns, a small numbers of voters can make the difference between winning and losing. Second, by using the phone banks, candidates can "put their support in the bank" as soon as it has been identified. Once a voter has been identified as a supporter, he or she is encouraged to vote as quickly as possible. And third, early voting programs have the potential to neutralize negative campaigns; most negative attacks occur during the last few days of the campaign, too late to have an impact on early voters.

Legislative Lobbying   Although political phone banks have been traditionally viewed as a campaign tool, advancements in telephone and computer technology have increased the effectiveness of phone banks as a force in the legislative arena. If a party or interest group is concerned over a specific legislative issue, phone banks can encourage voter support for that position. A typical format involves a telephone call to a targeted voter, asking for his or her position on the issue. If the respondent agrees with the position held by the phone bank's client, the voter is told, "Did you know that the legislature is considering a bill to..." and is asked to contact his or her representative to express that opinion. If the voter agrees to do so, the phone bank can then immediately connect the respondent to the office of the targeted representative, at no cost to the voter. By continuously repeating this process, the representative can receive a barrage of phone calls in support of or in opposition to the legislation.

This is another way in which telephone banks "fly under the radar screen," in the words of one phone bank consultant. In fact, academicians often overlook this feature themselves. For example, in an analysis of 5,000 constituent letters sent to Congress during the Iran-Contra debate, Thelan (1996) found there was a distinct difference between the tone of the letters and the public opinion polls on the issues at the time, particularly in terms of the writer's attitude toward Colonel Oliver North. Thelan concluded that those communications represented the authentic voice of an American public that was outraged by the media's misrepresentation of their attitudes. What Thelan apparently overlooked was the extent to which many of those letters were the by-product of a coordinated lobbying effort, using phone banks and other media to stimulate letters to Congress.

Robo-Calls   One of the developments in telephone-bank operations during the first decade of the twenty-first century was the tremendous increase in the use of robo-calls. Officially referred to as integrated voice recordings, the technique quickly developed the nickname of "robo-calls," and the moniker stuck. Robo-calls can be used for a variety of purposes—for persuasion, reinforcement, GOTV, or other reasons. The public often views them as annoying, but campaigns like them because (a) they allow the campaign to be associated with a high-profile public official, and (b) the cost is minimal, since little labor is involved. The absence of live callers means the major cost of phone contacts is reduced, and computers can quickly reach a large number of telephones within any voting district.

The process is relatively simple, with a typical project running something like this:

1. A candidate convinces a high-profile person to endorse his campaign.
2. The person records a 30–60-second message using a script developed by the campaign but approved by the person doing the endorsement.

3. The recording is sent via the Internet to the phone house, which uses its audio system to clean background noise from the recording.
4. The digital version of the recording is uploaded to a computer.
5. A list of phone numbers is uploaded to the computer.
6. The recording is keyed to call those numbers within specified hours.

Thus, the process is relatively simple and inexpensive. A typical computer can make more than 600 calls simultaneously (Cauchon, 2008b) and that will increase as technology improves. The only complicated part is cleaning the tape of background noise. The individuals who make these recordings are often busy, with little time to devote to studio quality recording. Many are made in automobiles, with background noise including outside traffic and conversations from within the vehicle. The authors know of at least one instance where a phone bank had to filter out the sound of a toilet flushing during the recording.

Endorsements can have a positive, muted impact on a campaign (Powell, 2007). When done sparingly, robo-calls can be highly effective in linking a well-known person to a candidate. They seem to be most effective when left on answering machines, rather than when an individual picks up the phone.

Unfortunately, robo-calls are so easy and inexpensive that their use has proliferated to the point of annoyance. More than 5 million such calls were made during the 2008 primaries alone, with the total number for the campaign estimated in the hundreds of millions; voters in key states sometimes received as many as twenty-five calls in a day (Cauchon, 2008a). As early as 2007, there were efforts to legally limit their use (Saulny, 2007), and that call was repeated with the high volume of calls in 2008 (Cauchon, 2008a).

Calls for bans increased when robo-calls started being used as part of negative campaigns (Cauchon, 2008b). Again the low cost makes it attractive to use for such purposes. Further, they have the added advantage of anonymity. The recording can be made to sound like a legitimate poll (with negative information in it), or even as if it is coming from the campaign of the person being attacked. At the very least, robo-calls can be difficult to police and regulate, providing an additional incentive to use them for negative purposes.

The Telephone Bank Process

The first step in planning and executing a telephone bank effort is to define the groups with whom it is possible to effectively communicate. This is typically done on the basis of polling data that suggest groups that are persuadable and the issues that move them toward your campaign. The campaign then seeks to acquire relevant voter lists by group. For example, the campaign would design a list by demographic and/or behavioral type, for example, a list of voters, twenty-five to thirty-four years old, female, high school educated, all races, who have voted in four of the last five general elections.

The concurrent second step is message development. Perhaps the universe is uncharacteristically supportive of an opponent because its members do not know of his or her positions, and the data also indicate there would be a shift within the voter group if they learned of your candidate's position. For example: "Hello,

Ms. (____)? I'm calling for Charlie Whatnot's campaign for Congress. He wanted me to tell you how hard he has worked for all of us, particularly to keep the right-wingers from outlawing a woman's right to choose. You know Charlie trusts you to make that decision, unlike his opponent, Congressman Squishy, who wants to make that decision for you. Charlie really needs your help in the November election to protect your rights. Can I tell him you will support him in November?" ____YES ____NO ____Undecided.

The third step is to brief the callers concerning the task at hand. Emphasis is placed on delivering the message as designed and written. Many practitioners will instantly remove any caller who will not respect the integrity of the message.

The fourth step is to assess the effectiveness of the message. This is done by reviewing the results of the calling and comparing them in a general way to the poll. With respect to the prochoice message and the "calling universe," perhaps the polling data indicated that the campaign should be getting 80 percent "yeses." If the bank is only getting 50 percent yeses, the message is likely ineffective. It is then adjusted and reassessed.

Concurrent with message adjustment is the process of compiling the results. Those who answer "Yes" are added to a database of those who will be called or otherwise contacted in the waning days of the campaign to remind them to vote. Those who answer "No" are discarded; if they are unresponsive to this message they will not support your candidate. Those who answer "Undecided" are added to a later contact list to be called after the main list is completed. These will be mailed a solicitation, perhaps signed by the candidate asking them to be considered. This is a classic telephone bank. It may be augmented by recruiting "YESes" as headquarters volunteers, as financial contributors, as precinct workers, or as workers in a programmatic effort to further aid the campaign.

Other Types of Telephone Banks

Telephone banks can be used to assist in the management of large numbers of influentials. Perhaps the campaign has recruited a large finance committee. In an effort to maintain communications with them, the campaign arranges for three or four callers to call them with an inspirational message and to remind them of specific deadlines. In this way, the campaign can closely coordinate with its key organizations.

Specialty calling can be undertaken. It is possible, using new technology, to leave messages with and only with targets who have telephone answering machines. This was developed to deal with the problem of the increasing use of voice mail type–answering devices in general use. It is possible using the technology to use a recording of the candidate's voice as the message, "Sorry I missed you, because I really need your support next Tuesday. If you get a chance give a call…."

A "blind" telephone bank, or "push poll," is a telephone bank that, more or less, obscures the sponsor of the call while providing, more or less, a very negative message about the opponent. As mentioned in the chapter on polling, its goal is persuasion, not information. Although presented in a format similar to a public opinion survey, its intent is to impart information, not gather it.

The Weaknesses of Telephone Banks

Telephone banks take considerable time to make phone calls. A persuasive bank might take two or three weeks to make its initial call-around. When the opponent gets wind of the message, he or she can plow under the message of the phone bank in a matter of days with an electronic advertisement. Using telephone banks exclusively, therefore, is a risky undertaking. Using them in conjunction with electronic advertising, analogous to "air cover," reduces the risk. Electronic advertising is often aimed at main persuadable publics. For an opponent to attack your candidate's telephone banks to get you to abandon an effort to attract persuadables is risky. At worst such attacks on obscure targets can result in a catastrophic outcome by leaving the great field uncovered.

Telephone banks are susceptible to special problems. The caller's accent and dialect can immediately sour a voter. For example, a caller with a Brooklyn accent is unlikely to be able to persuade a voter in Tennessee. It is considered generally ineffective to have whites call African Americans or to have African Americans call white voters. This fact has led some telephone bank operators to design blind telephone banks where African American callers call upscale voters with a false message from the opponent. The resulting anger and/or confusion may satisfy a given campaign dynamic.

SOMETHING NEW UNDER THE SUN

In recent elections fewer and fewer targeted voters are responding to standard telephone banks. The phone rings at an inconvenient time, the caller is obviously reading some standard message, and these are often the most that can be expected because many people have elected to have unlisted telephone numbers. Large numbers of people are using cell phones as their only telephone service. Consequently, the cost to persuade voters has increased exponentially. More money is being spent on fewer voters.

Smart professionals spent a decade trying to find an answer to these problems. Many settled on using social media to supplement their telephone calls, which in many ways deals solely with the problem of availability of targeted voters and voters available to "get out the vote" calls.

The problem facing professionals was how to think "out of the box," increase profitability, and improve the response of persuadable voters. The development of VOIP (Voice over Internet Protocol), which places powerful computer servers between the caller and the person being called, is the latest technological advancement. This requires telephone knowledge such that the server can take in the voter lists, manipulate them, accept entry calls by the caller, dial the voter, provide the connected call to the caller, and monitor the results provided by the caller. Lists of likely persuaded and likely voters are compiled by the computer for later recalls. Others are compiled by issues for recalling when the issue heats up.

Using VOIP means that the capable server can utilize predictive calling techniques and can direct the call to nearly every kind of telephone connection. And by not having to actually dial, keep records, or even wait for the remote phone to ring, vast amounts of time can be saved. Further savings are realized by utilizing volunteers, their phones, or other supporter telephones. Added savings are realized by using VOIP and not incurring toll costs. The costs of this concept of telephone bank are most likely to be less than $.10 per call.

Using volunteers for this kind of campaign calling is in many respects a return to the future. The advantage of using volunteers is simple. They are self-motivated. In short, they are working for the candidate or the issue because they want to. They are true believers. They care about what they are doing. Professionals in this kind of phone bank are estimating that such calls are executed five times faster.

For campaigns to use this kind of system, they will need a knowledgeable volunteer coordinator capable of recruiting the volunteers, finding supporters' telephones, and organizing the timing of the calls.

To date, most professionals with an investment in call centers and paid supervisors believe such systems are best utilized for GOTV efforts. This may be underselling the virtual predictive capabilities of such systems. Generally, such systems are just power dialers.

DIRECT MAIL

Long-time political consultant Matt Reese (1975) once said, "You have four ways to contact the voter,... and the intelligent campaigner uses all four of them in proper ratio" (p. 162). Reese's fourth option, direct mail (the others were media, personal visits, and telephones), is an often overlooked and maligned form of mass communication with voters, yet is an important communication tool. Together with phone banks, direct mail makes up the discipline of direct voter contact. Direct mail often supplements phone banks and electronic advertising, but many campaigns will also use it as a stand-alone means of communicating with highly targeted audiences. Either way, it can be an effective campaign tool.

In high population locales where television time is very expensive, programmatic direct-mail campaigns may replace television advertising because it is more cost efficient. In such cases where television advertising is very expensive and the relative number of voters is small (for example, the Los Angles media market and a race for city council), direct mail is the preferred means of communicating with voters because of the massive expense of the alternative. In other instances, direct mail is used to communicate with key, marginal voter groups with a persuasive piece delivered in the regular mail. Campaigns that use direct mail usually use many mailings to accomplish the goal of capturing a vote, thereby approximating the advertising effect of television.

When multiple mailings are employed, some campaigns will use direct mail for the distribution of attack messages and/or responses to attacks. As a response, or refutation, mechanism, direct mail is generally ineffective; but it works well as an inoculation tool to combat future attacks from the opposition (Pfau et al., 1990). Direct mail has also been used in voter turnout programs, with some success. Schmidt and Schmidt (1983) analyzed direct mail by four Republican candidates in the 1982 elections, noting that the most successful letters were those that used only two compliance-gaining techniques. They attributed the success to the brevity of the two-message format: the short letters were easier to understand and more straightforward.

> ### ◣ CASE STUDY: ELECTION DAY IN FLORIDA, 2000
>
> November 7, 2000. Voters went to the polls for one of the closest presidential elections in American history. At the end of the day, neither Republican George W. Bush nor Democrat Al Gore could definitely be declared the winner. The outcome depended on the results in Florida, where Bush had an early lead in raw votes while the Gore campaign was poised to protest the voting process in at least one Florida county—Palm Beach.
>
> Sometimes overlooked in the hoopla that followed was that of the role of phone banks in the process. In an unusual move, the Democratic party hired a phone bank on election night to call thousands of voters in Palm Beach to raise questions about the disputed ballot and to urge them to contact local election officials. The Democratic National Committee paid TeleQuest, a Texas-based firm, to make the calls and describe the problem to voters in the area. "If you have already voted and think you may have punched the wrong hole for the incorrect candidate, you should return to the polls and request that the election officials write down your name so that this problem can be fixed," the calls said.
>
> The confusion resulted from the design of the ballot in Palm Beach. The Gore-Lieberman ticket, listed second on the ballot, was assigned to the fifth punch slot on the ballot. The second slot was assigned to Reform party candidate Pat Buchanan, and news reports indicated that some Gore voters were mistakenly voting for Buchanan.
>
> The party had been making routine Get Out the Vote calls all day, but they shifted to a crisis management call on short notice. Those calls started shortly before 6 P.M., EST, giving TeleQuest only one hour to make the calls before the polls in Florida closed. During that hour, they made 5,000 calls, contacting 100 voters who had not yet voted and identifying 2,400 who said they felt they had made a mistake on the ballot. ■
>
> *Source:* Solomon, J. (2000, November 11). "Florida, we've got a problem." *Birmingham News,* pp. 1A, 6A.

The sophistication of the use of direct mail tends to vary dramatically. Ringer (1986) analyzed the differences between the language of direct mail used by national and local political campaigns, finding three key differences: national letters were more emotional and personal in style, while local letters were shorter, more general, and maintained a more professional style; letters from national campaigns were easier to read than local campaign letters; and national letters contained multiple persuasive devices—compliance appeals, explanations, and warnings—while local letters concentrated only on explanations. Ringer attributed the differences to writing style—the national letters appear to have been written by professional consultants, while most of the local letters appear to have been written by volunteers with little experience in direct mail. That was probably an accurate assessment, but his conclusions might be different today. The 1990s saw an increasing number of local campaigns that employed direct-mail consultants, and that trend is likely to continue.

Direct mail is costly, with the campaign incurring costs at four different levels: list development, design, assembly, and postage. Voter lists must be obtained in a format that can be used to address the mail. In its simplest form, this is a collection of address labels, but it can also include computer disks or tapes that can be used to address envelopes, letters, personalized messages, and so forth. Such lists can be vetted to produce the desired subgroup. For example, a campaign can request a list of elderly voters from their list providers. They may want, however, elderly voters, older than sixty-five who live in a particular geographic area, and who also have college education. Each subgroup, while reducing the total number of a given mailing, will increase the unit cost of its list. The reason is simple: more computer work is needed and is therefore more expensive. And, as always, to achieve a subgroup sort, the entire master list must be run through the computer. Some political consultants are dealing with this problem by maintaining their own lists through cooperative arrangements with computer service bureaus; or by having their clients maintain such lists. Advances in small computer technology in recent years have made it possible to handle and manipulate very large lists, particularly when located on CD-ROM. Such systems, however, require well-trained operators and managers to assure effectiveness, which affects costs upward.

The second step is to design the mailing piece. For some campaigns, this can be as easy as printing a letter on campaign stationery. Nearly every political consultant advises candidates to use heavily produced, graphically communicative designs that will catch the attention of the voter, punching through the junk mail with which it arrives to the voter. The design incorporates the campaign logo and message. The targeted message is developed on the basis of survey research like any other large investment of the campaign. Cutbirth and Rasmussen (1982) examined more than seventy examples of direct mail used for fund-raising during this period. They identified four major content norms, which typified most such letters. Typically, they first begin with a startling or dramatic opening statement that is intended to motivate people to read the letter. Second, there is an early introduction of an enemy, either a specific individual (the opponent) or an abstract group. Third, there is an attempt to assure the reader of the credibility of the organization sponsoring the letter, typically by casting the sponsoring organization as a defender of some traditional value and thus ensuring that their support will be put to effective use. Finally, there is a closing appeal for financial assistance.

The third step is assembly. Larger campaigns use "mail shops." A mail shop is literally an assembly line that puts the mailing together. Their task includes printing the mailer, affixing labels, and bundling the finished products by zip code and carrier route (to facilitate mail delivery and comply with postal regulations).

In most cases, the fourth step—postage—is provided through bulk mail permits arranged by the campaign directly with the U.S. Postal Service, a process that reduces the mailing costs. Sometimes, though, campaigns prefer to use full postage (often with commemorative stamps), based on the assumption that voters are more likely to open a stamped envelope than one bearing a permit. Because of the added expense, stamped mail pieces are more likely to be used for fund-raising letters; permit-imprinted pieces are heavily used in the final days of a campaign, using headlines and designs that are eye-appealing. Most readers simply scan printed material. Loken (1983) found that only 14 percent of the target group had read a community campaign mailing, and only 20 percent remembered receiving it. To be effective, the mail piece must have a memorable headline that quickly and clearly conveys the campaign's message. That gives the piece a potential impact, even if discarded by the voter, who must at least glance at the headline to decide whether to read it or not.

Direct mail can be used to supplement and complement television advertising. While using the look and feel of the campaign's electronic advertising to capitalize on its weight, such mailings may hone the campaign message for subgroups that might otherwise disturb the larger audience. In other cases, when attacking the opponent, for example, pains may be taken to give the mail a completely different look so as to reduce possible negative blowback on the campaign's larger financial investment, television advertising.

DeVries (1975) estimated that direct mail has a potential impact of 3.3 percentage points among ticket splitters, a rating that puts them above billboards (2.1) but below television ads (6.8). Still, the impact of direct mail can vary widely, and its effect can sometimes exceed that of the broadcast media. The 1970 Michigan gubernatorial campaign of William Milliken monitored its advertising effectiveness using experimental test precincts throughout the campaign. Their research indicated that direct mail was totally ineffective in the early stages of that campaign; later, however, during the same campaign, the mail resulted in a 9-point swing for Milliken among undecided voters, while television was relatively ineffective (DeVries, 1975, pp. 78–81).

DeVries's data came from the early 1970s, a time when many consultants were starting to appreciate the value of direct mail as a communication tool. At about the same time, consultant Richard Viguerie (1975) called direct mail "campaigning's sleeping giant" and parlayed his expertise with the medium into a fund-raising and communication mechanism that could be used to target and activate voters with strong conservative leanings. The primary use of direct mail was to simultaneously raise funds for a media campaign while also developing a list of conservative voters who could be targeted for other campaigns. The success of direct-mail campaigns became obvious to most political observers during the early 1980s when it was used as a potent weapon by groups associated with the religious right, often in conjunction with broadcast media (Kitchens & Powell, 1986).

SUMMARY

While television and radio ads are the most visible communication efforts of many campaigns, they are far from being the only communication channels used by modern campaigns. Many campaigns, particularly those at the local level, may be conducted entirely through alternative media.

When campaigns move away from using the broadcast media, the media they most frequently prefer are telephone banks and direct mail. Both phones and mail allow for more precision in targeting than is available from television ads, and both approaches can communicate a candidate's message without generating high profile messages. As a result, many campaigns devote a major amount of their financial resources to both means of communication.

The growth of the Internet has provided an increased opportunity to use online media to both communicate with voters and to organize supporters. Currently, the Internet's potential has exceeded its actual use in campaigns, but that is likely to change quickly. Future elections will likely see an expansion in Internet campaigning.

QUESTIONS FOR DISCUSSION

1. The incumbent mayor, an African American, is being challenged in a primary by a former African American mayor and a white city councilman. The voters in the city are about 53 percent African American and 42 percent white, with the rest Hispanic and a few of Asian descent. Design a telephone bank program for the incumbent that maximizes his support among all groups. How would you create a telephone bank program for the white candidate that maximizes his support among African American voters? Create one for the African American candidate that maximizes his support among African American religious and community leaders. In each case, assume that the incumbent is a former get-tough police chief; the former mayor is widely considered to have been corrupt even though he was never charged with a crime; the white candidate is a young politician who is considered to be a reformer.

2. A candidate for governor discovers that her opponent has an accused child abuser as a member of his education issues steering committee. Design two approaches that bring this fact to the attention of the parents of school-age children.

3. Your candidate has spoken out on the issues using television commercials. Using the Internet, what can be done to extend the effect of the message? What role would e-mail play?

4. Your job as the campaign's field director is to harness grassroots support. During a presidential primary in the South, your opponent has launched a vicious attack ad on television in a midwestern state. Your job is to use the campaign's e-mail list to generate an effective grassroots reaction and drive the ad from the airwaves. Describe your resulting program in detail.

5. Can the Internet facilitate a substantive exchange on issues? How? What is the likelihood that the campaign that has more sophisticated features such as streaming video and audio will more favorably impress voters on the basis of its visual features instead of the merit the argument?

6. Name five ways to acquaint voters with the name of your Web site. Why is this necessary?

Political Speeches

On December 5, 1955, Martin Luther King, Jr. stood before 4,000 people in Montgomery, Alabama. The civil rights movement was at a critical juncture. Rosa Parks had been arrested four days earlier for refusing to give up her seat on a Montgomery bus, and the crowd that had gathered was primed to do something to express their disapproval. King inspired the audience by comparing the Montgomery situation to the biblical exodus of the Israelites from Egypt (Selby, 2001), proclaiming, "Now we are reaching out for the daybreak of freedom and justice and equality." The speech was the mobilization call for the Montgomery bus boycott, the first of numerous civil rights protests led by King and other African American leaders. Selby (2001) argues that the speech was a critical element of that protest, with King's inspired oratory mobilizing the protesters and instilling in them a conviction that they would succeed. Years later, that conviction was rewarded at the political level with the passage of the Civil Rights Act of 1964.

Not all political speeches have such a dramatic impact. Some observers, in fact, approach the topic of political oratory with an obvious touch of cynicism. Writer George Orwell (1949, p. 363) once described political speeches as "...the defense of the indefensible." Corcoran (1979, p. xv) complained that political speeches are often used "not to convey information, but to conceal or distort it..., (bearing) no relationship to the organization, coherency and clarification of information and ideas."

Such comments aside, though, political speeches are an integral part of the campaign process. As Martin Luther King, Jr. and others have demonstrated numerous times, political speeches can play a vital role in inspiring and uniting people around a common cause. Furthermore, as Trent and Friedenberg (2000) noted, "Speechmaking is fundamental to political campaigning. The politician cannot reasonably expect to campaign without continually facing audiences" (p. 182). Speeches are used for a variety of reasons that extend beyond pure transmission of information. They also serve important roles in political leadership and governance (Campbell & Jamieson, 1990; Hart, 1987). Their use comes closer to what Graber (1976) describes as "political linguistics," a means of creating, sustaining, and communicating political reality and of directing or constraining action toward that reality.

Words matter. The meanings of words can make a difference in people's lives. Spoken communication can spell the difference between a venture's success and failure. Colleges and universities often encourage (and sometimes require) that their students take at least one course in public speaking. Corporations spend thousands of dollars to train their executives and junior executives to obtain those skills. In the face of such widespread training, political speeches become an easy target for criticism. Jamieson (1988) complained that speechwriters interfere with the open debate of political issues: "When a politician enters a forum clutching a text," she wrote, "public discussion is likely to be replaced by declamation" (p. 216). Indeed, political speeches are usually inherently biased, with candidates using the public forum to promote their agenda or their version of events. Others associate a lack of integrity with political speeches, particularly those written by a professional speechwriter. Sometimes even the candidates feel guilty; as Jamieson noted they "are reluctant to confess that the words they speak are not their own" (p. 210). Regardless, in a modern political world, speeches and speechwriters are a necessity for major candidates.

The nature of the media is partly responsible. The modern press corps requires that advance copies of speeches be available, and the text of televised speeches have to be put into the TelePrompTer in advance of the actual delivery. Both features require a written text (Jamieson, 1988, p. 211). Furthermore, particularly for presidential speeches, carefully prepared speeches, with each word carefully chosen, are necessary to ensure that the speech is not misinterpreted (Bormann, 1960; Campbell & Jamieson, 1990, p. 10). As Noonan (1998) noted, "...a president really can't be winging it a lot because everything he says...has implications, sometimes serious ones" (p. 124).

The sheer number of speeches that an elected official must deliver prohibits them from writing each one. Presidents may give numerous speeches every day (Jamieson, 1988, pp. 212–213), creating a need for more than half a million words every year (Bonafede, 1972). Elected officials simply don't have enough time to do all that writing themselves. They must have a speechwriter to help articulate those ideas. The speechwriter's function is not to change the speaker's platform but merely to communicate those ideas to others. How they do that will vary with the writer and the candidate. Jamieson (1988) noted that the major job for George McGovern's speechwriters was to "replace his long, complex sentences with shorter ones" (p. 212). For some, it may be a relatively simple task of organizing the candidate's ideas around a major theme. For others, the candidate must focus instead on developing rhetorical techniques that can communicate the candidate's ideas to the voters.

THE NATURE OF POLITICAL SPEECHES

Part of the criticisms come from the inherent differences between political speeches and other forms of public speaking. This book assumes that those differences include the following features.

■ *Political speeches are more complex than most other forms of public speaking.* Issues such as abortion, civil rights, economic theory, and international relations have generated years of debate and argument, far too much for any such issue to be addressed in a single speech. Although a thirty-minute speech offers more time to discuss an issue than does a thirty-second commercial, it is still rarely enough time to go into the details of a complex topic. Typically, the political speechwriter doesn't even try; instead, they are content with defining and examining an issue or situation in limited terms (typically those that are most beneficial to them). Political speakers will often describe the problem in emotional terms without seriously examining its solutions.

■ *Great political speeches are often developed more than written.* Jamieson (1988) wrote that "those who study a modern president's speech are analyzing not a single person but a syndicate" (p. 217). Indeed, several people may contribute to the development of a political speech over an extended period of time. Candidates often take preliminary drafts of their speeches and try them out on small audiences. Some aspects may be pretested with focus group or polling research, but even these are not typically implemented until they have been tried on small audiences. Over time, a number of people may contribute by helping to refine the wording, delivery, and organization of the speech until it becomes a natural extension of their campaign activity.

Ronald Reagan became active in politics in the 1960s in California, but he started working on his stock campaign speech in 1954—a decade earlier (Ritter, 1968). His speech notes numbered in the thousands and included anecdotes, jokes, and one-liners on a variety of topics (Brinkley, 2011). Special event speeches often incorporate and refine successful elements of campaign speeches; John F. Kennedy's inaugural address, probably the product of speechwriter Ted Sorenson, included a polished version of a line previously used by Kennedy in a Labor Day campaign speech in Detroit (Carpenter, 1999, pp. 14–15). The memorable line today ("Ask not what your country can do for you. Ask what you can do for your country.") started out as: "The new frontier is not what I promise I am going to do for you. The new frontier is what I ask you to do for your country." Similarly, in 1968, Richard Nixon campaigned during the general election with a speech that had first been honed during his primary campaign (White, 1969, p. 378). Nor is such refinement limited to candidates; issue advocates often take a similar approach in developing their message. Martin Luther King, Jr.'s "I Have a Dream" speech is best known for his delivery of it at a giant rally in Washington, D.C., but King had previously previewed the same theme at a less well-known event in Detroit (Smith, 1999).

■ *Political speeches are part of a process, not an individual event unto themselves.* Bitzer (1968) places persuasion in the context of the rhetorical situation, contending that a rhetorician must create a fitting response to a situation. The political speech is illustrative of that situational approach. Political speeches are only one element of a larger rhetorical process, one in which the entire goal is to communicate with a mass of voters. A classroom student develops a speech with the intent of making a grade on a specific assignment, while a corporate sales presentation may be aimed at getting an immediate response. Political speeches must take a broader view, planned to play a vital role within the context of an entire campaign. They are written to provide verbal support for the paid advertisements. A sentence or paragraph may be inserted that makes little sense at the time to a local or outside observer but may be there for future strategic purposes—either to set up a later strategic move, for use in a later advertisement, or to "bait" the opposition into making a strategic mistake. During the 2000 New Hampshire primary, George W. Bush frequently inserted new lines into his speech, responding to the issue of the day. His campaign taped those lines and edited them into a "news actuality" commercial for use forty-eight hours later. In Buddy Roemer's 1987 campaign for governor of Louisiana, Roemer's campaign speech included the phrase, "I hate Louisiana politics, but I love Louisiana. That's why I'm running for governor." That phrase was first used in the campaign speeches, and later appeared in his television spots.

The essence of the speech as "part of a process" is the mantra to "stay on message." The fear of many campaigns is the unscripted comment that gets away from the campaign message (Bosman, 2007). Bosman once noted that many "candidates want to go down a campaign trail as predictable as 'The Truman Show.'" The press, and perhaps the public too, prefer those "moments of spontaneity [that] provide a valuable peek behind the curtain of campaign stage managing, allowing voters to see truer glimpses of a candidate's ability to handle unscripted challenges" (p. WK5).

■ *The audience for political speeches extends beyond the immediate crowd.* Traditional speech preparation emphasizes the importance of audience analysis and adaptation, presenting the speech using language and a delivery style that is most effective for the immediate audience. Political speeches can rarely do that, aiming instead for an extended audience, or composite audience that is highly heterogeneous (Myers, 1999). At the very least, the campaign speaker must remember that an extended audience is monitoring the speech, an extended audience composed of voters, the press, and the opposition. Noonan (1998) argued that the press is the most important of these extended audiences. "[E]very speech a candidate or leader makes is serious and important, because every speech is an opportunity to succeed or fail in front of an audience that just may include the press," she wrote (p. 115). That's why, she noted, political speechwriters must "be devoted to keeping an eye on the press—what will interest them in a speech, what will impress them" (p. 133), since the press communicates the ideas in the speech to the rest of the extended audience.

Because of this extended audience, politicians frequently use a discrete campaign audience as a means of reaching a larger target, even if that message is not well received by the immediate audience. In 1999, for example, while campaigning for the Republican presidential nomination, George W. Bush criticized his own party for its lack of compassion to the poor and needy. The speech, made during the Republican primaries, was not well received by its immediate Republican audience, but it did generate a positive response from a crucial general election target—independent voters. Bush was willing to take criticism from the immediate audience in order to broaden his appeal to general election voters.

■ *The success of a political speech is often judged by its sound bites, not by its overall impact.* Noonan (1998) defines the sound bite as "the little snippet of videotape that television news shows use when they show a politician talking" (p. 88). Both scholars and consultants have criticized this aspect of modern political rhetoric for placing more priority on thirty-second messages than on thirty-minute speeches (Kern, 1989; Noonan, 1998). Others argue that sound bites can be an effective way of synthesizing the ideas behind a speech. Jamieson (1988), for example, commented on "the ability of a small unit of discourse to stand for an entire piece" (p. 91), and in a latter work she argued that sound bites and slogans can be effective at communicating the candidate's ideas (Jamieson, 2001).

Since the target audience for a political speech extends beyond the immediate audience, its success depends on the message of the speech reaching that extended audience. The press rarely passes along the entire speech to its news audience, opting instead for quick summaries that include a limited number of quotes (usually just one). As Jamieson noted, incumbents must "say or do something that is concise, memorable and relevant to the day's news agenda" if they have any hope of getting news coverage for their issue (p. 214). Special emphasis should be placed on the word "concise." Jones (1988, p. 53) notes that TV stations typically use only about ten seconds of what the speaker says. To politicians, it often seems even shorter than that. Speechwriter Peggy Noonan (1998) recalled one incident when Ronald Reagan's frustration with sound bites surfaced. While reviewing the text of a speech, he said, "You know, I'm going to give this whole long speech but they're going to show two seconds of me and then Lesley Stahl's gonna stand there giving her version of what I said" (p. 90).

Maybe so, but those sound bites become the memorable part of the speech, the cornerstone by which they are remembered and identified by both the press and the public (Carpenter, 1999). Few people remember John F. Kennedy's entire inaugural address, but they do remember its key line: "Ask not what your country can do for you. Ask what you can do for your country." While many voters missed George Bush's speech at the 1988 Republican convention, many of them can still recite his key line: "Read my lips. No new taxes." The bites chosen by the media may not be the ones hoped for by the campaign. During the 1976 presidential election, while campaigning in the New York primary, Jimmy Carter responded to a question about housing in the suburbs by saying, "I see nothing wrong with ethnic purity being maintained. I would not force a racial integration of a neighborhood by government action. I would not permit discrimination against a family moving into the neighborhood." One television network (CBS), focused on the phrase "ethnic purity" from that quote, creating an issue that dogged the Carter campaign for weeks (Schram, 1976, pp. 143–144).

There's nothing particularly new about the idea behind sound bites. They've been used in American politics since the Revolutionary War. Patrick Henry aroused a nation with his "Give me liberty or give me death" line, and other slogans have been used by numerous politicians through the ages. Jamieson (1988) describes such lines as "a memorable statement that capsulizes the speech and serves as the hook on which we hang it in memory" (p. 90). But there is an important difference between those early slogans and modern sound bites. In modern campaigning, those short phrases may be all that the voters ever hear of the speech. As Jamieson noted:

> Good reporters search for the news segment that reveals as much of the whole as possible. But where, in the past, the audience experienced the event or the whole speech and used the synecdochic statement as a memory-evoking digest, now the audience is often not exposed to the whole for which the part stands. When this occurs, the part simply stands for the part. (p. 112)

Problems can also occur if the speechwriter focuses too much on sound bites. If that occurs, the speech may sound like a series of sound bites and little else. That's why Noonan (1998) argued that speeches need sound bites, but the speechwriter should "never ever try to write one" (p. 88). Speeches written around sound bites, she argued, are boring, lack coherence, and have little to say. Instead, she emphasized the need of the writer to have a topic worth talking about. If the topic is worthwhile, she argued, good sound bites will naturally occur. "Great sound bites of political history are great *sentences* and *phrases* of political history," she wrote, "they weren't trying to self-consciously fashion a phrase that would grab the listener. They were simply trying to capture in words the essence of the thought they wished to communicate" (p. 93). Instead of writing sound bites, she recommended reviewing the speech after it is written, looking for lines that would work as a sound bite:

> If a sentence jumped out at me..., I'd make sure that it ended a paragraph or started one, so that when producers got the written transcript of the speech before it was delivered they'd be more likely to notice it, underline it, listen for it. If I saw a sentence that I thought producers might like, but I didn't want them to choose,...I'd make sure it was surrounded by sentences and therefore less noticeable. (Noonan, 1998, pp. 90–91)

Still, even this process recognizes the importance of sound bites in modern campaigns. As Jamieson (1988) noted, "The speaker who is able to reduce situations and issues to synoptic statements...exercises the power that comes from helping to shape the media's definition of key events. The speaker unable to do this will cede control of the event to those who can or to the media" (p. 114).

■ *Sound bites from a speech may be open to multiple interpretations.* Slogans and memorable lines often employ language with a variety of positive connotations. The multiple meanings that can be attached to the phrases allows for the audience to become a participant in the persuasive process. John F. Kennedy's classic line ("Ask not what your country can do for you...") illustrates this point. The final version was actually somewhat more ambiguous than the version it replaced, allowing for multiple interpretations. Some people viewed the quote as a call for self-reliance and a challenge for citizens to stand on their own. Some others saw it as an indictment of the welfare state. In the end, it meant many things to many people, a typical attribute of a successful political speech. Martin Schram (1976) gave a similar assessment of Jimmy Carter's discussion of the amnesty issue during the 1976 presidential election: "Carter on amnesty. It is not an answer; it is an art form—carefully constructed so as to diffuse the emotions of the subject and come up with something for everyone" (p. 97).

■ *The effectiveness of the speech can be enhanced or diminished by the candidate's delivery of it.* The importance of delivery is a staple in basic public speaking textbooks. Its role is intensified in campaign speeches. How the candidate delivers the speech is central to the impression formed by the voters. Ronald Reagan, for example, converted his skills as an actor into superb presentation skills of his speeches. He rehearsed every presentation and always reviewed his stump speech before every appearance. As Michael Deaver, Reagan's communications adviser, once said, "Reagan felt that his job was the speech. Everyone in the campaign had a job to do, and his was to communicate his vision, and the way he did that was through his speeches" (quoted by von Drehle, 2000). Presentation skills are particularly important to presidential candidates; the voters' ideal image of the presidency is someone who speaks eloquently, coming up with the right word or phrase, without being packaged to do so. A professional actor such as Ronald Reagan can succeed at both of those sometimes contradictory goals, but others have problems. George W. Bush, for example, generally opted for a "home-spun delivery"—"complete with stumbles and swallowed words"—because he felt that such an approach conveyed both sincerity and authenticity (von Drehle, 2000). For major occasions, candidates must also learn to use a TelePrompTer for delivering the speech. This device displays the text of a speech on transparent panels positioned on each side of the podium. Experienced speakers scan a passage with one glimpse and stare directly at the audience or camera while tossing out the sentences in a conversational tone. Few can do that effectively. Both Ronald Reagan and Bill Clinton were masters of its use.

THE SPEECHWRITER AND THE PROCESS

Speechwriters have been on the American political scene from the beginning of the nation. George Washington considered his own speaking style to be awkward (Brigance, 1956), so Alexander Hamilton, James Madison, and John Jay ghosted some of his orations (Einhorn, 1981). Andrew Jackson got help with his speeches from his secretary of state, Edward Livingstone (Gunderson, 1960). Woodrow Wilson had help from Robert Lansing (Fleming, 1959), while Raymond Moley wrote Franklin Roosevelt's 1933 inaugural address (Jamieson, 1988, pp. 201–204). Schlesinger (2008) argues that those presidents generally considered the best communicators—FDR, Kennedy, and Reagan—were also the ones who worked most closely with their speechwriters. Given such a tradition, it's not surprising that in today's political world, major candidates don't decide if they will use speechwriters—merely how they will be used.

Trent and Friedenberg (2000, p. 174) note that each candidate faces two different decisions regarding campaign speeches: which audience or audiences should be addressed and what messages should be used. Audience selection is partly a matter of targeting (which groups are potential supporters) and partly a matter of broader influence (what message will an appearance to this group send to those who are not there). Identifying those target groups and the messages is often the job of the pollster. Expressing those concepts is the job of the speechwriter.

The ideal speechwriter has superb rhetorical skills and can write in an easily read, conversational tone that includes vivid and quotable phrases; add in versatility in subject matter and the capacity to work under pressure, and that person can be a political speechwriter (Persico, 1972). Speechwriters in the past were more likely to come from a journalistic background rather than a rhetorical background. The nature of the journalist's job requires them to write constantly, and they work daily to hone their conversational style. Journalists also have a better appreciation of what sound bites would appeal to other journalists.

Rhetoricians usually have a better sense of the persuasion process, but are less practiced at the use of conversational writing.

The speechwriting process typically starts with a conference attended by the candidate, the campaign manager, the issue experts, the media consultant, and the writer (or writers). Sometimes these conferences will be held on a regular basis; at other times, the meetings may be called as needed. After the meeting, a first draft is developed. It is then checked by the issues experts and other campaign consultants for accuracy, and edited (or rewritten) to conform to the candidate's style. This process is repeated until both the candidate and the experts are satisfied with the product. That product, by the very nature of its development, is a complete expression of the campaign, but not necessarily an ideal one. Ronald Reagan's speechwriter, Peggy Noonan (1997), has written of the problems that a writer faces in crafting a speech that is acceptable to the speaker and their aides. The result may be a compromise, but it is usually at least a well-considered compromise. President Barack Obama usually offers input regarding ideas and arguments that he wants in a speech, but his director of speech writing (Jon Favreau) oversees much of the process (Zeleny, November 27, 2008).

A basic decision to make during this process is the nature of the arguments to be used in the speech. Three general options are available—positive arguments, attacks, and defensive arguments (Benoit, Blaney, & Pier, 2000). Positive messages (or "acclaiming") are those messages that praise the candidate or their party. Attack messages or those that focus on negative information about the other candidate or party. Defensive messages are those that respond to an attack from the opponent. Consultants generally prefer to use the first two, and defensive arguments are generally reserved for situations that require an apology. In normal campaign discourse, most consultants recommend responding to an attack with another attack, rather than a defense. Regardless of which approach is used, the writer needs information on what the candidate has previously said on the topic and research data to support the arguments (Schram, 1976, pp. 181–182).

Trent and Friedenberg (2000) note that most political campaign speeches are written as "speech modules," short segments that can be reassembled and adapted for use in a variety of situations. Shadow and Peck (1991) note that, in terms of organizational structure, the typical speech module aims to gain attention, describe a problem, present a solution, and visualize a solution. These four elements correspond to the first four elements of the classical "motivated sequence" organizational pattern for persuasive public speeches. The motivated sequence represents a five-step organizational pattern: gain attention, describe a need, offer a solution that will satisfy the need, visualize the impact of that solution, and suggest an action that the audience can take. For the purposes of individual speech modules, that last concluding step is not needed. Instead, it is reserved for use in the conclusion of the speech, when the suggested action is to support, vote for, and/or donate money to the candidate.

Message Framing

Message framing is news priming on a holistic level. If the media accept the way a candidate has framed an issue, then subsequent coverage of that issue tends to be beneficial for that candidate. Most academic research on framing has focused on news coverage, with the results indicating that the way the media frame an issue can have a major impact on public opinion and voter behavior (Devitt, 1997; Gamson, 1996; Gitlin, 1980; Graber, 1987; Iorio & Huxman, 1996; McCombs & Shaw, 1993; McLeod & Detenber, 1999). More specifically, framing can have an impact on candidate credibility by framing voter attributions of blame or praise (Iyengar, 1996). Framing works because political attitudes are expressions of underlying arguments recalled from memory (Chong, 1993, 1999; Kelley, 1983; Zaller, 1992).

While researchers have focused on the role of the news media in the framing process, the role of the speechwriter in this process sometimes gets overlooked. An effective speechwriter understands that the speech will serve as an initial framing device that will influence press coverage. If the speechwriter can influence which underlying arguments are recalled from the speech, then the frame will be successful. But, "all frames of reference do not lead to the same response" (Chong, 1999, p. 220). The frames chosen by the speechwriter must be carefully chosen to elicit the desired response.

On a campaign level, framing is achieved with the campaign theme. Miller (1999) noted that campaign themes attempt to construct a reality by framing the interpretation of external events and providing a suggestion as to how the electorate should decide the election. The theme expresses an attitude, defines the rhetorical situation, and provides a mechanism for addressing external aspects of the campaign. A campaign theme, then, acts as a controlling concept, naming and revealing attitudes toward events, providing a "strategic answer" to questions posed by situations (Burke, 1973, p. 1). The frame simplifies external events, defining them with cues for decision making. Bill Clinton's 1996 campaign theme, "Bridge to the twenty-first Century," framed the election context as a decision about the future. It simultaneously expressed confidence in his earlier programs, optimism, and excitement about the ambiguous future of the next millennium (Miller, 1999). Ronald Reagan's "common culture" evoked benevolent capitalism and civic virtue as elements of the cornerstones of the American myth (Patterson, 1999). When he needed a political scapegoat, Reagan often framed the federal bureaucracy as a "benign political scapegoat" that could be the target of his verbal assaults (Braden, 2001).

Word Choice

Framing is also affected by word choice. Careful attention is placed on choosing the right word or words to use in a speech. Words can simultaneously create labels, convey a speaker's feelings on a topic, and signal emotional distance between the speaker and the issue (Fraser & Gordon, 1994). Given that complexity, the goal of the speechwriter is to select the "right" word: "the word that does exactly what you want it to do, and nothing else" (Perlman, 1998, p. 129). In some instances, the search for the right word is so critical that drafts with blanks inserted will be circulated, so that multiple suggestions for the right word are obtained. There is nothing new here. Mark Twain once wrote, "The difference between the almost right word and the right word is really a large matter—It's the difference between the lightning bug and the lightning."

Speechwriters generally avoid long words that may be hard for the speaker to pronounce and harder for the audience to understand. As Noonan (1998) noted, "big things are best said, are almost always said, in small words" (p. 54). Long words can also create other problems. She recalled a speech on volunteerism that she wrote for President George H. W. Bush. Her first draft included the phrase "muscular altruism," referring to the need for people to lend a hand and help others. Campaign aide John Sununu vetoed the term (rightly so, she says), "Because it sounds like a disease" (p. 37). Use of the phrase could have made the president the target of ridicule.

Once a word or phrase is identified, it may be used repetitively as part of a process known as "staying on message" (Norris et al., 1999). The authors worked on one campaign in which the guidelines for a candidate's radio interview included working in the phrase "fiscal conservative" three times. During the 2000 presidential election, George W. Bush never attacked Al Gore for "lying" when he made statements that were incorrect, but he repeatedly said the vice president's behavior was "disappointing"; similarly, Bush never talked about spending "cuts" to reduce government expenditures, but always used the word "savings" as his euphemism (Bruni, 2000). During the 1980 New Hampshire primary, Ronald Reagan's consultants countered concerns that Reagan was too old (then sixty-nine) by using the phrase "oldest and wisest" in speeches and in conversations with reporters, thus putting a positive connotation to the age issue. Deborah Tannen (2000) noted that George W. Bush's campaign rhetoric was filled with words that would appeal to women voters, including references to "children," "dreams," "hope," "love," and "hearts." In a December 1999 speech on tax cuts, Bush referred to "children" or "child" eleven times.

Sound Bites

Two content darlings of public speeches, examples and illustrations, play a relatively small role in political speeches. They are still used because the use of examples and illustrations add interest and clarity to speeches. But while such elements are favored by live audiences, they are often eschewed by the press. They simply take too long to replay on the evening news. Instead, the content darling of the media is the sound bite, a short concise statement that reflects a candidate's message in a memorable manner. As Jones (1988, pp. 31–32) noted, "the secret to getting an idea broadcast on television is to 'condense, condense, condense' until you have a statement that can be said in twelve seconds or less."

A variety of techniques are used, but four tend to dominate: the antithesis, the metaphor, the quotation, and the anaphora. The antithesis is perhaps the most memorable of these techniques. It involves the positioning of words with opposite meanings, either in a parallel or inverted format. Antitheses come in a variety of formats. The simplest is the single antithesis, where a single set of antonyms are used to express the statement. The antiwar slogan of the sixties, "Make love, not war," fits this category with the antithesis created on the words "love" and "war." A double antithesis positions two sets of words in opposition. Democratic consultant James Carville's admonition that "We're right, they're wrong" fits into this category. In the double antithesis, each key word in the first half of the statement is followed by similarly placed antonyms in the second half. This format is diagrammed as ABAB: "We're (A) right (B), they're (A) wrong (B)." Roemer's "I hate (A) Louisiana politics (B), but I love (A) Louisiana (B)" is another example. More recently, in his 2001 inaugural speech, George W. Bush praised his opponent Al Gore for a campaign that was "conducted with spirit and ended with grace."

An inverted antithesis takes the word and reverses their order to that of an ABBA format; John F. Kennedy's most famous quote falls within this category: "Ask not what your country (A) can do for you (B), ask what you (B) can do for your country (A)." Carpenter (1999, p. 39) noted that the impact of an antithesis is influenced by balance, brevity, and placement. Balance requires that approximately the same number of words and antonyms be in each of the dual phrases. Brevity is important because brief statements are easier to remember. Placement is important because the second half of the statement has the strongest impact; the crucial point of the message ("Ask what you can do for your country") should come in the second phrase of the line.

Carpenter (1999, p. 83) describes the metaphor as a form of "rhetorical shorthand," an attribute that makes it particularly useful for sound bites. In one short word or phrase, a metaphor can evoke essential meanings with relatively few words. Although a variety of metaphors are available for the rhetor, political speechwriters are more likely to use one of three versions—synecdoche, metonymy, and the archetypal qualifier. Synecdoche is the use of a part of an object to represent the entire object, much like teenagers who refers to their "wheels" when talking about their car. Metonymy uses a tangible object to refer to an intangible concept. Winston Churchill's use of "blood, sweat, and tears" served as a tangible reference for suffering. Similarly, George W. Bush used two metaphors as a means of contrast in his inaugural speech: "Through much of the last century, America's faith was a rock in a raging sea. Now it is a seed upon the wind, taking root in many nations."

Archetypal qualifiers are metaphors that have commonly accepted connotations. Common uses of this type include those founded upon references to disease, the appeal of light and the avoidance of darkness, high and low, and changes of season. Thus, George H. W. Bush referred to a "thousand points of light" to refer to volunteerism as a program that could "illuminate" the nation. Similarly, Bill Clinton used the last line of his acceptance speech at the 1992 Democratic convention to cast himself as the candidate of optimism; his approach was to refer to his childhood home in Hope, Arkansas, closing with the line, "I still believe in a place called Hope."

Quotations are popular among political speechwriters, but they have to be used judiciously. Too many quotes can be interpreted as the words of a candidate who has few original ideas, while too few might indicate a candidate who is not well educated. A few, though, carefully placed and used, can simultaneously increase a politician's credibility by demonstrating that their knowledge of a subject exceeds their own opinion on it. Furthermore, the source of the quote can be used to identify with an audience. Candidates who speak to predominantly black audiences, for example, almost invariably use a quotation from Martin Luther King, Jr. Quotations can also provide an eloquent way of opening or concluding a speech. When Peggy Noonan wrote a speech for President Reagan in the aftermath of the Challenger explosion, she closed with words from a sonnet by James Gillespie Magee to honor the astronauts who had "slipped the surly bonds of earth to touch the face of God" (Noonan, 1998, pp. 82–87).

Quotations can make profound points. When Florida gubernatorial candidate Buddy MacKay was addressing a crowd in a joint appearance with President Bill Clinton in the midst of the Lewinsky scandal in 1998, he quoted Dr. Martin Luther King, Jr. "In the end it is not the words of our enemies we will remember. It is the silence of our friends." In a sentence, MacKay made his feelings known with great emotional depth.

Anaphora is a technique in which a sequence of sentences begins with the same word or phrase. Martin Luther King, Jr. used this technique effectively in his "I Have a Dream" speech, with that phrase serving as the starting point for several expressed dreams. Similarly, George W. Bush's 2001 inaugural speech (by speechwriter Mike Gerson) used an anaphora based on the word "citizen": "I ask you to be citizens. Citizens, not spectators. Citizens, not subjects. Responsible citizens, building communities of service and a nation of character."

One simple form of a sound bite is the dramatic statement. It can be particularly effective if used as the introduction of a speech. For example, speechwriter Robert Hartman opened Gerald Ford's speech on the end of the Watergate controversy with the direct statement, "My fellow Americans, out long national nightmare is over." Those words became the headlines in many newspapers providing coverage of the speech (Hartmann, 1980).

Humor

Mario Cuomo once began a speech to the New York Press Club by relating last-minute advice from his wife, Matilda. "I know they're a tough group, but don't be intimidated. And don't try to be charming, witty, or intellectual. Just be yourself." That introduction is an example of the effective use of humor in a political speech. It establishes a positive start to the speech, diffuses any perception of arrogance on the part of the speaker, identifies the speaker as a witty person (Chang & Gruner, 1981), and establishes a mood that will make the immediate audience more receptive to the rest of the speech. Noonan argued that every political speech needed humor near its beginning because it provided a "quick victory" for the candidate and "shows the audience you think enough of them to want to entertain them" (p. 11). Files (2000) argues that humor has become one of the standards by which voters judge major candidates, particularly those running for president. "Humor has become another proving ground, especially for anyone who wants to be president," he wrote. "Besides handling stand-up at the annual Washington dinners of powerful media barons, politicians and lobbyists, politicians are expected to appear on the late-night Leno and Letterman shows, as well as on 'Saturday Night Live'" (p. A24).

Much of the candidate-based humor is directed at themselves. At the 1994 Gridiron dinner, Al Gore had himself wheeled to the speaking stand on a handcart, thus poking fun of his reputation for stiffness. At the 2000 dinner, he acknowledged the controversy over White House fund-raising with the question, "This isn't a fund-raiser, is it?" The second primary theme for campaign humor is an attack on the opponent. These humorous attacks typically use "gotcha" one-liners, such as Al Gore's campaign line that claimed George W. Bush "thinks fettuccine al fredo is the Italian prime minister."

Humor, when done well, can also become the sound bite that is replayed by the press. One highlight of the presidential debates between Ronald Reagan and Walter Mondale was Reagan's joking approach to the age issue by insisting that he would not make an issue out of his opponent's "relative youth and inexperience." Humor can also be an effective device for inducing inoculation against persuasion; once people start laughing at an opponent or concept, it is difficult to alter their opinions in the future (Powell, 1975). But jokes that don't work are disasters; during the presidential debates leading up to the Iowa caucuses in 2000, Steve Forbes tried several jokes that were unsuccessful, either because of missing on a punch line or missing the timing on his delivery. There's a lesson there: not everybody can use humor effectively in political speeches. Noonan (1998, p. 106) warns that politicians should be particularly wary about using sarcasm in their speeches; they rely heavily upon effective delivery and might still be misunderstood. Sarcasm that backfires can be particularly harmful to a candidate.

TYPES OF CAMPAIGN SPEECHES

The Stump Speech

The stump speech is the basic campaign speech used by candidates in most campaign appearances. Nimmo (1970) described it as "the prepared speech repeated endlessly..." (p. 119). Reporters who follow a candidate quickly identify those elements that are common to all appearances, and those common elements quickly become old news to veteran reporters. In fact, one way to identify the key components of a presidential stump speech is to compare press coverage of the speech by local reporters and by national reporters. The national reporters typically do not cover the stump material, reporting only on new elements added to the message. Local reporters, though, often provide detailed coverage of the entire speech.

An ideal stump speech is really a collection of topics usually generated by survey research from which the candidate pulls those that are most appropriate for the immediate audience. Ronald Reagan's initial stump speech was contained on a file of three-by-five notecards; he would select a series of cards for use at any specific appearance, resulting in the use of different material at different places and varying the length according to the situation (Ritter, 1968). Each speech was different, and yet themes and ideas were consistently repeated. Nimmo (1970) noted that stump speeches are not designed to sway voters' attitudes or to provide an in-depth view of the candidate's position. Its principal purpose instead is credibility enhancement. "By quoting facts and details on a variety of issues the candidate leaves the impression that he possesses the knowledge, sophistication, and acumen to hold public office" (pp. 119–120).

The Issue Speech

The purpose of an issue speech is threefold: to define the candidate's position on an issue, to frame the issue in a manner that is advantageous to the candidate, and to generate positive news coverage for the candidate on that issue. Issue speeches are often presented at occasions that are associated with the issue selected. Thus, a speech on increasing the minimum wage might first be presented to a labor union, while one on changes in capital gains taxes might be offered to a business group. For that reason, the speechwriter must compose the speech with both the immediate audience and the extended audience in mind. The presentation must be organized well and argued coherently, so the immediate audience will attend to and follow its content. It must also contain a condensed version of the issue proposal (preferably in a sound-bite format) that will make it easy for the press to provide coverage.

A number of different formats can be used for issue speeches, but the most common approach is relatively simple:

1. State a voter-held premise about the issue ("Education is the key to our future")
2. Link the issue to the position ("Your governor must take the lead in improving our schools")
3. Link the candidate to the position ("John Doe will make sure that gets done")
4. Support the argument with:
   a. the candidate's record on the issue ("As a legislator, I sponsored the bill that raised teachers' salaries to the national level"), or
   b. a proposal on what to do ("I'll put together a statewide lottery with the funds dedicated to improving education")
5. Appeal for support, with that support linked to the issue ("But I need your help. Vote for me in November, and together we can improve education in this state.")

To generate coverage of the speech, the candidate must have something newsworthy to say. That decision is often based on how much risk the candidate is willing to take. The more risk involved in the message, the more likely it is to receive coverage and the more legitimate the message becomes (Garlick & Mongeau, 1992). But taking too big of a risk opens the candidate to criticism. The candidate must also evaluate the degree of rigidity he or she will hold on an issue; the politician who appears too rigid is seen as too ideological, while the one who shifts too often is viewed as an opportunist who lacks values (Denton & Woodward, 1985, p. 11).

One advantage of the Internet is that issue speeches can be delivered and then posted online to generate further analysis and consideration. Speechwriter Peggy Noonan (2011) sees this procedure as offering new hope for a revival of issue speeches in politics. "Speeches are back," she wrote. "They have been rescued and restored as a political force by the Internet" (p. A15).

The Event Speech

Politicians are often called upon to make speeches at special events, such as political conventions, holiday celebrations, or celebrations to honor other people or historical figures. Speeches at party events are often full of praise for the party's candidates and attacks on those of the opposition (Benoit, Blaney, & Pier, 2000), but speeches at nonpartisan events are more complex. The event offers a chance for positive publicity, but the focus of the news coverage is likely to be on the event rather than the candidate. Any overt attempt to take advantage of such events often creates a backlash. The general rule here is that the speech should be written to focus on the event rather than the candidate, a goal that will naturally benefit the candidate if done well. To do otherwise is to risk the development of a self-serving image.

Combs (1980) used the terms "political ceremonials" and "political rituals" to describe many such event speeches. Political rituals, he noted, can dramatize the cohesion of a political group, separate it from another political group, and link "the group to a guiding myth" (p. 25). Some—including the inaugural addresses, State of the Union addresses, and farewell addresses—are institutional in nature and serve specific purposes (Campbell & Jamieson, 1990). The inauguration ceremony, for example, comes complete with an inaugural speech. The ceremony itself is a ritual of political succession that invests the new president with power, duty, and privilege (Mair, 1962). Not all political rituals involve political speeches, but many do. The speakers may be "long-winded orators" who speak on predictable topics (Combs, 1980, p. 28), but even cliches can serve a communicative purpose. After all, the very nature of political rituals is to celebrate political symbols (Duncan, 1968), and ritualistic speeches provide that opportunity.

The most visible of event speeches for presidents and governors is their inaugural speech. George Washington started the tradition, and Abraham Lincoln used the inaugural speech to define his presidency. Franklin Roosevelt used his to unite the nation (Seelye, 2009). Harry Truman's was the first to be televised, but that started the tradition of the speeches as media events.

Playing Defense

Since a candidate's image plays a critical role with the voters, an attack on that image can prompt a self-defense speech (Gold, 1978). Such speeches have a long history in American politics, but the modern era of media-based apologies can probably be traced to Richard Nixon's "Checkers" speech. Nixon, besieged by charges that he had misused donations from campaign contributors, went on television to defend his actions; the only gift he had accepted, he claimed, was a puppy his family had named Checkers (Cornog & Whelan, 2000).

From the consultant's perspective, the best guideline for responding to attacks is "The truth is the best defense." The first action is to discuss the action with the candidate, identify the facts in the matter, and develop a defense based on those facts. If the candidate denies the action, or provides some justification for the action, then a variety of options are available. Most of these have been described, under a variety of labels, by a number of communication scholars.

Kenneth Burke's (1973) theory of dramatism states guilt as the primary motive behind such speeches. The major means of not accepting such guilt, according to Burke, was a process he called "Victimage." Victimage, or scapegoating, discards the guilt by transferring it to someone other than the accused. Scott and Lyman (1968) identified two other types of account behavior for self-defense speeches: excuses and justification. Excuses involve admitting to a wrong act but not accepting full responsibility for it. Scott and Lyman identify five subtypes of excuses, one of which is scapegoating. The other four can be added to Burke's limited list—accidents, defeasibility, biological drives, and justification. A candidate uses an "accident" argument when they claim that unexpected factors influenced the behavior or act. Defeasibility is used when a candidate argues that they could not have committed an action because of a lack of knowledge or completed it because of a lack of will. The biological drive category is better known as the "I couldn't help myself" argument. Justifications are perhaps the most complex form of excuses; in this approach, the candidate accepts responsibility for the act, but does not accept the fact that the act was wrong.

Benoit, Gullifor, and Panici (1991) identified four types of defensive speeches, those based on denial, evasion of responsibility, minimization, and mortification. Denial claims that the speaker had no responsibility for the act, evasion tries to reduce responsibility for the act, and minimization tries to reduce the salience of the act. Mortification occurs when the candidate admits the wrongful act and asks for forgiveness.

Ware and Linkugel (1973) identified four types of rhetorical self-defense: denial, bolstering, differentiation, and transcendence. Their definition of denial is similar to that of Benoit, Gullifor, and Panici (1991), which is that denial occurs when the candidate disassociates him- or herself from the act. Bolstering attempts to offset the source by associating the speaker with something for which the audience has positive affection. Differentiation takes the speaker's image out of a negative context in the hope that it is the context and not the speaker that caused the displeasure. Transcendence tries to place the object of disapproval in a more favorable context.

A similar taxonomy was identified by Kennedy and Benoit (1997) when they examined Newt Gingrich's defensive rhetoric following the controversy that erupted after he signed a multimillion dollar book deal; they identified five strategies used by Gingrich: denial, good intentions, bolstering, attacking accusers, and corrective action.

The Apology—The Mea Culpa

"The truth is the best defense" maxim applies to the apology also. Voters are more tolerant of wrongdoing than many candidates might realize, and they are particularly tolerant when a candidate is willing to accept responsibility and acknowledge wrongdoing. However, their tolerance is strained if a candidate denies an action and later facts reveal the denial to be a lie. When an apology must be given, the simplest and most effective approach is to say, "I shouldn't have done it and I won't do it again." The technical term is *mortification*, which is the admission and acceptance of wrongdoing (Burke, 1973, p. 39). The goal of the speech is to seek forgiveness, and—more often than not—it usually works. Such a speech shows that the candidate is human, and voters are willing to forgive—particularly if it is a first offense.

Apologies are effective but not necessarily easily elicited from candidates. Benoit, Gullifor, and Panici (1991), for example, noted that Ronald Reagan dealt with the Iran-Contra controversy by first using denial; after that his arguments shifted to the justification of his actions as being well-intentioned. After the release of the Tower Commission Report detailing the activities, though, Reagan finally issued an apology—one based on mortification (acknowledging that he had traded arms for hostages) and victimage (announcing changes in people and policy to prevent a similar event from happening again). Benoit, Gullifor, and Panici noted that the latter approach was the most effective.

The Nonspeech

Speechwriters sometimes write speeches that are never given. Sometimes these are written merely as a draft of ideas, a starting point for the discussion of how issues or themes are addressed. More often, these are anticipatory in nature, written for situations in which the outcome is not yet known. For example, two speeches are typically written for election night—one should the candidate win and another if he or she loses. Presidents often have disaster speeches ready for tense situations that could go awry, hoping they will never need to use them. In 1969, for example, William Safire (1999) prepared a speech for President Richard Nixon's use if Neil Armstrong and Buzz Aldrin became stranded in space during the historic first trip to the moon.

▶ THE SPEECH NOT GIVEN

William Safire wrote a speech for President Nixon to deliver in 1969, in case the Apollo XI astronauts were stranded on the moon. It never had to be delivered.

The request for the speech came not from Nixon but from astronaut Frank Borman, NASA's liaison to the White House. Borman called Safire to say, "You want to be thinking of some alternative posture for the president in the event of mishaps." When the stunned Safire did not respond, Borman added: "Like what to do for their widows."

Borman then explained that the most dangerous part of the trip was not landing on the moon, but in launching it back up to the mother ship. If that failed, Neil Armstrong and Buzz Aldrin could not be rescued, Mission Control would have to cut off communications, and the doomed astronauts would be left to starve to death or commit suicide. Nixon aides H. R. Haldeman and Peter Flanigan told Safire to proceed with a plan for that tragic contingency.

On July 18, 1969, two days before the astronauts reached the moon, Safire recommended a contingency plan. In the event of a disaster, the president should telephone each of the widows-to-be. After NASA cut off contact, a clergyman would perform a ceremony equivalent to a burial at sea, commending their souls to "the deepest of the deep" and concluding with the Lord's Prayer. A draft of a speech for the president was included with the plan. Here is a selection from the speech:

> "Fate has ordained that the men who went to the moon to explore in peace will stay to rest in peace," the speech began. "These brave men, Neil Armstrong and Buzz Aldrin, know there is no hope for their recovery. But they also know that there is hope for mankind in their sacrifice.... In ancient days, men looked at the stars and saw their heroes in the constellations.... In modern times, we do much the same, but our heroes are epic men of flesh and blood. Others will follow, and surely find their way home. Man's search will not be denied. But these were the first, and will remain foremost in our hearts.... For every human being who looks up at the moon in the nights to come will know that there is some corner of another world that is forever mankind."

Safire based the final line of the speech on lines from a poem by Rupert Brooke, who died in the British royal navy in World War I. "If I should die, think only this of me: That there's some corner of a foreign field that is forever England." ∎

Speeches that are not used are not necessarily wasted. The writer typically files them away, using its prepared material for a later situation that is more appropriate. On other occasions, private distribution of a never-delivered speech can have positive benefits for the campaign. One of the authors once wrote a speech for a candidate to use at a rally honoring a civil rights leader; a last-minute change in the schedule resulted in the speech never being presented, but a copy was distributed to some of the participants. That led to an important endorsement for the candidate.

INFLUENCING THE SITUATION

How important is control of the immediate speech environment? Quite important, judging by how much emphasis consultants and candidates place on influencing that environment. Campaigns typically go to great lengths to generate large crowds for campaign appearances; if numerical numbers are expected to be low, the appearance will be scheduled for a smaller location so that the crowd will at least appear to be larger. Collateral material is distributed and placed in strategic spots (within range of the television cameras) to enhance the festive and optimistic mood of the event. What about hecklers? They're okay too, if properly placed. George Wallace used to insist that hecklers be placed closed to the stage, making it easier for them to verbally attack him. Wallace felt confident in his ability to outwit the hecklers and knew that the television cameras would capture the entire exchange for the evening news.

Campaigns also choose the music that will be played at such events. That's nothing new. Franklin Delano Roosevelt campaigned to the strains of "Happy Days Are Here Again," a tune that reflected the optimistic promises of his campaigns following the sad days of the Great Depression. More recently, candidates have been choosing pop or rock songs to represent their campaigns. Decisions on which song or songs to use are carefully made. The song can't be too popular (people will get tired of hearing it) and must be politically correct (McFetters, 1999). And, most important, it must underscore the campaign message in a positive manner. Thus, both Ronald Reagan and Bob Dole campaigned to the beat of "God Bless the U.S.A."; Bill Clinton relied heavily on the Fleetwood Mac tune, "Don't Stop Thinking About Tomorrow"; And George W. Bush opened his campaign for the 2000 presidential election with "Signed, Sealed, Delivered, I'm Yours." Most of those worked well, but some candidates have run into problems. President George H. W. Bush wanted to use "Don't Worry, Be Happy," but songwriter Bobby McFerrin publicly said he didn't support Bush. Similarly, Bruce Springsteen objected to Reagan using "Born in the U.S.A.," a song he had originally written as the plaint of a Vietnam veteran.

SUMMARY

Political speeches are an integral part of the political communication process. They reflect the candidate's expression of ideas and form the basis for mass media messages. Still, they differ from many other forms of public speaking in terms of how they are developed, written, presented, and used. Many political speeches are developed over time, as different units (or modules) of the speech are written, tested, and rewritten as the expression of a message on a particular issue is refined. In the process, though, political speeches offer verbal opportunities for candidates to define their positions on issues, speak out on current events, defend their records, and offer apologies for misdeeds.

The format for such speeches will vary, ranging from the rough informality of a stump speech in a small town to solemn occasions that involve the death of citizens. The political speech may be an informal presentation to a small group of supporters, introductory comments at a press conference, or formalized statements delivered in a televised public address. In any situation, the political speech plays a vital role as a primary source of material that is reported by the media to the voters. As a result, the political speech speaks to both its immediate audience and to an extended audience, conveying messages that can have an important impact on framing issues and defining the images of political candidates.

QUESTIONS FOR DISCUSSION

1. At its best, political rhetoric is the politician's voice and the voice of his or her campaign. Analyze examples from one particular campaign and try to identify to what extent the rhetoric of the campaign was a key part of the campaign plan? Were there any examples that you believe were simply a reaction to unexpected circumstances on the campaign trail? The random musings of the candidate? The result of careful research?

2. A candidate expresses a popular desire in a well-received speech. Behind the rhetoric, however, there is little to suggest the sentiments expressed by the candidate have any grounding in the candidate's own life and experiences. Can such a speech be successful? How can an opponent attack such rhetoric? Can you cite an example?

3. A candidate in Pennsylvania for the U.S. Senate suggested that if criminals have a right to an attorney, why can't the people have a right to quality health care. Is this an effective argument? Why or why not?

4. Special interest groups, speechwriters, political consultants, candidates, their spouses, supporters, and contributors: Which of these is likely to be a source of political rhetoric? Which of these is likely to be a source of *good* political rhetoric?

Cyberspace: The Internet and Political Communications

In June of 2007, online visitors to the YouTube Web site could watch an independent video called "I've Got a Crush…on Obama." A relatively unknown actress and model, Amber Lee Ettinger, was supposedly the star of the production, but the real star was arguably the Democratic candidate for president, Barack Obama. Or at least his photo was the star. The video had Ettinger lip-synching to a song, while dancing in a bikini, and pining over a photo of Obama that pictured him on a beach wearing no shirt.

Ettinger quickly became an Internet star known as "Obama Girl." Her video became an Internet sensation, triggering more than 13 million views—a number that was more than double the best total of any of the Obama campaign's official videos. The original posting was followed by a number of sequels featuring the same actress/character and marked the opening of an unofficial online campaign for the candidate. More importantly, it signaled the increasing use of the Internet as a medium for political communication (Kluver et al., 2007).

In this instance, YouTube and its ability to offer the public viral videos was the unit for distribution. But independent videos were not the only Internet elements to emerge in the 2008 election. Candidates increased their Web presence in 2008, with campaign Web sites becoming obligatory rather than a signal that the candidate was trying to deal with the new media. The fund-raising focus of the Internet used by John McCain was refined and expanded by Barack Obama, resulting in an unprecedented level of fund-raising in a presidential campaign. Candidates started using social media to reach out to voters on a level that was simultaneously a mass effort and was also more personal. The Internet also became a substitute for news conferences, with candidates releasing major announcements via Twitter and Facebook. Meanwhile, some candidates became victims of the Internet, caught on camera in "gotcha" moments that they did not expect and which they did not know how to handle. In the span of one election, it seemed, the Internet had changed politics (Hendricks & Denton, 2010).

THE EARLY YEARS OF INTERNET AND POLITICS

Jesse Ventura helped put the Internet on the map as a political force in 1998 when he used the Web to organize his successful independent campaign for the governorship of Minnesota (White, 2000). Since then, nothing has fired the imaginations of political operatives and academicians in recent years more than the Internet and its possibilities as a means of communication with voters. As the *New York Times* (Kelley, 1999) noted, "The Web page is the new whistle-stop, a way for candidates to carry their messages daily to more people than they can reach on the campaign trail." Larson and Psystrup (2000) wrote that "the Internet promises to change politicking by involving more citizens in the democratic process" (p. 159). Selnow (2000) noted that the Internet "threatens to upset the balance (of power) by granting users the power to send information cheaply" (p. 205). Owen and Cutbirth (2000) saw its potential in engaging more young people in the political process. Chicksand and Carrigan (2006) viewed it as a way to target young voters. Others saw its potential to be a significant channel for the exchange of political information (Hacker et al., 1996; Whillock, 1997). As Republican Jim Nicholson (2000), chairman of the Republican National Committee, noted, "Two decades ago, voters were passive receivers of information, dependent upon the judgment of editors and reporters to decide what was newsworthy. But the Internet changes that, offering interested voters the ability to go online and actively seek out the information they desire." Initially, the role of the Internet has been that of a supplemental campaign medium (Benoit, Benoit, & Hansen, 2000), but it has the potential to be much more. Tedesco, Miller, and Spiker (1999) noted that the Internet feeds a desire for information. Selnow (1998) called it a "master medium" that includes text and photos like newspapers, audio like radio, and video like TV. The Net offers distinct opportunities for audience adaptation and the personalization of campaign messages. The audience size has been constantly increasing and the communication is potentially interactive. By the 1998 elections, more than two-thirds of those running for political office had Web sites (Selnow, 2000).

Still, others were skeptical. Davis and Owen (1998) questioned both the accuracy of political information on the Net and the quality of its public affairs reporting. Political Web sites tend to be highly partisan in nature (Benoit, Benoit, & Hansen, 2000), a factor inhibiting a full discussion of issues. Furthermore, the Internet appears to have a split political personality; Internet users tend to be political liberals, but most political content on the Web is conservative (Hill & Hughes, 1998). Such a dichotomy reflects the concerns of Goldzwig and Sullivan (2000) on the role of the Internet in local communities, particularly for those who were "socially and economically disenfranchised" (p. 53). Boyle (2000), furthermore, argued that the Internet "will be used mostly by journalists and others with an existing investment in the campaign, while undecided voters are likely to continue receiving information from traditional sources" (p. 27).

Davis (1999) agreed, noting that the press and politicians have adapted to the Internet and were using it to maintain the status quo. At first, political campaigns used Web sites as a sort of proof that they, as candidates, were up to date, "with it," and able to deal with the problems of the twenty-first century. With the explosion of Web sites and the vast improvement in modem technology, cyberspace is becoming more directly useful to political campaigns. Campaigns regularly check one another's Web sites for information, particularly about issues and travel schedules. A campaign can often thus intercept where and when the opposing campaign will make an appearance to discuss an issue. With this information, the campaign can prepare an answering statement or press release that can be handed out at the opponent's appearance.

The press also found the Internet to be a source of news, and some candidates have taken advantage of that. In 1999, George W. Bush became the first presidential candidate to make updated lists of campaign donors available online. Similarly, Arizona senator John McCain made news when he used his Web site to criticize congressional pork projects (Kelley, 1999).

Radio and television commercials were increasingly transmitted to broadcast outlets through the Internet, resulting in time and cost savings. The Internet is a vast research resource and most campaigns use it to access both free services such as the Federal Election Commission and various news media paid subscription–only sites such as Lexis/Nexis and the more prosaic Encyclopaedia Britannica. While not all information about a given individual or a given issue exists on the Internet, at least a good start can be made with a relatively small expenditure of time and effort.

E-mail was a very fast way to communicate with campaign insiders. Moreover, because it is relatively easy to use, the circle of those included for such communication is large when compared to traditional systems. There are also many Internet-based fax services. The campaign can send one memo or newsletter that can be faxed to many thousands of others. Finally, Web sites are able to reach non-English-speaking voters who desire detailed information if the campaign uses a Web-based translation program.

While some politicians are still leery of technology, some are using it as a way to let constituents be in touch with them. For the technologically savvy, e-mail is an easy and convenient way to contact their representative, easier than mailing a letter. For the politician, it ensures public input on a regular basis. U.S. Senator Conrad Burns (Rep. Montana) used the Internet as his personal multimedia station, offering a live, weekly video and audio broadcast to answer questions from constituents. Florida Governor Jeb Bush's fondness for e-mail was disclosed to the public in a June 1999 news report. The next day, Bush was inundated with 500 electronic messages—five times the number he usually received in a day (McPherson, 1999).

The 2000 elections saw an even bigger increase in Internet campaigning (White, 2000). In Pennsylvania, Governor Tom Ridge established a Web site for his reelection campaign that attracted more than 150 visitors a day (Tomlinson, 2000). In North Carolina, Republican gubernatorial candidate Richard Vinroot greeted his Web visitors with a survey; respondents could obtain the results by providing the campaign with their e-mail address and Zip code—information subsequently used for targeting purposes. Others asked the visitor to sign up and to provide the e-mail addresses of three friends as well.

Individuals also used Internet Web sites to parody politicians (Lowy, 1999). There were at least four anti-Gore Web sites during 1999, but the parody site that drew the most attention was the "gwbush.com" Web site that parodied Republican George W. Bush's official Web site (www.georgewbush.com). Bush's campaign responded by filing a complaint with the Federal Election Commission, a move that prompted a reporter to ask the Texas governor whether the parody site should be shut down (Black, 2001). When Bush replied, "There ought to be limits to freedom," his quote became the buzz of the Internet for weeks.

No other campaign technology was growing as fast as the Internet. Some remarkable endeavors were accomplished by using it. During the Bush–MacKay campaign for governor of Florida in 1998, the campaigns were very active in using the Internet for rhetorical volleys. Typically, one campaign would post a campaign position on its Web site. The other campaign would research and craft a response, often within an hour. The result was that campaign exchanges occurred entirely in one news cycle. Both campaigns would make the news media aware of the exchange through e-mail, faxes, or telephone calls.

One advantage of the Web is that much more information about a given issue could be made available. There is no practical limit on the length of issue papers, allowing for access to the entire text of speeches, legislative proposals, and organizational details (Browning, 1996). That's one reason that Peggy Noonan (2011) saw the Internet as having the potential for more in-depth discussion of issues. Furthermore, Web site visitors spend an average of eight minutes browsing through any public official's site; that is considerably more voter attention than can typically be obtained by any other political medium (Kelley, 1999). Phone banks, for example, can typically maintain a voter's attention for only forty-five seconds, while television ads are usually limited to thirty seconds.

The Internet has proven to be a successful fund-raising tool. John McCain's presidential campaign raised $6.4 million over the Internet in 2000, a number that accounted for more than 25 percent of his campaign budget. Contributors like the ease with which it can be done (using a credit card) and the ability to make donations based on recent campaign activities. Campaign contributions can react instantly to daily news with a response that can be translated into immediate financial support. That can be particularly true for candidates who lack institutional support or a strong initial base. In 1999, Bill Bradley faced an uphill battle against Vice President Al Gore for the Democratic nomination for president. In the first half of the year, the Bradley campaign signed up 15,000 volunteers and raised more than $200,000 through mostly small contributions over the Internet; at one point, the Internet was bringing in an average of $7,000 a day for the Bradley campaign (Kelley, 1999). On the Republican side, John McCain's presidential efforts raised more than $100,000 from online contributions in the early days of his campaign, and half a million dollars came in within a few days of his victory in the New Hampshire primary from online contributions alone. In the state of Washington, Republican John Carlson's challenge of incumbent governor Gary Locke included a "LockeSmith" Web page to "help unLocke Washington." Voters who signed up through the site were asked to raise $500 in 100 days.

As a vehicle of mass communication, though, the Web is still problematic. Davis and Owen (1998, p. 254) noted that it is still in "an adolescent stage" and has yet to reach its full potential. Cassidy (2000) argued that the Internet's promise of increasing voter interest "... wrongly assume[s] that civic participation is a function of access to technology, when it is more likely to be related to much deeper social issues" (p. 57). Part of the problem is that it is passive, which means that the voter has to seek it out. A 1999 study by Nielsen Media Research and CommerceNet reported that nearly half of American adults were online, a significant number but far short of the pervasiveness enjoyed by television. Furthermore, nearly 40 percent of those online do not bother using the Web at all, and most others do not seek out political information. In a time when voters are increasingly turning away from TV advertisements (which are very easy to view), turning on a computer, finding the correct Web site, and then reading several pages of issue-related material seems unlikely at best. As Curtis Gans (1999), director of the Committee for the Study of the American Electorate noted, "The Internet is a fragmenting medium, in which everything is self-selected. If you're not motivated to go to a particular site, it doesn't matter that the site exists and is wonderful."

In fact, the Web seemed to serve elites who could afford computers and had the needed personal interest and time to access it. If anything, the Internet had lured the cream of viewers away from television, resulting in further fracturing the group of habitual voters available to receive campaign messages. Twenty-nine percent of Internet users had decreased their reliance on television for political information, while their newspaper usage has dropped by 18 percent. Other researchers (Coffey & Stipp, 1999) predict that TV usage will decline even more in the future as more viewers turn to their personal computers.

Another problem was credibility of information. As Selnow (2000) noted, "Much of the information on the Web is undocumented, put up for no other reason than that someone has a wild idea and $25 to set up a Web site" (p. 220). This problem was accentuated by the fact that many people don't realize that Web site information can be uploaded with no editorial control or review by legitimate media outlets. Voters who have become highly media savvy about television, radio, and newspapers have not yet developed those skills for the Internet. As Selnow (2000) noted, "They have learned to draw a distinction between the *New York Times* and the *National Enquirer*, but many have not yet understood the difference between one Web site and another" (p. 226).

Commercial advertisers generally rate the Internet lower than television but higher than direct mail as an effective advertising medium (Huang, Leong, & Stanners, 1998). Its advantages are its ability to convey information and detail at little cost. Furthermore, it seems to be most effective for people who are verbally oriented, while voters who prefer visual media appear to be hampered by the interactive nature of the Internet (Benzjian-Avery, Calder, & Iacobucci, 1998).

There was a feeling that the Internet had a big future in campaigns (Bush, Bush, & Harris, 1998), but exactly what it would do was unclear. As Selnow (2000) said, "The role of the Internet in American politics is presently uncertain but potentially promising" (p. 204). Surely, the lines between television, radio, computers, and telephones will be blurred. At the very least, all these instruments (and more) were combined in the same machine. The fusion of that technology finally happened in the 2008 campaign, where the Internet demonstrated that it was a vehicle that could deliver political communication to the public and have an effect on their political attitudes. It made huge strides as a medium to draw together the main players of a campaign—the candidate, staff, consultants, volunteers, opponents, news media, and public officials (DeFleur, 1997; Garrison, 1998).

TV critic Alessandra Stanley described the 2008 election as one "that changed the way we watch and drew new audiences ... including younger people who mostly ignore the news and download their entertainment from the Internet" (2008). Joe McGinniss (2008) noted that while the Internet was drawing only a small percentage of advertising dollars, it was still having an impact—particularly among young voters. As Democratic consultant Will Robinson noted, "if you're under twenty-five you don't watch television that much. You're just as likely to be on YouTube, making videos, or text messaging friends as doing anything else" (quoted by Graff, 2007, p. 262).

Academic research supported that conclusion. Several studies reported that Internet media were effective in reaching young voters (Blom, 2009; Kushin, 2009), particularly for young African American voters. Further, not only were young voters seeking political information on the Internet, but they were also using the Internet to pass along videos of Barack Obama's speeches to their friends. As Stelter (2008, March 27) noted, "younger voters tend to be not just consumers of news and current events but conduits as well—sending out e-mailed links and videos to friends and their social networks" (p. 1A). As a result, the Internet is now a major means for campaigns to communicate with voters (Warnick, 2007).

FUND-RAISING

Advances in fund-raising were among the most significant improvements in the political campaign use of the Internet in the most recent presidential campaign. Many campaigns vastly exceeded their fund-raising targets and vastly exceeded the level of political speech normally associated with presidential elections. The Internet permitted highly organized contacts and, more importantly, recontacts of small contributors as well as the gathering of high levels of information about their likes and dislikes. Contacts took the form of social media, text messages, and e-mails.

Selection of universes was easily accomplished using the fast accumulation of data. High levels of success could be realized by contacting potential small contributors at the times when issues that concern them most are in the forefront among the daily discussion. For example, groups that were particularly concerned about "climate change" or "gun control" could be communicated while that issue was actually being discussed in the national marketplace of campaign issues. This communication would take the form of a brief message from the campaign, followed by a request for more funds. Contributions are usually accomplished through credit cards, which makes giving painless, especially in the context of the issue you care about. And, each contribution will result in many follow-up requests for contributions.

John McCain was the first to use the Internet as a major source of fund-raising, but Barack Obama's campaign raised it to an unprecedented level (Pollard, Chesebro, & Studinski, 2009). Obama's approach used the Internet to solicit both small and large donations from supporters. Small donations were appealing to many voters who had not contributed to campaigns previously. All they had to do was provide a credit card number and authorization to charge $25, $50, $100, or some other amount to their account. The campaign gets the money, while the computer also gathers information necessary for filing forms with the Federal Election Commission. In addition, the computer could also keep up with the total amount that the individual donated, thus allowing the campaign to (1) file full disclosure on everyone who met the minimum reporting requirements and (2) monitor the possibility that the person could donate again in the future. If the latter were the case, another e-mail solicitation could be sent at later dates.

Obama's use of the Internet to raise money was successful at an unprecedented level, prompting some observers to predict that it would mean the end of public financing for presidential elections (Luo, 2008). By the end of the election, Obama had received donations from more than 3.1 million voters, collecting nearly $70 million in September 2008 alone. John McCain, who took public financing, was at a financial disadvantage. The Obama campaign had the funds to refine messages and micro-target those messages for delivery through different media, while McCain had to rely on fewer messages with broader themes—sometimes having to put a positive and negative message in the same ad to save money (Kenski, Hardy, & Jamieson, 2010). McCain's shortage of money was particularly acute during the final month of the campaign (Wayne, 2008).

VIRAL VIDEOS

YouTube was created in February 2005 to provide people with a way to display videos, their own videos (Graham, 2005). The site was soon so popular that in less than one year after its official launch, it became a target for other investors. By July 2006, Internet users were uploading more than 65,000 new videos a day, while the site was recording 100 million viewers daily. Most users were individuals, people putting up home videos of themselves, their families, and pets. But some media companies—including CBS and the BBC—also became registered users and provided video footage. Political uses of YouTube generally fell into three different categories—campaign videos, independent videos, and "gotcha" videos.

Campaign Videos In the 2008 election, the most active users of YouTube were the Democratic candidates (Dalton, 2007). Democrat John Edwards shifted his entire campaign approach to adjust to the Internet presence (Nagourney, 2007), while Senators Hillary Clinton and Barack Obama announced their campaigns simultaneously on both TV and YouTube (Dalton, 2007). Still, not all campaigns fully embraced online campaigning. As Jill Lawrence (2007) noted, the general attitude for most campaigns was that the Internet was needed to compete, but "it's not a substitute for politics as usual" (p. 10A).

However, the Obama campaign was an exception; it viewed an online presence as critical to its campaign efforts. At least one observer described the Internet as a primary communication vehicle for Obama (Stallings-Carpenter, 2009). Obama's campaign created its own YouTube channel to raise funds and to provide supporters a place to post their own videos (Harper, 2009). The campaign posted more than 1,800 videos of the candidate's speeches on the site, encouraging comments and responses from supporters (Heffernan, 2009).

Obama's speech on race triggered more than 1.6 million views on YouTube within 24 hours of its posting, with pastors of some churches recommending that their congregation view the speech online (Rohter & Luo, 2008).

The campaign's first attack ads premiered online. Mitt Romney released an Internet ad attacking John McCain on the immigration issue, while McCain released one that described Romney as a "phony." On the Democratic side, John Edwards was the target of "I Feel Pretty," a video that depicted the candidate admiring himself in the mirror (Graff, 2007). Republican Mike Huckabee held a news conference to show an ad that his campaign had decided not to air—a spot attacking Romney. Huckabee showed the ad to reporters and then announced he was not planning to use it. However, he posted it on YouTube; *New York Times* reporter Katherine Seelye (2008) noted that "The circumstances of the commercial and the nature of free media, particularly now with YouTube, make it likely that the advertisement will be viewed far more often than if it had simply run" (p. 11A).

However, a successful online video is no guarantee of electoral success. As Santarelli (2010) noted, "Just because an ad moves up the rankings of YouTube, doesn't mean victory is guaranteed" (p. 13). In the 2010 Alabama election, Dale Peterson, a candidate for Agriculture Commissioner, had a popular video that depicted him with a gun and a horse. He rose from 5 percent to 28 percent in the polls after the video was released, but still finished third in a three-person race after his ad became most popular on YouTube.

Independent Videos   The Obama Girl video mentioned in the introduction to this chapter was produced by Barely Political, a Web content producer that specialized in producing online video. The release of "I Got a Crush on Obama," the first Obama Girl video, was followed by series of other Obama Girl releases—all on the same YouTube channel. That series culminated in "Red States, Blue States," released on inauguration day in 2009. The series represented a second use of YouTube—videos that were the product of independent producers. Independent groups also got involved, with most of them also using the standard ad formats. Health Care for America spent $40 million on a cable and online ad promoting comprehensive health care (Bosman, 2008).

Negative campaigns were also apparent, with some Web pages established for that purpose alone (Bennett, 2008). The AFL-CIO and Service Employees joined forces for an online video called "McCain's Mansions: The Real Elitist" that featured McCain's homes and condos in a manner that tried to portray the Republican as elitist and out of touch (Greenhouse, 2008). Another conservative group, "Vets for Freedom," released two Internet ads attacking Obama for his position on the Iraq War. After the initial GOP euphoria over Sarah Palin subsided, Palin also became the target of YouTube videos. The first came from a woman, Lisa Donovan, who did imitations of Palin on YouTube (Fairbanks, 2008). Some of these videos became so popular that they appear to have had some impact on the election (Powell, 2010), at least in terms of information. Others were designed as entertainment, yet they also could have contributed to a candidate's image.

"Gotcha" Videos   In 2006, YouTube was mostly a channel for "gotcha" journalism, a place where users could post videos of politicians saying or doing embarrassing things. At the beginning of the 2006 U.S. Congressional elections, Senator George Allen confidently campaigned for reelection to his senate seat in Virginia. Allen's election seemed very certain, and he had been mentioned as a possible presidential candidate for the Republican Party in the 2008 cycle. All of that started to change when he got captured making a racial slur ("macaca," a racial slur aimed at people with Indian heritage) on a "gotcha" video that was posted on YouTube (Allen, 2006). Eventually, Allen's campaign got buried by the YouTube video and its resulting publicity. As the election neared, one pundit noted that "If Jim Webb … wins in Virginia, technology will get credit," while another noted that Allen's gaffe "made the campaign competitive" (Marsh, 2006, p. 4A). By the end of the 2006 campaign, candidates had become aware of YouTube's influence on campaigns and were fearful that they might be the next victim of the "candid camera" moment (Allen, 2006). Labeled the phenomenon as "Macaca moments," which he defined as "high profile candidate gaffes that are captured on YouTube and receive a cascade of citizen viewing, leading to substantial political impacts" (p. 1). The threat was that amateur reporters might capture unscripted moments that caught the politician "off message" with a comment or behavior that could damage the campaign. In past elections, such mistakes were often minor problems that did no lasting damage to their campaign. For example, former Montana senator Conrad Burns had a reputation for being "gaffe-prone" in previous campaigns, but none had been captured on video before. YouTube had suddenly transformed those gaffes into major mistakes. As Steven Levy noted, "This new technology brings radical transparency to the Internet, where information is available immediately and anyone could end up an unwilling figure of shame and ridicule" (Levy, 2006, p. 17).

That role continued in the 2008 campaign, starting in the primaries. In some cases, campaigns used YouTube in an effort to take advantage of their opponents' gaffes. On the Republican side, John McCain's campaign tried to discredit Mitt Romney's shift on the abortion issue (moving to a strong antiabortion position) by posting a video on YouTube that showed Romney in a 2005 appearance saying he was "absolutely committed" to a pro-choice position (Memmott, 2009). After conservative commentator Ann Coulter called John Edwards a "faggot," Romney called the remarks offensive—only to have his reaction nullified by a video showing him and Coulter laughing backstage (Graff, 2007). One amateur reporter, Mike Stark, made a reputation by getting into speaking venues of conservative speakers (e.g., Rush Limbaugh and Bill O'Reilly) and asking embarrassing questions—with the exchanges posted online.

John McCain had problems when videos emerged of Rev. John Hagee, an evangelical preacher who had endorsed him, attacking the Catholic Church as "the Great Whore" (Rich, 2008b). McCain eventually had to disavow the endorsement, causing Hagee to disavow his support of McCain (Banarjee & Luo, 2008). One of the most devastating gotcha videos came at the expense of Democratic contender Hillary Clinton. The problem was a statement that she made several times during March 2008 about being threatened by sniper fire in a visit to Bosnia. Once CBS made a video of the event available, though, it showed Clinton calmly exiting from her aircraft and being greeted by local VIPs. That turned Clinton's remark into fodder for late-night comedians (Rich, 2008a). One conservative Web site,

The Drudge Report, provided a link to the YouTube video that became popular with conservative audiences. Even the winner, Barack Obama, got caught—although his problem was merely an auditory recording. In April 2008, Obama flew to San Francisco for a private fund-raising event. While speaking to the crowd, the candidate said that many small-town Pennsylvania voters were bitter over their economic circumstances and "cling to guns or religion or antipathy to people who aren't like them" (Zeleny, 2008a, p. 20A). Those remarks were audiotaped and subsequently posted on the Huffington Post Web site. That created a firestorm that the Obama campaign had to address. The result: Gotcha videos had a major impact on the 2008 elections.

SOCIAL MEDIA

The 2008 presidential election became the first presidential election in which both party nominees were positioned to use social networks as a campaign tool (Hendericks & Denton, 2010). Research on Internet communication has identified four primary motivations for seeking online political information: guidance, information-seeking, entertainment, and social utility (Kaye & Johnson, 2002). Social utility often emerges on the Internet through the use of social media such as Facebook. Social utility has been reported more often by individuals with a higher interest in political campaigns and issues (Kaye & Johnson, 2002). One by-product of social utility is that it can increase information seeking and knowledge of political events (Kitchens, Powell, & Williams, 2003). It becomes a means of gathering information that can be used when discussing politics with others. This behavior is particularly common among college students, since college students read more news online than their noncollege peers and turn to the Internet more often than any other source (Diddi & LaRose, 2006). Students who seek out news and political information on the Internet are more politically active than other students, are more likely to be politically involved, and reported higher informational motivation—including motivation for social utility (Park, Kee, & Valenzuela, 2009).

Voters who use social media as a means of gathering information on a candidate frequently relate to such candidates in a para-social manner. Campaigns use social media to tell voters about their campaign activities, keeping them involved by giving daily updates (Pearson & O'Connell, 2010). They tend to use interpersonal constructs such as homophily (similarity), interpersonal attraction, and interpersonal credibility in the development of their image of that candidate (Powell, Richmond, & Williams, 2011). Homophily is the key variable, with voters making judgments about candidates based on similarity with themselves. That, in turn, influences information-seeking on the Internet.

During the 2008 election, Barack Obama's campaign was the most adept at using social media to communicate with voters. The campaign's skill at the use of this media led Hendricks and Denton to label the president "Communicator-in-Chief." The Obama campaign used social networking to help build ideological unity and commitment from its supporters (Pollard, Chesebro, & Studinski, 2009). After the election, many elected officials used Twitter accounts to update their supporters on their activities (Parker, 2011). Nearly all politicians use Facebook to contact their "friends" (Kirkpatrick, 2010), although most hire someone to ghostwrite the material and do the actual postings (Rich, 2010). Conversely, the protests that ripped through the Middle East in 2011 were ignited by a Facebook page that fueled public anger (Preston, 2011).

VOTER CONTACT

Campaigns increasingly use the Internet to maintain contact with voters. They establish Web sites as virtual bulletin boards on which they post a wide range of information about their candidates, including candidate biographies, candidate travel schedules, downloadable photographs, radio and TV ads, press releases, position papers, fund-raising information and fund-raising pitches, attacks on opponent's positions, specific contact information (e-mail addresses, regular mail addresses, telephone numbers) for staff and local volunteers, links to Web sites whose positions coincide with the candidate's, and links to newspapers and television Web sites that have written or produced favorable pieces about the campaign or an unfavorable piece about the opponent. Some sites offer "fill-in-the-blank" e-mail that supporters can forward to their friends. Still, each campaign designs its Internet presence to reflect the candidate's or the staff's individual approach. In 1992, for example, Bill Clinton used the Internet primarily for posting campaign information, while Perot's campaign was more likely to use it as a means to post opinions (Hacker et al., 1996).

Still, 2008 represented a maturation of the process, particularly by the Obama campaign. His GOTV program, for example, used computerized contact and databases to increase enthusiasm and support for the candidate. An example of how they did this was in Ohio, which the campaign divided into 1,231 targeted neighborhoods (Zeleny, 2008b). Teams were assigned to each neighborhood, with the leader being someone from that neighborhood. The database for the contact included information derived from magazine subscriptions, shopping history, income levels, and the type of cars the family drove. Each name was bar-coded so that responses could immediately be fed back into a computer.

BACK TO THE FUTURE—VOLUNTEERS

One of the great losses to political communication has been the lack of comprehensive utilization of volunteers. Lost to the campaign is the natural dedication to cause and candidate volunteers bring to the campaign. Recent Internet applications are virtual predictive dialers and power dialers. Thus, the time volunteers spend calling goes entirely to calling by cutting out the time formerly taken in actually dialing, printing call sheets, or, even, waiting for the phone to ring. And, the calling system even records the amount of time spent on the phone so that volunteers can be appropriately monitored. All this, and by using VOIP (calls made via the Internet, see Chapter 8), all calls are made at vastly reduced cost. The final advantage is that complete reports can be generated immediately by caller, by universe, by candidate/issue, or by client. Estimates are that as many as five times as many calls can be made. Those calls may count for more because the natural enthusiasm of volunteers makes those calls far more effective.

POLITICAL BLOGS

One of the earliest intersections of politics and the Internet came in the form of political blogs. Blogs were often a combination of information and opinion pieces used to distribute information to voters. They first appeared in the political arena in the 2004 election (Lawson-Borders & Kirk, 2005). By the 2008 election, they had developed into a key communication unit that was comparable to political coverage from other, more traditional media (De Zuniga, Puig-i-abril, & Rojas, 2009).

Many blogs have a partisan bias, with both parties using blogs to develop their framing of an issue. During heated issue debates, leaders of the parties will discuss communication strategy late at night, develop key talking points, and then distribute those ideas to sympathetic bloggers. If it works the way they hope, their talking points appear on the national news by that afternoon. Some blogs have large followings. During the 2006 election, Politico averaged nearly 3 million visitors a month—a number that likely has increased ever since then (Peters, 2011). Some blogs provide polling data, while others treat themselves as if they were regular news sites. While older voters adapted to blogs slowly, young voters quickly moved in that direction (Sweetser-Trammell, 2007). Blogs have had an impact on the news agenda. For example, the uproar over the construction of a mosque near Ground Zero of the 9/11 attacks was sparked by a conservative blogger (Barnard & Feuer, 2010).

Political blogs have been primarily used to express opinions rather than to mobilize voters (Wallsten, 2007). Those opinions are usually negative attacks on the opposition, rather than positive information about the bloggers' candidates (Trammell, 2006). Further, those opinions are often biased and sometimes not supported by facts, yet the potential social influence of blogs is strong—particularly among conservatives (Meraz, 2011).

THE NEGATIVE SIDE OF INTERNET POLITICS

Despite the increased use of the Internet in politics, problems still remain. Morozov (2011) notes that there is nothing inherently liberating about the Internet, so it can create some delusions among its users. Further, there is still a problem in terms of editorial control. Anybody can put anything on the Internet, including blatantly false information, without any editorial review. Jones (2011), for example, expressed his concern about a loss of common information among the voting public, as each side creates its own view and data related to events. Similarly, Giridharadas (2009) noted that "Lies spread like wildfire on the Web" (p. WK5).

Further, the Internet can be used for negative purposes. For example, it has become a major means of communication for racist and white supremacy groups (Daniels, 2009). Warner (2010) argues that this will increase extremism because "The Internet provides people with an opportunity to preselect the ideological perspective of the political content they encounter" (p. 430). It is also possible to put up false Web sites that are hard to distinguish from real campaign sites. Giridharadas considered that to be the Internet's biggest problem, writing that "Perhaps most menacingly, the Internet's openness allows well-organized groups to simulate support" (p. WK5). Tomaszeski, Proffitt, and McClung (2009) went further, using the term "blog terror" to describe a situation in which "people are getting their understanding of the world from random lunatics riffing in their underwear, rather than professional journalists with standards and passports" (p. 72). Similarly, Fishkin (2009) was referring to the Internet when he wrote, "Many methods and technologies can be used to give voice to the public will. But some give a picture of public opinion as if through a fun-house mirror" (p. 1).

SUMMARY

The growth of the Internet has provided an increased opportunity to use online media both to communicate with voters and to organize supporters. Currently, the Internet's potential has exceeded its actual use in campaigns, but that is likely to change quickly. Future elections will likely see an expansion in Internet campaigning. As Pollard, Chesebro, and Studinski (2009) concluded, the Internet "increasingly appears to be functioning as an independent, if not discrete, sociopolitical system with unique modes of interaction, its own rules and procedures, and ultimately its own standards and guidelines for presidential campaigns" (p. 575).

Political Polling

The authors once met a local political activist who opened the conversation by saying, "I don't believe in polls." She then recounted the story of a local tax referendum that she led, noting that she campaigned in the wealthy section of the community by talking of how the area would benefit from a better school system. When campaigning in the low-income areas, her message focused on the structure of the tax—it would be paid by wealthy families. She summed up her story by smiling and saying, "We passed that without ever doing any polling."

No polling? Perhaps. But she did engage in audience analysis, and that is essentially what polling is—audience analysis (Gunter, 2000; Ruddock, 2001). With a small local electorate, one with which she was highly familiar, she was probably correct to reject formal polling. Her narrative indicated, however, that she did adjust her message to different target audiences based on her perceptions of those two audiences. Had she done a poll, the pollster would have recommended the same strategic approach that she used.

She didn't need a poll because she already understood her electorate well. Candidates in major campaigns lack that capability. A person from a wealthy Texas family may run for president, but it is unrealistic to expect that person to understand the problems faced by Hispanics in California, coal miners in Kentucky, ranchers in Montana, or African American voters in Mississippi. Polling fills that knowledge gap, providing a way for the candidate to analyze large and diverse audiences within the electorate. The resulting data are used for planning, evaluating campaigns, and developing campaign strategies (Ferguson, 2000). As the sophistication of the data-gathering process increased, candidates found a variety of uses for the information. First, polling provides a view of public opinion that can be compared with those of the candidate. Second, polling provides a basis for the expenditure of scarce campaign resources. Finally, a campaign can discover the standing of its candidate compared with an opponent.

Scientific polling in political campaigns began in the late 1930s, a development that coincided with a nationwide increase in the use of scientific approaches on communication variables. By the 1960s, polling techniques were used regularly in presidential campaigns. Veteran political pollster Bill Hamilton traced the beginnings of modern strategic campaigning to the successful use of telephone surveys in the 1970s (Hamilton & Beattie, 1999, p. 95). By then, most statewide candidates were regularly using polling techniques. By the early 1980s, several national polling firms had formed their own telephone banks, while several independent phone facilities were also formed for the purpose of conducting telephone surveys. Meanwhile, the use of polls had expanded to congressional candidates. By the 1990s, their use expanded further, with many local candidates starting to use polling services.

The news media also joined the bandwagon, with an increasing number of newspapers and television sources regularly using polls as a means of reporting on campaigns. From 1984 to 1988 alone, the number of news media polls on campaigns tripled (Taylor, 1990a, p. 261). Some argue that the release of such polls helps to construct public opinion, rather than just measure it. Generally, though, research indicates that polls can affect the perception of public opinion, but do not create a bandwagon effect that induces undecided voters to side with the probable winner (Daschmann, 2000). For that reason, political campaigns seldom release their data, even when they would report positive information for them. Instead, they prefer to use their polling resources to validate campaign messages and to discover the movement of public opinion on key campaign issues, information they would prefer that the opposition not have. When they do release information, it is highly selective, with information favorable only to their side typically released. As a result, those news outlets that wish to have polling data often gather their own data. The effect is that the news media regularly release their polling data showing who is leading and by how much, and political campaigns seldom offer theirs unless there is a vast and potentially destructive difference between their numbers and the media's numbers.

TYPES OF POLITICAL POLLING

Although most people use the terms interchangeably, there is a technical difference between a political poll and a political survey. A political poll is a relatively short questionnaire with a descriptive purpose; its intent is to describe voter attitudes and intentions with relatively simple questions. A political survey uses a longer questionnaire and seeks more in-depth information about attitudes and predispositions. The differences between the two are most apparent in the benchmark survey and a tracking poll. The benchmark survey seeks in-depth information about the voting public, with the intent of using that information to develop a campaign strategy. Tracking polls are a way of "keeping score," to know who is ahead at any given point in the campaign.

Benchmark Survey

The benchmark survey is an initial survey taken by the campaign to assess the political environment and develop a campaign strategy. The benchmark is a specific type of cross sectional survey, which is a survey that studies a cross section of a population at a particular point in time (Stacks & Hocking, 1998, p. 237). It makes no attempt to measure or observe changes among voters. It is more interested instead in obtaining a description of the attitudes and beliefs of the voting population as a whole, and identifying any demographic or psychographic differences among those voters. It is typically conducted early in the campaign (sometimes as much as eighteen months before the election).

Tracking Polls

A tracking poll is considerably shorter than a benchmark, usually consisting of only ten to fifteen short questions that can typically be asked in less than five minutes (frequently, only two or three minutes). Its primary goal is test ballot assessment, which is to learn which candidate is leading and by how much.

The most crucial part of the tracking poll is the test ballot ("If the election for Position A were held today, would you vote for Candidate X or Candidate Y?"). It gives the most direct test of the relative success or failure of the campaign, serving as an index of which candidate is ahead at that point in the campaign. Tracking polls may also test the campaigns' major messages to identify possible reasons for success or failure. The last set of questions typically included in a tracking poll are demographic questions about the voters themselves—age, partisan preferences, income level, ethnic background, gender, and geography. Each of these demographic factors represent something that can be used by the campaign for targeting purposes.

Tracking polls fall into two broad categories. The "One-Shot Track" is a short, cross sectional descriptive study. It takes a cross section of the voting population and describes their attitudes and voting intentions at one specific time during the campaign. The Moving Window Track "... provides the campaign with the most stable and accurate measure of a trend line and the base for timely strategic decision making (Hamilton & Beattie, 1999, p. 102). The "Moving Window" ("Rolling Average" or "Rolling Sample Survey") is an example of a cohort trend longitudinal study—a survey technique that gathers observations over time with the sample drawn from the same subgroup universe (Stacks & Hocking, 1998, pp. 238–239). In the case of a political moving window track, that subgroup is voters. The moving window allows for constant polling to gauge the effect of the opponent's ads, the effects of the candidate's ads, and assessments of whether new ads are needed for the campaign.

Like the one-shot track, the moving window track does not provide causal information. It lacks the presence of an external control group for making causal inferences. Still, while caution should be used in interpreting the data from any single day (John, 1989), moving windows offer the pollster multiple options for analysis (Moore, 1999). It is considerably more precise than a one-shot track because it allows the pollster to draw conclusions about which factors occur at which time. That additional information increases the reliability of the informed judgments made by the pollster and the other participants in the campaign. When something happens that causes a dramatic shift in voter responses, that shift can be detected immediately. That, in turn, allows for a quicker and more effective response on the part of the campaign.

Other Polls and Surveys

A number of pollsters use a variety of names to describe other polls and surveys that have specific purposes. Two of the most common are strategy adjustment polls and vulnerability surveys. A strategy adjustment poll is a relatively short questionnaire used to assess the effectiveness of the campaign's strategy, with the information used to make any necessary adjustments in that strategy. Hamilton and Beattie (1999) refer to this type of poll as a "brushfire survey," adding that they "...should be conducted when a strategic decision needs to be made" (p. 102). The questionnaire is typically midrange in length (about ten minutes), longer than a tracking poll, but shorter than a typical benchmark survey. The focus is on questions that measure the images of the candidates, their relative test ballot strength, and any refinements in issues that may need to be reassessed.

Vulnerability surveys are similar to benchmark surveys in terms of length, but differ in intent. This questionnaire is designed to measure the likelihood that an incumbent can be defeated by a strong challenger. If the vulnerability survey indicates that the challenger has a chance, it can help them develop a strategy for the campaign and assist in their fund-raising efforts. Sometimes, the vulnerability survey is done on behalf of the incumbent with the intent of identifying potential points of weaknesses; in those cases, the incumbent typically uses the information to reduce those weaknesses before a challenger has an opportunity to take advantage of them.

Exit Polling

One popular form of polling for media outlets is exit polling. Exit polls are on-site surveys conducted on the day of the election with voters as they leave the voting booth. Their purpose is to identify for whom they voted, and what factors influenced their voting decision. For campaign purposes, this is relatively useless information; the campaign is over, and it is too late to use the information for strategic adjustments. However, these data can be useful to media outlets by allowing them to project winners before the polls have closed and to provide some type of insight as to why one candidate won and another lost.

Exit polling was first developed by Warren J. Mitofsky for CBS News in the early 1970s and first used for election-night coverage of the 1972 election (Clymer, 2006). He then worked with the *New York Times* to design a broader method for the 1976 election. Since then, the national media have paid for a joint exit-poll system to aid them in election-night coverage of national elections.

Exit polling is not a foolproof system. It is subject to the same margin of error (usually plus or minus five percentage points) that limits regular polling approaches. Furthermore, since it is physically impossible to have interviewers at every voting site, the validity of the system depends on the representativeness of those voting precincts that are selected for interviews, which introduces a further possible margin of error. Those precincts or election districts are often chosen on the basis of turnout in previous elections, without considering whether the nature of the precinct has changed since that time. Even if representative precincts are chosen, if those precincts do not have voter turnout rates consistent with the election as a whole, its results may be invalid. Given all of these problems, it is really remarkable that exit polling is as effective as it is. Most of the time, the national networks get it right, and correctly project probable winners. Still, they occasionally miss. In 1984, for example, the national networks projected Senator Jeremiah Denton

(Rep.-Ala.) to win reelection; when the votes were finally counted, Democratic challenger Richard Shelby narrowly defeated him. In 1996, incumbent Senator Bob Smith, Rep.-N.H., was declared the loser, but he narrowly won reelection. In the 2000 election, exit poll projections for Florida led to a series of wrong predictions by the television networks. Early on election night, all of the major networks declared Al Gore the winner; they subsequently rescinded that and later credited the state to George W. Bush's win column. Eventually, they withdrew both predictions; the vote count was so close that it took weeks to decide a winner.

That problem caused the media and academicians to take a closer look at the problems of exit polls. One problem in 2000 turned out to be one what Mitofsky had warned about before, that is, flaws resulting from "premature leaks of incomplete data" (quoted by Clymer, 2006, p. A17). But later analysis also revealed another potential problem when McDonald (2007) reported that the samples for exit polls tend to be biased toward younger voters, minorities, and women. Older white men, it appears, are less willing to consent to an exit poll interview. Further, exit polls can be influenced by the same poor methodology that can beset other forms of polling. In the 2004 election, for example, poorly written questions were blamed for diminishing the level of analysis provided by the networks during election coverage (Langer & Cohen, 2005).

Some critics also fret over the impact of exit poll projections on voter turnout. If the networks declare a winner early, based on exit poll results, will that cause some voters to decide that there is no reason to vote? Research has generally found that releasing such results early can decrease voter turnout, but not in close elections (Sudman, 1986). Thus, exit polls have not been found to change the outcome of elections. Critics have also wondered if exit polls sufficiently represented absentee voters, but that concern has also been researched and deemed unfounded (Barreto et al., 2006).

Focus Groups

A focus group is a group of people who are gathered together at a common location to discuss some topic under the direction of a moderator (Merton, 1987; Merton, Lowenthal, & Kendall, 1990; Stewart & Shamdasani, 1990). Krueger and Casey (2000) note that focus groups are about listening. When used properly, the process improves listening, the results can be used to benefit the participants, and those participants leave with a good feeling about having been heard. In most cases, the size of the group is relatively small (usually ten to fifteen participants). As a result, data from focus groups lack the generalizability of similar responses obtained from a poll. That weakness aside, in-depth information can be obtained. In essence, polls and surveys provide a "quantitative" assessment of a political situation. Focus groups provide "qualitative" data about the same event (Denzin & Lincoln, 2000; Morgan, 1988; Silverman, 2001). Joseph Glick (1999, p. 121) noted, "The strength of the focus group is that it allows people to be people." Surveys can tell a candidate what is happening and focus groups can tell them why. As Hansen et al. (1998) noted, the semi-structured nature of the focus groups allows the researcher "a potentially much richer and more sensitive type of data" (p. 258).

Two factors are critical to the success of a focus group: a good research question and a good facilitator. The research question is essential, because it is unlikely that the researcher will elicit useful information when they do not know what they are seeking. The research question guides both the development of the group discussion and the selection of the participants, who are usually selected on the basis of some demographic or psychographic criteria (undecided voters, ticket splitters, and so forth).

Similarly, the facilitator is a key person in the process (Glick, 1999, p. 119). The facilitator's job is to encourage discussion by all participants, guide the discussion along the topic of interest, but not to influence the discussion in any manner. He or she often has a guide or a questionnaire to remind them of the information being sought, yet they must use some personal research skill to guide the discussion without letting the questionnaire become an artificial part of the process. As the discussion progresses, the facilitator must ask effective questions to draw out a group, and then refine those questions based on the group's responses. Doing that requires a skillful moderator, who can then produce useful information. As Glick (1999) noted, "When nonconsensus and disagreements are encouraged, two things generally emerge in group discussion: opinion becomes nuanced in ways that begin to reveal underlying thought frameworks, and people often invoke powerful images" (p. 117).

Facilitators often have materials with them that can be used to stimulate discussion. The most popular of these are copies of television ads, with group participants serving as critics and explaining their responses to the ads. The pollsters and other campaign officials typically monitor the entire process. The monitoring frequently occurs at the same time as the discussion, with the researchers and campaign officials observing the discussion behind a one-way mirror. In addition, the entire process is videotaped, providing for frequent viewings at a later date to verify conclusions.

As mentioned before, because of the small sample size, the representativeness of focus group results is questionable. The general rule of thumb is that you need at least two groups, for comparison purposes, with ten to fifteen participants in each group. Usually, though, the campaign is not looking for generalizable answers. Instead, the goal of focus group research is to obtain new insights into the electorate and their views, which works to supplement the work of the media consultants. For instance, focus groups have led to the development of campaign slogans, using terminology provided by the focus group participants. Or, campaign ads may be reedited based on the participants' comments. Other times, focus group discussion can lead to the development of new ideas or messages that are subsequently tested with survey research (Wimmer & Dominick, 1994, p. 148).

The most common uses of focus groups in political campaigns are to pretest television ads, monitoring audience responses to presentations, and identifying audience language habits that can be used in campaign messages. One Republican pollster who frequently used focus groups is Richard Wirthlin, who provided data for former president Ronald Reagan. Every time Reagan gave a televised speech, Wirthlin had focus groups watching and using hand-held devices to record their responses to the speech, second by second. Wirthlin used the resulting data to identify what worked and what did not work for each speech. The information was then used in preparing the next speech (Taylor, 1990, p. 218).

Focus groups have limitations. Wimmer and Dominick (1994, p. 149) argue that, considering the small sample size and qualitative methodology, gathering quantitative data are inappropriate for a focus group. Along this line, most academicians argue that focus group data should be viewed as only preliminary data that should be verified with more in-depth research.

Another problem is their representativeness. Focus groups consist of volunteers who are often provided monetary incentives to participate. Such groups may not be representative of the overall population from which they were selected. That is particularly true if those participants are "professional subjects," who are constantly used by research organizations for a number of projects. Once someone volunteers to participate in a focus group, the research organization often keeps the name (complete with phone number and demographic data) on file. When they need another participant with those demographic criteria, the research organization may first call people who have participated before, creating a sample of people who are frequently used for similar research. Constant repetition of this process leads to focus groups composed of unrepresentative samples.

Cyberpolling

Cyberpolling is a relative newcomer to the field of polling. It relies on voters providing their responses to the pollster through e-mail or some other online technology. Pollsters Gordon Black and Humphrey Taylor used the Internet to conduct polls for the 2000 election (Terhanian, 1999), with varying results. The Internet provides for surveys composed of larger samples, while computer technology allows for an almost instantaneous tabulation of results. That can provide a polling service that is both faster and cheaper than conventional methods while also attaining a similar level of reliability and validity. Other Web sites, such as speakout.com and survey.net are being developed as a way of offering voters a direct means of expressing their opinions. The number of sites available for that purpose is likely to increase in the future, even though their main purpose is entertainment instead of research. The most popular sites today, though, are Survey Monkey and the Knowledge Network.

Early efforts at cyberpolling had the same problems as call-in surveys—difficulty in controlling the sample in a systematic manner (Couper, 2000). The response rate on e-mail surveys is dramatically lower than those of both telephone surveys (Taylor, 2000) and mail surveys (Couper, Blair, & Tripplett, 1999; Schaefer & Dillman, 1998). While efforts have been made to correct that problem, their success has not yet been dramatic (Dommeyer & Moriarty, 2000). Furthermore, even if the response rate problem is corrected, cyberpolls still do not provide a sample that is representative of the general population (Flemming & Sonner, 1999; Taylor, 2000). Finally, responses to online surveys are heavily influenced by the design of the Web page (Dillman et al., 1998) and the layout of the questionnaire (Smith, 1995).

Some problems were merely growing pains that were eventually eliminated or reduced. Some researchers worked to develop systematic methodologies for the Web that can provide a consistent means of evaluating its data (Schaefer & Dillman,

1998). The Harris Poll Online, for example, has the potential of providing longitudinal data from panel studies that can be useful in identifying attitudinal trends (Couper, 2000, p. 482). But most of the online surveys currently available fail to reach such levels of sophistication. The voting public will have to learn to separate trivial and entertaining surveys from those that develop sophisticated methodology.

And pollsters have found a way to get past the major problem—a lack of representativeness in the sample. The process is relatively simple. Pollster now simply oversample the universe of voters that interest them. For example, if a sample of 800 is needed for the survey, the pollster will use his cyberpoll technique to gather 1,000 interviews, or maybe more than that. Once the over-sample is completed, the results are then weighted down to meet the stratification desired for the survey. That approach has worked well and saw extensive use in the 2008 campaigns. In fact, two dominant versions of cyberpolling have emerged—robo-polling and Internet polling.

Robo-Polling

The Integrated Voice Recordings first used for direct voter contact via telephone (see Chapter 8) have since been utilized by pollsters for quick tracking polls. The response rate is low; most voters don't want to bother to answer a computerized telephone poll. Those that will don't like to stay on the line too long. Still, since the computer is never demoralized by rejection, the process can work merely through the ability of the computer to call everyone within a voting district.

The process is simple. The script for the questionnaire is read and the recording is uploaded to a computer in a digital format. The script is slightly different from a traditional poll in that it uses "push" instructions rather than coded responses. Thus, both forms would be similar to, "Would you vote for Candidate A or Candidate B." The traditional poll would record the verbal answer of the respondent and check the appropriate category (A or B). In a robo-poll, the script would follow the question with "Push 1 for Candidate A or Push 2 for Candidate B." Thus, the computer both asks the questions and records the answer using the responses on the telephone touch pad.

This approach can gather information quickly, often having the capability to complete an entire poll in one night of calling. It is particularly valuable at tracking polls, since campaigns often want tracking responses quickly.

Still, there is one major problem with robo-polling. It only works on short polls, not long surveys. Some voters enjoy responding to such polls, but they will not stay on the line for an extended length of time. As a result, most robo-polls are limited to less than 10 questions. That means that robo-polling can be useful for tracking purposes, but has limited utility in benchmark surveys or other long-form approaches.

One secondary problem must be considered too. Robo-polling cannot use an extensive list of options as responses to questions. A traditional image question, for example, might begin with the name of a public figure and the request to rate the individual in terms of "very positive, positive, neutral, negative, or very negative." That five-item response is too long for most people who respond to a robo-poll. Instead, the options work more effectively if there are only three choices: "positive, neutral, or negative."

Polling in the Twenty-first Century

John Anzalone has been over twenty years in the polling business—helping candidates, associations, and corporations all across the country with message development, strategic planning, and targeting. John has helped build a firm that helped elect Barack Obama as President and now represents two U.S. Senators, eleven U.S. Congressmen, and dozens of other statewide and local elected officials in over twenty states. He regularly works with the DCCC, DSCC, and the DGA. The Washington Post *recently has called Anzalone Liszt Research one of the "hottest in the nation" and John Anzalone "the best pollster you've never heard of";* Politico *named him "one of the five most important people not running for president." Anzalone is regularly quoted in* The Washington Post, Roll Call, Politico, The Los Angeles Times, *and the national Associated Press. Anzalone started his own polling firm in 1994 and has offices in Washington, DC, and Montgomery, AL. Anzalone was a campaign operative whose experiences include working for national democratic strategists James Carville and Paul Begala in U.S. Senator Frank Lautenberg's (NJ) 1988 campaign and managing gubernatorial, congressional, and mayoral races. He began his political career as a research assistant to David Wilhelm (who later became DNC Chairman) at Citizens for Tax Justice, and then went on to manage campaigns in five different states, before concentrating his energies on polling for campaigns.*

Q: How would you describe the role of polling in a typical campaign?

A. Polling is like the message bible. Polling has its tentacles in each part of the campaign. You do a poll and it gets made into a TV ad, a radio ad, or a direct mail piece, or even a speech. We consider ourselves the watchdog of the message, and that becomes important. It's also vital in targeting. We help campaigns spend their money wisely and efficiently. We're able to target and project upon those voters who aren't with you, but who may move toward you, or who are currently with you and you need to solidify, or those who will never be with you. We can parse those out and make sure we're communicating either through how you place your TV and radio or which mailboxes you send your mail to, or where the candidate actually schedules himself. So polling is fundamentally an efficiency tool. You either solidify voters or persuade them to move toward you. Polling is often helpful with the field program with targeting, and—over the last few years—with micro-targeting in terms of how people on the ground will use their field resources. We actually also, more and more, are part of the fund-raising team. Our polling gets turned into fund-raising memos to insiders, the PAC community, and donors in general. We also, at times, sit down with funders, or do dog-and-pony shows with big funders. Also, we find ourselves helping to design press strategies based on the power of issues and how they resonate in the polls. Polling is an efficiency tool for the campaign. It's a product that really pays for itself, and it touches every part of a campaign. So it becomes your playbook, your bible, that you go back to everyday to make sure that you're on message, that you're talking to the right people, and doing the right things.

Q: Some first-time candidates are reluctant to spend money on polling. But you're saying that it doesn't really cost much.

A: In a cost-benefit analysis, it really doesn't. But polling is expensive. It's labor intensive to do it right. It's expensive. The phone bank costs have gone up quite a bit in the last decade because of things like cell phones, caller ID, and voters becoming less likely to spend 10–20 minutes answering questions over the phone. It is still possible to do it—and do it right, but getting an interview is more expensive now than it was just a few years ago. So it's an expensive tool, and it's an expensive tool to do correctly, but in the overall scheme of things, it's a very valuable investment. The general rule of thumb is that polling will consume 5–7 percent of a campaign's overall budget.

Q: Has it become harder to get a good sample, because of cell phones?

A: It has. As good pollsters, we're constantly trying to refine our methodologies to compensate for changes in technology and voter behavior. We're aware now that a quarter of all voters use cell phones as their only or primary way to communicate. We're now starting to have a quota or a percentage of our interviews that are cell phone-only or cell phone as a main use of communication. It's going to be a huge part of the future of polling, as will the Internet. And, I'm sure, at some point, so will be texting.

Q: Do you see any problem with Internet polling?

A: I don't see any problem. I think it's actually underused. Even phone polling is imperfect. People have to accept to take part in a poll. The same thing with the Internet. The biggest problem is getting probability-based samples from the Internet. It can be done, through companies such as Knowledge Network. Still, to do Internet or cell polling correctly is expensive. Some cell phone interviews can be two or three times as expensive as landline calling. And sometimes, when you're using the Internet, the costs can be even higher. It can also be lower. It just depends on what kind of methodology you use.

Q: What kind of different polling services do you offer?

A: If it's a campaign, we usually start with a benchmark—a messaging poll. It's usually about twenty minutes long. If it's a congressional campaign, it's usually a 500 sample. If it's a statewide campaign, the sample could be 600, 800, or a thousand. Sometimes you follow that with focus groups either before or after the benchmark. Depending on the timeline and the budget, you will sometimes go in with what we call a trend poll a few months later for message refinement. You might do that if you've got more things that need to be tested from opposition research, or when it's just time to go in and take another look. We're doing more ad testing, after the media folks have put ads together based on the benchmark. We're also doing focus groups on the Internet as well as in live in-person groups. We also do ad testing in person as well as on the Internet. Before the campaign goes up on TV, we usually do another trend poll just to be sure we know where we are before we start communicating. Then we do a series of tracking polls during the campaign. Again, the polls depend on budgets. In a high-end campaign, you would do the full program. But there's plenty of campaigns in which we do a benchmark, a track, and maybe that's it.

Q: To what extent have automated polls become a factor?

A: They're not a factor in the sense of making strategic decisions. Automated polls are very cheap, very inexpensive. They're not very regulated. Most campaign consultants won't use them. They're mostly done for news organizations. You can't use them to make strategic decisions. It's mostly who's ahead, who's behind, but it's almost impossible to use it for message development. There are a lot of news media, such as the *Washington Post*, who won't report on an automated poll. They don't think they're sufficiently valid.

Q: What about the charge that you're doing push polls?

A: There is a lot of confusion about push-polling versus message testing. A real push poll calls thousands of people and the sole purpose is to disseminate negative, often false information about an opponent. A legitimate message testing poll may test unflattering information about an opponent—or even your own candidate—to determine that

(Continued)

(*Continued*)

candidate's most serious vulnerability. But just because a poll has negative information in it, doesn't make it a "push poll" in the sense that it's underhanded or contains malicious information. The confusion usually comes from a campaign trying to muddy the waters and take advantage of a real poll. AnzaloneLiszt has nothing to do with push polls. A push poll is when you get a voter list, go down the line, and disseminate negative information. What we do is pull random samples and get valid questions answered. Push polling is not valid at all. It's not a real poll. The opposition may criticize a real poll that has someone testing something about a voting record, and that's nonsense.

Q: Does it hurt your credibility when you put something out for the press?

A: The press knows who's credible and who's not. I think mostly Republicans stand up and cry "push poll" when they can, but it's mostly a political ploy. Sometimes it gets some press, and sometimes it doesn't. Ultimately the credibility is in some level of transparency in terms of the methodology, and also in a firm's track record in previous cycles.

Q: Assuming that it's a major campaign, how often and to what extent are you in touch with the campaign?

A: If we're doing a major campaign, like a U.S. Senate race or governor's race, we're in daily communication with either the campaign manager or one of the consultants—the TV guy or the mail guy. It's daily and sometimes multiple daily. If you count the Internet, it's going to be multiple daily. But even with the phone, it's going to be daily. On big congressional races, I'd say that's the case too.

Q: To what extent do you watch out for trends and suggest changes that are not consistent with the original strategy?

A: There's always the X variable that's in every campaign. It's something that's going to happen that you can't see today. It's usually out of your control. Sometimes it is something that your opponent does, either in the primary or general [election]. But sometimes it's the national dynamics. There are certain things out of your control and all of a sudden you're talking about an issue that you hadn't anticipated talking about. Things just happen. In that case, you might do a shorter tracking poll, to keep a pulse on voters in almost based on what is happening in real time. But at the end of the day, you want to get back to your core message. Pollsters are often thought of as the "numbers people" and polling is certainly more science than art. But most pollsters can write a good poll and get numbers correctly, but a good pollster also needs to have street smarts and a gut feel for campaigns and how to turn the numbers into a real-world strategy.

Q: What about the different levels of professionalism in the field?

A: We have professional standards, we have professional organizations, but at the end of the day it's more difficult to be credible in the polling business than it is in hanging up a shingle for a media or mail consultant. There's a certain weightiness to polling—that it's a science, it's difficult, it's statistical and math based. You usually have to have some basis of intelligence in that field. The bigger issue is college professors who get some polling software and they're soon zipping out polls. But at the end of the day, if you're going to break in, credibility is a high bar to meet. We work on a national level, but on a very local level, you'll have people who do polling who're not necessarily qualified to do polling.

Q: One academic criticism of polling is that it leads to candidates catering to voters rather than leading them.

A: I don't necessarily buy that. At the end of the day, the general public's opinions are important. I think all elected officials would agree that knowing what people think on issues is important, because they're representing those people. In that sense, I think polling can be very helpful. Where it's detrimental is when you get a candidate who is a blank slate, and he says, "Tell me what I should say." That doesn't benefit anyone. We don't like working with that type of person. What we like working with is a person who has a high level of character and drive and accomplishments and who wants to help his constituents. The poll helps to separate the wheat from the chaff on those things that he's done or the vision that he or she has—which of those things resonate more intensely with voters. At the end of the day, voters are only going to capture so much of what any individual will say. So it's not a matter of telling them what to say, it's what of their vision, their traits, their accomplishments are things that can help them get elected.

Q: One final question. What's the future of polling?

A: I think the future of polling is debatable. I think that, quite frankly, the system in which we rely on is broken. We can't rely on just landlines anymore. Unless this industry is willing to move forward and experiment with future methodologies, we're going to be in trouble. The future is, I think, interviews by landlines, by cell phones, by Internet, and maybe even by text. You'll have to get a combination of these things to include everyone. Otherwise, we're going to get bad data. I think we're in a precarious situation. For the media consultant, the advances in digital are great. They purchase the studio equipment and their stuff looks great. It's a little more difficult with what we're trying to do. We're trying to deal with science. Therefore, we have to be much more careful in how we approach technology. Advances in technology are continuing to advance and change in real time. That's going to be a real hurdle for the industry. ■

Internet Polling

For decades, pollsters relied on telephone surveys or in-person interviews as the media for gathering data. That approach worked well in an era in which nearly all households had at least one telephone, but the ever increasing use of cell phones knocked a hole in that assumption. An ever-growing number of people are dropping their landlines entirely, relying on their cell phones as their only means of telephone communication. This trend is particularly strong among young people, resulting in a situation in which traditional polling techniques don't adequately represent this group in their samples.

One solution has been to rely on Internet polling. Prior to 2008, Internet polling was viewed with disdain by communication critics who put it in the same category as pseudo-polling (Kent, Harrison, & Taylor, 2006). But its extensive and successful use in the 2008 elections muted that criticism. The procedures associated with Internet polling have been gradually developed (see, for example, Couper, Conrad, & Tourangeau, 2007; Heerwegh & Loosveldt, 2008; Porter & Whitcomb, 2007). Internet polling had already worked well in traditional marketing research, particularly when marketing online merchandise. Further, researchers have also used Internet polling to successfully gather data relating to employee satisfaction. As of this writing, Internet polling has not been fully implemented into political polling. There are, however, two major exceptions to that trend. First, some pollsters use Internet polling to supplement their traditional polling technique. After completing a round of calls using telephone surveys, they may supplement the data with Internet polling to ensure that they reach a sufficient sample of young voters or some other subgroup not adequately represented in the telephone sample.

Second, Internet polling allows for longer answers than can be gathered with a telephone survey. Thus, the Internet can be used to gather information from in-depth interviews with a smaller sample. The medium can even be used for online focus groups (see below), which allows the participants to express their opinions about a product or a political candidate.

Finally, the latest research indicates that the sample quality for an Internet survey is similar to that of a telephone survey. Ansolabehere and Schaffner (2011) compared landline/cell phone surveys, mail surveys, and opt-in Internet surveys. They found little differences in the samples between the phone surveys and the Internet surveys. The average difference was five percentage points, and both techniques produced similar correlational structures.

THE PROCESS OF POLITICAL POLLING
Questionnaire Development

The process of political polling begins with the questionnaire development. Typically, the pollsters and the candidate (and media consultant) discuss the issues and circumstances surrounding the campaign. As a result of the discussion, the pollster develops a first draft of questions to test these relevant factors. This is followed by subsequent rounds of discussions and revisions until all parties are satisfied that the questionnaire will provide the information sought.

Guidelines for Writing Questions Designing a questionnaire requires that the pollster be careful in constructing and writing the questions themselves. Questions need to be direct, clear, and unambiguous. Furthermore, unless there is a specific reason for testing audience biases, most questions should be phrased in an unbiased manner. This can be difficult, because many candidates prefer only to phrase questions from their own perspective, not that of their opponent. Still, the pollster has been of little use to the campaign if the survey does not provide unbiased information.

Most pollsters use some version of forced-choice options or Likert-type questions. Forced-choice options are closed-ended questions that limit respondent options (such as "Yes" or "No"). Likert-type questions expand the options slightly to cover a broader continuum of responses, but still offer limited options (such as "strongly agree, somewhat agree, undecided, somewhat disagree, or strongly disagree").

Other techniques have sometimes been attempted, but with limited success. Some pollsters use a "feeling thermometer," in which respondents rate candidates and issues on a scale ranging from zero to one hundred. Generally, most voters have trouble making such fine distinctions. Research, in fact, indicates that voters make their most optimum distinctions about candidates and issues if the options are limited to no more than nine intervals. Furthermore, some voters interpret the zero to one hundred scale differently; some view it as if it is an academic scale. As a result, the midpoint of "fifty," which should be an average rating, is considered a "failing grade" by some respondents.

Zaller and Feldman (1992) oppose both the Likert-type scales and alternative scales like the feeling thermometer, arguing that attitudes on issues are particularly difficult to measure as precise preference points. They argue that issue positions may be based on a number of considerations that might move them toward any number of positions on an issue. These "considerations" are underlying arguments that are recalled from memory and may vary with time (Chong, 1993). Zaller (1990) also argues that responses to survey questions are influenced by the political sophistication of the respondents, and that pollsters err by giving the same weight to the responses of uninformed voters and the responses of political sophisticates. The only way to counter this, they argue, is to measure attitudes within a range of possible responses that are either acceptable or not acceptable to the voter. From an academic perspective, Zaller and Feldman have a valid point. From a consulting perspective, attempting to measure attitudes within ranges of responses is expensive and may produce limited additional information for the client. Few candidates are willing to pay for the extra expense to do so.

Several different types of survey questions are often employed. These include the greeting, the screen, favorability ratings, test ballots, issue questions, message questions, open-ended questions, and demographic questions.

The Greeting   The greeting is a brief statement that introduces the interviewer to the telephone respondent and leads to a question about their interest in responding to the survey. Typically, the greeting starts with an introduction ("Hello, I'm John Doe,...") and identification of the research unit ("... and I'm calling from JLP Research"). As Stacks and Hocking (1998) noted, these two elements serve "as a credibility inducement and provides indication that the project is important" (p. 251).

The Screen   If the respondent agrees to participate, the next job for the interviewer is to determine whether they qualify for the survey. This qualification element is operationally defined by the survey's screen, a question that verifies their eligibility. For political polls, the minimal and basic screening question is one that asks whether or not the respondent is a registered voter; if not, the phone call should be terminated. Most pollsters add additional screens, however, depending on the nature and circumstances of the campaign. These might include questions regarding whether the respondent plans to vote in the election, and the likelihood of their doing so.

Favorability Ratings   The first questions asked on many political surveys are favorability questions designed to measure positive and negative evaluations of candidates. Favorability ratings are typically phrased as, "Do you have a very favorable, somewhat favorable, somewhat unfavorable, or very unfavorable opinion of Candidate X?" Voters who are unable to offer an opinion on a candidate might be coded into one of several other categories ("unsure," "don't recognize," and so forth). Campaigns monitor favorability ratings for themselves and their opposition closely on tracking polls, since communication impacts often show up on these ratings before they are noticed in the test ballots.

Test Ballots   The most frequently cited questions on a survey or poll are usually the test ballot questions ("If the election for Position A were held today, would you vote for Candidate X or Candidate Y?"). The test ballot gives the most direct test of the relative success or failure of the campaign, serving as an index of which candidate is ahead at that point in the campaign. Its true value to the campaign varies, though, depending on when the survey is taken.

Another version of the test ballot, one that frequently appears on vulnerability surveys, is the "definite reelect" question: "If the election were held today, would you definitely vote to reelect Candidate X, like to consider someone else, or would you definitely vote against Candidate X?" This version of the test ballot is used when testing the vulnerability of incumbents. It can be used even when there is no known opponent for that incumbent. Responses give pollsters an indication of the size of core support and core opposition to the incumbent.

Mood of the Electorate   These questions are designed with the intent to identify underlying trends that can have an influence on the election. The classic question of this type is the standard "right direction–wrong direction" question, which is used to measure satisfaction with the political system. A typical wording is, "Generally, do you believe things in America are headed in the right direction, or have things gotten off onto the wrong track?"

Issue Questions   Issue questions are intended to measure voter reactions to the major political issues of the day. Although the question formats vary considerably, the most common techniques for measuring issues are in terms of support or opposition of an issue, agreement or disagreement with a position, or forced choices on major positions. Support and opposition questions generally use a Likert-type approach such as "Do you strongly support, somewhat support, somewhat oppose, or strongly oppose requiring a three-day waiting period for the purchases of handguns?"

Image Questions   Some survey questions measure specific areas of the candidate's image, an area that Hamilton and Beattie (1999, p. 99) refer to as "personalities." Although the format of image questions can vary, many use an "agree–disagree" format or a rating format, such as one to ten, which provides a range of possible image dimensions.

Message Questions   Frequently, the candidate and/or the media consultant will test messages that might be used in the campaign. Furthermore, the campaign can often anticipate the messages that the opposition is likely to use. Both elements are included in the survey so that the candidate and the consultants have some estimate of the relative strength of each message. Message questions are sometimes phrased in a "more or less likely to vote for" approach, which asks, "Would you be more or less likely to vote for a candidate who … ," with the specific message used as a tag line.

Open-Ended Questions   One problem with most survey questions is that the respondents can only answer what is asked. When only closed (or forced) option questions are used, the pollster cannot identify what other issues or factors may be operating within the electorate. One way to counter this problem is to use open-ended questions that allow the respondents to express an opinion with no guidance from the pollster.

Demographic Questions   Demographic questions measure attributes of the respondents such as age, income, party affiliation, gender, and ethnic background. They are usually delayed until the end of the survey, and they serve three purposes. First, they allow the pollster to stratify the sample and verify its representativeness. Second, cross-tabulations of the results, by these demographic questions, are the primary statistical analyses for the survey. Third, the demographic breakdowns provide crucial targeting information to the campaign.

Sampling

Ideally, political polling is a scientific process for describing the attitudinal and demographic makeup of a voting population at any given point in time. Polling is based on the mathematical principles of sampling, a process that projects that the responses of a representative portion of the electorate can be used to gauge the responses of the electorate as a whole. The accuracy of any political poll, though, will depend upon the extent to which the sample represents the actual voting turnout on election day. For that reason, the use of some means of random sampling is essential, and a variety of techniques have been developed for that purpose. Still, there is no such thing as a perfect sample technique. All have limitations, although most are minor.

The most common approach, regardless of how the list is generated, is to use a process called stratified random sampling. In this approach, the pollster predetermines how many responses are needed in each category of one major demographic variable (usually geography), and then respondents are randomly selected from within each of the subgroups of that category. As the survey progresses, calls are monitored to ensure that they correspond to the projected participation on one other variable (usually gender). After the survey is completed, the other demographic variables are tested to ensure that each category of those factors is adequately represented. This approach is the preferred choice of most pollsters because it guarantees that certain groups within the population will be sampled. As Hansen et al. (1998, p. 241) noted, stratified random sampling "allows for the appropriate representation of different groups in the population" to ensure that the sample represents the population under study.

Interviewing

Most political polling involves the use of telephone interviews and professional callers. Professional interviewers know to read the questions as they are written, know when to repeat questions that are not understood, and know to refrain from commenting or reacting nonverbally. Even then, there will be problems, because not everyone reached by telephone will agree to respond to the survey. Yu and Cooper (1983), in an analysis of surveys reported in academic journals, found that the average completion rate for telephone surveys was about 72 percent, and that that estimate applied only to those who did not refuse to participate during the greeting or screening stage. Wimmer and Dominick (1994, p. 121) recommend that telephone surveys be limited to a maximum of twenty minutes in length, since there is a significant increase in the breakoff rate (hang-ups) when interviews exceed that length. Electronic surveys have to be even shorter, since it is easier for people to hang up on a machine than another human (Havice, 1990).

Data Analysis

Data analysis for a political poll is considerably simpler than similar types of analyses conducted for academic polls. The basic level of analysis is a simple cross-tabulation, with crosstabs conducted on each individual survey question. The independent variables for the analysis are typically the demographic questions and the test ballot. The primary statistical analysis used is the Chi-Square (χ^2), but this statistic is often not reported to the campaign. Instead, the data analysis is provided to the campaign in the form of tabular columns (banners) that identify, by frequency and percentages, the responses of the overall sample and of each demographic subgroup.

LEVEL OF CONFIDENCE AND THE CONFIDENCE INTERVAL

Confidence level (or level of confidence) refers to the extent to which the pollster has confidence that the findings obtained from any one particular survey will fall within a specified interval. The width of that specified interval is referred to as the margin of error. The minimum level of confidence for social science research is usually 95 percent. As the sample size increases, the margin of error decreases. Thus, the margin of error for a sample of 300 is ±4.9 percentage points, but that drops to ±4.0 for a sample of 600. The margin of error for a sample of 1,000 is ±3.1 percentage points, and that for a sample of 1,200 would be ±2.8 percentage points. Reducing the margin of error any lower than that requires considerably larger sample sizes.

As a result, few surveys employ sample sizes larger than 1,200. It simply becomes cost prohibitive, with relatively few resulting benefits. Such larger sample sizes can typically be justified only if there is some specific need to analyze some of the subgroups in more detail.

Report Writing

The utility of polling information largely depends on the pollster's ability to interpret the numbers and provide that interpretation to the campaign. This is typically done in a written report. Most reports include a summary of conclusions and a set of crosstabs that report the frequency of responses to each question from each respondent in a particular demographic category. The harder task is assigning meaning to the numbers. Sometimes small numbers may be a sign of a bigger or growing trend. Democratic pollster William Hamilton notes that the public may exhibit a "low-grade fever" for change that may have a dramatic impact on eventual voting behavior (Taylor, 1990, p. 224). In October 1989, for example, President George H. W. Bush received a 75 percent positive rating in a Time/CNN poll, even though most voters (between 72 percent and 86 percent) consistently opposed his public policy agenda. By 1992, that discrepancy had grown to the point that the incumbent president was eventually defeated by Bill Clinton.

WHAT CAN GO WRONG

Any number of things can confound the results and lead to unreliable poll numbers. The most common problems are sampling errors, question framing, ordering effects, and interviewer effects.

Sampling errors are perhaps the most common mistake. If the sample in the survey is not representative of those voters who will vote on election day, the survey is likely to be inaccurate. Other times, the pollster may use a stratified random sample based on turnout patterns of previous elections; if those turnout patterns are altered in future elections, the survey will be inaccurate. In addition, the sample can be affected by the use of improper screening questions. Some media surveys, for example, screen only for "head of household" or for "registered voters." Most pollsters believe a more accurate sample is generated by what is known as a "tight" screen in which only "probable voters" are selected for the survey. Even then, overreporting can occur if nonvoters get through the screen.

Question framing is another major factor that affects the results (Box-Steffensmeier, Jacobson, & Grant, 2000; Hansen et al., 1998, pp. 244–246). Ideally, questions used in the survey should be clear and simple, requiring a minimum amount of effort on the part of the respondent. Lengthy questions create confusion, with the respondent often forgetting the first few options by the time the last ones have been recited (Wimmer & Dominick, 1994, p. 109). Responses can also be influenced by the verbs used in the question; people often agree with questions that ask whether they believe something should be "allowed" or "forbidden," regardless of the topic (Holleman, 2000). During the controversy over the Obama healthcare proposal in 2010, for example, different polling organizations reported different results primarily because they asked different questions (Sussman, 2010).

"Interviewer effects" refers to those responses that are produced as a result of the behaviors of the interviewer. In general, telephone interviews have minimal interviewer effects if the calls are made by professionals (MacLin & Calder, 2006).

Further, experienced callers can conduct such a survey faster and more efficiently than amateurs (Olson & Peytchev, 2007). Research has indicated that face-to-face interviews can be influenced by the type of clothing worn by the interviewer (Hickson & Stacks, 1992; McPeek & Edwards, 1975), his or her ethnic background (Finkel, Guterbock, & Berg, 1991), a number of nonverbal cues (such as nodding, smiling, or tone of voice), and by verbal cues (Conrad & Schroder, 2000). Most political surveys are conducted by telephone, which at least eliminates those factors related to the personal appearance of the interviewer. But telephone interviewing does not eliminate all interview effects. Gubrium and Holstein (2001) note that, even over the telephone, the respondents' answers can be influenced by their perception of the interviewer and the interviewer's perception of the respondents. Additional control can be obtained by using professional interviewers who are not connected to the campaign. Preferably, the telephone personnel who conduct the survey should not even be aware of which candidate is paying for the survey, thus limiting their ability to influence the results. Another technique is to use callers who do not know any of the candidates. This is frequently done by subcontracting the phone calls to a phone bank in a state different from that of the campaign.

One common demonstration of how interviewer effects alter a poll can be seen with the use of "volunteer" polling. To save money, some low-budget campaigns will sometimes use volunteers to conduct their own in-house polling for the campaign. This approach invariably overinflates support for the candidate. Even if extensive training is conducted for each of the volunteers, it is still impossible to eliminate all of the subtle cues that they will give to respondents. Consequently, the survey results will be tainted.

THE ETHICAL CONTROVERSY GENERATED BY POLITICAL POLLING

From the consulting perspective, polling has a positive impact on political campaigning. It provides campaigns with a sense of audience analysis, or at least an impression of the public's perception toward any number of issues. Others argue that polling contributes to the democratic process by identifying the areas of most concern to the voters (Jacobs & Shapiro, 2005), an effect that may be even stronger when applied to issue polls related to specific states (Turner, O'Connor, & Rademacher, 2009). Other research has reported that the polling results had an impact on the policy developments of both Presidents Nixon (Druckman & Jacobs, 2006) and Reagan (Murray, 2006). Jacobs and Shapiro (2000) argued that polling has played a major role in presidential crafting of policies.

Still, several observers have criticized polls, arguing that the poll results have too much impact on campaigns and candidates. Taylor (1990) argued that polling has had a negative impact on the political process because "politicians have become increasingly dependent on the technologies of political market research… to guard against ever uttering an unpopular word in public (p. 218)." Taylor quotes Democratic pollster Stan Greenberg as saying, "The dialogue has become more sterile because the campaign ads are designed to repeat back to voters what they already know."

Such attitudes are not particularly new. Former President Harry Truman similarly lambasted the use of polls during his term in office. "How far would Moses have gone if he had taken a poll in Egypt?" Truman asked. "What would Jesus Christ have preached if he had taken a poll in the land of Israel? What would have happened to the Reformation if Martin Luther had taken a poll? It isn't polls or public opinion of the moment that count. It's right and wrong and leadership." Dionne (1991) gave a similar assessment of focus groups, but the comments could easily be applied to polling research. "The focus group may be the perfect symbol of what has happened to democracy in America. Insofar as 'the people' are consulted by political leaders these days, their reactions are of interest not as a guide to policy but simply as a way of exploring the electorate's gut feelings, to see which kind of (usually divisive) message might move them the most. The approach to politics is not even Machiavellian; it is Pavlovian" (p. 311).

Others argue just the opposite. Jacobs and Shapiro (2000) question whether political leaders base decisions on public opinion or poll data. They argue instead that politicians increasingly ignore public opinion in favor of their own views and those of their major supporters. The result, they would argue, is politicians have become less responsive to public opinion than in the 1960s and 1970s, while the use of polls has increased over the same span of time. Similarly, Fishkin (1995) complains that the voice of the public is often never heard by political elites. Herbst (1998) agreed, concluding that many political elites reject the voice of the people as uninformed or nebulous.

Ryan and Wentworth (1999) argue that polling has a negative impact on news coverage of political campaigns, with the media "focusing more on who is ahead and who is behind than the substance of political issues" (p. 81). Research supports that criticism. The number of poll-related stories has increased in recent years. Stories about polls have also been given a higher priority within newscasts, and reporters have increasingly defined campaigns as based on the success of the candidate's campaign activities, as measured by polls (Craig, 2000). One reason is that many reporters are not well informed on the issues themselves, and coverage of polls is easier to do. Others argue that the public is also more interested in the ups and downs of political careers, or relative changes in candidate positions in the polls, than they are in specific issues. Regardless of the cause, though, today's media (newspapers, magazines, radio, the Internet, and TV) do indeed have a strong focus on "horse-race" coverage, with many media outlets now conducting their own surveys (thus creating their own news).

In at least one instance, polling has influenced a campaign. During the 2004 presidential election, Democratic challenger John Kerry frequently complained about incumbent George W. Bush's "stubbornness" during the campaign. That led the *Los Angeles Times* to include the trait in one of their national polls on the campaign, with the poll finding that Bush was viewed as more stubborn than Kerry. The result, according to Hardy and Jamieson (2005), was that the poll "produced an attribute agenda-setting effect that strengthened the link between that term and Bush" (p. 725).

Herbst (1998) questioned the validity and neutrality of polling. She argued that the validity was in question because the impact of polls is based more on the assessment of political elites (journalists, political activists, legislative staffers) than upon the attitudes of the mass public. The neutrality of polling is also open to criticism, she added, because numbers do more than convey neutral information, but also serve as a basis of authority. Those numbers can be influenced by the manner in which public opinion is measured. Political polls often work within a "file drawer" model that incorrectly assumes that attitudes are stored in memory and retrieved when a question is asked during the survey (Tourangeau, Rips, & Rasinski, 2000). That model leads to surveys that ask questions that the respondent may have never considered. When that occurs, the survey may be creating and constructing an attitude for the respondent, rather than measuring it. Fishkin (1995) recommends a technique he calls a "deliberative poll," in which a large representative sample is gathered at one location; he polls the participants only after one or two days of intense discussion and education on an issue.

Cantril and Cantril (1999) identified a "mixed signals" effect that is often present in polls, noting that public opinion polls often produce contradictory results. Not only will polls from different candidates have different numbers, but contradictions often exist within the same poll. Voters will often, for example, say they oppose an increase in taxes while supporting increased government spending. They attribute the phenomenon to a subgroup of voters called the "ambivalents." They also identified another subgroup (largely conservative Republicans) called the "steady critics," who have little confidence in government but are highly involved in politics. Their responses can also send mixed signals in a poll.

Former Democratic pollster Paul Maslin believes polling contributed to the rise in negative campaigns, a criticism that has received some research support (Daves & Newport, 2005). As quoted by Taylor (1990), Maslin said, "It's like taking a shot, because you can see the way they [negative ads] move the numbers. The techniques have gotten so refined, the weapons so powerful, that if you don't use them, you'll lose" (p. 218). Maslin's comment seem to echo the pragmatics of polling in modern political contests. The ethical issue to be addressed is not whether to use them, but merely how to use them in an ethical manner. Polling is merely a sophisticated form of audience analysis—a basic skill taught in nearly all communication courses. If audience analysis is important for other forms of communication, why not for political campaigns? Political candidates have a right and, ideally, an obligation to consider the beliefs and values of the people they represent. In a time when a single officeholder may represent thousands or millions of people, polling provides a means of assessing those beliefs and values.

Sometimes polls are wrong. At their best, they are snapshots of an election at a specific point in time. Still, more often than not, they are remarkably accurate. Consider the 2004 presidential election, for example, where polls became a hotly debated topic during that campaign (Frankovic, 2005), but still accurately predicted a close race between incumbent George W. Bush and Democratic challenger John Kerry (Traugott, 2005).

Research indicates that concern over the impact of polls on elections is over stated. The concern appears to arise from what is known as the third-person effect, that is, perceptions that media will have an impact on other people by not on one's self. Price and Stroud (2006) reported that most of the concerns resulted from perceptions of "untoward effects" that respondents feared might influence other voters (p. 393).

PSEUDOPOLLING

One form of polling sometimes used in unethical ways is the category known as "pseudopolls." These include call-in surveys, push polls, and cyberpolling.

Call-in Surveys

Call-in surveys are a popular media feature in which the public is provided a question and asked to phone in their responses, a technique first used by ABC News during the televised Carter–Reagan presidential debate on October 28, 1980 (Frankel & Frankel, 1987). While call-in surveys can produce interesting results, they have no scientific validity and may contain substantial errors (Gerhard, 1990). The sample is a process of self-selection rather than a random sample. Although call-in poll participants are demographically similar to the population as a whole, they are more opinionated than telephone survey respondents (Cotter, Perry, & Stovall, 1994) and more likely to be activists with a prochange mentality (Bates & Harmon, 1993). Furthermore, participation in some call-in surveys costs money (sometimes fifty cents or a dollar per call); that monetary intrusion biases political responses for Republicans, who are typically more able to afford the call and spend the money. Finally, call-in surveys cannot control how many times a particular person responds; any one person could make multiple calls to the computer, and they could get their friends and relatives to do the same. If a call-in survey addresses a "hot" issue, its results are more likely to indicate the relative organizational strength of the candidates than it is their popular support. Unfortunately, despite their problems, call-in polls tend to be credible to media audiences. As many as one third of newspaper readers believe they are credible sources of information, especially for readers with less formal education (Gerhard, 1990).

Push Polls

Push polls are not polls at all, but merely a questionable form of phone bank persuasion. This approach takes advantage of the public's familiarity with the polls by calling a respondent under the pretense of conducting a poll. Once the person agrees to participate, they are read a list of questions designed to imply negative information about an opponent. Thus, instead of eliciting unbiased information from the respondents, the survey is merely used as a form of negative or smear campaigning.

A typical push poll was used in the 2000 South Carolina Republican presidential primary by George W. Bush. A phone bank in Houston, Texas (Voter Consumer Research), called South Carolina voters and asked a series of carefully scripted questions. The initial questions were simple and straightforward— Will you participate in the Republican primary? How much attention have you paid to the Republican race? Are things better or worse in the country?—but the later questions were used as a means of providing negative information on Bush's competitor John McCain. The questions were not really questions, but merely messages disguised in a question format that attacked McCain's position on tax cuts, told the voters McCain had been reprimanded by the Senate Ethics

Committee, and argued that his campaign finance plan would give more influence to unions and to the press (Yardley, 2000).

An earlier example emerged in a 1996 issue debate in Texas over the tobacco issue. A tobacco company (Phillip Morris) hired Public Opinion Strategies, an Alexandria, Virginia, firm to develop a push poll against the state's attorney general, Dan Morales, who was preparing to file a lawsuit against several tobacco companies. The script "included more than a dozen negative statements about Mr. Morales's record as attorney general" and the resulting information was used in an attempt to get him to drop the lawsuit (Van Natta, 2000).

SUMMARY

Polling and survey research has become an integral part of modern campaigns, one that is so integral to the process that the informed voter should have a basic understanding of its role in the democratic process (Asher, 1992). What began as new technology for presidential elections during the 1970s has since become standard practice in most major campaigns. Its use has gradually filtered down to lower-level elections, and is now commonly used in many state and local campaigns. Most successful campaigns use polling, and those that do not are at a strategic disadvantage.

Is that good or bad? Some critics complain that modern polling techniques have motivated political candidates to alter their campaign practices. No longer do they lead the voters on issues of concerns; they merely follow the voters' concerns instead. Polls are used to identify voter priorities, and those priorities are mouthed back to them in the campaign. In its most essential form, though, polling is merely an extended form of audience analysis. It provides the political rhetor with an understanding of the attitudes and values of the audience to be addressed. Such a function has always been performed in political campaigns. In the past, though, candidates would go out to talk with voters individually to seek their feedback, with no way to ascertain whether what they were hearing was representative of all of their constituents. Polling provides more precision to that effort. The function hasn't changed, merely the precision with which it is done.

Pollsters have refined their techniques over the past decade. In addition to live telephone surveys, they now solicit voter input via the Internet and through computerized robo-calls. Focus group data can also be gathered over the Internet to provide further insight into voter attitudes.

Even some of the critics of polling accept its utility. Sociologist Alan Wolfe (1998) prefers to use ethnographic methodologies in which in-depth interviews are conducted with a large number of participants. Such methodologies, he believes, move beyond poll data and provide a better understanding of the people's beliefs (p. 278). Still, even he noted that "America is rightly guided by its polls; besides the results of the previous election, ... politicians have little else to go on in formulating their views than the polls" (p. 277). After all, to represent the public, they should have at least some sense of what the public believes.

QUESTIONS FOR DISCUSSION

1. To what extent do political polls shape and influence public opinion instead of merely measuring it? How and why might this occur?

2. Some political theorists argue that the success of democracy rests upon public opinion. If so, to what extent does political polling add to or detract from a successful democratic process?

3. Political polls usually make no attempt to survey the entire public, but only the voting public. To what extent does this add to or detract from the democratic process?

Campaign Concerns

During any political campaign, a number of issues and concerns will arise that must be addressed. Many of these will be campaign specific, with too many variations to discuss in this book. However, some general elements typically must be addressed by all campaigns. Some of these factors represent campaign thresholds or contingencies, conditions that must be achieved if the campaign is to be competitive.

Chapter 12 discusses a major communication concern of the campaign: press coverage. Press coverage of presidential campaigns has the potential to influence the outcome of the election. Coverage of statewide elections can influence what issues candidates discuss, and which candidates are best known to the voters. At any level, press coverage can have an impact on whether a candidate is viewed as a legitimate contender for a position. This chapter will discuss press coverage in terms of the factors affecting press coverage, topics covered by the press, and the types of events that can generate press coverage. The campaign team member who is most heavily involved in this aspect of the campaign is the press secretary, and special attention is devoted to that role.

Chapter 13 looks at the financial side of politics. Political campaigns are often massive money machines, with part of the organization raising funds while the rest spends it. Money is more than just the fuel of the campaign organization, though. Campaign fund-raising can have a persuasive impact that influences press coverage, bestows legitimacy on a campaign, and reduces the competition. The financial side of politics represents a threshold that must be met if a campaign is to be effective, but it is also at the center of an ethical debate that should be addressed. This chapter looks at those elements and their impact on campaigns, candidates, and the political process.

Chapter 14 looks at the role of interpersonal communication from several viewpoints. Interpersonal communication is a key part of the opinion leadership process, with citizens discussing their views with friends, neighbors, and coworkers while refining their voting decision. Interpersonal communication plays a key role in the diffusion of information from political elites to the public. Communication between candidates and political elites influences legislation and other public decisions. Political lobbying illustrates the role that interpersonal communication can have in the drafting of legislation. Legislative cue-giving looks at the impact of interpersonal communication on legislative votes, as one lawmaker talks to another.

Chapter 15 looks at a specific way of analyzing campaigns: critical events analysis. Critical events analysis is the study of major discrete events that test the relationship between media and politics. From a campaign perspective, critical events analysis is a rare convergence of academic and consulting perspectives, albeit each approaches the topic from a different perspective. Scholars seek to identify major events—debates, convention speeches, major public appearances—that can influence a campaign. For consultants, critical events are predictive factors, points and events within a campaign that can be anticipated to have a major impact; special care and attention are given to preparing for them.

This book ends with Chapter 16 and its discussion of ethical questions in political communication. Included in this discussion is a look at several different types of unethical behaviors in campaigns, the controversy surrounding negative campaigning, and the role of consultants. The chapter ends with a section devoted to the primary goal of the book: becoming critical observers of the process. We hope that by the end of Chapter 15, the reader will feel more qualified to make critical and ethical judgments about the political campaign process.

Press Coverage and Media Relations

If he had to campaign today, George Washington might not win the presidency. He didn't like to make public presentations, sometimes writing his presidential speeches but never delivering them. And, forced to wear uncomfortable dentures, he had trouble smiling in public. All in all, he would not have made a good media candidate.

Compare that to the press campaigns of Bill Clinton. During his eight years in office, Clinton was beset by both financial and moral controversies that threatened his presidency and triggered an impeachment process. During it all, Clinton maintained relatively high ratings with the public, enough to remain in office for two full terms. Kurtz (1998) attributes Clinton's success to a highly effective team that effectively influenced press coverage to the president's advantage. Their primary techniques were the use of controlled leaks, carefully worded briefs, and avoidance of some questions. Simple techniques, really, but ones that allowed the Clinton administration to control the scope and coverage of news stories.

Or consider the 2008 campaign of Barack Obama. His presidential campaign was the most media intensive in history and covered a wide range of media outlets. He overmatched his Democratic opponents in the primaries and, in the general election, his skills served to highlight the relative weaknesses of Republican John McCain's media image.

The skills possessed by candidates such as Clinton and Obama took decades to develop. They build on a media tradition that included, in its early stages, the "fireside chats" of President Franklin Roosevelt. Dwight Eisenhower became the first president to use televised press conferences and the first to establish a television studio in the White House (Allen, 1993). That early development has evolved into a government–press relationship that includes talk radio (Bobbitt, 2010; Holbert, 2004), cable news (Brubaker & Hanson, 2009), and reporters embedded in military groups (Pfau, Haigh, & Gettle, 2004). Indeed, today's candidates have to be media savvy both for the press and for entertainment venues (Holbert, 2005), such as movies (Riegert, 2007); and a variety of television shows (Giglio, 2005), such as *Saturday Night Live* and *The Daily Show*, have entered the political arena.

In today's political environment, saying that someone is both a "good candidate" and also "effective with the media" is unnecessarily redundant. Television is the "window on the world" through which most people follow political activities (Ansolabehere, Behr, & Iyengar, 1993). In most major campaigns, the candidate must have media-friendly characteristics to even be considered as a contender. Altschull (1995) argues that the power of the news media includes a social control function that influences campaigns and public policy. Nimmo (1970) noted that news coverage influences voter impressions of the candidate's credibility and character (p. 130). Neuman, Just, and Crigler (1992) see it as a vital agent in the construction of political meaning. Gunther and Christen (1999) found that voters rely on news coverage as a source for assessing public opinion. Chaffee, Zhou, and Leshner (1994) found that news coverage, including coverage of special events, interviews, and talks shows, added to the predictability of election outcomes. Simon (1996) found that newspaper use is related to the likelihood that a person will vote in an election, while Leshner and McKean (1997) noted that TV news played a critical role in providing knowledge about candidates. Gunter (1998) noted that the media have at least an indirect impact resulting simply from the pervasive assumptions that the media make about society, and the effect is particularly strong for television news (Wilson & Howard, 1978). Ryan and Wentworth (1999) noted, "Whatever the magnitude of the effect on voters' behavior, media coverage now plays a major role in political campaigns" (p. 80).

There is nothing new about that concept. Campaigners have long recognized that voters placed more credibility in news coverage of the campaign than they did in the campaigns' self-created propaganda. Campaign efforts to take advantage of that trend have also been part of the process for centuries; supporters of both John Adams and Thomas Jefferson printed ads disguised as news (Seib, 1994). But the complexity of modern news organizations has made the task considerably more complex. Multiple factors go into a decision by a news organization when they must consider how much coverage should be devoted to a candidate or an issue. Some argue that the best coverage goes to those who are most adept at playing the "media game" (Ansolabehere, Behr, & Iyengar, 1993). Inevitably, some are covered while others—including some that might be of equal importance—are not; those who understand and adapt their message to the press are more likely to get press coverage and the credibility that is associated with it. As Sigal (1986, p. 15) noted, "News is not what happens, but what someone says has happened or will happen."

One role of the consultant is to plant the seeds for stories that will increase positive coverage for their client. Hamilton Jordan, a consultant for President Jimmy Carter, expressed the consultant's view: "Stories in the *New York Times* and *Washington Post* do not just happen, but have to be carefully planned and planted" (quoted in Schram, 1976, p. 67). German (1995) recognized the rhetorical edge that could be gained in the press by power and rhetorical skills, skills that Duffy (1997) referred to as "the role of rhetorical artistry in gaining desired news coverage" (p. 117). Journalists, she added, can get "caught up in the fantasy themes and rhetorical visions produced by (public relations campaigns of) corporations and powerful interest groups, (and) the underlying ideologies they represent are rarely questioned" (p. 130).

Shogan (2001) went even further, arguing that the modern press plays the role of enablers by allowing candidates and their consultants to use the press to abuse the political process. Didion (2001) agreed, calling the entire process one of "political fiction" that resembles Hollywood more than an American democracy. National politics, she argued, is a carefully choreographed drama that is created by political professionals (politicians, consultants, reporters) for the consumption of a public that has little impact on the drama. Similarly, Bennett (2001) describes political press coverage as the "politics of illusion." Political news, he argued, is a romanticized version of events that hide the actual political circumstances involved. "Indeed," he wrote, "the mark of skill in the political trade is the ability to make the public version of a situation convincing, no matter how far removed from actuality it may be" (p. 114). At the very least, then, an understanding of political campaign communication requires an understanding of how politicians and candidates interact with news organizations for the purposes of news coverage.

FACTORS INFLUENCING NEWS COVERAGE

Candidate Credibility

Perhaps the single most important factor influencing coverage of a candidate is the credibility of the candidate. With only rare exceptions (when a candidate is so outrageous that he or she is interesting for example), news organizations provide little coverage to candidates whom they perceive as having little chance of winning an election. In most cases, their assessment of candidate credibility is based on two factors: previous political experience and financial support. Experience through serving in previous political positions provides automatic credibility to most candidates, particularly if one is the incumbent officeholder in a "stepping-stone" position. For example, the press will nearly always provide coverage to gubernatorial candidates who are incumbents in such positions as lieutenant governor, attorney general, or secretary of state. Congressmen who decide to run for the U.S. Senate have a similar, out-of-the-starting-gate credibility with the press. Experience is not limited to experience in public office; it can also be applied to public experience at dealing with high-profile issues. For example, individuals who have spent most of their career promoting education might choose to run for a public position related to that issue. Their long-time career in that arena would be enough to bestow automatic legitimacy to their candidacy, thus ensuring press coverage.

Perhaps the biggest factor that can establish credibility with the press for a candidate is that of financial resources. Press coverage of candidates tends to correspond to how much money they spend during the campaign. Any candidate who demonstrates an ability to raise significant financial resources becomes a legitimate candidate. Similarly, any candidate who has enough personal financial resources to finance his or her own campaign will receive similar significant press coverage. In 1992, for example, Independent presidential candidate H. Ross Perot received extensive media coverage despite his small chances of winning the election. His personal fortune guaranteed his ability to mount an extensive campaign, regardless of its odds for success, and thus led to heavy coverage by the press. At the state level, self-financed candidates have sometimes been successful, with successful businessmen who were political novices winning election as their state's governors (e.g., John Warner in Kentucky and Fob James in Alabama).

Nature of the News

Newspapers and the broadcast media cover things that are "newsworthy," but not necessarily things that are "news" and/or "worthy." The press is more likely to cover a story about an individual than it will one about an issue, something that Jamieson and Campbell (1997) called the "tendency to focus on people rather than processes" (p. 41). News is also a daily commodity. Roughly the same amount of time and space is devoted to news each day. Unfortunately, not as much happens on some days as it does on others. On slow news days, reporters are looking for stories to cover, and an energetic candidate's chances of getting coverage increases. Even then, though, reporters are also more likely to be event driven rather than issue driven; for example, they are more likely to report on a protest against an insurance company (a one-day event) than to report on issues related to the insurance industry.

Reporters are also drawn to conflict, so candidates and groups seeking coverage often look for ways to express their issue as a conflict. A candidate complaining about unfair labor policies has less chance of getting covered than does a group that calls for a labor strike against a company. A strike is an event representing conflict; a candidate's press conference is merely rhetoric. The attractiveness of conflict for reporters leads to another maxim of news coverage: "Typical news is not news." Reporters prefer nontypical, unusual, out-of-the-ordinary stories. As Jamieson and Campbell (1997) noted, "Resource-poor groups often have to depend on deviance and disruption in order to receive media coverage" (p. 47). Candidates face a similar dilemma, but are sometimes successful in overcoming this barrier by looking for unusual ways to dramatize their campaigns. Florida's Lawton Chiles launched a political career that took him to Florida's governorship and to the U.S. Senate by walking the length of the state as "Walkin' Lawton." Florida's Bob Graham campaigned with work days, eschewing normal campaign activities once a week to work eight hours in a normal job. TV news is highly visual in nature, so television reporters are more likely to cover events that offer interesting visual footage or stories for which they have available footage. Candidates sometimes provide prepackaged feeds to meet that requirement, or they choose highly visual locations for a press conference.

Finally, the last word that can be used to describe news is "easy"—easy to write, easy to understand, and easy to cover. A typical news story is short and simple (Jamieson & Campbell, 1997, p. 69). A newspaper reader will scan through it in a matter of minutes. A major television story may only be forty-five seconds long. Reporters are going to be more likely to cover stories that can be condensed into a brief time span. They are also more likely to cover a story that can be easily and quickly covered. That usually means stories that are on assigned beats, or those that can be developed and put on the air or on the front page quickly. As Jamieson and Campbell (1997, p. 47) noted, "Reporters ... have a low tolerance for the long haul of a complex story that may take years to develop."

Nature of the Office

In the eyes of the press, all political offices are not created equal. Some warrant more coverage, and therefore more scrutiny, than others. As Jamieson and Campbell (1997) noted, "An event is more likely to be covered and published if it involves people in positions of authority" (p. 61). Candidates for federal office, incumbency, and the population base of the electoral district all influence the extent to which an election will receive news coverage (Havick, 1997). As a result, some topics that are not newsworthy in some campaigns can receive extensive coverage in others. For example, a decision by a candidate to adopt a dog as a family pet is usually not newsworthy information; however, if that candidate is the president of the United States, it may become a national news story.

Location

In assessing the potential impact of news coverage, one question frequently asked by consultants is, "Where are the cameras?" The location of a press conference or interview can have a dramatic impact on the credibility of the information, the amount of coverage, and the performance of the candidate.

The first two factors—credibility and coverage—are interrelated. If the press views the information as credible, then the amount of coverage devoted to an issue will increase. The reverse is also true: more coverage increases credibility. For example, a candidate who wants to address the issue of waste in highway construction would increase his or her chances of getting press coverage by holding a press conference at a location that demonstrated the problem, such as at the end of a paved road that connected with no other road. The use of such a location provides a visual demonstration of the message and also provides television crews with interesting footage that can be used in the newscast.

The location can also be critical to the performance of the candidate. Most candidates feel more comfortable, and thus perform better during television interviews, if they are in familiar surroundings. Furthermore, the toughness of questions from reporters tends to lose its edge when they ask those questions on the candidate's home territory. During a 1987 congressional campaign in Tennessee, front-runner Bob Clement was sued for alienation of affection by a man who claimed Clement had an affair with the man's wife, thus leading to their divorce. Clement denied the allegations, but reporters had more questions. Rather than holding a news conference to address the allegations, Clement and his wife together met with reporters individually, in their home, and answered their questions on the charges. Despite the stress associated with responding to such charges, Clement was perceived as at ease and honest during the individual interviews, and the press shifted their attention to whether his opponents might be behind the allegations. Their investigations subsequently revealed that one of the opponents had indeed been behind the charges, and Clement went on to an easy win in the campaign.

Location can also have an impact on which reporters cover a candidate. After Al Gore moved his campaign headquarters from Washington, D.C., to Nashville, Tennessee, the campaign found that it was subjected to less press scrutiny. After revelations that Naomi Wolf consulted with the campaign, offering advice on how Gore could appeal to women as an "alpha" male, the Washington press leaped on the story. But Gore's campaign representatives in Nashville found that they could continue campaigning and ignore the issue, because none of the local reporters asked about it.

The 2000 presidential campaigns also demonstrated how location can affect candidate performance. During many of George W. Bush's early TV appearances, questions from reporters "caused him to send a panicky look into the camera" that contrasted sharply with the "easy charm" exhibited during his first appearance on CNN's *Larry King Live* (James, 1999). Much of the difference was due to the location of the camera; instead of speaking at a press conference, where Bush often felt like an open target, the Larry King interview was conducted in "the warm, woody setting of a Nashville saloon." Democrat Bill Bradley made a similar use of location to soften his image. During some early campaign events, Bradley often sounded aloof and abstract. Those negative tones disappeared, however, when the ex-professional basketball player shot baskets at Madison Square Garden with Ed Bradley for a *60 Minutes* interview and when he sat on the court for an interview with Wolf Blitzer on CNN's *Late Edition.*

Candidate–Reporter Relationships

One factor, sometimes unspoken, that influences political coverage is the relationship between reporters and the candidates. Weaver and Wilhoit (1980) noted that candidates and reporters often have a symbiotic relationship that benefits both partners. The candidate provides the reporter with useful information, while the reporter provides the candidate with coverage. Some reporters simply like some candidates, as individuals, more than they do others, and this can create an unconscious bias in coverage. Such an effect is nothing new. Crouse's (1974) analysis of presidential reporting noted that reporters riding the campaign train with Franklin Roosevelt shared a relationship with the president that is often absent in the modern era of negative press coverage. Furthermore, such positive relationships still exist in the world of political journalism, though they may be increasingly rare. During the 2000 presidential campaign, Republican senator John McCain gained the respect of the national press by his accessibility and willingness to bluntly answer questions (Mitchell, 1999). Cornfield (2000) noted that maintaining good relationships with reporters remains an important factor, even as the nature of information dissemination changes. "The Internet enables you to bypass the news media more easily than ever. But that's no cause for poisoning relations with them," Cornfield wrote. "They can still help you compensate for weaknesses in name identification …, cash, incumbency and reputation with your targeted audience" (p. 55).

Indeed, a negative relationship can also be engendered, with predictable results. President Richard Nixon was never the darling of the Washington press, but he did nothing to change that relationship. Instead, the Nixon White House attempted to dominate the press through harassment. Some reporters had income tax returns audited after they published an unfriendly story, while others were barred from the White House newsroom (Crouse, 1974). That antagonistic relationship hurt Nixon when the Watergate scandal began to unfold.

Objectivity can be impaired even if the candidate is not the source of the news. Journalists rely heavily on confidential sources within campaigns and bureaucracies for information. Sources are often built up over years through the development of interpersonal relationships, and reporters often have to trust their source for the veracity of that information. In most cases, that trust is well placed; the source would not violate the relationship by intentionally providing false information. Still, that source can have a crucial impact on objectivity by guiding reporters to some stories and avoiding others (Turow, 1992, p. 159). Furthermore, the relationship can potentially influence the slant on the story, a decision that can significantly influence public reaction to the news; Gunter (1998), for example, found that the slant of a news story had a direct effect on perception of public opinion and an indirect effect on perceptions of changes in public opinion.

Objectivity is a rather recent ideal in journalism; in the past, reporters were often open in their bias toward candidates (Schudson, 1978, p. 157). During the Truman administration, the president constantly attacked the press for their lack of objectivity, while the reporters who covered him openly considered him incompetent and over his head in the White House (Mitchell, 1998). At lower levels, money sometimes exchanged hands as a way of sealing the reporter–candidate relationship. Grover Smith, press secretary to Senator John Sparkman during the 1950s, reported that rumors abounded that some reporters were soliciting bribes, particularly television crews and their cameramen, with the word reaching the campaign through their advertising agencies. In that instance, Smith reported that he stopped the requests by passing word back through the ad agency that any requests for bribes would be reported to the FBI (Smith, 1999).

Objectivity can create its own bias, however. In an attempt to maintain objectivity, some reporters may go overboard to report divergent views—even absurd ones. By reporting a dissenting view, they maintain the appearance of objectivity, even if the opposing view lacks merit. As Joseph Turow (1992) noted, "the routines of objectivity are not the neutral recording instruments journalists like to believe they are" (p. 158).

Pack Journalism

Generally, reporters report what other reporters report. As Jamieson and Campbell (1997) noted, "Hard news reports events linked to issues prevalent in the news at the time" (p. 50). Granted, each reporter strives to have a unique angle, a different development, or some new information on the issue of the day. But, with rare exceptions, such angles are merely variations on the same topic. During the 1970s, for example, television news relied heavily on newspaper coverage for prioritizing which stories the broadcast outlets would cover (Shaw & McCombs, 1977). Today, because of competition, each TV network monitors the others closely, and any issue covered by one is quickly picked up by another, with the agenda of one news organization influencing the others (Roberts & McCombs, 1994). Such a mentality led to dominant issue coverage at various times in U.S. history—civil rights in the sixties, Watergate in the seventies, and the Clinton–Lewinsky controversy of 1998–1999. Pack journalism also extends to candidates and others who are already in the news; any specific news event is more likely to be covered if it involves people who have been newsworthy in the past (Jamieson & Campbell, 1997, p. 61). New candidates, as a result, sometimes find it difficult to get news coverage; once they get coverage from one news source, however, the other outlets usually follow suit.

Pack journalism also shows itself in the realm of breaking news. The desire to be first with new information often produces errors, but those errors may stay within the process for an extended period of time. Once an error has been reported as a fact, other news sources repeat the error. It may eventually become an accepted "fact" for audiences that don't know better. In many instances, that mentality comes not from the reporters themselves but from editors. Crouse's (1974) analysis of news coverage of the 1972 presidential campaign found that many of the reporters on the campaign had a story refused or questioned because the wire service did not carry a similar report. Such uniformity in coverage can create a uniform, but not necessarily accurate, image of the candidate.

Some candidates take advantage of the pack journalism mentality. The most common technique for doing so is the use of "spin doctors" who interpret news events in a manner beneficial to their candidates. The goal of the spin doctor is "spin control," a term popularized during the Reagan administration. Maltese (1994) defined spin control as "twisting (a story) to one's advantage, using surrogates, press releases, radio actualities, and other friendly sources to deliver the line from an angle that puts the story in the best possible light" (p. 215). Spin doctors are most effective at spin control in the area of breaking news. Coverage of breaking news is considerably more difficult for reporters (particularly TV reporters), because they often lack the time to verify how other media outlets are covering the same story. That offers spin doctors a chance to define the story positively for their client, hoping that other news outlets will pick up on the same spin.

Embedding

For years, campaigns have sent supporters to public events featuring their opponents, hoping to learn something or to hear something that could be used against that candidate. With the development of inexpensive video cameras, though, that technique has multiplied. The goal is to catch the candidate on video saying something that is "off message." Further, in major campaigns, the technique has been used by major journalism organizations. They hired young journalists with a camera to follow presidential candidates in the 2008 elections; the young people followed the candidates across the nation, filing regular video and blogs on the campaign. The individuals who shot the video rarely appeared on camera, but their reports became the fodder of news stories presented on the air by more seasoned journalists (Stelter, February 11, 2008). As Stelter wrote, "A single person can now shoot video, edit it and quickly send it to the Web" (p. C1).

News Priming

Iyengar and Kinder (1987) argued that the media establish standards used by voters to evaluate the government, the president, and political candidates. These standards are developed as a set of expectations that are used as the basis of judgments of the political activity that the voters see and hear in the media. This theory was subsequently supported by research regarding extensive 1986 media coverage on the Reagan administration's covert diversion of funds to the Nicaraguan contras. Voters' evaluations of Reagan were strongly linked to the amount of coverage that the issue received (Krosnick & Kinder, 1990). The news priming function is the primary reason that elected officials and candidates want to dominate the media agenda (Perloff, 1998, p. 218).

Reporters themselves can become victims of news priming, sometimes falling into the habit of reporting events not in terms of results but in terms of expectations. If previous news coverage has indicated that a candidate is expected to win a primary, then victory in that primary is not particularly newsworthy. Reporters instead look to see whether the victory was by a margin that was bigger or smaller than anticipated. If the margin of victory is too small, then the "win" may be treated as a "loss" in the resulting news coverage. Consultants typically participate in this process by trying to deflate expectations before an event and making positive comparisons with the expectations on a post hoc basis. Even in the absence of such expectations, consultants consider news priming to be an important factor in spin control.

TOPICS FOR NEWS COVERAGE

Events

During nonpolitical months, most news outlets (broadcast and print) assign reporters to "beats" based on topics (such as crime, health, city government, and so forth). That typically changes during election time, with most reporters assigned to cover specific candidates—not topics or issues. The natural by-product of this approach is an increased emphasis on coverage of campaign events like appearances and speeches rather than issues. Schram (1976) described the media event from the candidate's perspective:

> A media event is a by-product of the performing arts that is often without cultural, social, or even aesthetic value. It is the sort of thing that does not necessarily look impressive in person—it may, in fact, look perfectly ridiculous and may even *be* ridiculous. But if it guarantees that the candidate will get in one of the local news shows that night, then it is good. (p. 207)

Jamieson and Campbell (1997) explained why such events appeal to the press: "An event is concrete and discrete; ordinarily it can be explained clearly in a limited time or space. A single event is more likely to be intelligible and to be a novel, dramatic event involving specific individuals" (p. 46). The media event meets both the visual and time criteria for the press, providing them with a story that is relatively easy to report. For that reason, most campaigns devote considerable time to advance work and preparation of their campaign events to make them more conducive to press coverage (Schill, 2009).

Issues

Overall, the media have a relatively poor record of covering political issues, generally making it a lower priority than covering the campaign itself (Ryan & Wentworth, 1999, p. 81). Even during nonelection times, the media's success at covering issues is questionable. Keefer (1993, p. 412) concluded that "the news media serve to hinder—rather than facilitate—citizen participation" in the policy-making process. Another concern is that coverage of personal issues may replace coverage of campaign issues. Recent elections have not reduced the criticism. Shogan (2001) chastised himself and other reporters for their tendency to cover personalities instead of issues during the 2000 presidential election.

Most political candidates also believe the press should provide more coverage of issues—as long as it is their issue. This is particularly true of candidates running a single-issue campaign, regardless of the issue topic. Most political consultants tacitly accept the findings of agenda-setting research and its importance to campaigns. If their issue of choice becomes the major news story of the campaign, their chances of winning will increase. Thus, a Republican campaigning on an antitax campaign is always enthused about any news coverage related to taxes. Similarly, a Democrat campaigning on a pro-lottery campaign always benefits from coverage of lottery issues during the campaign. The effect of such coverage decisions can be dramatic. By putting issues in the public spotlight, the media can influence party preferences (Brosius & Kepplinger, 1992) and influence the actions that people take on those issues (Roberts, 1992).

Scandals and Controversies

The news media salivate over a political scandal. Like a moth drawn to a bright light, the media will quickly focus on a scandal, even if getting too close to the scandal can damage the media itself. During 1999, when controversy broke out over Republican George W. Bush's possible use of drugs, one reporter noted that "the frenzy that is gripping the Washington press comes from the merest whiff of scandal" (Fillippeli, 1999). Sabato (1991) described the trend as a "feeding frenzy" in which journalists destroy a candidate. Similarly, Patterson (1994) has argued that the focus on scandals has made the political system ineffective by destroying trust in political institutions.

In most cases, neither the candidates (both the target of the scandal and the opponent) nor the media look good during scandal coverage, since nobody appears interested in a serious discussion of the campaign. The candidates focus on spin control, trying to put the scandal in the best possible light for themselves and the worst possible for their opponents. The press focuses on sensation, often offering serious issues only as justification for sensational images and controversy. As Yardley (1999) noted, "It is a shootout in which there are no good guys" (p. 6C).

The Horse Race

Ryan and Wentworth (1999, p. 81) have noted that the news media's emphasis on polls has led to a horse-race approach to political coverage, with the media focusing more on which candidate is ahead and who is behind than on the issues of the campaign. Farnsworth and Lichter (2010) have found that horse-race coverage has been a major part of election coverage since 1988. Such coverage is so intensive that it can have a greater impact on the outcome of an election than coverage of policy issues (Serini, Powers, & Johnson, 1998). Johnson (1993) noted that the press generally follows a two-step phase in campaign coverage, focusing initially on general indicators of candidate strength and then shifting to event-specific horse-race coverage. There are several reasons for this type of campaign coverage. First, it's relatively easy to do. Relative positions in the polls are fairly easy stories to write and report, requiring little investigation into issues by the reporters themselves. Second, many viewers and readers like this approach. Early studies of the Uses-Gratification theory identified "excitement" as one reason that people seek out political issues. Political junkies often view campaigns as the ultimate sporting event, played on a statewide or national field, with poll results giving the "score" at various points during the campaign. Many critics, though, question the value of horse-race coverage, arguing that it detracts from coverage of issues and encourages self-centered voting patterns (Capella & Jamieson, 1997). Increased focus on who's winning means less coverage on important issues that could affect the voters.

Personal Lives

During the 1884 presidential campaign, Grover Cleveland was beset by accusations that he had fathered an illegitimate child. Cleveland's only response to reporters who approached him about the issue was "Tell the truth," and most reporters did not pursue the matter. Not so today. Modern campaigns often represent a "politics of intimacy" (Parry-Giles & Parry-Giles, 1996) in which a candidate's personal life is considered fair game. During the 2000 presidential campaign, candidates were asked a multitude of questions that had little to do with the issues of the office, but a lot to do with what they did in private. During Hillary Rodham Clinton's campaign for the U.S. Senate from New York, a radio talk show host in Buffalo asked the First Lady if she had been "sexually unfaithful" to her husband (Hu, 2000); Clinton called the question "out of bounds," but answered it anyway (she denied the charges). Topics considered appropriate by reporters ranged from the sometimes controversial to the mundane, including questions about their sex lives, religious views, physical and mental health, income, advisers, friends, favorite books, movies, and political philosophers.

Two issues seemed to be raised by this type of political reporting. At what point do reporters cross the line, delving into matters that are none of their's or the public's business? To what extent does such intrusion keep highly qualified candidates from even running for public office? The latter is difficult to answer; during the Clinton–Lewinsky controversy, Republican governor George W. Bush speculated that he might not seek the Republican nomination for president if he and his family would have to be subjected to such scrutiny, but he ultimately decided to run anyway. Right or wrong, though, the press seems intent on examining candidates' private lives, and the pressure to do so increases with the increased visibility of the office being sought. Candidates who run for public office today have to expect some news coverage of their private lives.

Some public figures, in fact, take advantage of this effect by using their public exposure to increase coverage for issues that are of interest to them. The most obvious situation in which this occurs is with the presidential first ladies, some of whom fought to protect their privacy while others used their public recognition as a forum for favorite issues. Some, such as Barbara Bush, become celebrities in their own right (Wertheimer, 2000). Eleanor Roosevelt became a famous public figure whose public persona was quite distinct from that of husband Franklin Roosevelt (Lash, 1971); by using the public exposure that came with her position, she was able to promote the causes of a number of issues that concerned her. Conversely, Betty Ford's personal bouts with alcohol started out as a private problem that evolved into a public crusade for others to seek rehabilitation (Gutgold, 2000). More recently, Laura Bush used her position as First Lady to promote such medical issues as AIDS and malaria and children's rights (Dubriwny, 2005; Jackson, 2008). Michelle Obama went further, using her popularity to promote some of her husband's programs (Swarns, 2009). Other first ladies, such as Edith (Mrs. Teddy) Roosevelt (Hastings, 2000) and Lou Henry (Mrs. Herbert) Hoover (Atkinson, 2000), sometimes fought against public intrusion into their lives, preferring instead to focus on a sense of home life for themselves and their families.

Campaign Advertisements

Campaign ads sometimes become news, particularly if they are sufficiently controversial or targeted toward a specific group. Over the past few years, in fact, coverage of campaign advertisements has increased. This factor can be both a boon and a bane to campaigns. On the positive side, news coverage of the ad can extend the message to larger number of voters. On the negative side, "when the message is aimed at one constituency, it can backfire if it is replayed in the news and critiqued by press pundits in the view of other groups of voters" (Stone, 1999, p. 150).

In the past, media outlets have done a relatively poor job of evaluating campaign advertisements. During 1988, for example, 17 percent of newspaper coverage focused on campaign advertising content, but less than 2 percent of it dealt with the accuracy of advertising claims (Jamieson, 1992). One innovation of campaign coverage during the 1990s that attempted to deal with this problem was the introduction of "adwatches," a name for news coverage of campaign ads. The idea behind the adwatch program is an admirable one. Given the impact that campaign advertising has on elections, the media have a responsibility to report on those ads, including a recounting of any inaccuracies that might be present. Unfortunately, reality often misses the ideal of this goal. Between 1972 and 1988, network news coverage of ads were often negatively slanted (Kaid, 1996). Since then, most television news coverage has been neutral; however, when there is a slant, it is largely negative (Kaid, Tedesco, & McKinnon, 1993; Tedesco, McKinnon, & Kaid, 1996). Newspaper adwatches tend to be neutral in focus (Tedesco, McKinnon, & Kaid, 1996), providing little evaluation one way or the other to the reader.

Generally, adwatches seem to have minimal impact on voter decisions. Geiger (1993) found that adwatches usually produced no effect. In other instances, adwatch coverage can mitigate the intended effects of the candidate's ad. Capella and Jamieson (1994) found that adwatch coverage of a 1992 Pat Buchanan attack ad against George H. W. Bush caused viewers to consider the ad as less fair and less important, and they were more likely to have a negative view of Buchanan than of Bush. Still, the latter effect tends to be an exception. More often than not, the effect of adwatch coverage of an ad is to enhance the sponsoring candidate. O'Sullivan and Geiger (1995) found that the enhancement effect was particularly pronounced when the adwatch supported the claims in the ad. The impact seems to be more pronounced with negative ads than with positive ones (Ansolabehere & Iyengar, 1995a), even if the adwatch coverage criticizes the ad as unfair. Pfau and Loudon (1994) reported that critical adwatches can produce a boomerang effect, further enhancing the ad itself. Jamieson may have explained why in her study, which found that, after viewing an adwatch, voters remembered the ad itself better than the corrections made by the media commentator. Another possible explanation is that adwatch coverage may help to legitimize false or misleading advertising claims by airing messages in a credible news environment (Jamieson, 1992; West, 1993).

The growing importance of ads as news content may have been best represented by the Mike Huckabee campaign during the 2008 presidential primaries (Seelye, 2008). In February, Huckabee called a news conference to show an ad that his campaign produced that was a negative commercial attacking Republican Mitt Romney. Afterward, he announced that he was not going to run the ad because of its negative nature. The result: The press covered the ads content, allowing Huckabee to get the negative message out "while he claimed the high moral ground" (Seelye, 2008, p. A11).

Narrative Examples

Modern television news focuses heavily on the use of a narrative story line, a trend that has contributed to the increased use of the horse-race coverage mentality mentioned earlier. Apart from horse-race mentality, though, much political coverage focuses on the narrative element. Many individual political stories use a narrative example, or exemplar, to drive home the point of a story. Brosius and Bathelt (1994) defined exemplars as illustrative single cases used to reflect an issue being discussed. On broadcast television, their use is almost an art form. A story on the loss of rural lifestyles might be prefaced with a few statistics about farmland development, but the meat of the story would likely be an exemplar: a story of a Midwest farmer who was losing his farm to encroaching development. Such narrative examples have a strong impact on both personal opinions and perceptions of public opinion (Daschmann, 2000).

TYPES OF NEWS COVERAGE

Straight News

The most frequent form of coverage available to politicians, candidates, and campaigns is that of straight news. The story is reported, hypothetically in an unbiased manner, and presented as information that will keep the readers and listeners informed. As noted before, consultants are unofficial proponents of the agenda-setting hypothesis, particularly its news-priming implications, so most make conscious efforts to seek such coverage (Ansolabehere, Behr, & Iyengar, 1994). Success in achieving news coverage is typically referred to as free media, or earned media. The latter term, although somewhat pretentious and inaccurate, is particularly popular among consultants, since it indicates they have done something on behalf of the client to generate coverage for them.

Regardless of whether that coverage is defined as "free" or "earned," the hope of every candidate is that their stories are not only covered, but covered in a way that is beneficial to them (Graber, 1987). The easiest indicator for this is placement of the story in relation to others (Nimmo, 1970, p. 130). They hope that newspapers will give their positive stories front-page treatment. Their prayer is that negative stories are buried with small headlines, somewhere in the back of the paper. Whether in the newspaper or on radio, placement of the story is critical. The lead story on TV news is often used as part of the promos, or teasers, used to entice viewers throughout the night to stay tuned to the news. As a result, lead TV stories tend to get more coverage than others that are on the same night. Similarly, individuals with only a minimal interest in politics might scan the front page of the newspaper.

Editorials

Consultants usually assume that editorials and op-ed (opinion) pieces in newspapers have little direct impact on election outcomes. Few people read the editorials, and those who do tend to be politicos who have already decided how they will vote. Still, endorsements can have an impact on down-ballot campaigns. Furthermore, newspaper editorials can have a major, indirect, impact if the campaign chooses to use editorial content in its campaign advertisements. Being able to cite a newspaper brings instant credibility to a television ad, and candidates love to use headlines as a visual association for a verbal message.

One particular form of editorial that draws a great deal of attention is the editorial cartoon, a visual and humorous part of the editorial page (Brinkman, 1968; Carl, 1968; Riffe, Sneed, & Van Ommeren, 1985; Wheeler & Reed, 1975). Some scholars view cartoons from a historical perspective (Steakley, 1983), while others consider them merely a social barometer that reflects public opinion (Penner & Penner, 1994). Still, a significant number of scholars view political cartoons as a form of persuasion that can influence public attitudes (Morris, 1993; Turner, 1977). Morris (1993) identified three communication functions of the cartoon: condensing a complex issue into a single image, combining elements from different domains into one, and domesticating (making the abstract or distant seem familiar). Some have argued that such rhetorical functions imbue political cartoons with the ability to change public opinion (Brinkman, 1968) and influence perceptions of political figures (Bosdorff, 1987).

At the very least, their structure and intent fall within the realm of traditional rhetorical form (Medhurst & DeSousa, 1981), and several scholars have approached them from that perspective. Bosdorff (1987), for example, looked at the rhetorical implications of political cartoons attacking former presidential cabinet member James Watt. Similarly, Holm argued that political cartoons about the Clinton–Lewinsky sex scandal had a positive impact on Bill Clinton's image because many of the drawings identified him with the common man. That factor could have contributed to keeping Clinton in office despite the threat of impeachment.

Not all scholars agree with this approach. Despite their humor and political insight, political cartoons are often ignored by the average voter and misunderstood by many. Those who most appreciate political cartoons tend to be political insiders, a trend that prompted Bormann, Koester, and Bennett (1978) to conclude that cartoons were essentially inside jokes that few people understood. Research generally supports the latter conclusion (Carl, 1968); average readers often miss the point of the cartoon. Still, when the point is driven home, a political cartoon does so in a graphic and memorable way.

Sunday News Shows

In national politics, some of the most influential news television occurs on Sunday mornings (when few people are watching television) on interview shows such as NBC's *Meet the Press*, CBS's *Face the Nation*, and ABC's *This Week with Sam Donaldson and Cokie Roberts*. As TV commentator Roger Simon (1987, p. 4) once noted, those shows are all based on the assumption "that important political and government figures, faced with vigorous questioning, just might slip and commit news."

The formats of the shows are similar. Each has a reporter or reporters directing questions at public officials or other newsworthy individuals. In most cases, those guests are either high-ranking administration officials or people who are in leadership positions in Congress. The oldest of the shows, *Meet the Press,* made its debut in 1951. For the remainder of that decade, the questions were gentle, with reporters typically showing respect toward their guests. Simon (1987) noted that, in the beginning, "persistent follow-up questions were somehow considered bad manners" (p. 5). Today, tough questions are the rule, not the exception. Furthermore, appearances on the shows may offer little opportunity to reach undecided voters; the audience tends to be made up of active voters (Hofstetter et al., 1994), most of whom have already made their voting decision.

So why do politicians agree to participate? First, they want to get exposure for themselves and their ideas. Despite the small audience, all of the Sunday interview shows generate a great deal of spinoff coverage. Comments made on the show are reported on the evening television news and distributed in print to all of the major newspapers. An effective interview on any of the shows can dramatically increase recognition of an issue, pushing it to the forefront of the media's agenda.

Second, most of the guests are not afraid of the tough questioning. Most, if not all, have been interviewed thousands of times before they make their first Sunday-morning appearance. Their interview-response skills are often just as well developed as the interview-questioning skills of the reporters. As Simon (1987) wrote, "If they don't want to say something, it is hard to make them say it" (p. 6).

THE ROLE OF THE PRESS SECRETARY

The press secretary is the major conduit of news and information between the candidate and the news media. As Perloff (1998) noted, "It is a dicey job" (p. 69), one in which verbal missteps can have serious consequences. The role is such an integral part of today's political communication process that it is easy to forget that it is a relatively new role. For decades, most statewide campaigns did not bother to use one. Even at the presidential level, the position did not formally exist until the administration of Herbert Hoover (Nelson, 1998). Stephen Early's performance during twelve years as Franklin Roosevelt's press secretary generally defined how the job should be handled, at least in the eyes of the press (Mitchell, 1998).

Gradually, the role of the press secretary filtered down to other campaigns. Grover Smith served in the function of press secretary for Senator John Sparkman (Dem.-Ala.) during the 1950s. At the time, however, senators had no official press secretaries, and Smith's official title was "research assistant." Smith eventually organized the first press secretary association for the Senate, and got recognition for the group when newsman David Brinkley agreed to speak to them. Smith subsequently arranged for the official contact lists for each senator to include a person in each office who was identified as the press secretary (Smith, 1999). The most visible press secretary is the one working with the president, where that person deals with some of the top reporters in the nation. Jody Powell (1984), from the Carter administration, identified dealing with reporters as the hardest part of his job. As Ari Fleischer (2005), press secretary to George W. Bush, once wrote, "The White House Press Corps is one of the toughest, sharpest, most skeptical groups anyone will ever encounter. They're the best in the business, and that's why they're stationed at the White House" (p. x).

In most modern campaigns, the role is distinctly separate from other campaign functions, with the press secretary acting as both manager of the message and "messenger boy" (Grossman & Kumar, 1981, p. 130). The press secretary serves as a conduit for information to the press, keeping reporters alerted to the candidate's schedule, scheduling press conferences, and writing press releases for standard announcements. As a conduit, the press secretary serves as a gatekeeper between the candidate and the press. Using that "gate" to control access to the candidate requires a careful balance. Too much can be detrimental, offering too many opportunities for negative press; too little can be even worse, creating an antagonistic relationship that also leads to negative coverage. During the 1988 presidential campaign, for example, Republican George Bush was often kept away from the press based on the assumption that "with public access goes lack of control" (Winter, 1989, p. 3).

Although approaches to the role can vary, depending on the personality of the individual, most press secretaries aim for a positive working relationship with the press with the intent of maintaining that relationship through the ups and downs of the campaign. As a result, some campaigns use both the campaign manager and the press secretary in "good-cop/bad-cop" roles. When the campaign feels it is necessary to criticize the press, the criticism is more likely to come from the campaign manager; that way, the criticisms do not hinder the press secretary's working relationship with reporters.

As a conduit of information, the press secretary has several options for passing information on to the press. "On the record" refers to those comments that may be quoted in the press and the name of the source identified. If the information is released, "on background," the quote can be used but the source cannot be identified by name—only by status or position ("a source close to the president said…," for example). "Deep background" has even more control; reporters can use the information provided by the press secretary, but they cannot attribute it to a particular source. Some information is given "off the record." In those instances, the reporter is not to use the information in their story at all; it is provided merely to help them understand the larger context of an issue or situation.

Some information may bypass the press secretary entirely through the process of news leaks. Leaks are used on premature information that the source wants the press to have, but which they are unable to disclose through normal channels ("This reporter has learned …").

THE ISSUE OF MEDIA BIAS

The hostile media effect was discussed in an earlier chapter, but the topic continuously emerges under the topic of media relations too. Most of the perceptions related to hostile media can be chalked up to partisanship (Gunther & Schmitt, 2004). Some element of media bias has always been present (Sheppard, 2007). It can show up in elements as innocuous as the facial expressions of the commentators and anchors (Miller, Coleman, & Granberg, 2007). Still, given the proliferation of talk radio and cable news, the problem of media bias has increased over the years. Commentary on debate coverage, for example, typically includes comments regarding which candidate won the debate. Analysts on Fox News are more likely to identify the Republican candidate as the winner, while CNN is apt to credit the Democrat as the best debater (Brubaker & Hanson, 2009). During the Iraq War, viewers of Fox News were more likely to support the war than were viewers of CNBC (Lin, 2009). During the Bush administration, conservative talk-radio hosts consistently lauded the work of President George W. Bush (Holbert, 2004). Overall, Republicans are more likely to view the media as biased than are Democrats (Stalder, 2009), but arguments can be made that examples of bias by both sides occur. Sometimes the degree of bias was so apparent that candidates would base part of their strategy on running against the media, with Democrats attacking Fox News while Republicans did the same for MSNBC (Stelter, 2010).

POLITICS AND ENTERTAINMENT MEDIA

There was a time when political candidates merely had to worry about the press and the public's response to their speeches and campaign activities. But that approach disappeared toward the end of the twentieth century, perhaps pushed along by Bill Clinton playing his saxophone on *The Tonight Show* during his successful 1992 presidential campaign. Today's campaigns largely contend with a variety of television entertainment shows—particularly late-night comedians—who will joke about any misstep candidates make. And they often appear on such shows themselves. During the 2008 campaign, for example, Barack Obama, John McCain, and Sarah Palin made appearances on *Saturday Night Live*. McCain was scheduled to appear on David Letterman's show, but canceled because of campaign events and was heartily skewed by the comedian on the show that night (e.g., Leibovich, 2009). Eventually, McCain made another appearance to apologize for skipping out on this previous commitment.

Such events have led to a new field of communication research that looks at politics and entertainment media (e.g., Riegert, 2007). Scholar Lance Holbert (2005) has been a leader in the field, even establishing some criteria for such analysis. For example, during the 2004 presidential election, director Michael Moore produced and released a film called *Fahrenheit 9/11* that lampooned incumbent President George W. Bush in an attempt to limit the success of his reelection campaign. Bush won anyway, but several studies have looked at the film and its communication goals (Holbert & Hanson, 2006, 2008; Holbert et al., 2007a). Holbert has also examined politics in relation to the television show *The West Wing* (Holbert et al., 2003; Holbert et al., 2005; see also Parry-Giles & Parry-Giles, 2006) and *The Daily Show* (Holbert et al., 2007b), and the impact of police/crime dramas on attitudes about gun issues (Holbert, Shah, & Kwak, 2004).

SUMMARY

Despite the incursions of new media such as the Internet, the impact of media coverage will not dissipate anytime soon. Candidates will still be judged by many voters on their ability to deal with the press, the information that many voters get will continue to come from the press, and candidates will continue to be chosen, at least partly, on the basis of "their media-friendly characteristics" (Ryan & Wentworth, 1999, p. 80). That's why modern campaigns devote a significant amount of resources to developing and maintaining relationships with the press.

That relationship is a complex, ongoing process that is constantly in flux. News coverage of a candidate can be influenced by a number of factors. While some of those factors are under the control of either the campaign or the reporter, many others are triggered by events in a campaign environment over which neither the candidate nor the reporter has control. The resulting news stories can appear in a variety of formats with a number of different effects. Naive candidates can find their personal reputation damaged by selective reporting of facts about their past. Experienced candidates may find their pet issues are overlooked in favor of other issues that have grabbed and kept the media's attention. And, with the advent of the Internet as a new means of dispensing news information, the news cycle has been compressed into a shorter frame of time. Not surprisingly, the role of the press is growing increasingly complex in modern campaigns.

QUESTIONS FOR DISCUSSION

1. Your candidate has planned a series of news conferences highlighting his environmental proposals. The first one goes well, but on the way to the second event, the candidate's automobile is sideswiped by a patrol car driven by a deputy sheriff. Will the accident or the news conferences result in greater news coverage? Why?

2. In 1992, Bill Clinton, beset by charges of womanizing, placed second in the New Hampshire primary. He described himself as the "comeback kid," and the news media generally treated his performance there as a victory. What role did "expectations" play in this perception? If you had been the campaign manager for one of Clinton's opponents, what effective spin could you have used that might have led to a different interpretation?

3. On the night before election day, a television station carried the story that your candidate for mayor had been killed in a traffic accident. The story was false, and the report was corrected in the next news cycle. How can such a report damage your campaign? As campaign manager, what would you have done to deal with this story? What responsibility does the television station face?

4. Abraham Lincoln is cited as an example of a candidate who would have great difficulty winning the modern presidency. As his campaign manager, how would you muster arguments in his favor? What campaign preparations would you undertake to focus the news media on his strengths: his good sense of humor, strong values, and excellent political leadership skills? How would you spin a story on his lack of media skills? How would you get the media to cover the "Lincoln" issues?

The Role of Political Money

Political novice John Corzine altered the political landscape of the 2000 Senate election in New Jersey when he entered the election with a reported net worth of $300 million and vowed to spend as much as he needed to get elected. "Money has been a dominant theme in the New Jersey Senate race since Mr. Corzine announced his interest a year ago," wrote one reporter (Halbfinger, 2000). "His willingness to pay any price was cited by nearly every candidate who eventually withdrew, among them the governor, Christine Todd Whitman, a Republican, and Democrats Michael Murphy, Frank Pallone and B. Thomas Byrne."

For the academic community, political communication is an exercise in the democratic process in which different ideas compete for public support. For the consulting community, campaigns are a business. Not surprisingly, money is a pivotal factor in the consulting role, while it is often criticized by the academic community. Consultants focus on bending the constantly changing rules of the game so they can simultaneously do a more effective job for their clients and make more money for themselves. Academicians, meanwhile, often bemoan the role that money plays in modern campaigns.

The media might adopt both views. Their editorial departments toss out criticisms of the role of money in campaigns while their advertising departments eagerly compete for political advertising. A typical editorial comment notes that the presidential elections are likely to be won "by whichever candidate can get the highest number of wealthy people to write $1,000 checks," while adding, "This is no way to run a democracy, and it is a result of our sorry system of campaign finance" (Judis, 1999). Still, while the editorial department and television commentators rail at the system, as much as 70 percent of the money collected by campaigns is spent with those same media outlets.

An occasionally overlooked aspect of the financial side of politics is that the concern over money also creates problems and arguments within the campaign. Even though fund-raising plays a critical role in their careers, many candidates despise fund-raising. When former Illinois senator Paul Simon retired from politics, he cited the dislike for the almost daily routine of soliciting those contributions necessary to run for reelection. Many candidates have a similar distaste for seeking money, creating another potential source of internal conflict between the candidates and their consultants. While the candidate resists additional fund-raising activities, the consultants may be pressing for more money to use in more projects. Given that scenario, it is hardly surprising that Franzen (1999) noted that "many of the difficulties that arise between consultants and their clients revolve around money" (p. 300). The consultants argue for another round of media or another program as necessary for success, while the candidate projects the resentment they might face from donors who have already been more than generous with their contributions. Internal conflicts between consultants also often revolve around money. Most of the campaign budget typically goes to the mass media consultant, a situation that can build resentment among the other vendors. Polling, direct mail, telephone, and organizational consultants often find themselves fighting for the remaining dollars. Success at getting those monies helps to finance their business through another campaign cycle. Failure to win the fight gives them an easy explanation as to why any particular campaign did not win.

The reality of modern politics, though, requires some means of dealing with such conflicts, since money is an essential and necessary ingredient for most campaigns. As Perlmutter (1999) noted, "It is extremely difficult to run for higher office in America without an enormous war chest filled with one's own money or that of wealthy friends and partisans" (p. 2). The fact is that money buys the means of political speech. Without money political messages cannot be tested by pollsters; advertising spots cannot be created; ad time cannot be purchased; staffs cannot be hired; campaign schedules cannot be kept; and money cannot be raised. Without adequate funding there is less political speech. For the candidate who wants to win, money is an ever-present reality.

This means a fund-raising plan is essential to the campaign. Even those candidates who enter the process full of idealism will eventually learn about the financial side of politics. They enter the profession as civic-minded idealists who believe their views can have an influence on public policy. By the end of their first campaign, they have a healthy appreciation for the role of money—either because they had to spend so much time raising it, or because they were defeated by a better-financed opponent. For their messages to prevail, the candidate must have at least enough money to communicate those ideas to the voters (Broder, 1999). That means that fund-raising starts early, with presidential candidates typically starting their fund-raising efforts more than a year before election day (Drinkard, March 10, 2000).

THE ROLE OF POLITICAL MONEY

A sometimes overlooked aspect of political communication is the rhetorical effect that money has on the campaign (Jones, 2000). An effective fund-raising program provides at least four rhetorical advantages to a campaign by enhancing credibility, attracting media attention, increasing subsequent fund-raising, and diminishing the opposition. Early fund-raising is critical to candidate credibility. Early success draws media attention to the campaign, bestows legitimacy to the campaign efforts, and puts pressure on the competition to raise a comparable amount. The media attention can create a mushrooming effect; journalists tend to cover campaigns in direct relationship to how much money the candidate raises, and the increased visibility created by that coverage can spur even more donations. As the bank accounts start bulging, the pressure to compete drives some competitors away. Columnist Michael Kinsley (2007) summarized the idea when he wrote, "Candidates raise money not to purchase TV time and hire consultants. They raise money to prove that they can raise money" (p. 34).

The most dramatic recent example was Republican George W. Bush, who used the rhetoric of money to drive out and finally overcome his primary competitors and win the 2000 Republican nomination for president. Elizabeth Dole dropped out of the race, citing her inability to compete with the record $70 million raised by the Bush campaign. More than a year before the Republican convention, *USA Today* (Lawrence, 1999) cited the inevitability of Bush's nomination and quoted Larry Markinson, of the Center for Responsive Politics, on the rhetorical impact of Bush's campaign war chest. "It really shows the power of the purse," Markinson said. "The funders have decided who the next nominee is going to be six months before anyone casts a vote. The reality of these numbers has to be brutal for the other Republican candidates."

Jennifer Steen, of the Scholars Network of the Citizens' Research Foundation at the University of California at Berkeley, called political money a "self-fulfilling prophecy" that drives out competition. "The perception that a millionaire can buy victory exerts a chilling effect on electoral competition, discouraging would-be candidates from entering the fray," she wrote (Steen, 2000). That conclusion was based on data analyzed from four congressional campaigns over four election cycles that pointed to an "unmistakable pattern": "the richer the candidate, the fewer the opponents."

For reporters and editors, the amount of money becomes a scorecard by which candidates can be judged. Each side is so sensitive to the rhetoric of money that the release of any such information by one side often prompts a similar salvo from the other. When New York mayor Rudolph Giuliani's Senate campaign reported that it collected $12 million in 1999 for his 2000 campaign against Hillary Rodham Clinton, Clinton, who had refused to release her fund-raising totals at that point, announced she had collected $8 million during the same time period. As the *New York Times* noted, "It was emblematic of the pronounced role of money in the race that the advisers then sought to explain why her total was not higher, pointing out, for example, that she had been raising money only since the summer" (Levy, 2000).

Strategic decisions on the use of campaign finances can also have a critical impact on election outcomes. In 1996, Republican candidate Bob Dole started his primary campaign early in an effort to win the nomination with a growing momentum that could carry him to a November victory. Unfortunately, his campaign ran out of money before the primary season was over. Bill Clinton, meanwhile, was spending millions of dollars on ads touting his political agenda and building a lead among key constituencies that Dole was never able to overcome.

Sometimes the rhetoric of money can exceed its political impact, particularly in self-financed campaigns. Data from the Citizens' Research Foundation, a campaign finance research center at the University of California at Berkeley, have consistently found that millionaires who finance their own campaigns face an uphill battle in winning an election (Steen, 2000). As Steen noted, "Self-financers usually don't win. When they do, it isn't their money alone that puts them in office" (p. B1). Several factors contribute to this conclusion, including the millionaire's lack of political experience and their lack of a political network. Her study of five election cycles (from 1990 to 1998) found that only six of thirty-eight nonincumbent Senate candidates who financed their own campaigns with at least $1 million had won their campaigns, a success rate of only 16 percent. Meanwhile, 49 of the 155 nonincumbents who raised $1 million or more in contributions won their elections (a 32 percent success rate). Differences in House races were even more dramatic: The success rate among those who raised a million dollars (67 percent) was more than three times that of millionaires who used their own money to campaign for Congress (21 percent).

RULES OF THE GAME

Candidates cannot merely enter a campaign and immediately start to raise and spend money. Modern campaigns play by a sophisticated, complicated, and often confusing set of rules. Federal candidates (presidents, senators, and members of Congress) must adhere to federal laws that are monitored by the Federal Election Commission (FEC). State and local candidates have a different set of rules, although many of those local regulations are patterned after the federal guidelines. Although there are some exceptions for local regulations, the relevant laws generally fall into three different categories: limits on contributions, limits on spending, and reporting requirements (Schotland, 1992).

Campaign Contributions

For years, federal law limited contributions for federal elections—campaigns for president, U.S. senator, and the U.S. House of Representatives—to $1,000 from individuals and $5,000 from political action committees (PACs). That changed in 2003 when the McCain–Feingold Act changed the limits and tied future increases to inflation (Smith et al., 2010). In 2008, the individual limit was $2,300. That was increased to $2,500 for the 2012 election.

Once any election is completed, the contributor can donate again for the next election. The implication of this is that, for some candidates, the actual ceiling on individual contributions for one election cycle is $7,500, not $2,500. A contributor could donate $2,500 to the candidate's primary campaign, another thousand to the primary runoff, and still make a third donation for the general election. With the same setup, political action committees could potentially donate three times the maximum to campaigns.

Finally, the financial books close in each phase except in one important respect. Funds may be raised for a primary or runoff or general election to the extent of debt. If a campaign owes money at the end of any of these periods, it may continue to raise money to pay off that debt. Often a financial contributor of a beaten opponent will contribute to a winner by helping to raise funds to pay off earlier debts. Potential contributors who might not want their support known might pledge a later contribution to pay off debt. The same contributors may then contribute in subsequent phases of the campaign.

Spending Limits

The goal of spending limits is to create a more level playing field for candidates. Ideally, the winner of the election should be the candidate with the best ideas, not the one with the most money, and spending limits are an attempt to provide more parity on this front. However, neither the federal nor local governments may unilaterally limit expenditures for all candidates. Candidates may spend their own money without limits. In *FEC* v. *Buckley*, the Supreme Court held that doing so would be to interfere with those candidates' right to freedom of speech. As a result, spending limits can be placed only on those candidates who choose to raise their funds or, in the case of presidential campaigns, those who accept matching funds from the government. If the candidate accepts governmental funds, or otherwise chooses not to use personal funds then the government has the right to place rules on how those funds are spent.

Congressional and senatorial candidates are typically not eligible for matching campaign funds, unless they qualify under regulations for their individual states. As such, there are rarely any spending limits for those races, only the individual contributions limits. For presidential candidates who choose matching funds, the first $250 of each individual contribution can be matched by federal funds. In the 2000 presidential primary campaign, for example, candidates who accepted matching money were limited to spending $40.5 million during the primary campaigns (that amount varies with each election). If the candidate chooses not to accept matching money, they are not bound by any spending limits. During the 2000 election, for example, Republican George W. Bush raised more than $70 million in individual and PAC contributions; he chose not to accept federal matching funds and spent much of that total during the primary season. Democrat Al Gore accepted federal funds and was limited to the $40.5 million ceiling on primary expenditures.

In presidential elections, the general election campaign officially begins after the parties formally nominate candidates at their conventions in the summertime. That portion of the presidential campaign is funded by taxpayers. In 2000, the Democratic and Republican candidates each got $67.5 million, and both were prohibited from using other funds. Theoretically, a candidate could refuse the federal money and raise money under the same rules as for the primaries. That has not yet happened.

State and local candidates have a different set of rules, which often vary dramatically from state to state. About half follow the federal model and offer either full or partial public financing of statewide elections. Others require candidates to raise their own funds but have contribution limits similar to those for federal elections. Still others allow unlimited contributions but have strict reporting requirements. Reporting requirements also apply to spending the money, with some states limiting expenditures until an initial report has been filed. Others require reports at specific times, with enforcement penalties varying from state to state. The bottom line for the consultant is that he or she must become familiar with the local laws as quickly as possible. Not surprisingly, the most valuable volunteers the campaign can recruit are local lawyers and accountants who are willing to research the legal and financial aspects of the campaign game.

Reporting Requirements

To enforce campaign contribution laws, both the federal and state government rely on specific reporting requirements for monitoring purposes. Reporting requirements are strict, even those elections that are not subject to contribution limits. For that reason, most major campaigns employ both a lawyer and an accountant to make sure that the account books are in proper shape and that all reports are made in a timely manner. Keeping those books requires a sophisticated set of records. In federal elections, for example, the $1,000 limit is cumulative for each individual campaign. A contributor who donates $500 early in the campaign can later donate another $500, but not more than that. When a contributor reaches a cumulative total of $1,000, he or she has given the most allowed for that election and is not allowed to contribute again until the next election cycle begins. Thus, the campaign's accounting system must be sufficiently complex to keep up with individual contributions and the cumulative total of each individual's contributions.

CIRCUMVENTING THE RULES

The basic regulations provide only a broad framework for the legal side of campaign finances. Campaigns often look for ways to adhere to the letter of the law while expanding the amount of money they are legally allowed to raise and spend (Adamany, 1990). A number of avenues have been used for this purpose.

Hard Money vs. Soft Money The most common method for circumventing the rules—as of this writing—is through the distinction between "hard money" and "soft money." Hard money is the designation used for donations made to the candidate or the campaign; hard money is subject to all the restrictions of the campaign finance laws. When the campaign is actively engaged in activities aimed at seeking voter support or actively requests that voters vote against a particular candidate, it is required to spend hard money on those efforts.

Soft money refers to donations made to the candidate's party rather than to the candidates themselves (Corrado, 1997; Magleby & Holt, 1999; Smith, 1998). Soft money is usually donated by corporations, labor unions, and wealthy individuals. As long as it is donated to the party and not to individual candidates, soft money is not regulated and can be given in unlimited amounts.

There is also no limit on how much of this sort of soft money can be spent. The only limits on soft money are how it is spent. Soft money is viewed as the party's money, not that of the candidate. Theoretically, soft money can be used to promote party activities and party views, but is not supposed to be used to actively solicit votes for any specific candidate. It is supposed to be used only for getting out the vote and other general political activities. From a practical perspective, however, it is often used to a candidate's benefit by coming just short of using forbidden words, such as "vote for" or "vote against." In essence, such ads can say "Congressman X is one of us. He supports us with his vote by opposing abortion on demand and gun control. He supports us in the U.S. House of Representatives." A hard money ad can say, "Congressman X is one of us. He supports us with his vote by opposing abortion on demand and gun control. Vote for X and keep him in the U.S. House of Representatives."

One of the most open uses of soft money during the 2000 elections came from the Virginia-based Republican Majority Issues Committee, which sought to raise $25 million in donations that ranged from $500,000 to $3 million while promising its donors that they would remain anonymous. Such an approach is legal, provided that neither the group nor its ads explicitly tell voters which candidates to vote for or against, the committee receives no guidance from Republican congressional or party leaders, and it does not coordinate its efforts with any of the candidates it supports. If a group meets those three requirements, it is not required to register with the Federal Election Commission and, as a result, not required to report its donors nor restrict the size of donations from individuals.

When using soft money, the campaigns walk a fine line adhering to the legal requirements while maximizing expenditures. Some of the techniques they use include the following.

Staff Transfers   Once a candidate has received the party's nomination, they typically shift most of the campaign staff to the party headquarters. That allows campaign workers to continue to draw regular paychecks without any of the funds counting against the hard money spending limits.

Consulting Services   Many consulting services are not considered to be direct efforts to solicit votes. Polling is considered a form of research that is separate from the advertising efforts. Voter turnout programs can be organized to help all of the party's candidates, not just individual candidates. Consequently, payment for such services can come from the party, thus giving the campaign more room to operate under the spending limits.

Issue Ads   While soft money is—theoretically—not supposed to be used for campaign ads, both parties have frequently done so under the guise of "issue ads" (Magleby & Holt, 1999). Issue ads are legal; both parties have the right to communicate their position on issues that they deem important. To be within the legal guidelines, however, the ads cannot solicit voter support for a candidate. Typically, the parties get around this requirement by simply using the issue ad to address a campaign theme deemed important by the campaign, and then merely omitting the traditional "Vote for Candidate X" line at the end of the ad.

The first major use of issue ads came during the 1996 presidential campaign when both Bill Clinton and Bob Dole used their national party organizations to buy millions of dollars worth of TV spots. The Clinton ads, paid for by the Democratic National Committee, ran almost continuously for more than twelve months before the election in key markets and totaled more than $46 million dollars; the Republicans joined the fray later and spent a similar amount.

Multipack Ads   Some states have regulations that allow for soft money to be used for candidate advertisements as long as more than one candidate is depicted in each ad. The regulations vary, but a typical requirement is for a "three-pack," which means at least three different candidates must be mentioned in the ad. The intent of such regulations was to allow party advertisements that argue for the election of a partisan "team" of candidates, but both parties have used the law to support individual candidates. The technique is simple. The thirty-second ad is designed with twenty-six seconds devoted to the targeted candidate; the names and postage stamp–sized photos of two other candidates (sometimes candidates who have no opposition) are flashed during the final four seconds to make the ad a legal use of soft money.

Both issue ads and multipack ads skirt the intent of the original law, but the candidates generally go unpunished because of the ambiguity of the amended versions of the laws. In 1998, auditors at the Federal Election Commission ruled that both Clinton and Dole had exceeded their spending limits by using the soft money ads, but the commission decided not to pursue enforcement because of the vagueness of the legislative requirements (Drinkard, 2000). The practical effect of that decision was to give the presidential candidates of both parties almost total control of the budgets of their party's organization.

Third-Party Independent Expenditures   Despite the limits on campaign donations and expenditures, most court decisions have interpreted the freedom of speech principle to mean that the government cannot limit the political activity of groups who wish to participate in the political process as long as the group's activities are not coordinated with those of a campaign (Magleby & Holt, 1999). As a result, starting in the late 1970s, the involvement of friendly interest groups in campaigns has increased dramatically (Smith, 1996). Kitchens and Powell (1986) reported on early third-party campaigns by New Right organizations on behalf of Republican candidates. Since then, as Drinkard (2000) noted, "They have grown more active with phone banks and ads that praise candidates who agree with them and rap those who don't." The 2000 campaigns saw such activities on behalf of candidates from both parties. The AFL-CIO, the Sierra Club environmental organization, and several abortion-rights groups spent millions to help Democratic candidates, while the National Right to Life Committee, the Republican Leadership Council, Americans for Tax Reform, and several other groups did the same for Republicans.

PAC and Candidate Donations   Contributors who have donated the limit to the candidate of their choice can still make donations to group and individual political action committees. Those PACs, in turn, can potentially donate up to $5,000 to an individual candidate. Furthermore, contributors can also donate the legal maximum to other candidates, even if those candidates have no competition. Those unchallenged incumbents can then legally donate their collected funds to other candidates within their party who do face opposition. Consequently, many powerful incumbents maintain major fund-raising organizations; by raising huge sums of money, they discourage challengers from taking a serious look at them while simultaneously raising funds that can be used by other candidates with tougher campaigns. By using their money in that manner, incumbents can become "political benefactors" to other candidates in their party (Baker, 1989).

CHANGES FOR 2010

Prior to the 2010 election, the U.S. Supreme Court issued a ruling on campaign finance laws that changed the restrictions imposed on campaigns and corporations that participate in the campaign process—particularly in terms of third-party participants such as the 527 groups (Liptak, 2010). The decision also reignited the debate of "Freedom of speech versus the ability of the rich to buy elections." Naturally, both sides immediately started seeking ideas for either (a) getting a different ruling or a different law, or (b) taking advantages of the new leniencies suggested by the ruling (see Smith et al., 2010).

The ruling involved a documentary (*Hillary: The Movie*) released during the Democratic primaries of 2008 that was largely an attack on Hillary Clinton's 2008 presidential candidacy. Lower courts had ruled that the movie was a work of advocacy journalism and thus in violation of that part of the Bipartisan Campaign Reform Act of 2002 which banned the broadcast or mass transmission of "electioneering communications" paid for by corporations or labor unions within thirty days before primaries and sixty days prior to a general election. Instead, the Supreme Court considered the case on the broader issue of corporate contributions during elections. The 5-to-4 ruling broke on ideological lines, with the five conservative judges in the majority and the four liberal judges in the minority ("*Citizens United ...*", 2010). The result, though, was a ruling that *USA Today* described as one that would lead to "a new era for campaign spending" (Schouten & Biskuic, 2010, p. A1). *The New York Times* wrote that the decision "handed lobbyists a new weapon" that would "increase the power of organized interest groups at the expense of candidates and political parties" (Kirkpatrick, 2010, p. A1). As Zeleny (2010) concluded, the "ruling upends the nation's campaign finance laws, allowing corporations and labor unions to spend freely on behalf of political candidates." *USA Today* agreed, writing in an editorial, "Think American elections are already grossly distorted by special interests? ... It's about to get a lot worse" ("Court's campaign ruling ...", 2010, p. 8A).

Indeed it did. The 2010 midterm elections saw the most use of corporate cash and anonymous donations seen in any election since the Watergate Era, when Richard Nixon's secret list of donors was kept by his secretary, Rose Mary Woods (Abramson, 2010). The Supreme Court ruling will likely be the subject of additional legal appeals and legislative action. Still, as Smith et al. (2010) noted, "It opens up new avenues for funneling more money into campaign efforts, even if that money is still 'hands off' for the campaigns themselves" (p. 140).

FUND-RAISING TECHNIQUES

Techniques for raising campaign funds are unlimited, but a few tried-and-true tactics have been employed for a number of years in various combinations. Among the most common are host events, direct mail, online contributions, and bundling.

Host Events

A favorite fund-raising technique at all levels is the hosted fund-raiser. In most cases, the event is treated as a social occasion in which a select few have an opportunity to mingle with the candidate and to show their support for the campaign. The host is a major donor who typically sets an example by making a sizable donation to the campaign. At the local level, the event may include informal receptions, teas, or coffees (Thomas, 1999, pp. 68–72). As the size of the campaign grows, so does the guest list and the formality of the event. At statewide or presidential levels, the event may be a dinner with a celebrity guest speaker (or, in some cases, several), with rival campaigns touting their various celebrity donors. During the 2000 Democratic primary, Al Gore was supported by actors Kevin Costner and Chevy Chase, musician Quincy Jones, and TV executives Norman Lear and Grant Tinker. Republican George W. Bush counted actor Chuck Norris among his financial supporters.

In May 2000, the Democratic National Committee set a one-day fund-raising record of more than $23 million with its "Gala Tribute to President Clinton." The event featured a visit from the president and performances by singer Stevie Wonder and actor-comedian Robin Williams. Ten unions donated $500,000 each to the event, twenty other groups or individuals anted up $250,000. Other tickets sold for as little as $50 each.

The prime example of a hosted fund-raiser for an individual candidate belongs to the losing Democratic contender in the 2000 campaign, Bill Bradley. Bradley listed actors Tom Selleck, Paul Reiser, and Steve Guttenberg among his supporters, but his most visible supporters were former professional basketball players whom Bradley knew from the days when he played the game. A number of those former players collaborated to host a fund-raiser for Bradley at Madison Square Garden that garnered more than $1.5 million (Dao, 1999).

Direct Mail

Richard Viguerie's (1975) description of direct mail as a "sleeping giant" is based largely on the capacity of the medium for raising money. During the late 1970s and early 1980s, Viguerie's consulting firm raised millions of dollars for Republican causes and candidates using direct mail. But Viguerie has not been alone in using direct mail for political fund-raising. In the 1972 presidential election, the Nixon campaign raised money using a mailing list of 65,000 contributors, while Morris Dees developed a mailing list of 165,000 names to raise money for George McGovern and Jimmy Carter (O'Leary, 2000).

Justifications for a direct-mail solicitation are limited only by the imagination of the candidates and their consultants. During the 2000 Republican primary,

Arizona senator John McCain sent out 40,000 letters before his wife's birthday, asking supporters to send a special birthday contribution to his campaign; the approach raised more than $63,000.

California's Republican congressman Jim Rogan used a similar approach, but in reverse; the letter to supporters came from his wife, who included a birthday card addressed to her husband for the supporter to sign and send along with their donation. The Rogan piece was the work of direct mail consultant the Lukens Cook Company; the same company produced a piece for Kentucky congressman Jim Bunning that featured a letter written in a child's scrawl and was reportedly signed by Bunning's eight-year-old granddaughter. It included one line that read, "I talked with Miss Debbie (Grandpa's campaign manager) and Mr. David (his finance director) and they told me we must raise $50,000 to get Grandpa on TV more."

One of the most memorable uses of direct mail, though, came in a 1999 effort by the House Republican Campaign Committee. In early 1999, the committee spent more than $30,000 to send out a computerized fund-raising letter, but ran into trouble when a computer foul-up mistakenly sent some of the letters to the wrong people. No problem. In June, the committee sent out another letter asking for donations to cover the snafu and to save the job of the person who got blamed for the error (Drinkard & Pound, 1999).

Online Contributions

One major change in the 2000 elections was the extent to which the Internet became an avenue for raising campaign funds. Overall, the four major candidates in the 2000 presidential election (John McCain, Al Gore, George W. Bush, and Bill Bradley) raised more than $9 million from online contributions. Three (Gore, McCain, and Bradley) raised more than a million dollars each online, and one (McCain), more than $6 million. Online contributions accounted for about 25 percent of McCain's total campaign budget, but less than 0.5 percent of George W. Bush's funds came from the Internet (Noble & Kennedy, 2000).

The advantage of the Internet as a fund-raising mechanism is that it is politics' version of an "impulse buy" (Drinkard, 2000). Supporters can show their enthusiasm for a candidate by going online and using their credit cards to express their support and approval immediately. Not surprisingly, then, the biggest influxes of cash from online sources tend to come after major events. The thirteen Republicans who led the U.S. House's impeachment efforts in the Senate trial of President Clinton also used the Internet to try to raise campaign funds for Republican congressmen who supported the impeachment ("Impeach This," 2000). John McCain collected more than $400,000 online within forty-eight hours of his victory in the 2000 New Hampshire Republican primary (Drinkard, 2000) and more than $2.8 million in the weeks that followed (Noble & Kennedy, 2000). McCain also broadened the use of the Internet, scheduling a live online fund-raiser that was the first event of its kind—a $100-per-person "town hall" meeting online at the College of Charleston.

An additional advantage of online fund-raising is that it develops a database of individual donors who can be asked to donate again at a later date. Forty percent of the online donors were first-time givers to a presidential campaign, and the typical donation was between $105 and $115—well below the maximum level of allowable donations. To be successful, though, the candidate's Web site must be designed to facilitate fund-raising activities. Jalonick (2000) noted that the three crucial elements of success were to ask them to donate, don't make them search for a place onscreen to contribute, and don't use technology that you're not equipped to handle. In essence, the Web site must make it easy for potential contributors to donate their money and easy for the campaign to handle the money that comes in.

The Internet was such a major source of campaign funds in Campaign 2000 that it caught the Federal Election Commission by surprise (Whillock, 2001). The commission found itself having to issue a number of rulings on issues that it had never faced before. Generally, though, campaign Web sites are subject to similar sponsorship requirements as are other campaign media (FEC Advisory Opinion #1988–2, 1998), but those requirements are not placed on individuals using their home equipment (FEC Advisory Opinion #1999–17, 1999). The most important ruling, though, for fund-raising purposes was the revision that allowed credit card contributions to be eligible for federal matching funds, with the provision that the campaign report the name of the donor, and the donor's occupation and employer for any contribution over $200 (FEC Advisory Opinion #1999–9, 1999).

Bundling

Limits on campaign contributions are also intended to limit the influence that any one contributor can have on a candidate. One by-product of the laws, however, is that the relatively low ceiling on the limits makes it impossible for the candidates to seek such contributions on an individual basis. A presidential candidate with a budget of $30 million, for example, would have to meet individually with more than 30,000 different people to have a chance to solicit funds in that amount. Campaigns handle that (and simultaneously get around the intent of the law) by using a process known as "bundling."

Major contributors are asked to provide "bundles" of campaign contributions that include their contribution, contributions from other family members, and contributions from their employees and/or business associates. In the 2000 election, for example, George W. Bush raised more than $70 million for his primary campaign; while all of the individual contributions were within the legal limit, most of that money was raised by only 200 people, super-fund-raisers who were known in the Bush camp as "Pioneers" (Hitt, 1999). Al Gore used a similar technique in the 1996 election when his visit to a Buddhist temple served as the impetus for a bundling event. Legally, there is nothing wrong with the approach, but it represents a tactic that the framers of the law had not anticipated. As a result, there is no legal requirement for the candidate or the campaign to identify who the super-fund-raisers are. In fact, some reformers approve of bundling (*Nixon* v. *Carver*, U.S. District Court 518, U.S. 1033, Springfield, MO, 1996). In essence, then, bundling is a process that simultaneously makes it easier for campaigns to raise money while also allowing major contributors a chance to provide campaigns with major sources of funds. The latter factor, in essence, circumvents the intent of the campaign finance laws.

SUMMARY

Money has become such a major part of campaigns that even the political parties have looked at ways to cut back on expenses (Drew, 2007). Still, an effective campaign must have an effective fund-raising unit. Such a program is usually the result of a well-planned and executed program that involves a great deal of time and labor devoted to that effort. Perhaps that's why consultant Carl Silverberg (2000) described "discipline" as the most important ingredient in fund-raising efforts. If the effort is successful, the campaign gains at least four rhetorical advantages. Fund-raising enhances credibility, attracts media attention, increases subsequent fund-raising, and decreases the opposition. Early fund-raising enhances a candidate's credibility, draws media attention to the campaign, bestows legitimacy to the campaign efforts, and puts pressure on the competition to raise a comparable amount. Increased media attention can generate even more donations, putting pressure on the competitors and possibly driving some of them out of the race.

Campaign funds are raised amid a set of rules that govern campaign contributions, reporting, and spending limitations, but campaigns often use "soft" money to circumvent at least some of these requirements. Traditional techniques for raising funds include the use of host events, direct mail, and "bundling" plans in which major donors serve as surrogate fund-raisers. More recently, the Internet has provided a means of online fund-raising through which supporters can use their credit cards to make "impulse donations" to a campaign.

Overall, though, the financial side of political communication is full of potential ethical and legal potholes that can create problems for the candidate, the campaign, the donors, and the voters. As new campaign laws have been developed, loopholes have always been detected and unintended consequences emerged that have affected the campaign process (Smith, 1996).

QUESTIONS FOR DISCUSSION

1. A multimillionaire candidate for governor, who had lost several major statewide races that he had largely funded himself, was determined to be successful in a political endeavor. Beginning very early, he raised funds for his gubernatorial race from all possible sources. Seven months before the election he had raised four times as much money as all other candidates. As campaign manager for one of his opponents, what would you do to counter this financial advantage? As his campaign press secretary how do you keep news coverage of his financial success continuing?

2. Why do the news media spend so much time reporting how much money a candidate raises?

3. One candidate for governor raised more funds than were permitted under the laws of his state. As a result, his opponent received a windfall in the final two weeks of the campaign in the form of a cash payment from the state—one of the penalties placed on a candidate for exceeding fund-raising limits. As a result, in the last two weeks of the election, the first candidate was criticized for his excessive funds and poor campaign management. Meanwhile, his opponent was able to purchase more advertising and visibility than anyone expected. Was this fair? Why or why not?

4. In an open city council race, one candidate raised very little money. However, third-party advertisements supported him unanimously. Generally, the amounts of money actually spent on the campaign were same on both sides. Was this fair?

5. Your campaign has decided to use the Internet as the major fund-raising avenue for a secretary of state campaign. As campaign manager, what strategies and tactics do you use to maximize contributions? As campaign manager for the opponent, what strategies and tactics do you use to minimize the value of those contributions?

The Role of Interpersonal Influence

As he arrived for work one morning, John remembered a story on the evening news the night before about a presidential candidate's position on an environmental issue. John was an assistant manager of an automotive tire plant, and petroleum-based waste was a common by-product of the production process. Would the candidate's new position on this issue affect his industry? His job? His paycheck? He would have to see what others at the plant thought.

John's inquisitiveness illustrates the importance of interpersonal influence, or opinion leadership, in modern political persuasion. Most modern theories of political influence assume that opinion leadership plays a pivotal role. Voters evaluate the opinions of others while forming their own opinions (Mutz, 1998). As they move toward and make their individual political decisions, they argue with and inform one another about the candidates and their issues (Huckfeldt & Sprague, 1995). Various theories disagree on the specifics of its role and the relationship of opinion leadership to media use, but nearly all specify a significant relationship of some type. The limited effects model views interpersonal opinion influence as a mitigating factor that limits the impact of the media. Agenda-setting views interpersonal discussions as reflective of media priorities. Uses-Gratification views "interpersonal utility" as one of the reasons that voters seek information from the news. In each case, the theory proposes a link between what voters see or read in the news and what they discuss with other voters. What people discuss with others, it turns out, may be more influential than what they receive as information from the media.

The topic represents one area of political campaign communication research in which there are major divergences between the views of academicians and consultants. Most academic research on the topic has focused on the role of interpersonal opinion leadership as it affects public opinion, an approach represented by the example at the beginning of this chapter. But the concept of interpersonal influence has a much broader view among consultants, one that includes interpersonal opinion leadership, diffusion of information, elite leaders, lobbyists, and legislative leadership. Regardless, interpersonal communication can have a major impact on elections and sometimes can be the difference between winning and losing. As pollsters Mike Mellman and Michael Bloomberg (January 6, 2008) concluded, "While 30-second spots will remain a central means of persuasive communication, we have to recognize the power of individuals to influence one another" (p. WK12).

INTERPERSONAL OPINION LEADERSHIP

The Two-Step Flow

The concept of interpersonal influence was first introduced into modern political communication theory as an explanation of the "rule of minimal effects," or limited effects model, discussed in an earlier chapter (Klapper, 1960). Katz and Lazarsfeld (1955) suggested the "two-step flow" as one explanation for these minimal effects whereby more knowledgeable and active opinion leaders processed and passed on campaign information to their friends and associates. Berelson, Lazarsfeld, and McPhee (1954); and Lazarsfeld, Berelson, and Gaudet (1968) reinforced this view, arguing that one reason the media had a limited effect on voting behavior was because the media were subordinate to interpersonal influence. When faced with voting decisions, many voters simply did not rely on information from the media and instead sought advice from people they respected, either to find out how to vote or to reinforce a decision already made (Rogers & Cartano, 1962). Thus, much political information reached the public only after it had passed through interpersonal channels. Interpersonal opinion leaders interpreted the media in light of the social predispositions of their community and passed those interpretations along to other members of the social groups. The result of these interpersonal discussions was that the media reinforced attitudes rather than changed them. Mass persuasion, it was argued, was subordinate to interpersonal influence. In this framework, opinion leaders are an essential element for the effective transmission of media information to the public. Information first reaches opinion leaders, who subsequently pass their interpretation of the information along to their followers.

Problems with that notion soon became apparent. Researchers had trouble identifying who were opinion leaders and who were not. Opinion leadership differed from topic to topic, and designating a particular person within a social group as the opinion leader became difficult. Furthermore, data from the original study by Katz and Lazarsfeld (1955) indicated that most of the interpersonal discussions generated by the media were horizontal in nature—between social equals—rather than a downward transmission from leaders to followers. As a result, researchers in opinion leadership soon shifted their focus to an analysis of social influence produced by those horizontal interpersonal discussions.

Interpersonal Utility (*Anticipated Communications*)

One approach to studying interpersonal discussion is interpersonal utility, a concept developed in the Uses-Gratification approach to media effects. Interpersonal utility refers to the idea that information obtained from the media serves as a storehouse of data for interpersonal discussions between friends and in the workplace. The function springs from our needs to have information to use when talking with others. The media are viewed as sources of information, outlets that provide verbal ammunition for future discussions or arguments with others. For those who actively participate in elections, interpersonal conversations about politics is a frequent activity. Election time stimulates a round of coffee-shop, e-mail, and telephone exchanges as political junkies seek to stay up to date on the latest political information. Their talk will include exchanges of information, political arguments, and issue-specific news as political activists express their views and exchange information with others (Wyatt, Kim, & Katz, 2000).

Several subcategories of interpersonal utility have been identified. Swanson (1976) divided it into three subcategories: political discussions with friends, offering advice to others, and asking others for advice. Other suggested uses have included information-seeking and opinion-leadership needs (gathering information so we can offer opinions on an issue). Nor is the interpersonal utility of political information limited to information or decision-making purposes. Voters also use political media as a source of information for informal discussion and entertainment. Political jokes are frequently exchanged in this manner. Television comedians such as Jay Leno and David Letterman become the source of new jokes that later become fodder for the interpersonal context. During 1998 and 1999, the controversy surrounding President Clinton's relationship with a White House intern eventually led to impeachment proceedings against the president; the late-night television shows, meanwhile, provided jokes that were later retold in interpersonal and work-related environments (Powell & Kitchens, 1999).

Interpersonal utility views the process from the view of the voter, not the political candidate. Voters discuss political stimuli when it is useful for them to do so, not when campaigns want them to do it. Neuman (1986) argues that voters use discussions with opinion leaders as a filtering mechanism that allows them to bypass most of the political information that comes from campaigns. As Neuman (1986) wrote, "It is unnecessary to recompile and reevaluate all the available political data when a trusted friend or colleague has already completed the task" (p. 173).

Rumors

Rumors refer to interpersonal communication constructed around unauthenticated information (Rosnow & Fine, 1976, p. 11). They can have a dramatic impact on political campaigns. Some political rumors occur spontaneously, but others are carefully constructed by consultants or other campaign agents. When they develop spontaneously, they typically reflect a group effort to define what is occurring. In those instances, Allport and Postman (1947) argue that the foundation of rumors is laid when events are important and news is lacking or ambiguous; the resulting rumors reflect a normal desire to find meaning in events, even though the attempt might prove dysfunctional (p. 144). Spontaneous political rumors often surface during times of political turmoil. For example, rumors continue to circulate regarding the assassinations of President John F. Kennedy, Martin Luther King, Jr., and Robert F. Kennedy.

In other instances, campaign rumors may be a packaged story that is deliberately planted as a political whispering campaign (Rosnow & Fine, 1976, pp. 27–29). Such campaigns are nothing new. Andrew Jackson's campaign for the presidency was tainted by rumors spread by the opposition that he and his wife lived together in adultery. Martin Van Buren was rumored to be the illegitimate son of Aaron Burr. During the 1972 presidential election, the Nixon campaign used a number of "dirty tricksters" to spread rumors about George McGovern and the other Democratic presidential hopefuls. Sometimes such campaigns can be dramatically effective; the Nixon campaign succeeded in driving Senator Edmund Muskie out of the race. The manipulative use of rumors can continue even after the elections. Government officials initiate rumors on a number of issues as a trial balloon to test public reaction. News leaks are an organized form of rumor initiation that allows officials to release information without attribution.

Political rumors can be especially powerful because of the rhetorical situation in which they occur. Allport and Postman (1947) noted that the seeds for rumors are planted when the issue is salient and information is ambiguous. The emotional content of many political campaigns, coupled with the equivocation that often dominates political speeches, provides a fertile field for rumors to grow. As a result, organized efforts to spread rumors can be dramatically effective. And, with the advent and anonymity of the Internet, campaigns have a quick and effective means of planting such information.

POLITICAL ELITES

Political observers watched with interest in 1999 and 2000 as Arizona senator John McCain ran a surprisingly strong, although ultimately unsuccessful, campaign for the presidency. Many pundits attributed McCain's early success to shifts in public opinion, arguing that his campaign addressed themes that generated frequent interpersonal discussions about him among friends and coworkers. Sometimes overlooked is that McCain's very presence in politics was at least partly due to a different form of opinion leadership: elite leaders. McCain had no ties to Arizona until he married Cindy Hensley and moved there in 1981. His wife's father, beer baron James W. Hensley, helped finance McCain's first race for Congress in 1982 (Frantz, 2000). Adding to McCain's edge was the support of another political elite, Darrow Tully. Tully, the publisher of Arizona's biggest newspaper (*The Arizona Republic*), ensured that McCain was the darling of the state's business establishment. With Hensley's money and Tully's endorsement, McCain was able to outspend and defeat better-known opponents.

That early success illustrates the role that political elites play in political campaigns. This collection of active politicos and members of social and professional groups who are active in the political process has been tagged with a number of descriptive labels including the "para-political system" (Easton, 1965), a "para-political subsystem" (Donahue, Tichenor, & Olien, 1972), "grasstops" (Ciglar & Loomis, 2006, p. 1), and "intermediate relations and ties" (Suine & Kline, 1976). Some critics view political elites as part of an influence-peddling political system that hurts the democratic process (e.g., Harwood & Seib, 2009).

Still, research has generally viewed political elites as a stabilizing force that balances the upward and downward communication between government and voters (Donahue, Tichenor, & Olien, 1972). As an upward channel, the intermediate relationships increase active participation. As a downward channel, the parapolitical ties provide a context for processing and receiving messages, thus serving as "social anchors for evaluating and contextualizing messages" (Siune & Kline, 1976).

These power brokers have an influence on public opinion that can extend beyond their financial help and personal ties. Neuman (1986) calls them political elites, a subgroup of political sophisticates who participate in political activities and "respond to political stimuli" (p. 103). They are distinguished from other voters by three variables: their knowledge of politics, the salience of political issues to them, and the complexity of their conceptualization of politics and campaigns. Despite the potential powers of political elites, they are limited by the sparsity of numbers. For the democratic process to work, Neuman argues that "it remains important to balance the specialized knowledge of the elite and the generalized common sense of the mass polity" (p. 189).

Politicians value and seek out political elites to enhance their chances of electoral success (Nimmo, 1970; Shadegg, 1972). As such, political elites become persuasive targets of a political campaign effort, resulting in them serving an intermediary role in which they are both sources and receivers of information. As a result of elites' direct contact with politicians, subordinates view the elite as a secondary source of information, someone who can obtain data and can pass them on to them. At the same time, as targets of the persuasive efforts of politicians, elites are receivers of campaign messages and not simply channels for further diffusion.

The communication process between politicians and elites differs in channel, style, and goals. In most cases, politicians prefer to communicate directly to the elite, either through personal contact or personal letters (Powell & Shelby, 1985). There is correspondingly less reliance on television or other forms of mass media. When the mass media are used, the persuasive goal often differs from that of normal campaign communication. In a process known as "laying cover," politicians or special-interest groups may use a mass media campaign in an effort to convince political elites that popular opinion is on their side. Even there, though, the ultimate argument is made through direct contact instead of through the media.

The style and goal of candidate-elite communication also differs from other campaign communications. Politicians feel less need to be friendly, representative, or easy to talk to when conversing with elites, as compared to contacts with voters (Powell & Shelby, 1985). As less attention is paid to these skills, the effective candidate is likely to increase his or her active listening skills when dealing with political elites (Joy, 2001). It becomes more important that candidates understand the elite's position on issues. Part of that shift in skill usage is a by-product of the directness of the messages exchanged in such settings, and part may come from the interpersonal channels used. The personal contact represents an affirmation of the political elite's worth, as acknowledged by the politician. Such acknowledgment may be the crucial communicative goal for both the politician and the political elites.

Still, the role of interpersonal influence is not limited to politician-elite inter-actions. Some groups and individuals have developed programs that target political elites for lobbying efforts. An Alabama estate lawyer who launched a campaign to repeal the federal estate tax used political elites as a crucial part of his campaign effort. Birmingham lawyer Harold Apolinsky identified fifty congressmen who were not yet supporting the bill and targeted thirty of their donors who had given the maximum $1,000 contribution. He contacted each of those contributors and asked them to call the legislators and urge them to support the repeal of the tax (Brumas, 2000).

POLITICAL LOBBYING

A very specific type of political elite who is actively involved in the political process is the political lobbyist. Lobbyists are an often overlooked factor in the political process, and yet their influence likely exceeds that of any other type of political consultant. Washington, D.C. is the working home of more than 20,000 lobbyists. That number far exceeds the number of professionals who make their living as campaign consultants, and represents nearly forty lobbyists for each member of Congress. The money involved (more than $1.4 billion in 1999) makes even George W. Bush's campaign war chest seem small, and that number only covers the federal government. Add in the massive number of lob-byists in each state capital, and a staggering number of people are involved in the lobbying process.

Nature of the Profession

Dexter (1969, p. 4) defined lobbying as a process of addressing or soliciting support from a legislative body. Their job is simple: to have influence over legislation (Lane, 1964, p. 4) and to validate the role that their group plays in policy making. They remind legislators that they are around and that their views should be considered when policy decisions are made. They keep in touch with interest group allies and try to spur them on. The constant inter-action is a means of exchanging information, developing strategy, and politely supporting and pushing other groups. When the process works ideally, the lobbyists have a "reconciliation" impact on legislation that improves legislation before it is finalized (Brasher, March 21, 2010, p. 1F). When it doesn't work, the lobbyists strive to ensure that the legislation helps (or does not hurt) their inter-est group, without necessarily considering the good of the general public (see, e.g., Kirkpatrick, 2009).

Despite the commonality in goals, lobbyists often differ in the way they do their job. Some rely on letters written by their constituents. Others prefer direct contact with the legislator. For all, they have the responsibility of being the eyes and ears of their organization. They must keep the members of their group aware of policy developments and legislative changes that may affect their clients. Lobbyists are the nerve endings of an interest group, and they spend most of each day carrying messages back and forth between their environment and the organization.

The profession is both maligned and misunderstood. Hamm (1991) noted that few lobbyists engage in unethical activities, and most work long hours to represent their constituents. But the negative images remain anyway, with many being seen as backroom operators with an unethical influence on the laws of the land. Contrary to that image, most try to be as visible as possible. They attend congressional hearings even though nothing much of consequence is likely to happen there. They'll make repeated visits to different Capitol Hill offices, even if they can only leave a message with a secretary. Interminable after-work receptions are a chance to exchange a word or two with legislators. One retired lobbyist was quoted as saying: "I used to get irritated when I'd see my colleagues in on a Tuesday, Wednesday, or Thursday afternoon (Congress's usual days in session). I'd ask them why they weren't on the Hill. You have to be seen. Even if the legislators don't know who you are, if they see you often enough, they'll start to feel you belong" (Checkoway, 1993).

Many professional lobbyists don't even describe themselves as such, referring to their work instead as "public affairs" or "government relations." Aberbach (1990) noted that many resent the "lobbyist" label "because of its unflattering connotations (and) also because it doesn't adequately describe what they do." As a group, they are highly educated (Salisbury, 1989). Many hold advanced college degrees in law, business, or political science.

Turnover, among both lobbyists and politicians, makes the job even harder. Turnover among lobbyists is frequent, with a great deal of movement in and out of lobbying jobs. The typical lobbyist has been in the job for five or fewer years (Orren, 1989). Part of the turnover is likely due to frustration, for theirs is a job in which most policy outcomes are determined by factors beyond their control (Salisbury, 1989). Part of the turnover comes from opportunities in other organizations; competent lobbyists frequently say that their professional contacts within the political arena makes other job opportunities available to them (Checkoway, 1993). Even when there is stability among the lobbying forces, there can still be significant turnover among the legislators with whom they must work. Each new election brings a new group of representatives, initiating a process known as "courting the rookies." When new faces reach the nation's capitals, lobbyists emerge to court these legislators. The basic forms of courting include dinners, sporting events, trips, and gifts. Trips may consist of hunting, fishing, and some trips that might include a small amount of business. Lobbyists send cards on special days, mail flowers to secretaries, give candy and cigars to politicians. Some lobbyists offer services to political officials that include massages from therapists or chiropractic services.

Tools of the Trade

Several factors contribute to their effectiveness. Not surprisingly, those factors share some commonality with other persuasive situations.

Interpersonal Relationships   The primary communication tool of the lobbyist is interpersonal communication. Their main objective is to build solid relationships and connections with as many legislators as possible. Once a relationship is established, it becomes a means for lobbying issues later. As one New Jersey lobbyist said, "Before I ask for anything from them, I try to make friends" (Rosenthal, 1993). Athletics is a major tool, with many lobbyists jogging, golfing, or playing basketball with legislators. Relationships are developed and maintained even if the legislator generally opposes the lobbyist on most issues. Issues shift and coalitions change, and a lobbyist who may be at odds with a legislator on one issue may need his or her support on another (Sethi, 1993). A positive relationship is continued for as long as possible.

Credibility   One reason that lobbyists are, as a rule, highly ethical in their professional behavior is that credibility is an essential component of what they do. Their job is persuasive in nature, and credibility is essential to the persuasive process. They readily admit this; the need to protect their credibility is the top priority for the job (McCaid, 1989). If they lose that credibility, for whatever reason, their job (and their reputation) is threatened. "Washington is a village," Aberbach (1990) wrote. "You are known by your good name and integrity." Similarly, as one lobbyist told Orren (1989), if you mislead a member of Congress, "you can expect a member never to listen to you seriously." Another corporate lobbyist told McCaid (1989), "all you have is your word." The emphasis on credibility starts early during the development of the relationship. As the lobbyists get to know an individual legislator, they look for ways to demonstrate their friendship and credibility to the legislator.

Money   Lobbyists are a generous source of campaign contributions (Rosenthal, 1993, p. 129) and frequently set up political action committees for that purpose. Big groups, such as the National Rifle Association, can have a major influence on elections (Patrick, 2002). Money helps them to elect friendly legislators, candidates who are more likely to share their philosophical leaning. Campaign contributions open doors for later lobbying efforts and create obligations that a legislator can repay by at least listening to the lobbyist's position. Decisions regarding allocation of candidate funds is usually based on what Lowery and Brasher (2004) call an "an access strategy—rather than an electoral strategy" (p. 171), that is, lobbyists support a candidate based on how much access they have to that candidate. Such decisions can be particularly important to a new candidate, because interest groups can "offer new candidates access to vital resources that they need to win" (p. 20). The money factor is not limited to campaign contributions. Lobbyists also lavish money on entertainment for legislators— "fact-finding" trips to vacation spots, receptions, and meals. Phone giant AT&T once organized a lobbying campaign based on providing cupcakes to key government officials (Wyatt, 2011). There are a number of restaurants in Washington, D.C., for example, where a member of Congress can enter at nearly any time, knowing that they are unlikely to have to buy their own meal. Some lobbyist who is also dining there will invariably pay for the meal.

Research   Aberbach (1990) noted that the lobbyists' messages are guided by one principle: "The more factual the better." Some staff members spend all or most of their time gathering information, separating the useful from the unnecessary (Salisbury, 1989), and compiling it in a manner that is most useful to both the lobbyist and the legislators. Messages must focus on specific facts. If a lobbyist hopes to persuade a legislator to change his or her vote on a piece of legislation, he or she must have new information. No legislator will be influenced without factual support, regardless of how close the relationship is with the lobbyist. Sometimes new information comes from polling data. Many lobbyists maintain relationships with political pollsters for that purpose. If a legislator is wavering on a particular vote, lobbyists might provide them with a poll to illustrate how a vote on legislation might affect their reelection chances. Others seek public support by focusing media attention on the issue (Yanovitzky & Bennett, 1999).

Hamm (1991) argues that the goal of the lobbyist should be to create a dependency by providing the legislator with the right kind of information at the right time. Typically, the "right kind of information" will be arguments that point out the consequences of the proposed legislation (Lau, Smith, & Fiske, 1991). Sethi (1993) noted that the optimal role for lobbyists is that they become trusted sources of information when legislators need data. For that to occur, lobbyists must become experts in their subject of concern. Once they have mastered a complex policy issue and the consequences of policy changes, they become part of the legislative process. Legislators seek them out for advice, and many lobbyists actually assist (sometimes heavily) in the writing and wording of new legislation as policy makers draw on their knowledge to solve difficult issues. Lobbyists will also help a legislator by working to get support from other legislators.

Compromise The lobbying profession is one in which most tasks are doomed to failure. Ideal legislation, as defined by the lobbyists and their constituency, is rarely achieved. Instead, most legislation is produced as a compromise between competing positions. As noted earlier, Brasher labels this process "reconciliation" and describes it as "a tool for getting things done" (p. 1F). Successful lobbyists recognize this fact and aggressively seek workable compromises that are acceptable to all parties (Checkoway, 1993).

The Revolving Door

One unusual aspect of the lobbying profession is the extent to which the roles of legislator and lobbyist are often a revolving door through which former legislators become lobbyists. As of 1999, 138 of Washington's registered lobbyists were former members of Congress, two-thirds of whom left the Hill after 1990. Twenty-five percent of those congressmen defeated in the 1994 elections subsequently landed jobs in Washington lobbying firms. Rosenthal (1993, p. 113) noted that 20 percent of the lobbyists in California were former legislators or governmental staff workers. The advantage of the revolving door is that most legislators have an intimate understanding of the legislative process and preexisting relationships with their former colleagues. But the practice has raised ethical questions about its effect on legislation. Would legislators who might want a high-paying lobbying job after they retire be influenced in their relationships with lobbyists? Under current law, former members of Congress cannot directly lobby their colleagues for one year after leaving office. But they can go ahead and establish their lobbying position or business while indirectly lobbying on issues. Thus, the effect of the law is merely to delay direct lobbying for one year.

LEGISLATIVE CUE-GIVING

Cue-giving research focuses on how legislators decide how they will vote. Most research has indicated that the primary cue is partisan in nature (most legislators vote in concert with other members of their party), a trend that makes the lobbyist's role even more difficult. Legislators, however, are sometimes faced with issues on which their party has no formal stance. In those instances, they may resort to personal beliefs or they may rely upon any number of other cues. Cues that could influence their vote are the position of other legislators, input from legislative leaders, influence from the executive branch, information from interest groups and their lobbyists, and attitudes among the legislator's constituents. Regardless of which specific cue influences the final decision, most arguments for voting for or against a bill fall into one of two categories—arguments based on the merits of the proposal, and warnings of the political consequences of voting the "wrong" way.

Research into "cue-giving" was pioneered by Kingdon (1973), who interviewed sixty members of Congress in 1969. The results of the survey found that most legislators followed partisan lines on noncontroversial legislation, but broke party lines to vote with the apparent majority on controversial issues. Matthews and Stimson (1975) subsequently defined cues as "any communication—verbal or nonverbal—intended or unintended" that influences voting (p. 51). They described cue-givers as colleagues with attributes of trustworthiness, similar views, friendship, and reciprocity. By the 1980s, studies in cue-giving were shifting from Congress to state legislatures, with the reporting of different results. Ray (1982), in a study of legislatures in Pennsylvania, Massachusetts, and New Hampshire, found that the most important cues were fellow legislators and interest groups. The executive branch, conversely, had little impact.

A number of studies have examined the role of friendship as a cue-giving factor. Patterson (1959), in a study of the Wisconsin state assembly, argued that legislative friendships were a function of geographic location, length of tenure, earlier political alliances, and seating arrangements on the floor. In a study of the Iowa legislature, Caldeira and Patterson (1987) demonstrated that legislators who sit next to one another tended to develop friendships. Uslander and Weber (1979), in a study of all fifty state legislatures, found that legislators cited friends in the legislature as the largest source of cues on how to vote. Matthews and Stimson (1975) found that friendship was frequently mentioned as an attribute of friendship in the U.S. House of Representatives. Ferber and Pugliese (1999), however, in a study of the New York State Assembly, found that the influence of seat proximity was largely a function of party. Proximity tended to influence cues because members of the same party are seated together.

Ferber and Pugliese (1999), in an examination of controversial roll call votes, found little relationship between communication among legislative members and their votes. There was such a relationship on one issue—the death penalty—with members who "stuck to business" when talking with colleagues demonstrating more influence on that issue. But there was little support for other issues (abortion, health care, surrogate parenting for example). Generally, state legislators rely on party leaders for "narrow" issues, but shift to other cues on issues with a broader appeal. Similarly, in the U.S. House of Representatives, members of Congress rely on cues from staff, party leaders, committee chairs, ranking members, and other colleagues on issues that are of an internal nature to the legislature. If the issue is of a broader, external nature, however, the parties' use of cues differed according to the subject at hand.

CAMPAIGN IMPLICATIONS

From a campaign perspective, the importance of interpersonal communication has been widely accepted, if not always implemented. Diffusion theory, for example, is rarely used by campaign consultants. Kraus and Davis (1976, p. 125) have pointed out a number of theoretical weaknesses to diffusion research, and some of those bear directly on why consultants have generally ignored this element. Specifically, the diffusion model is primarily descriptive in nature. Research has focused on what happens to information on a post hoc basis, rather than predict how any specific information will be diffused. Lack of predictability is its major academic weakness, which also reduces the utility of the theory to consultants. Diffusion theory cannot predict when barriers might appear, how long the diffusion will take, how widespread it will be, or what stages it might pass through. Such an ambiguous conception of what might happen simply reduces its utility to consultants and campaigns.

But the general concept of interpersonal influence has been incorporated into a number of campaign efforts and techniques. Typically, campaigns first target elite opinion leaders, with major campaign efforts directed at getting their support. Still, the importance of interpersonal opinion leadership has not been overlooked. Some campaigns, including George McGovern's 1972 primary campaigns, placed a major emphasis on interpersonal communication programs (Devlin, 1973). As early as the 1960s, Republican consultant Stephen Shadegg (1972) often touted the value of interpersonal influence on campaigns. He recommended two distinctly different approaches in which the two-step flow could be used in campaigns. The "Social Precinct" program began with a mail campaign in which supporters wrote to their friends, asking them to provide advice and support to the candidate. If they agreed, they were added to a computerized list; the campaign would regularly provide those people with information about the campaign that could be used in interpersonal discussion. Although he provided no empirical support for the success of the program, Shadegg's plan aimed at reaching 3–5 percent of the voting public with the program. That formula was based on an assumption that each member of the social precinct was able to influence ten other voters on behalf of the candidate.

The social precinct survives today in electronic form, with many campaigns distributing such information to supporters by e-mail. In fact, the Internet offers campaigns their first capability of establishing an interpersonal network based on a global communication system (Carey, 1998). Since the modern process starts with computers, with new names and e-mail addresses easy to add, it likely sees more use today than it did in Shadegg's time. Its impact can be diminished, however, when all members of the social precinct come from the same or similar social groups. When that occurs, the "insider" information exchanged at the interpersonal level is merely a repetition of the information that each received by e-mail. Reinforcement occurs, but only among existing voters. To be successful, the social precinct program must spread its reach into a variety of social groups. The ultimate measure of its success is not the number of people who are reached, but the number of different social groups that are represented.

Shadegg's other plan, the "Block Captain" program, is also still around. The block captain is a program in which telephone workers call potential supporters in an effort to recruit interpersonal opinion leaders. When a person is contacted who agrees to become an interpersonal worker, a personal letter is sent to them. Campaign brochures are included, along with a request for the volunteer to distribute the information to the neighbors who live on the same city block. As new issue materials are developed, these may also be mailed to him or her with a request to distribute them. On election day, the telephone bank contacts each of the individual block captains again, asking them to knock on their neighbors' doors and remind people to vote. The value of the block captain program hinges on two factors, the value of interpersonal influence and its capacity to increase turnout within targeted areas. During the 1970s, Texas-based Democratic consultant Hugh Palmer adopted a variation of Shadegg's plan and used it to start a telephone-based consulting firm for Democratic candidates. Palmer eventually used the technique in a successful campaign as a candidate himself, winning election as mayor of Fort Worth.

The use of such programs indicates that most consultants place some value on the role of interpersonal influence on political voting behavior. Most consultants generally accept its value and like to use that process to their advantage. Implementation of such programs on a large scale can be difficult and costly, however. As a result, the organized use of such programs is often restricted either to small elections or to targeted areas of a larger electorate. Ultimately, when campaigns have to reach masses of voters, consultants will focus their efforts on the mass media.

SUMMARY

While mass media still dominate most political campaigns, the role of interpersonal influence cannot be overlooked. Interpersonal influence operates on multiple levels in political campaigns. Voters discuss campaigns with one another, seeking information or expressing a commonality of opinion in a manner that validates their lifestyles. Among political activists, interpersonal discussions are an integral part of daily conversations, but political topics will often be sprinkled into the conversations of those with even a moderate level of interest in politics. Consultants have tried to take advantage of this phenomenon by developing programs that can use voters' natural tendency to talk about politics. In the past, these programs have relied on organizational frameworks that used telephones and direct mail as the main communication channels. With the increased presence of the Internet, campaigns can now maintain one-to-one contact with supporters by e-mail.

Interpersonal communication is also a factor in candidate interactions with elite opinion leaders when the candidates seek donations and support that will legitimize their campaigns. While only a small percentage of the voters may ever see the candidate in such an informal setting, the candidate's ability to communicate on a one-to-one level can potentially influence the success or failure of their campaigns.

Lobbyists engage in an ongoing process in which interpersonal communication plays a key role. For them, interpersonal contacts with legislators is a means of influencing legislation. Although often unseen by the voting public, the communication exchanges in this forum have a major impact on legislative packages that affect the public. Further, major special interest groups, such as the National Rifle Association (Patrick, 2002), can influence election outcomes.

Finally, legislators use a variety of interpersonal cues when deciding how they will vote on much legislation. In addition to talking with lobbyists, most legislators exchange information with their colleagues, seeking to either learn more about a particular piece of legislation or to broker deals that will be beneficial to some legislation that they support. Again, the interpersonal communication process exercises a vital role on legislation that affects the public.

QUESTIONS FOR DISCUSSION

1. In 2001, the state of Mississippi held a referendum on whether the image of the Confederate battle flag should be removed from the state flag. Those who wanted to change the flag spent more than $700,000 in their campaign, while expenditures by the keep-the-flag side were minuscule by comparison (estimated at about $10,000). Still, in the subsequent referendum, voters supported keeping the old flag by 66 percent to 34 percent. How could the effects of interpersonal influence explain why a poorly financed campaign could be so successful?

2. One of the Democratic candidates in a primary received the endorsement of a prominent Republican. The Democrat played the endorsement very prominently in advertising, spending more than the other two Democrats. However, polls taken with three weeks left showed the candidate running third among Democratic voters. The campaign manager immediately removed the references to the Republican endorsement in the campaign advertising. The candidate won the primary. What led the campaign manager to make this decision? What is one explanation for this effect?

3. The city government decides to bring to a vote a proposal to build a new professional basketball arena. Enthusiastic fans, the chamber of commerce, and city officials support the proposal. Those who oppose higher taxes and "corporate welfare" oppose the proposal. Design a campaign plan to defeat the arena that will mobilize the most opponents while using only limited financial resources. Be sure to use an interpersonal communication and opinion leadership component in the plan.

4. A proposal is made to outlaw union agreements throughout the state that require union membership. How can the unions prevent the proposal from passing, using their membership as an activist core of support?

Critical Events
Analysis

On November 4, 1979, Iranian demonstrators overran the guards at the American Embassy in Tehran and captured a number of American personnel as hostages. When initial diplomatic efforts failed, President Jimmy Carter wrote a letter to the Iranian leader Ayatollah Khomeini, arguing that the embassy personnel were not spies and should be freed. As the press waited for presidential actions, little else was done. As press secretary Jody Powell said, "They think we're doing more than we are. They don't know how lousy our options are" (quoted by Jordan, 1982, p. 36). As negotiations dragged on, the Carter administration froze all Iranian assets in the United States, put other sanctions in place, and saw a United Nations commission formed to deal with the issue.

Nothing worked. Finally, the president attempted to free the hostages with a dramatic military rescue operation. That failed too, in an embarrassing manner, when U.S. helicopters had trouble flying in the sands of the Iranian desert. Eventually, Iran requested a $24 billion payoff for releasing the hostages. Carter refused. Unfortunately for Carter, the whole debacle continued through all of 1980—including the 1980 presidential election campaign. His inability to free the hostages was viewed as an indication of his weakness in the presidency. When the dust settled and the votes were counted, Ronald Reagan had been elected president. Iran freed the hostages on the day of Reagan's inauguration.

From a political campaign perspective, the Iranian hostage crisis would be classified as a critical event, which is an event that becomes a focal point of media coverage and thus influences the political environment. Researchers study the phenomenon using a technique known as "critical events analysis" (Kraus et al., 1976). A number of research studies have used the approach, with many looking at high-profile political debates, such as the 1960 Kennedy–Nixon debates (Kraus, 1962), or provocative events such as the assassination of President John F. Kennedy (Greenberg, 1964; Mendelsohn, 1964) and the attempts on the lives of candidate George Wallace (Steinfatt et al., 1973) and President Ronald Reagan (Gantz, 1983; Weaver-Lariscy, Sweeney, & Steinfatt, 1984). Others have looked at key speeches during the campaign, including keynote speeches at the parties' conventions (Benoit, Blaney, & Pier, 2000).

From the campaign perspective, critical events analysis is a rare convergence of academic and consulting perspectives, albeit each approaches the topic from a different perspective. For the academic community, critical events analysis is primarily a post hoc process; scholars seek to identify major events—debates, convention speeches, major public appearances—that could have influenced the campaign. Identifying and analyzing those events provide scholars with an opportunity to examine the campaign process as a microcosm, identifying key points within a campaign and studying how they influenced the outcome of an election. For consultants, critical events are predictive factors, points, and events within a campaign that can be anticipated to have a major impact. Special care and attention are given to preparing for those that can be anticipated. Those that are unexpected are referred to in the field as "game changers," that is, "those campaign-shaking events that can alter the dynamics of a race" (Rutenberg, 2007, p. A25)

ANTECEDENT CONDITIONS

Not all campaign events are critical to the success or failure of a campaign, but critical events analysis, as outlined by Kraus and his associates (1976), assumes that campaign events can have an impact when certain social conditions are present. The most common characteristics that must be present are dissemination of information about the event, either concurrently with its occurrence, or extended over a period of time after it occurs, or both; and voter interest in the event, either at the time it occurred, after it occurred, or (more often) both.

Dissemination of Information

The dissemination of information about any campaign event is usually defined by its media coverage. Such coverage frequently occurs before, during, and after the event. Anticipated critical events, such as presidential debates, receive advanced publicity from the media, extensive on-site coverage of the event, and even more extensive postevent coverage. Still, on-site coverage by the media is not essential for an event to be considered a critical one. Sometimes all or most of the coverage occurs well after the event, particularly if the event was not anticipated by the news media. The Watergate break-in, for example, received only a small amount of coverage at the time it was discovered, and it had no appreciable effect on the Nixon–McGovern presidential campaign. However, subsequent coverage over the next two years was extensive, eventually leading to President Nixon's resignation.

In some small and local elections, media coverage of a critical event may be minimal or nonexistent; dissemination of the information about the event is limited to those in attendance and to the subsequent interpersonal discussions that follow. Still, that may suffice; when the electorate is small, the interpersonal discussions that follow may quickly spread the information. The authors, for example, are familiar with one state senate campaign that was decided on the basis of a critical event that never received news coverage. In that incident, the son of the candidate got involved in a fistfight with an elderly man over the placement of a campaign sign. The event received little news coverage, but rumors about the incident spread quickly. Campaign polling subsequently revealed that the incident was the major reason the candidate lost the election, with more than 60 percent of the electorate aware of the incident.

Voter Interest

For an event to be critical to the election, it must capture voter attention. The reasons for that attention may vary. Sometimes it may result from the news-priming function of the press. The news media's advance coverage of the event may serve to heighten awareness of it, leading to close attention being paid to the event. The intense scrutiny given to presidential debates, for example, falls within this category. Speeches at political conventions play a similar role; the media often provides gavel-to-gavel coverage of major convention speeches, priming them with advance notice of what the speaker might say. The most striking example of the role of news priming in political events, though, may be the undue impact that the media place on early presidential primaries and caucuses. Typically, all of the major newspapers and TV networks provide extensive coverage leading up to and following the Iowa caucus and the New Hampshire primaries. As the first two major electoral events in a presidential campaign, these two events are critical to the success of any major candidate. Straw polls are sometimes promoted by the media to the point that they become a critical event. Jimmy Carter used a 1975 Democratic straw poll in Ames, Iowa, as a springboard in his winning presidential campaign a year later.

Sometimes an event becomes critical because it becomes a symbolic representation of a larger issue. Martin Luther King, Jr. made this attribute a hallmark of the civil rights movement; rather than campaign for civil rights as a broad ideological issue, King based his protests on specific incidents that represented the larger issue—Rosa Parks's refusal to sit in the back of a Montgomery, Alabama, bus; sitting at a public lunchroom counter in North Carolina; a voter registration drive in Mississippi. More recently, during the 2000 presidential campaign, George W. Bush's appearance at Bob Jones University became representative of his ties to the religious right of the Republican party (Bruni & Kristof, 2000), leading to a subsequent apology from the candidate (Berke, 2000). President Clinton's decision to participate in the thirty-fifth anniversary of the Selma march resulted in extensive news coverage of that annual event (considerably more than in past celebrations) and served to highlight his concern over the fight for civil rights.

At other times, an event may play a watershed role because it plays a critical role in defining a candidate's image. During the 1988 presidential campaign, the vice presidential debate between Dan Quayle and Lloyd Bentsen included Bentsen's tart criticism of Quayle, "You're no Jack Kennedy." The line helped to define Quayle as a political lightweight, an image he was never able to overcome, and thus limited his ability to seek the presidency himself. Quayle was subsequently hurt by another critical event that hurt his image and credibility when he incorrectly spelled "potato" at a public school appearance. Nor is the damage of such events limited to Republicans. The Monica Lewinsky controversy was a critical event in the presidency of Bill Clinton. Even though Clinton survived the impeachment effort that resulted, the event had a lasting impact on his personal image as president.

IDENTIFYING CRITICAL EVENTS

Most studies that use critical events analysis have examined provocative events and the dissemination of information that followed them. These topics have included assassinations, speeches, and major protests. One of the earliest was a study of a parade to honor General Douglas MacArthur in Chicago, and every presidential debate since 1960 has garnered such academic attention. From the academic perspective, one purpose of this research is to identify those events that will produce the most useful explanation and prediction of social change. If the key points of a campaign can be reduced to one, or perhaps just a few, critical events, then analysis of the entire campaign or of any social change process can be simplified. In essence, critical events analysis makes the study of social change feasible. Otherwise, the enormity of the interaction of variables and events could overwhelm any single research effort.

Given that goal, then, a key aspect of the analysis is the proper identification of critical events. Important events that made a difference in a campaign must be identified, and all must be included. Just as important, those events that had little or no impact on the campaign must be eliminated from the analysis; their presence could unnecessarily complicate the analysis with extraneous variables and information. Ideally, that filtering process is most productive if it is conducted before the event, because advance notice of an event allows for a more thorough analysis of it. Presidential debates are the most obvious events that can be routinely anticipated; not surprisingly, they are among those critical events that have been the most thoroughly studied, beginning with the Kennedy–Nixon debates in 1960 (Kraus, 1962). Since then, the debates have produced a number of memorable moments—Bentsen's dig at Quayle, Ford's miscue on eastern Europe, and Ronald Reagan's affable joke about his age when paired against Walter Mondale.

The problem, of course, is that not all critical events can be anticipated. Sometimes critical events are planned by one of the competitors, but revealed to the public and the press without advance notice. This is frequently done through the paid media, with a campaign using an ad that aims to catch the opposition in a "surprise attack." Holding the surprise until the last minute gives the opposition less time to plan a response, and gives the press less time to thoroughly examine the issue. Another form of unanticipated critical event are campaign blunders. The frequent campaign appearances by candidates allow for multiple opportunities to make a mistake; if that mistake is documented, it can play a pivotal role in the campaign. In 1986, Alabama Republican Senator Jeremiah Denton was heavily favored to win reelection until he complained in a campaign speech that he "didn't have time" to talk to voters and also do his job. While the speech received little news coverage, a campaign worker for challenger Richard Shelby filmed the speech, and Denton's words became the topic of subsequent news coverage and a major commercial for the Shelby campaign. Shelby subsequently won the election.

Remember Howard Dean? The former governor of Vermont was a major contender for the Democratic nomination for president in 2004. That essentially ended after an unexpected fourth-place finish in the 2004 Iowa Democratic caucus. The disappointing finish was bad enough, but it was highlighted by his infamous "Scream" speech after the results were in—a speech broadcast nationwide and that effectively ended his chances for the nomination (McSweeney, 2007).

STUDYING CRITICAL EVENTS

As Kraus et al. (1976) noted, "The ultimate purpose of critical event analysis is to provide a scientific explanation of how elite actions have social consequences and how certain social processes constrain elite actions or negate their intended impact" (Kraus et al., 1976, pp. 199–200). That rather comprehensive goal cannot be achieved easily or with data that only approach the event from a limited perspective. Instead, critical events analysis attempts to use a variety of methodologies integrate data collected at both the individual and societal levels. At the individual level, these might include interviews with individuals and/or a broader range of participant-observation research. At a societal level, it might include public opinion research or an analysis of societal trends. The particular methodologies used have often varied depending on the extent to which prior notice was available and to what extent political elites were involved in the creation of the event. As noted earlier, identification of a critical event cannot always be anticipated. If the importance of the event is only recognized after it occurs, then some form of ad hoc research design must be employed to gather what information is available. If political elites are involved in the planning and execution of the event, the researchers can often mine their memories for useful information leading up to the event, even if that information was not public knowledge before the event. Political elites, however, sometimes have minor roles in truly critical events. Some may be well planned, but others, such as the Kennedy assassination, are outside the control of the politicos. The methodology also has to be adjusted on the basis of how the information was disseminated. In the past, major coverage was almost an essential ingredient in the diffusion of information about a major national event, but the extent and type of coverage may vary, depending on journalistic anticipation and evaluation of the event. The advent of the Internet has led to an increase in alternative sources of information.

A Design for Critical Events Analysis

An ideal analysis of a critical event gathers four types of information, data from the locale, the public response, media output, and opinion trend indicators.

The Locale   The goal for the researcher who studies the locale can vary, depending upon the nature of the event. Still, a few research questions seem to apply to most situations. The major ones are as follows:

1. What happened? Understanding the event requires a re-creation of the sequence of individual events that constituted the major event. At this stage of the research, the researcher approaches the critical event much like a detective or accident investigator, first trying to get a sense of what happened before any conclusions about "why" can be drawn.
2. What was the goal of the participants? This element of the analysis is essentially a post hoc strategy analysis in which the rhetorical intent of the

participants is identified. Why did they do this? What goals were they trying to achieve? This is a crucial stage in the research process; a misidentification of the participants' goals likely dooms the rest of the study to unproductive analysis.

3. Who was the target audience? This element of the process recognizes that the audience with which the event has the greatest effect may not be the immediate one. To understand the participants' intent, you must also understand whom they were trying to reach.

Answering these three questions usually involves one or more of three different techniques: direct observation, indirect observation, and focused interviews with elites. Direct observations may come from researchers positioned at the locale themselves. In the "MacArthur Day in Chicago" study, some members of the research team were stationed at points along the parade route to observe the reactions of others in the crowd as MacArthur's entourage passed by. Indirect observations may use unobtrusive data that might provide information about the size and nature of the immediate audience—how many beverages were consumed, how much trash was later collected, how many pro and anti signs were present at the event. Focused interviews with elites are necessary, though, to get a better understanding of their intent and target audience. Even that may not be sufficient for an ongoing campaign, since political strategists are reluctant to reveal their strategy while it is still being deployed. But an experienced interviewer can glean significant information about the participants' goals and targets, and that must be done to make the research valid.

Public Response Understanding the impact of a critical event requires an understanding of the public response to it. The issues in analyzing such responses are threefold: What is the public's perception and awareness of what happened? What sources of information did they use to form those perceptions? and Were there any perceived changes in opinions and attitudes as a result? The most common means of collecting these data is with some form of interview methodology, typically either a public opinion survey or a series of focus groups.

Collection of Media Output Public response to a critical event is often based on both the event and media coverage of the event. Critical events analysis thus places a major priority on collecting the media output related to a critical event. In the past, this has primarily meant collecting newspaper clippings and video copies of network news coverage. Electronic news sources have been particularly important, since—in the past—most people first heard about any one critical event through television or radio news, or from an interpersonal contact with someone who had heard about it there. More recently, the Internet has started to play a larger role in early dissemination of news about breaking events. Regardless of which medium dominates early coverage, the impact of critical events is often determined by news coverage of those events. In debates, for example, postdebate designation of a "winner" increases the likelihood that the public will view that candidate as the winner (Lowry, Bridges, & Barefield, 1991). That, in turn, has a positive influence on perceptions of that candidate's image, particularly his or her trait attribution (Ferguson, Hollander, & Melwani, 1989) and related vote decisions (Elliott & Sothirajah, 1993).

Collection of Opinion Trend Indicators When a critical event occurs, academic researchers are often poised to quickly conduct a public opinion survey to analyze audience response. But they are not alone in their pursuit of the topic. Many news organizations and national public opinion companies, such as the Gallup Poll and Harris Poll, also follow suit. The plethora of surveys that typically result serve as a data bank for an intensive analysis of public opinion trends. These can prove crucial in developing an understanding of the event and its impact on the public.

DEBATES AS CRITICAL EVENTS

The most visible of the anticipated critical events in presidential campaigns (and some statewide races) are televised debates. Debates have been major components of every presidential campaign since the Ford-Carter debates of 1976 (Hess, 1988). They are now such an institutionalized and ritualistic part of presidential campaigns that voters expect them to occur (Kraus, 2000), even though they are not legally required as part of the campaign. Furthermore, despite concerns over political malaise and lack of interest among voters, televised debates typically have a large viewing audience, larger than any other presidential campaign event (Buchanan, 1991).

Presidential debates are truly critical events. They offer candidates a chance to enhance their credibility while addressing issues that the media might have overlooked (Hellweg, Pfau, & Brydon, 1992). Furthermore, although such elements are merely one of several sources of voter information, debates typically have some type of impact on the voting public (Chaffee, 1978). For candidates, debates can orient voters about the personalities of the candidates, highlight differences in political philosophy, and focus attention on the candidates (Glenn, 2001). For voters, debates can increase interest and participation in a campaign (Buchanan, 1991; Carpini, Keeter, & Webb, 1997), increase voters' information about the campaign (Becker et al., 1978), enhance their ability to discuss the campaign with others (Miller & MacKuen, 1979), and trigger increased interpersonal communication about the campaign (Jamieson & Birdsell, 1988). For the media, debate allows some reporters access to the candidates in a situation that allows for cross examination–type questioning, thus allowing the voters to see how the candidates respond under pressure (Glenn, 2001). One immediate effect is a short-term impact on the salience of issues (Atkin, Hocking, & McDermott, 1979; Swanson & Swanson, 1978). In the immediate aftermath of the debate, the issues addressed by the candidates are likely to receive increased coverage from the news media and an enhanced perception of salience by the voting public. Debates can also influence the image and perceptions of the candidates, although the impact does not typically alter any voting intentions (Abramowitz, 1978).

Still, debates are not perfect forums for candidate–voter communication (Jamieson & Birdsell, 1988). Media questions can be superficial; even persistent questioning may reveal little information. The questions are also often biased, with front-runners getting more negative questions than the other candidates (Ben-Porath, 2007). Candidates often resort to repeating segments from their stump speeches or use the debate as a forum for attacking their opponent (Glenn, 2001). Voter response to these factors is often affected by three factors: the expectations of the candidates, the performances of the candidates, and the political ideologies of the voters. The expectations of the candidates often come from other elements of the campaign, depending on the image that the candidates project and the issues they discuss (Hellweg, Pfau, & Brydon, 1992). In the 2000 election, George W. Bush entered the debates following a series of campaign mis-statements that had raised doubts about his ability to perform well during the debates. While his resulting performance was not particularly stellar, it wasn't bad either. He subsequently came out of the debates with an improved image with the voters.

The performance of the candidates is also a factor. Debates present the candidates to the voters for a longer and more intense view of the candidates than either news or through advertising, giving the public a chance to familiarize themselves with the candidates (Jamieson & Birdsell, 1988, p. 28). Vancil and Pendell (1984) noted that the candidates can use that opportunity to demonstrate a presidential image; if they succeed at doing that, they will typically be perceived as the winner of the debate. Candidates can also lose debates with poor performances. As is discussed later in "mistake-based critical events," a candidate who blunders during a debate can suffer serious damage. As Lawrence (2000) noted, "Mistakes are replayed endlessly on news and TV." During the Bush–Gore debates, for example, Al Gore drew negative attention from the press with a series of inaccurate statements, including the claim that he had visited Texas following a natural disaster in the state. The resulting news coverage about the misrepresentations occupied the news agenda for several days and necessitated a subsequent apology from Gore. Similarly, in 1988, Michael Dukakis lost ground when he was asked whether he would favor capital punishment for the killer if his wife were raped and murdered. Instead of expressing emotion, he listed the policy reasons behind his opposition to the death penalty (Lawrence, 2000). Mistakes are not always verbal in nature. In 1992, President George H. W. Bush was criticized for glancing at his watch during a debate, as if he were anxious for it to be over.

While the press will focus increased attention on factual errors, voters often react negatively to personal mistakes. Personal behavior during the campaigns are often evaluated through the lens of voter expectations. Hinck and Hinck (1998) argue for evaluating such responses through their politeness theory. Their work is an expansion on Brown and Levinson's (1987) theory that politeness is a universal value that operates across cultures. According to politeness theory, one standard used by voters to evaluate candidates is the expectation that the candidates maintain an attitude of respect for the opposing candidate. Any deviation from this standard makes the voters uncomfortable and can cause a negative reaction toward the candidate who violates the norm. The candidates used politeness strategies in both the 1992 and 1996 debates (Hinck & Hinck, 2000). The factor emerged again, in a negative manner, for Al Gore during the 2000 debates. At times, Gore made the voters uncomfortable with his overly aggressive debate style, his audible sighs, and his tendency to move closer to Bush when the latter was answering a question. Such moments become pivotal points in the debate because the viewers are attuned to potential violations of politeness and they view behaviors at that moment as indicative of broader values and competence. They recognize key moments when a candidate's public face is threatened, and how the candidate handles those moments affects the voters' perception of his or her competence in handling dramatic conflict within the debate.

Finally, voters' impressions of the debates are based heavily on their political ideology, position on issues, and prior support of a candidate (Martel, 1983). Despite the secondary impact that debates can have on voters' information, they typically have little effect on voter decisions (Abramowitz, 1978). Decided voters typically score their candidate as the winner. For them, the debates are more like a pep rally. Rather than changing their vote, it merely reinforces their support, particularly if the candidate meets their expectations. Even the positive impact of increased knowledge and information is tempered by the voters' predispositions. Although they generally increase their knowledge of the campaign, the voters may still misunderstand much of the information in the debate (Jacoby, Troutman, & Whittler, 1986). Ultimately, debates have a pivotal role in campaigns, but their impact can be muted by other campaign factors.

THE CONSULTANT'S VIEW: PLANNING AND COPING WITH CRITICAL EVENTS

For campaign consultants, critical events are what the name implies: critical to the election. Despite the overall complexity of preparing and running a campaign, consultants generally assume that there will be two or three critical points within a campaign that will serve a watershed function. How those crises are handled often determines the success or failure of that campaign. The consultants' view of this process, however, tends to have three distinct differences from the academic perspective. First, consultants typically approach critical events from a predictive perspective. If critical events can be anticipated, perhaps the campaign can make preparations to handle them more effectively. Some critical events are obvious—the campaign announcement, televised debates, convention speeches, and speeches on major issues. Preparation for these events is often extensive, with the candidate and the staff preparing for the event with research, review, and preparation. Research is conducted on the audience and issues that must be addressed. Topics and ideas are reviewed in discussion sessions involving the candidate, consultants, and other campaign workers. For events in which press questions are anticipated, the consultants employ role-playing, adopting the role of reporters and tossing increasingly difficult questions at the candidate.

Debate preparation frequently includes at least one person who plays the role of the opponent, seeking to throw the candidate off balance with an unanticipated question or challenge.

Lawrence (2000) noted that debate contenders also typically rehearse a few "gotchas." Noonan (1998) traces the trend to 1976 when Walter Mondale criticized the substance behind Gary Hart's positions by asking, "Where's the beef?" "After the success of Mondale's line," Noonan noted, "the word went forth: candidates needed to be supplied by their staff with zippy sound bites before they went into a debate or an interview" (p. 98). In 1984, Ronald Reagan faced concerns about his age with a response that he had planned in advance: "I want you to know that I will not make age an issue of this campaign. I am not going to exploit for political purposes my opponent's youth and inexperience," he said. Everybody laughed, including opponent Walter Mondale, and the issue never arose again. Jamieson (1988) noted that the line also functioned as a cover for weak performances by Reagan in other parts of the debate, particularly a somewhat rambling closing statement. "What saves him ... is the brevity of the light-hearted joke contrasted with the four-minute length of the final speech," Jamieson wrote. "The former lends itself to the news clip, the latter does not" (p. 113).

A different type of "gotcha" was used by Lloyd Bentsen in the 1988 presidential debate with Dan Quayle. After Quayle said he had as much experience as John F. Kennedy had when Kennedy sought the presidency, Bensten responded, "Senator, I served with Jack Kennedy. I knew Jack Kennedy. Jack Kennedy was a friend of mine. Senator, you are no Jack Kennedy." The line is still remembered as the classic example of a put-down in campaign politics. Still, such one-liners are rare in presidential debates, since it is typically difficult for any candidate to accomplish his or her goals with a single answer or line. Noonan (1998) credits that rarity to the media literacy of the voters: "The American public has become very sophisticated about such lines," she wrote, "so sophisticated that they now discount them" (p. 97).

Preparations for the candidate may include both verbal and nonverbal training. Seiter et al. (2009) found that the nonverbal behavior of candidates in the background of a shot could influence voters' impression of those candidates. Further, Goodman and Gring (1999), in an analysis of the 1992 and 1996 presidential town hall debates, noted that Clinton often repositioned himself so that each television image of him either included the American flag in the background (in 1992) or pictured him with the audience (in 1996). They concluded that Clinton "made a conscious effort to maximize his visual impact during the town hall debates," a factor that implied that he had planned and practiced the positioning in advance of the actual debate.

A second major difference for consultants is that, from the campaign perspective, not all critical events are public in nature. The public nature is essential to the academic community and its efforts to study the public impact of critical events. Without a public component, the event can have little impact on public opinion. From the campaign's perspective, though, the campaign may experience one or more nonpublic critical events that could potentially spell the difference between winning and losing. Typically, unless the campaign is a well-documented presidential campaign, these critical turning points may never become public knowledge. Still, while the public may be unaware of them, they are critical to the campaign. These might be more accurately classified as "critical decisions" or "critical maneuvers": deliberate choices or strategic moves that have a disproportionate impact of the rest of the campaign. Elements that fall within this category could include fund-raising decisions, endorsements, and allocation of resources. For example, the decision to seek funds from an unpopular source could have a positive impact on campaign finances but a negative one on public image. The endorsement of a major African American leader could result in the support of many of that person's followers. Campaigns are often won or lost on the basis of how resources are allocated for the campaign.

A third distinctive element of the consultant's view of critical events is that consultants often make assumptions about the probable timing of critical events. Critical points in the campaign typically occur very early or very late in the campaign. The early stages of the campaign establishes the strategic base of the campaign, and decisions that are made during this time have an effect that often lasts throughout the entire campaign. First impressions are critical; the candidate's introduction to the public often sets the tone for subsequent responses to the candidate's message. The announcement provides the first major instance of media exposure for the campaign, demonstrates the ability of the campaign to execute its basic campaign function, and provides a frame for interpreting later messages from the campaign.

The second major timing for critical events is late in the campaign, within the last two weeks of the election. Numerically, this time frame appears to be when most critical events occur for three reasons: external organizations, such as those who organize and coordinate campaign debates, often time their events for these latter stages; most campaigns save their most important strategic moves for the latter stages; and the public pays more attention to the campaign as election day approaches. Thus, during this time, the candidates must perform well in debates, execute critical moves in their own campaign strategies, and respond to similar moves by their opposition. For many campaigns, then, something happens in the last two weeks that is of critical importance. How the candidates respond to that event often determines who wins the election.

Between that early starting point and the late stages of the campaign, there is a span of time in which are produced few critical events. While the campaign must be alert to problems, this stage is often spent raising money, conducting routine campaign activities, and fleshing out the details of issues and strategies for later use in the campaign.

MISTAKE-BASED CRITICAL EVENTS

One frequent characteristic of critical events in a campaign is that their impact is intensified if a candidate makes a mistake. Diamond and Cobb (1999) refer to this phenomenon as "the candidate as catastrophe." Part of the phenomenon rests in the psychological processing of negative information. As Lau

(1982) noted, voters appear particularly sensitive to negative information about candidates. When that negative information is triggered by a critical event, it can have a major effect on a campaign. During the 1976 Ford–Carter debates, for example, President Ford incorrectly identified which nations in Eastern Europe were under Communist control, an error that was repeatedly pointed out by subsequent commentators. Given the importance of negative information in critical events, the goal of many candidates is often to escape from such events with as little damage as possible. As Diamond and Cobb (1999, p. 242) noted, "the battle is not to convince citizens that one's policy is *right,* but simply that it is *not unreasonable,* that a favored candidate's election … does not portend catastrophe."

Another example of mistake-based critical events are those instances in which candidates go "off message." As Bosman (2007) wrote, "Some observers say that moments of spontaneity provide a valuable peek behind the curtain of campaign stage managing, allowing voters to see truer glimpses of a candidate's ability to handle unscripted challenges" (p. WK5).

SUMMARY

Critical event analysis simplifies campaign analysis by focusing on major, discrete events that had significant impact on the election. The approach offers a way to view the campaign in a holistic way that might replicate the decision-making process many of the voters may go through. Several conclusions have already been drawn from previous works, many of which could be useful to the consultants in the industry.

One by-product of critical event analysis is an understanding of the importance of the message communicated by the event. Such messages are not always verbal in nature, but the impact is significant anyway. The ultimate impact of the critical event on public opinion is often symbolic in nature: what the event communicates about the people involved. In addition, those critical events that can be anticipated are likely to involve a great deal of campaign preparation and creative effort; the creative side of that equation is often directed at the message, or finding a symbolic way of having an impact on voters. In most cases, the mass media provide a critical link in conveying that message to the public.

There is, however, an implication of the watershed impact of critical events that is discouraging to both the candidate and the professional consultant. Given the inordinate effect that watershed events have on an election, the success of their campaigns is typically based on how they handle a relatively small number of tasks. Both the candidate and the consultant can perform admirably 90 percent of the time, but if their miscues occur on critical events, they are likely to lose the election. Conversely, they can both make a lot of mistakes on minor aspects of the campaign, but still perform well by winning the critical events. Because of that, the study of critical events is likely to remain an important factor for both the academic and the consulting communities.

QUESTIONS FOR DISCUSSION

1. A small down-state newspaper has reported that your opponent was asked the question, "Is withholding too much for the working man?" Your opponent answered, "What's withholding?" Is this a critical event? If it is, how do you communicate it to voters? How do you communicate it to opinion makers?

2. During a debate, one of the candidates for the United States Senate walked over to his opponent's lectern and demanded that she sign a pledge not to accept soft money. She refused. Later he attacked her for refusing to sign the pledge. Was this a critical event? How would each candidate spin this as a turning point in their respective campaigns?

3. In a runoff election, a self-described "law and order" candidate for attorney general is revealed to have a police record as a college student for assault. The crime occurred twenty-five years earlier and the victim and other witnesses have died. What can the candidate do to keep this information from becoming a critical event? What can the opponent do to make it a critical event?

4. During a campaign for the U.S. House of Representatives, Cold War tensions escalated when a U.S. surveillance aircraft disappeared without a trace near the borders of the Soviet Union. The incumbent made a statement in support of the U.S. Air Force and the families of the crew. His opponent condemned the Soviets and accused them of breaking international law. Is this a critical event? If yes, how can each candidate respond to the situation? If no, how should each candidate proceed?

Ethical Questions in Political Communication

In June 2000, the sheriff and circuit clerk of Winston County, Alabama, were accused of buying votes with money and moonshine whiskey. Federal indictments against the officeholders charged that they passed around cash to potential voters. The going rate for a vote, according to press reports at the time, was $2 or $3, with liquor tossed in as a bonus (Associated Press, 2000). Their defense for their actions was that they were merely engaging in the promotion of voter turnout, but a grand jury disagreed. Several of the participants were subsequently found guilty of voter fraud.

That case is only one example of how ethical and legal issues become involved in the political campaign process. The motivation to win sometimes drives participants to use a variety of questionable techniques that might enhance their electoral chances. Many cross the line and are clearly illegal. Others may fall within the boundaries of law, but still raise questions of ethical behavior.

Somewhat surprisingly to some outside observers, the consulting community and the academic community generally hold common views on this issue—although for different reasons. The academic community justifiably deplores unethical campaign activities as an affront to the democratic process that may succeed in overriding the will of the majority. Consultants generally share that sense of moral indignation when they see unethical behavior; in fact, their reaction may be even stronger than that of the academic community. To them, unethical behavior is both an affront to their profession, and a factor that could cause them to unfairly lose an election. Consultants who develop a reputation within the community for unethical campaigning are reviled as snakes who perpetuate the worst of the negative stereotypes of the profession while making it increasingly harder for their opponents to win an election in the face of such tactics. Where the two communities disagree is in the development of criteria for moral behavior. While the specifics of such criteria vary with individuals in both communities, a few points of agreement defining campaign ethics can be identified:

1. Philosophically, academic views of political ethics are usually based on democratic idealism, while the value criteria for consultants is campaign

pragmatism. The philosophy of ideal democracy is based on the concepts of freedom of speech and the ability of the truth to dominate and win an argument—those with the best argument will win. Candidates who use unethical tactics undermine that ideal, creating a situation in which the "sneakiest" candidate might win. The consulting philosophy of pragmatic democracy is based on the concepts of communicating with the voters—those who communicate the best have the best chance of winning. From the consultant's point of view, victory can be obtained through either message advantage (winning an argument because you have truth on your side) or through rhetorical advantage (winning an argument because you can explain your side of the argument better than the other side can explain its side). Again, though, unethical tactics undermine both assumptions. Message advantage and rhetorical advantage may be lost if unethical tactics prevent the campaign from communicating with the voters.

2. The academic goal of the dominance of truth is based on an assumption of an open and equal debate of ideas. Consultants believe that the use of inequities in access is an acceptable and ethical form of behavior. Some campaigns simply lack the finances, media exposure, and name recognition to present a viable message that articulates their side of an argument. For the academic community, such inequities of resources invariably mean that the message of one side is underrepresented in the media. Consultants, conversely, view the lack of resources as an indication of lack of legitimacy. An inability to raise resources reflects the lack of acceptance of a message among opinion leaders. As a result, they feel no qualms about presenting their message in a vacuum created by a lack of opposition from the other side.

3. Academics fear that unethical campaign practices can lead to the selection of unqualified leaders and the development of faulty governmental policy. Consultants fear that unethical campaign practices could cost them an election. Long-time political consultant Steven Shadegg (1972) often preached that consultants should be careful not to let the other side "steal" elections. From the consultants' point of view, unethical behavior is not merely an attack on morality, but also an attack on the consultants' win-loss record (and, indirectly, their future income).

TYPES OF UNETHICAL BEHAVIOR

Unethical activities in campaigns can occur at any point in the campaign process, but a few stand out as more frequent and easy to identify. These include ballot stuffing and vote buying, scandals, conflicts of interest, dirty tricks, issue avoidance, negative campaigning, and the role of consultants.

Ballot Stuffing

The case cited at the beginning of this chapter is an example of an illegal practice known as ballot stuffing. There is nothing historically new about the practice. Lyndon Johnson's opponents claimed he won his first election because of ballot stuffing in one Texas county. Chicago mayor Richard Daley was accused of stuffing the ballot box in Illinois to secure the presidency for John F. Kennedy in 1960 (Cohen & Taylor, 2000). Similar examples could be cited from nearly every state in the union.

In the past, the most common form of ballot stuffing was "graveyard voting." Campaign workers would scour tombstones for names of people who were still listed on voter registration rolls and find a way to cast a vote on their behalf. Such actions occasionally prompt remarks from veteran political junkies who talk about somebody's uncle—a person who "voted a straight party ticket all of his life and for ten years afterward." The most common means of implementing ballot stuffing in modern campaigns is through the use of fraudulent absentee ballots. Following the 2008 election, election officials investigated three Alabama counties for fraudulent absentee ballots; in one case, the number of absentee ballots cast was six times the state average (Nossiter, 2008). A few states have implemented "early voting" systems, where anyone can go to the polls before election day and cast a ballot. Others have retained traditional absentee ballot laws that allow people to vote in that manner if they are ill, shut in, out of the area on election day, or have jobs that make it difficult for them to go to the polling place. In close elections, both parties actively solicit absentee voters in an attempt to swing the elections. Such campaign activity can have a direct effect on voter turnout in the absentee boxes, with absentee votes accounting for as much as 10 percent of the total votes cast.

The weakness of the absentee system is that people who are ill or shut in will fill out their forms without the supervision of any election officials. That aspect makes the system open to manipulation, with unscrupulous operators filling out multiple forms and casting ballots on behalf of citizens who may not realize that they are even voting. Sometimes the results can be outrageous. In the 1994 election in Greene County, Alabama, three suitcases of absentee ballots were reportedly carried to the post office on election day. In that election, 34 percent—1,400—of all ballots cast in the county were absentees. Eleven people were eventually convicted of voter fraud after court testimony revealed that many of the ballots had been signed by the same person ("Greene County fraud," June 20, 1999). During the 2000 primaries, another Alabama county saw more than half (54 percent) of its votes cast as absentee ballots (Chandler, 2000).

Another simple way to stuff the ballot box is to pay voters for their vote. Although illegal, campaigns are occasionally caught giving money, alcohol, or other inducements for support. The Winston County, Alabama, example cited at the beginning of this chapter is typical of such tactics, with voters reportedly paid a few dollars and given liquor for their support. In other low-income counties, "where a third of the population lives below the poverty line and $100 is a fortune" (Nossiter, 2008, p. A10), there were reports of individuals receiving $50–$100 for their vote. One voter, questioned by a reporter, admitted that he had accepted such money, saying, "Well, yeah, I've accepted it. $100, $50. It's pretty common. Ain't no jobs around here. I know it's wrong" (p. A10).

While such tactics are obviously illegal, others skirt the law. Some candidates offer free post-voting parties, with food and drinks available, to those who show a form that indicates they voted. One group used voter participation as automatic inclusion in a lottery for a new sports utility vehicle. Such approaches are legal, since the voter is not required to support any specific candidate. Merely the fact that they voted, regardless of whom they supported, warrants admission to the party. Candidates, though, are unlikely to support such voter incentives for demographic and geographic areas they do not expect much support from.

Scandals

In 1998, scandal erupted in the White House when the media revealed that President Bill Clinton had engaged in a sexual relationship with a White House intern, Monica Lewinsky. The resulting controversy led to the impeachment of the president and sparked an avalanche of discussion about scandals, moral values, and the decline of ethics among government officials (Brito, 1999). Such scandals are nothing new in political life, including the presidency (Worland, 1998). During the presidency of Woodrow Wilson, rumors circulated that he had poisoned his first wife so he would be free to marry Edith Bolling Galt. Grover Cleveland served two terms (1885–1889 and 1893–1897) despite providing financial support to a baby boy who was born out of wedlock; his opponents mocked him with the chant, "Ma, Ma, Where's my pa?" Other presidents reported to have had sexual liaisons outside of marriage include James Garfield, Warren G. Harding, Franklin Delano Roosevelt, Dwight Eisenhower, and John F. Kennedy.

What is new about modern politics is the extent to which such scandals have expanded into the personal sphere, with the walls that separate one's public and private lives collapsing (Lee, 2000, p. 45). The personal lives and scandals of officeholders have become the subject of both press inquiry (Sabato, 2000) and campaign attacks (Sabato, Stencel, & Lichter, 2000). Except for Cleveland's paternity case, the sexual activities of most other presidents were considered off-limits by both the press and opponents. That tradition began to change with Gary Hart's candidacy in 1987. Hart was beset by rumors that he was having an affair while conducting his campaign for the Democratic presidential nomination. At a meeting with the press, Hart denied the charges and dared reporters to follow him around if they didn't believe him. Reporters from the *Miami Herald* accepted the dare and later revealed the story, one that knocked Hart out of contention.

That opened the door for closer scrutiny of Bill Clinton's personal life in 1992 when stories of his relations with a number of women were detailed. Still, some aspects of the gentlemen's agreement not to discuss such matters prevailed, at least for the '92 election. The national Republican Party was not openly involved in the accusations against Clinton. Instead, the charges came from local Republicans in Clinton's home state of Arkansas. Clinton's chief opponent, incumbent Republican president George H. W. Bush, distanced himself from the charges and never mentioned them in his own campaign appearances. That element of civility had disappeared by 1998 when Republicans in Congress were open in attacking Clinton's extramarital relationships.

The press, meanwhile, reported it all. The scent of such scandals often inspires a "feeding frenzy" of extensive coverage by newspapers, television, and Internet reporters (Sabato, 2000), with each hoping to "out-scoop" the others with the latest tidbit of gossip or information. The press was hampered in the 2000 election by having two major candidates—George W. Bush and Al Gore—who were not as colorful as Clinton, but they still found scandals to report. Bush was beset by rumors of drug use and a drunk-driving arrest, while Gore was targeted for questions about his fund-raising machinations. One local reporter (Yardley, 1999), in addressing the press scrutiny on Bush, called it "...a shootout in which there are no good guys." Yardley was particularly critical of how the press covered the Bush angle, but his assessment could apply to a number of other topics and candidates. "The parties to the immediate dispute are equally unappealing," he wrote. "On one side is the governor of Texas, whose flippancy is exceeded only by his self-righteousness; on the other side are the ladies and gentlemen of the press, whose self-righteousness is exceeded only by their hypocrisy. None of the participants is interested in serious, sober discussion of whatever consequential matters the presidential contest may entail...."

The focus on scandals has also led to increased coverage of politicians' personal lives, including their health (Purnick, 2000). Janet Reno's fight with Parkinson's disease is public information. On April 27, 2000, New York City mayor Rudolph Giuliani held a news conference to reveal that a biopsy of his prostate gland came back positive. Such intrusions into the health of candidates is a relatively new phenomenon. The public never heard about (and most knew nothing about) John F. Kennedy's struggle with Addison's disease or the extent to which a stroke felled Woodrow Wilson. Franklin Roosevelt was elected to four terms as president without most voters realizing that he was paralyzed from polio. The amount of coverage devoted to such issues probably portends that press coverage of political scandals and personal issues will continue to be a staple of the nightly news and the morning paper. What used to be private matters have now become public issues.

Conflicts of Interest

Another major ethical question is that of conflicts of interest. The financial side of politics is so vital that any legislature has the potential for voting on or representing issues in which they have a conflict of interest. In campaigns, opponents are often quite willing to point out such conflicts. Still, given the number of incumbents who face only token opposition, the extent to which such conflicts of interest exist may be underestimated.

One watchdog group that keeps an eye on this issue is the Center for Public Integrity. While the presidency has come under scrutiny from this group, its biggest criticisms seem to be aimed at state legislatures and Congress. The group's 2000 study of state legislators found that at least one in five helped regulate their own business or professional interests, had financial ties to organizations that lobby state government, and might receive income from agencies they oversaw; one in four sat on a legislative committee that regulated their own profession; at least 18 percent had financial ties to businesses or organizations that lobby state government; and nearly one in four received income from another government agency, often from agencies the legislature funded (Lewis, 2000). An earlier year-long study on Congress (Lewis, 1998) traced the decision-making process on major policy issues and concluded that "at critical forks in the road between the broad public interests of the American people and vested interests, Congress has taken the wrong path. That wrong path is illuminated by campaign contributions and other forms of political lucre."

Conflicts of interest are also a potential concern for the consulting industry. Consultants work for numerous candidates, some of whom have differing political philosophies. The conflict can become critical when differing candidates take different positions on the same piece of legislation and both solicit advice from the consultant. Whichever side loses that debate can, often justifiably, feel that they did not receive the best possible advice from their consultants. Some consultants handle this problem by offering services on a very specialized basis. In addition to those who work for only one party, others specialize by issues or special interest groups—business, labor, women's issues, the environment, and so forth. This effectively reduces the number of potential conflicts, but some will still arise. In those situations, the consultant has a professional obligation to tell the client (or potential new client) about the potential conflict. In some instances, the consultant should turn down a new client to avoid the conflict. At the least, if the client knows about the conflict, he or she could then evaluate whether the consultant is the best one for the job. In many cases, it would be to the candidate's advantage to talk to another consultant.

Dirty Tricks

During the 1972 presidential campaign, Richard Nixon's reelection efforts were centralized in a committee that was somewhat appropriately named CREEP, an acronym for the Committee to Re-Elect the President. A subunit of that organization known as the "plumbers" was in charge of developing strategies that would be disruptive to other campaigns. Their tactics set the standard by which modern dirty tricks are judged. Spies were placed into campaigns, unfounded rumors started and spread, and information contrived to place opponents into unsavory situations. The resulting jail terms for many of those campaign workers dampened the enthusiasm for such high-handed techniques on such a grand scale, but some chicanery continues in most campaigns. Many campaigns continue to place spies in the opposing camps, and some dirty tricks continue.

The most common dirty trick in local elections is sign destruction. Local candidates often find that their campaign signs simply disappear overnight. A candidate challenging an incumbent sheriff in Florida discovered that his four-by-eight plywood signs had been systematically torn down and used to build a hunting cabin by the supporters of the incumbent. At least one congressman came under scrutiny when his father was arrested for tearing down campaign signs of his son's opponent. One of the authors worked in a campaign in which the candidate was appalled to find that one of his supporters was defacing the signs of the opponent. When the staff was ordered to locate and identify the culprit, the candidate was further appalled to discover that the villain was his own son.

In the past, one common dirty trick involved making rude phone calls in the name of the opponent. Voters might be awakened at midnight by a phone call purporting to be from one campaign, with the resulting conversation leading to the caller insulting the unsuspecting voter. The advent of caller ID has reduced the use of this tactic; the turnaround came in 1996 when a number of campaign workers (for a number of different campaigns) were caught with the new device. Still, the telephone remains a popular means of using unfair influence in an election, and other nefarious techniques are limited only by the imagination of those who feel compelled to do something of that nature. A more modern version of this is electronic jamming of the opponent's telephones during the GOTV stage, a stunt that GOP operative Allen Raymond (2008) pulled in Republican John Sununu's successful 2002 Senate race in New Hampshire. Conversely, in a 2006 New York election, Republicans accused Democrats of calling Republican voters at the last minute and directing them to nonexistent or wrong polling places (Cohen, 2008). Then, in 2010, two young Republicans were arrested on federal wiretapping charges for trying to tap the phone lines of U.S. senator Mary Landrieu (D-La.) (Rutenberg & Robertson, 2010).

Dirty tricks sometimes come with a touch of humor. During the 1960s, political prankster Dick Tuck spent much of the year creating problems for Richard Nixon's campaign. He arranged for fortune cookies at a Nixon reception to read, "Vote for John Kennedy."

During a railroad whistle-stop tour in California, Tuck dressed as a trainman and signaled the engineer to pull away from the station just as Nixon began to speak. When Nixon visited San Francisco's Chinatown, Tuck erected banners that read "Welcome Nixon" in English but contained an anti-Nixon message in Chinese (Combs, 1980, p. 155). All in good humor? Not to the Nixon campaign, who used the actions as justification for forming their own dirty tricks squad.

Technological innovations now offer unethical campaigners with numerous other opportunities to mislead the public. Digital photography and video allow for film editing that can put candidates in places they never were and with people they've never met. Kaid (2000) noted that modern editing techniques, special effects, visual imagery, and computerized alterations can create a technological situation that "has the potential to interfere with the ability of an informed electorate to make rational choices" (p. 156). Furthermore, since the quality of digital editing can be extremely high, it can be difficult to detect such alterations. A vigilant public, a skeptical news media, and an outraged opponent are the only elements that must ultimately come into play.

Resume Inflation

Okay, "resume inflation" is a euphemism for "lying." Still, it's remarkable how many instances exist in which an individual takes credit for something that they never did. Sometimes it starts early in a person's career. They put an item on their resume that isn't quite right, nobody notices, and it stays there as they move up in their career. When they enter politics, however, the media quickly pounces on the candidate's qualifications to see if anything is improper.

Perhaps the most extreme example of this occurred in an Alabama School Board election in 2009. One of the candidates lied about his age, his education, and his experience during the campaign and on his Web site (Leech, 2009). The candidate claimed he was twenty-three years old, had graduated from high school in 2005, and had a bachelor's degree in elementary education from a state university. When the newspaper checked the facts, they found that he was only twenty-one years old, had dropped out of high school without graduating, and had never attended the university. Needless to say, he lost the election.

But that didn't keep others in the area from following his lead. The next year, a candidate from the same area claimed to have been endorsed by Alabama Crimson Tide coach Nick Saban in her campaign for mayor (Debro, 2010). She even distributed campaign literature showing her in a photograph with the college football coach. The University of Alabama and Saban denied the endorsement, prompting an investigation. The "photo" turned out to be a shot of Saban and his wife Terri that had been "photo-shopped" to delete Terri Saban and replace her with the candidate. Naturally, this candidate also lost her election.

NEGATIVE CAMPAIGNING

One area of political campaigning that attracts controversy is that of attack ads, or "negative campaigning." Such tactics are nothing new, going back to the early nineteth century. The first real presidential campaign occurred in 1800 (prior to that, George Washington was elected without controversy). There was trouble even then between candidates Alexander Hamilton and Aaron Burr, leading to the election of John Adams (Larson, 2008). That launched the trend of campaigns in which scandals were standard fodder (Daniel, 2011). Andrew Jackson's 1828 presidential campaign remains one of the dirtiest campaigns in American history. When political opponents discovered that Andrew Jackson had married his wife Rachel before the divorce from her first marriage was final, they attacked him as an adulterer. Jackson fought several duels to defend her honor, and the opposition distributed a "Coffin Handbill" that featured drawings of coffins representing men whom Jackson was accused of murdering or otherwise having done away with. Jackson responded in kind, accusing incumbent president John Quincy Adams of spending thousands of federal dollars to furnish the White House with gambling equipment.

Negative campaigns are standard practice in most modern elections (Garramore, 1984, 1985). Challengers may attack the incumbent with a "time for a change" argument (Trent & Friedenberg, 1995) or use some version of the In Man–Out Man attack strategy (Kitchens & Stiteler, 1979). Campaigns use negative ads because they believe they have an effect on voters, and research has generally supported that contention. Decades ago, tradition dictated that incumbents need not engage in negative campaigns, but that has gradually changed. Procter and Schenck-Hamlin (1996) found no difference in the types of negative attacks used by incumbents or challengers or open-seat campaigns. Others have argued that women candidates should avoid negative campaigning or incorporate strategies that "accommodate sex-based stereotypes of femininity" (Trent & Sabourin, 1993, p. 36) by softening or in some way disassociating themselves from the attack (Procter, Aden, & Japp, 1988), using humor (Kern, 1989; Taylor, 1990a) or drama (Johnson-Cartee & Copeland, 1991). Procter and Schenck-Hamlin (1996), however, found no difference in the negative attacks of women candidates and men candidates.

Procter and Schenck-Hamlin (1996) called negative ads "a normative advertising form" after they found that negative political ads were remarkably similar in both substance and style across all types of political campaigns. Their finding is not really surprising, given that all of the ads that they studied were likely all made by the same small cadre of consultants. They also suggested that negative advertisements were used more to blunt an opponent's chances of winning the election than to promote the sponsoring candidate's own images or characteristics—another conclusion that would not surprise consultants. The typical negative political ad, they noted, attacked the sponsoring candidate's opponent, had the appearance of a report, used a neutral reporter to present the attack, focused primarily on the opponent's ethics, and used undocumented facts and figures to support its claims. Nor are such negative ads limited to the verbal aspects of the ad; Kaid (1996) found that 42 percent of the spots contained some kind of video editing, special effects, or other technological distortion, and such distortions were more likely to occur in negative spots.

The ethical dilemmas associated with negative campaigning tend to fall within four different categories of criticisms: fairness, appropriateness, effectiveness, and impact on the political system.

Fairness   Some critics view negative ads as inherently unfair. Negative ads may focus on a single negative factor related to a candidate, oversimplifying the argument while disregarding the totality of that person's career (Hale, 1994). Lee (2000, p. 44) argued that "any system that creates such stark contrasts between good and evil will oversimplify problems, create a language of political resentment, and...increase the citizen's dissatisfaction with government." For example, incumbent members of Congress are frequently attacked by challengers who claim that they have voted against some issue that is popular with the voters. However, given the multiple votes that Congress takes on issues such as social security, budgets, and tax reductions, it is nearly always possible to find a recorded vote where a member of Congress voted "against" a popular issue. Procedurally, such votes are sometimes necessary to set up a vote on a stronger version of a bill. An even bigger fairness issue is when there is little or no justification for the charge. In the 1998 Alabama lieutenant governor's campaign, a lawyer and a private investigator were indicted for paying a prostitute to say she had sexual relations with one of the candidates (Huffington, 1999).

Appropriateness   Some critics argue that the topics of negative ads are inappropriate for true political debates. Such ads, the argument goes, cross the boundary of issue debate and become personal attacks that degenerate into name calling. During the early 1980s, conservative Republican groups attacked a number of Democratic incumbents, calling them murderers because they were prochoice on the subject of abortion. The name-calling nature of the attacks negated any attempt to discuss the complexity of the moral issue itself. Similarly, Democrats often label Republicans as the party of the wealthy, an approach that does little to discuss the intricacies of economic issues.

Effectiveness   Views on the effectiveness of negative ads tend to fall into two distinct schools of thought. One approach assumes that negative ads are highly effective, with voters responding in dramatic fashion whenever a negative ad is launched by one candidate against an opponent. Others argue that negative ads are not effective and are more likely to backfire on the candidate who dares to use them. Negative ads, this approach argues, merely give voters a reason to vote against the candidate who stoops to such mudslinging tactics. Consultants generally assume that there is validity in both points of view. There is little doubt about the first position; practical experience and academic research both support the view that negative ads are highly effective. Kaid and Boydston (1987) found that negative ads effectively damaged the image of targeted candidates; furthermore, the effect was significant across party lines. Similarly, Klein and Ahluwalia (2005) reported that voters weigh negative information more when evaluating candidates. Other studies have found that negative ads are effective at producing greater image discrimination and attitude polarization (Garramore et al., 1990). Negative ads can be particularly helpful in providing a cognitive frame for voters who are less attuned to the political system (Zhang & Buda, 1999). Even critics of negative ads have noted that comparative negative ads can assist voters in making rational choices (Gronbeck, 1992).

On the other side, negative ads can go too far and create a boomerang effect against the candidate who uses them. Consultants generally assume that a candidate who gets labeled as a "mudslinger" is likely to lose the election. The problem, of course, is identifying at what point a negative ad crosses the line that separates legitimate discussion of issues from unfair allegations. For the most part, the answer is relatively easy—the voters decide. If the attack goes against the ethical values and perceptions of fairness held by the voters, they consider it mudslinging. Many times, the voters' perception of fairness may differ from that of both consultants and academicians. For example, during 1999, Republican politicians were campaigning for the impeachment of President Clinton. Their public arguments for his removal from office were based on both personal and legal factors related to his relationship with a White House intern. A majority of the public, though, considered the effort to be an unfair intrusion into private acts. The result: the Republican effort failed, and President Clinton survived the impeachment.

Conversely, George H. W. Bush used ads in his 1988 campaign that academicians tend to view as unfair. The "revolving door" furlough ad focused on a Massachusetts inmate who was temporarily released under a program supported by Governor Michael Dukakis, and who committed a felony while away from the prison. Jamieson (1996) complained that the ad "invited the false inference that Dukakis had furloughed 268 first-degree murderers who had then committed other serious crimes" (p. 461). Furthermore, she noted, the ad had racial overtones since it depicted "dark-complected convicts," with one convict looking directly at the camera who is "more dark-skinned than the others" (p. 461). The issue was visited again by the "weekend passes" ad sponsored by the National Security Political Action Committee, a group that supported the Bush campaign. This ad associated Dukakis with Willie Horton, a murderer who had raped a Caucasian woman after being temporarily released on the Massachusetts furlough program. The ad, which compared Bush's and Dukakis's positions on crime from the Bush perspective, has an announcer saying, "Dukakis not only opposes the death penalty, he allowed first-degree murderers to have weekend passes from prison." The ad cites the example of Horton's furlough, adding, "Horton fled, kidnapping a young couple, stabbing the man and repeatedly raping his girlfriend." Again, academic critics considered the ad unfair; it cited only a single incident while implying that many others had occurred (Jamieson, 1996, p. 471). The public though, at a time when crime and repeat criminal behavior was considered a major issue, responded dramatically to the ad. Public perception that Dukakis was soft on crime rose eleven points to 63 percent. From the public's perspective, it was a legitimate issue that depicted Dukakis's views on crime.

Impact on the Political System   One of the most serious ethical issues raised by negative campaigns is their impact on the political system. Typical of these concerns is Gronbeck's (1992) allegation that negative campaigns undercut the electoral process. Ansolabehere and Iyengar (1995b) argue that negative campaigns polarize the electorate and drive people away from the polls, thus reducing political participation among the electorate. Jamieson (2001) disagrees, arguing that attack ads do not reduce voter turnout. Still, researchers have consistently reported finding high levels of apathy and low levels of public knowledge among American voters. Most critics of this persuasion argue that negative ads increase political cynicism by "turning off" voters who avoid political participation in ever-increasing numbers. The result, as Newsweek reporter Meg Greenfield (1999) noted, is that "politics has become less something in which people engage than something they watch."

The November 1996 election saw a turnout of less than 49 percent, the lowest voter turnout rate since 1924 (Doppelt & Shearer, 1999). Kanter and Mirvis (1989) described a process by which people become cynical in stages: a precondition of unrealistically high expectations, frustration of those expectations, followed by a sense of deception or betrayal. Unrealistic and harsh campaigns can add to this cynicism by focusing on deception and betrayal by other candidates. Critics argue that negative campaigns contribute to this cynicism while also engendering prejudice and disrupting communities (Domke, McCoy, & Torres, 1998).

Hollihan (2001) believes negative campaigning also affects those voters who remain part of the process. Negative campaigning, he argues, increases the likelihood that voters will make electoral decisions on the basis of self-interest rather than considering issues in terms of what is good for the nation. "If the candidates are depicted as primarily concerned with advancing their own interests rather than the public interest," he writes, "then why should individual voters not be concerned first and foremost with protecting their own personal interests?" (p. 182). Capella and Jamieson (1997) agree with Hollihan on the increase in self-centered decision making by modern voters, but they attribute it to another factor: horse-race news coverage. Regardless of the reason, the basic premise of both scholars is the same—when campaign decisions are made on the basis of candidate self-interest, then voters are likely to adopt a similar self-interest in making their voting decision.

The ultimate impact of negative campaigning has been a loss of civility between the two parties. For years, Republicans and Democrats disagreed with each other politically, but often remained friends behind the scenes. And they held to decade-long traditions of civility within the halls of legislatures. That has gradually eroded away. In June 2007, a Republican state senator in Alabama punched a Democrat in the face on the floor of the legislature (Faulk, 2007). In 2009, in a major breach of protocol, Republican congressman Joe Wilson blurted out, "You lie" in response to a statement by President Barack Obama to Congress (Sisk, 2009). Those are merely two examples of what has been described as a growing trend toward what's called a "partisan divide" (Holbert, LaMarre, & Landreville, 2009). It was a sign that the disagreement between the parties had gone so far that it extended beyond differences on issues. Not only was the opponent wrong on the issues, but there was a growing sense that members of the other party were actually evil people. That was a general Democratic view of George W. Bush during his administration (e.g., Rich, April 26, 2009), while Republicans had a similar view of President Barack Obama (e.g., Rich, June 14, 2009). At least part of this trend is attributed to negative campaigning, but other factors may also be involved. Klein (2006) believes that part of the problem is that politician are more interested in getting reelected than in doing something courageous for the nation. Rich (September 20, 2009) targets Republicans for much of the blame, with a heavy dose going to talk show hosts who like controversy to attract audiences. Columnist Peter Baker (2008) traced the beginning of what he called "political poison" to the Republican

▶ SETTLING AN ELECTION WITH DOMINOES

Elections don't have to be mean-spirited affairs. Consider the Democratic primary of County Commissioner in Pickens County, Alabama, in 2006. That disputed race was resolved with a game of dominoes.

Once the eight-candidate June primary was over, candidate Sentell Harper had a one-vote lead over his opponent Gene Worrell for the top position by a count of 283 votes to 282. However, when election officials reviewed provisional ballots for the contest, they found another vote for Worrell. The result: The vote finished in a tie with 283 voters each.

Rather than call for another election, the Pickens County Democratic Executive Committee asked the candidates to resolve the issue by drawing from a group of ten dominoes, with the winner being the one who drew the highest number.

Worrell was present at the meeting, and he agreed. Harper was out of town, but he sent W. D. Harris as his representative, and Harris also agreed.

The chair of the committee showed the candidates ten dominoes, all with different totals, and then turned them over, mixed them up, and asked the two men to draw. Harris (representing Harper) drew a domino with a 6/3 combo, or nine points. Worrell drew one with a 0/3 combo, or three points. Harper was declared the winner, the two men shook hands, and the issue was settled. ■

Source: Sanders, D. (August 2, 2006). Harper wins again: Draw of the dominoes ends tie for District 3 Commission slot. *Pickens County Herald*, 1–2.

attempts to impeach President Bill Clinton (p. WK1). Gormley (2010) essentially agreed, but argued that the impeachment effort was the end of a continuum that started with Robert Bork's nomination to the Supreme Court. Segal (2009) added that an essential element of a successful talk show was to attract "haters" and encourage "feuds" (p. WK3). Regardless of the cause, though, there appears to be a growing trend of viewing the other side as evil.

Despite all of the rhetorical concern, there are few empirical data to support these allegations. Hart (2000) used a computer analysis of campaign messages to show that political campaigns are not as negative as most people assume. Furthermore, the presence of negative ads in a campaign has no impact on involvement in the election, communication behavior regarding the election, or likelihood of turning out to vote in the election (Garramore et al., 1990). Political cynicism can be a problem, but it appears to be related to a broader range of issues than just negative campaigning. Miller (1974) argued that political cynicism was associated with alienation that comes from citizens who feel they have insufficient political influence to control outcomes. Neuman (1986) attributes it to low levels of political sophistication as evinced through knowledge, salience, and conceptualization.

Some authorities view the problem as an attribute of the voters, not the campaigns. Ehrenhalt (1996) complains that the American public no longer succeeds at balancing the demands of modern life with a feeling of community, resulting in a decline in civic virtue. Similarly, Erber and Lau (1990) view cynicism as a characteristic of the voter rather than an effect of the system; political cynics tend to be voters with chronic issues and those who perceived themselves as distant from both candidates; similarly, low levels of political trust are associated with voters who think about politics as represented by the people involved in it rather than the political system itself. Cynicism is inversely related to both external and internal political efficacy. External and internal efficacies are two distinct factors (Craig, Neimi, & Silver, 1990). External efficacy refers to an individual's beliefs about the responsiveness of governmental authorities and institutions to citizen demands (Balch, 1974; Coleman & Davis, 1976), while internal efficacy is based on beliefs about one's own competence to understand and to participate effectively in politics (Neimi, Craig, & Mattei, 1991).

Another frequently voiced concern is the possibility that negative advertising dampens the enthusiasm of qualified people to run for public office, resulting in a smaller (and less qualified) pool of candidates. There does seem to be an increased number of politicians who are more interested in personal power than in public service (Ehrenhalt, 1991), but a negative campaign does not appear to be the dominant cause. Potential candidates who decide not to run seem to be more concerned instead about press scrutiny than of negative attacks from the opposition. According to *Campaign & Elections* magazine, 81 percent of candidates surveyed say that press scrutiny keeps qualified people from running for office.

Another justification for negative campaigns is that such advertisements address issues that the public needs to know about. Negative ads frequently address character issues, the dimension that most voters consider most critical for people who hold public office. As Myers (1999, p. 305) noted, "...we believe possession of this ability (morality) to have a special value and expect this fact to be reflected in most people's desires." From this perspective, voters have a right to know about factors that might indicate serious moral deficiencies on the part of the people they are considering electing to leadership positions.

Efforts to Reduce Negative Campaigning

Negative campaigning has become such a common practice in campaigns that a number of groups have attacked their use. Kaid (2000) believes such reactions are unjustified. "It is often difficult to isolate the reasons that many find negative ads inherently unethical," she wrote. "There does seem to be an underlying assumption in the criticism…that somehow it is just prima facie unethical to engage in 'negative campaigning' or 'negative advertising' " (p. 160). Indeed, it's quite possible for a negative ad to meet all the standard criteria of ethical values: truth, honesty, and fairness. Consultants would generally argue that the best negative ads do just that—provide honest and fair information that the voters need to have before making their decision.

Still, as negative tactics have increased, a number have advocated that candidates take a more positive tone in their campaigns. The most visible efforts along this line have come from the Interfaith Alliance, a Washington-based group representing Catholics, Protestants, Muslims, and Jews that asks candidates to sign a pledge ("The Framework of Civility for Political Candidates") that they will "reject personal attacks, innuendo or stereotyping in describing or referring to your opponent." Political expediency almost dictates that a candidate has to sign the pledge; in the 2000 elections, more than forty candidates for federal office, including Hillary Rodham Clinton, George W. Bush, and Al Gore, signed the pledge. But whether the pledge does much to reduce negative campaigning is questionable. In the heat of the battle, the oath may be disregarded or a justification found for not abiding by it.

THE ROLE OF CONSULTANTS

Veteran Washington journalist Jules Witcover (1999) argues that professional consultants in campaigns have altered presidential politics for the worse. Their inclusion in the process, he believes, has led to an increase in negative campaigning and a win-at-all-costs mentality that is detrimental to the democratic process. Similarly, Newman (1999) argues that marketing, not ideology, drives America's contemporary political system, leading to an emphasis on image over substance, personality over issues, and thirty-second sound bites over meaningful dialogue.

Whether such critics are correct in attributing negative effects to consultants may be debatable, but there is no doubt that consultants have changed the process. During the 1960s, campaign managers were usually friends or political allies of the candidate who either took a job in the administration or went back to their regular job. Today that role is handled by professionals who move from campaign to campaign. As a result, Newman argues, campaigns become dominated by people who have no ideological allegiance and who justify amoral behavior on the basis of the need to win. Denton (2000) argued that television undermines democracy because candidates use media consultants and pollsters to subvert its watchdog role. Television, he wrote, "has been co-opted by politicians as an instrument of advocacy" (p. 93). Pohl (1971) took a more moderate view, arguing that consultants were "not necessarily evil men" but merely technicians whose participation is necessary to the modern political process; still, their roles should be limited. "Technicians should make only technical decisions, like how to implement a policy," he wrote. "When they are asked to *make* policies, they exceed both their proper responsibilities and their talents" (p. xiii).

Consultants have also contributed to a political environment known as the "permanent campaign" (Blumenthal, 1980). Pollsters recommend that incumbents start their survey work up to eighteen months before the election, a time frame that gives members of Congress only six months of noncampaign activity. In 1995, Bill Clinton began running TV ads for his reelection campaign a year and a half before the election. For the 2000 presidential election, George W. Bush and Al Gore both kicked off their campaigns in June 1999. Even in the absence of overt campaign activities, incumbents may be tempted to look at each legislative or executive move for its political impact on future campaigns. Members of Congress use the congressional franking privilege to constantly remind supporters of the good job they are doing, thus making it harder for opponents to mount a viable challenge.

Other critics have argued that modern campaigns have become rhetorical exercises in issueless politics, with voters seeking pseudoopinions to justify their choices. Cloud (1997), for example, argued that political discourse was merely the "rhetoric of therapy," and its primary purpose was healing, coping, adapting, or restoring an existing order—not a discussion of issues. Such political rhetoric, she argues, distracts from real issues or flaws in the system by encouraging voters to focus on themselves and their private lives. Hart (1998) draws a similar conclusion, arguing that television trades political wisdom for five lesser emotions: intimacy, discernment, cleverness, activity, and importance. As a result, he concludes, the primary effect of television is to make the public feel good about feeling bad about politics. Given such an environment, voters can hardly be expected to make rational decisions in choosing their leaders.

These criticisms have merit, but the system may not be quite as bad as the critics may think. For one thing, the pragmatics of business alone is enough to hold some consultants in check. Little is more damaging to one's business than having to testify before a grand jury. Unflattering press coverage of a consultant's negative campaign is enough to deter some potential clients. Also, despite its problems, the campaign process still seems to be rather effective at informing voters. As noted elsewhere, campaign messages are frequently more informative than news coverage of a campaign. Furthermore, voters are remarkably adept at figuring out which candidate best represents them and their values. As Neuman (1986) noted, the paradox is that the system works because the public has learned to bypass the glut of political information available in campaigns; they rely on the opinions of others or look for nonissue cues to identify which candidate will best represent them.

BECOMING CRITICAL OBSERVERS OF THE PROCESS

The authors hope this book has helped to explain the role of consultants and the academic community in campaigns. While describing the role of consultants, we have tried to avoid presenting this information as if it were "cookie-cutter" instructions on how to win an election. Such instructions don't exist. Those consultants who offer such advice to their clients soon find themselves with losing clients. There are simply too many variables that must be taken into consideration for any single approach to always work. In some ways, then, we end by agreeing with Plato in his debate with the Sophists. Students of rhetoric will recall that the debate with the Sophists centered on whether teaching should just involve a "how-to" approach to rhetoric (the Sophists' approach) or whether it should involve a more in-depth teaching style that engaged the student into understanding the theory behind the how-to approach. Media consultants are the modern-day Sophists, professionals who advise their client on what to do without necessarily explaining the theory behind their advice. We would agree with Plato, though, that they would give better advice if they at least understood why themselves.

The goal of a book such as this is to enhance the reader's understanding of the campaign process, for only by understanding the process can we become effective observers of it. Critics abound, but critics who have no understanding of campaign processes may not have a firm foundation for their criticisms. Conversely, those who best understand the system—its participants—have little impetus to criticize it. Their economic past and future has come from the system, and they have been successful primarily because they understand it better than most people. If the system changes, they will adjust to those changes; but they will rarely take steps to change that system themselves.

Academic critics provide objective insight into political outcomes, but they often must make those judgments in the absence of confidential internal information. It's simply hard to make an accurate evaluation of an event without all the facts, particularly if some of the participants take efforts to hide some of those facts. Academicians also have the luxury of conducting their analyses after individual political events (elections) are over. Those insights can be helpful to both consultants and other academicians, but their post hoc nature limits their applicability in the observation of current events. Those who are adept at such analysis can translate academic interpretations into current applications, but they may still lack the confidential information that is critical to a decision.

The goal, then, is to reach some type of synthesis in which the individual has the analytical skills of the outside observer and the understanding of the process provided by campaign insiders. Even then, being an objective observer of campaign events can be difficult. At the very least, though, observers should be able to identify those factors that can interfere with their objectivity.

The Sour Grapes Syndrome

Practically anyone can be a critic of political communication. And most are. Our own experience has been that the most vocal critics of political communication are those candidates (or their supporters) who lose. They often blame their loss on the failure of the media to cover the issues they were addressing, the failure of the voters to appreciate the issues that matter, the use of campaign consultants who unfairly used a tax vote against them, or…well, you get the idea. Nor is the sour grapes syndrome limited to candidates; blaming the system makes a convenient scapegoat for consultants (to explain why they lost a race they were expected to win), pollsters (to explain why their predictions were wrong), academicians (to explain why the "best" candidate did not win), and nonvoters (to justify their lack of participation).

The catch, of course, is that each of them might be right. Sometimes the media do make choices about issues that influence election outcomes. Voters don't always appreciate the complexity of issues facing the nation or a state. And sometimes a candidate's record is unfairly used against him or her. The problem for the casual voter is to identify which times such criticisms are warranted and which times they are merely the political version of sour grapes. We can't give a cut-and-dried method for making such distinctions, but we can point to some guideposts that might help.

Understanding the Media

The media is a frequent target for criticism, some of it deserved and some undeserved. Understanding the media, how they function, and their role in modern society helps in identifying those criticisms that are justified. Overall, we live in a highly media-literate society. Most citizens have grown up watching so much television and listening to so much radio that they are artfully attuned to many of the media's techniques and shortcomings. Still, some myths about the impact of modern media exist, and dispelling some of these myths is essential to understanding its role.

Myth no. 1: Modern media have changed politics by diluting the impact of issues by simplifying messages into thirty-second ads   That's only half true. It's true that the media often simplify messages; modern campaigns are often fought with exchanges of messages that are short, simplistic (sometimes overly so), and that overlook the complexities of many issues. The mythical part of the statement, though, is that this effect is a product of the modern media. In fact, such practices have been around for centuries. Patrick Henry's pre–Revolutionary War speech inspired the American colonists to take up arms against the British. But all that most people remembered from Henry's oratorical gem was one line: "Give me liberty, or give me death." It was that simple phrase that served as a rallying cry for the colonists. Similarly, the Texans of 1836 won a war against Mexico behind the rallying cry of "Remember the Alamo." Sound bites, it seems, predate modern media.

Myth no. 2: Modern media have more impact on other people than on ourselves   This myth has been extensively studied by modern scholars under the title of the "Third-Person Effect." Specifically, the third-person effect is a tendency among voters to believe that the media have a greater influence on other people than they do on themselves. It is a vital factor in understanding criticism of the process. Research has consistently shown that critics who call for change in the process do so not because they have been unduly or unfairly influenced by a campaign, but because they believe other voters have succumbed to misleading campaign tactics. The third-person effect, then, is the common impetus behind criticisms of the media, particularly those criticisms that call for restrictions on campaign messages (Salwen, 1998). In other words, fear that others might be influenced by the media is the impetus for censorship campaigns. That creates a paradox: for some people, the media's biggest impact may be fear of potential impact.

Identifying One's Own Biases

You can never eliminate your own biases from any analysis. This set of recommendations, for example, is based on the biases of both authors and their experiences at participating in and observing political campaigns. We have omitted other standards that other scholars prefer. Readers, in turn, will develop their own criteria for evaluating campaigns and their messages. Regardless of which specific standards a person uses, though, there should be an attempt to identify what biases are present. Each person can become aware of his or her own biases and look for those biases that may influence his or her observations.

SUMMARY

This chapter has provided an overview of some of the ethical issues involved in political communication. Despite the examples provided in this book, the number of actual cases in which the law is broken is relatively small. As of 2007, the Justice Department had obtained eighty-six convictions for voter fraud, but concluded that there was no evidence of organized efforts to disrupt the electoral system (Lipton & Urbina, 2007). Ethical issues are often philosophical arguments between democratic idealists and political pragmatists. Agreement between the two can sometimes be reached. Philosophically, both sides agree on the repulsive nature of ballot stuffing, dirty tricks, and unnecessary intrusions into people's private lives. Consultants must also contend with the pragmatic impact of ethical questions on their careers. They risk their careers if they ever do anything illegal. They risk their income if they lose a race with advice that leads to charges pertaining to ethics. Ethical questions are still hotly debated on such issues as negative campaigning and the role of consultants in campaigns. Becoming a critical observer of the process involves recognizing the sour grapes syndrome, understanding campaign strategy, understanding the media, and developing the ability to recognize one's own biases.

Ultimate control of political ethics lies with the voters. Acceptable behavior is, at a basic level, defined by the values of the voters and what they find acceptable. The voters can serve as effective monitors, though, only if they have the requisite information to evaluate candidates and their campaigns. Fortunately, they are apparently more adept at making those judgments than many politicians would give them credit for being. After all, ethical judgments about public behaviors are complex value decisions.

Republican partisans found the public's acceptance of Bill Clinton's sexual misconduct unthinkable. Democrat partisans could not understand public acceptance of Newt Gingrich's antagonistic approach to legislative issues. But neither partisan side understood the complexity of such issues as well as the public. Gronbeck (2000) argues that public judgment of candidates is based on candidates' motives and actions, their character, and their competence. Each of these factors, in turn, is evaluated by its message source, the audience, the message, and situational expectations. Taken together, these two dimensions create a three-by-four matrix that reflects twelve distinct judgments that individual voters must make before reaching a value-based conclusion about any candidate. Given the complexity of such decisions, it's no wonder that the voters found value judgments about Clinton and Gingrich to be considerably more complex than did the partisans themselves. That doesn't mean, of course, that the voters' judgments are necessarily more "right" than those of the political players, because the voters' judgments can also be clouded by personal biases. Overcoming those biases can be a key element if the public is to be successful at monitoring the ethics of its leaders.

One goal of this book was to make the reader more adept at monitoring political activities by offering two ways of looking at campaigns—an insider's view of those who work in the trenches of campaigns and an outsider's view offered by those who observe and analyze campaigns and their implications. A combination of both views, the authors believe, will make the average citizen a more informed voter. The insider view enables the observer to understand the how and why of some campaign decisions. The outsider view maintains a focus on the ethical and rhetorical implications of campaign activities. If the ideal model of an informed electorate is to be reached, both viewpoints must be appreciated.

QUESTIONS FOR DISCUSSION

1. In the course of researching your opponent's record, you are given a copy of his FBI "rap sheet." It comes from an implacable enemy of your opponent and says he was arrested for theft three decades ago. Clearly, it is genuine. Because your race is for state attorney general, it is clear that the document could help your candidate's campaign. On the other hand, it is illegal to use an FBI criminal record for a political purpose. What do you do with this document to help your campaign? If you make the document public, what is the likely response of your opponent?

2. Down the stretch of the campaign, you become aware that the campaign field director is probably getting a kickback on lawn signs from the printing company. It is possible he is sharing the money with your candidate. Do you undertake a further inquiry to discover the truth? Do you turn the information over to the authorities?

3. To reduce the impact of money on his campaign, your candidate has declared he will take no contributions greater than $100. In the course of the campaign the treasurer reports to you that the candidate gave him some 6,000 checks of $100 each. It is clear the checks are from a well-known special interest in your state and that the candidate intends to accept the contributions. Is acceptance of these contributions right or wrong? What is the downside when your opponent discovers this contribution? As campaign manager, what course of action do you follow?

4. While campaigning in a small county, your campaign receives the endorsement of the local sheriff. On two occasions he has received more votes than there are people registered to vote. It is widely assumed he is stuffing the ballot box and he promises you he will deliver for your candidate "just like in my campaigns." What do you tell him? What is problematic about accepting this sort of endorsement?

REFERENCES

Aberbach, J. (1990). Lobbying for the people. *American Journal, 22*, 161–167.

Abramowitz, A. I. (1978). The impact of a presidential debate on voter rationality. *American Journal of Political Science, 22*, 680–690.

Abramowitz, A. I., & Saunders, K. L. (1998). Ideological realignment in the U.S. electorate. *Journal of Politics, 60(3)*, 634–652.

Abramson, J. (2010, October 17). Return of the secret donors. *New York Times*, WK1, WK4.

Abramson, P. R., & Aldrich, J. H. (1982). The decline of electoral participation in America. *American Political Science Review, 76*, 502–521.

Abramson, P. R., & Ostrom, C. W. (1991). Macropartisanship: An empirical reassessment. *American Political Science Review, 85*, 181–192.

Adamany, D. (1990). The unaccountability of political money. In M. L. Nugent & J. R. Johannes (Eds.), *Money, elections and democracy* (pp. 95–118). Boulder, CO: Westview Press.

Agranoff, R. (1976). *The management of election campaigns.* Boston: Holbrook Press.

Allen, C. (1993). *Eisenhower and the mass media.* Chapel Hill: The University of North Carolina Press.

Allen, M. (2006 August 28). On candid camera. *Time, 168(9)*, 17.

Allport, G. W., & Postman, L. J. (1947). *The psychology of rumor.* New York: Holt, Rinehart and Winston.

Allyn, R. (1999). The good that political consultants do. In D. D. Perlmutter (Ed.), *The Manship school guide to political communication* (pp. 304–310). Baton Rouge: Louisiana State University Press.

Altschull, J. H. (1995). *Agents of power: The media and public policy.* White Plains, NY: Longman.

American Institute for Political Communication. (1970). *Anatomy of a crucial election.* Washington, DC: American Institute for Political Communication.

Ansolabehere, S., Behr, R., & Iyengar, S. (1993). *The media game: American politics in the television age.* New York: Macmillan.

Ansolabehere, S., Behr, R., & Iyengar, S. (1994). Riding the wave and claiming ownership over issues: The joint effects of advertising and news coverage in campaigns. *Public Opinion Quarterly, 58*, 335–357.

Ansolabehere, S., & Iyengar, S. (1995a). Can the press monitor campaign advertising? An experimental study. *Harvard International Journal of Press/Politics, 1*, 72–86.

Ansolabehere, S., & Iyengar, S. (1995b). *Going negative: How political advertisements shrink and polarize the electorate.* New York: Free Press.

Ansolabehere, S., & Schaffner, D. (2011). *Re-examining the validity of different survey modes for measuring public opinion in the U.S.: Findings from a 2010 multi-mode analysis.* Paper presented at the annual meeting of the American Association of Public Opinion Research. Phoenix, AZ.

Archibald, S. J. (1975). A brief history of dirty politics. In R. E. Hiebert, R. F. Jones, J. Lorenz, & E. A. Lotito (Eds.), *The political image merchants* (pp. 230–236). Washington, DC: Acropolis.

Arnold, M. (2000, April 27). The long history of the attack book. *New York Times*, p. B3.

Arterton, C. (2000). New relationships. *Campaigns & Elections*, 22–23.

Asher, H. (1992). *Polling and the public: What every citizen should know.* Washington, DC: Congressional Quarterly Press.

Associated Press. (2000, June 12). Winston county case not first for vote fraud. *Birmingham Post-Herald*, p. D2.

Atkin, C. (1975). Communication and political socialization. *Political Communication Review, 1*, 2–6.

Atkin, C., Hocking, J., & McDermott, S. (1979). Home state voter response and secondary media coverage. In S. Kraus (Ed.), *The great debates: Carter vs. Ford, 1976* (pp. 429–436). Bloomington: Indiana University Press.

Atkinson, A. (2000). *Lou Henry Hoover and the rhetoric of place: Building a sense of home and hearth.* Paper presented at the annual meeting of the Eastern Communication Association. Pittsburgh, PA.

Atwood, L. E. (1994). Illusions of media power: The third-person effect. *Journalism Quarterly, 71,* 269–281.

Bai, M. (2010, June 6). Obama and the chaos perception. *New York Times,* WK1, WK5.

Baker, P. (2008, December 14). The lasting effects of political poison. *New York Times,* WK1, WK3.

Baker, R. K. (1989). *The new fat cats: Members of congress as political benefactors.* New York: Priority Press.

Balch, G. I. (1974). Multiple indicators in survey research: The concept 'sense of political efficacy.' *Political Methodology, 1,* 1–43.

Banerjee, N., & Luo, M. (2008, May 23). McCain chides pastor over sermon on Holocaust. *New York Times,* pp. 15A–16A.

Banning, S. A. (2006). Third-person effects on political participation. *Journalism & Mass Communication Quarterly, 83,* 785–800.

Banning, S. A., & Sweetser, K. D. (2007). How much do they think it affects them and whom do they believe?: Comparing the third-person effect and credibility of blogs and traditional media. *Communication Quarterly, 55,* 451–466.

Baran, S. J. (1999). *Introduction to mass communication: Media literacy and culture.* Mountain View, CA: Mayfield.

Barber, J. D. (1964). *Political leadership in American government.* Boston: Little, Brown.

Barber, J. D. (1972). *The presidential character.* Englewood Cliffs, NJ: Prentice-Hall.

Barnard, A., & Feuer, A. (2010, October 10). Outraged, and outrageous. *New York Times,* pp. A27, A29.

Barone, M. (1996, September 30). The rise and fall of Spiro Agnew. *U.S. News & World Report, 121(13),* 28.

Barreto, M. A., Streb, M. J., Marks, M., & Guerra, F. (2006). Do absentee voters differ from polling place voters? New evidence from California. *Public Opinion Quarterly, 70,* 224–234.

Bates, B., & Harmon, M. (1993). Do "instant polls" hit the spot? Phone-in vs. random sampling of public opinion. *Journalism Quarterly, 70,* 369–380.

Beck, P. A., & Jennings, M. K. (1991). Family traditions, political periods, and the development of partisan attitudes. *Journal of Politics, 53,* 742–763.

Becker, L. B., McCombs, M. E., & McLeod, J. M. (1975). The development of political cognitions. In S. H. Chaffee (Ed.), *Political communication: Issues and strategies for research* (pp. 21–63). Beverly Hills, CA: Sage.

Becker, L. B., Sobowale, I. A., Cobbey, R. E., & Eyal, C. H. (1978). Debates' effects on voters' understanding of candidates and issues. In G. F. Bishop, R. G. Meadow, & M. Jackson-Beeck (Eds.), *The presidential debates: Media, electoral, and policy perspectives* (pp. 126–139). New York: Praeger.

Becker, R., Amundson, N., Anderson, D., Wenzel, K., Yakubova, M., Sajaia, N., & Frannes, R. (2009). Political participation, efficacy and the 2009 Minnesota presidential caucuses. *Qualitative Research Reports in Communication, 10,* 38–45.

Bennet, J. (2000, February 27). The fear of loathing on the campaign trail. *New York Times Magazine,* pp. 52–55.

Bennett, K. (2008, March 7). Attack sites as strategy. *New York Times,* p. A12.

Bennett, S. (1988). 'Know-Nothings' revisited: The meaning of political ignorance today. *Social Science Quarterly, 69(2),* 476–490.

Bennett, W. L. (1977). The ritualistic and pragmatic bases of political campaign discourse. *Quarterly Journal of Speech, 63(3),* 219–238.

Bennett, W. L. (2001). *News: The politics of illusion.* New York: Longman.

Benoit, W. L. (2007). Own party issue ownership emphasis in presidential television spots. *Communication Reports, 20(1),* 42–50.

Benoit, W. L., Benoit, P. J., & Hanson, G. J. (2000). Political advertising on the Internet. In D. Bystrom, D. B. Carlin, L. L. Kaid, M. Kern, & M. S. McKinney (Eds.), *Communicating politics: Engaging the public in campaign 2000 and beyond* (pp. 11–20). Washington, DC: NCA Summer Conference Proceedings.

Benoit, W. L., Blaney, J. R., & Pier, P. M. (2000). Acclaiming, attacking and defending: A functional analysis of U.S. nominating convention keynote speeches. *Political Communication, 17,* 61–84.

Benoit, W. L., Gullifor, P., & Panici, D. A. (1991). President Reagan's defensive discourse on the Iran-contra affair. *Communication Studies, 42,* 272–294.

Ben-Porath, Eran N. (2007). Question bias and violations of comparability in intraparty debates: Iowa and new hampshire, 2004. *Communication Quarterly, 55,* 375–396.

Benton, M. (1976). The agenda-setting function of the mass media at three levels of information holding. *Communication Research, 3,* 201–273.

Benze, J. G., & Declercq, E. R. (1985). Content of television political spot ads for female candidates. *Journalism Quarterly, 82,* 278–283, 288.

Benzjian-Avery, A., Calder, B., & Iacobucci, D. (1998, July/August). New media interactive advertising vs. traditional advertising. *Journal of Advertising Research, 38,* 23–32.

Berelson, B. R., Lazarsfeld, P. F., & McPhee, W. N. (1954). *Voting: A study of opinion formation in a presidential campaign.* Chicago: University of Chicago Press.

Berinsky, A. J. (2009). *In time of war: Understanding American public opinion from World War II to Iraq.* Chicago: University of Chicago Press.

Berke, R. L. (2000, February 28). Regrets well placed, if questionably timed. *New York Times,* p. A10.

Bernays, E. L. (1947). The engineering of consent. *Annals of the American Academy of Political and Social Science, 250,* 113–120.

Berne, E. (1963). *The structure and dynamics of organizations and groups.* New York: J. B. Lippincott.

Bernstein, A. G. (2000). The effects of message theme, policy explicitness, and candidate gender. *Communication Quarterly, 48(2),* 159–173.

Beville, H. M. (1988). *Audience ratings: Radio, television, cable.* Hillsdale, NJ: Erlbaum

Bineham, J. L. (1988). A historical account of the hypodermic model in mass communication. *Communication Monographs, 55(3),* 230–246.

Bitzer, L. F. (1968). The rhetorical situation. *Philosophy and Rhetoric, 1(1),* 1–14.

Black, J. (2001). *Battling cyber parody in the political arena: A case study of the rhetorical clash between George W. Bush and gwbush.com.* Paper presented at the annual meeting of the Southern States Communication Association. Lexington, KY.

Blom, R. (2009). *Reaching the young and uninvolved.* Paper presented at the conference on YouTube and the 2008 Election Cycle in the United States, University of Massachusetts. Amherst, MA.

Bloom, M. (1973). *Public relations and presidential campaigns: A crisis in democracy.* New York: Thomas Crowell.

Blumenthal, S. (1982). *The permanent campaign* (2nd ed.). New York: Touchstone Books.

Blumler, J. G. (1979). The role of theory in uses and gratifications studies. *Communication Research, 6(1),* 9–36.

Blumler, J. G., & McQuail, D. (1969). *Television in politics.* Chicago: University of Chicago Press.

Bobbitt, R. (2010). *Us against Them: The political culture of talk radio.* Lanham, MD: Lexington Books.

Bonafede, D. (1972). Speech-writers play strategic role in conveying, shaping Nixon's policies. *National Journal, 19,* 311–320.

Bormann, E. (1960). Ghostwriting and the rhetorical critic. *Quarterly Journal of Speech, 46,* 284–288.

Bormann, E. G., Koester, J., & Bennett, J. (1978). Political cartoons and salient rhetorical fantasies: An empirical analysis of the '76 presidential campaign. *Communication Monographs, 45,* 317–329.

Bosdorff, D. M. (1987). Making light of James Watt: A Burkean approach to the form and attitude of political cartoons. *Quarterly Journal of Speech, 73(1),* 43–59.

Bosman, J. (2007, November 25). When campaigning strays off script. *New York Times,* WK-5.

Bosman, J. (2008, July 3). New group to spend $40 million. *New York Times,* p. 16A.

Box-Steffensmeier, J. M., Jacobson, G. C., & Grant, J. T. (2000). Question wording and the House vote choice: Some experimental evidence. *Public Opinion Quarterly, 64(3),* 257–270.

Boyle, T. P. (2000). Political Web sites: Who will come to visit in 2000? In D. Bystrom, D. B. Carlin, L. L. Kaid, M. Kern, & M. S. McKinney (Eds.), *Communicating politics: Engaging the public in campaign 2000 and beyond* (pp. 22–33). Washington, DC: NCA Summer Conference proceedings.

Braden, S. W. (2001). *The rhetorical use of the benign political scapegoat: Ronald Reagan attacks the federal government.* Paper presented at the annual meeting of the Southern States Communication Association. Lexington, KY.

Bradley, B. (1996). *Time present, time past.* New York: Vintage.

Brasher, H. (2010, March 21). Reconciliation a tool for getting things done. *Birmingham News*, pp. 1F, 4F.

Brigance, W. N. (1956). Ghostwriting: Before Franklin D. Roosevelt and the radio. *Today's Speech*, pp. 10–12.

Brinkley, D. (Ed.) (2011). *The Notes: Ronald Reagan's private collection of stories and wisdom.* New York: Harper.

Brinkman, D. (1968). Do editorial cartoons and editorials change opinions? *Journalism Quarterly, 45,* 724–726.

Brito, R. B. (1999). *Values or facts: The impeachment debate as a struggle to define American morality.* Paper at the National Communication Association Convention, Chicago, IL.

Broder, D. (1999, August 8). Campaign lessons: Candidates quickly learn they need lots of money. *Birmingham News*, p. 3C.

Brosius, H. B., & Bathelt, A. (1994). The utility of exemplars in persuasive communications. *Communication Research, 21(1),* 48–78.

Brosius, H. B., & Kepplinger, H. M. (1992). Beyond agenda-setting: The influence of partisanship and television reporting on the electorate's voting intentions. *Journalism Quarterly, 69(4),* 893–901.

Brown, P., & Levinson, S. C. (1987). *Politeness: Some universal in language usage.* New York: Cambridge University Press.

Browning, G. (1996). *Electronic democracy.* Wilton, CT: Pemberton Press.

Brubaker, J. (2008). Best supporting actor: The third-person effects of celebrity political endorsements. *Ohio Communication Journal, 46,* 1–13.

Brubaker, J., & Hanson, G. (2009). The effect of Fox News and CNN's postdebate commentator analysis on viewers' perceptions of presidential candidate performance. *Southern Communication Journal, 74,* 339–351.

Brumas, M. (2000, April 4). Attorney's death tax crusade gets attention. *Birmingham News*, p. 4B.

Bruni, F. (1999, November 1). For Bush, an adjustable speech of tested themes and phrases. *New York Times*, pp. A1, A14.

Bruni, F. (2000, May 8). Bush runs, with a lexicon of his own. *New York Times*, p. A11.

Bruni, F., & Kristof, N. D. (2000, February 28). Bush rues failure to attack bigotry in visit to college. *New York Times*, pp. A1, A10.

Brydon, S. R., & Scott, M. D. (1994). *Between one and many.* Mountain View, CA: Mayfield Publishing.

Buchanan, B. (1991). *Electing a president: The Markle Commission research on campaign '88.* Austin: University of Texas Press.

Burgess, D., Haney, B., Snyder, M., Sullivan, J. L., & Transue, J. E. (2000). Rocking the vote: Using personalized messages to motivate voting among young adults. *Public Opinion Quarterly, 64(1),* 29–52.

Burke, K. (1973). *The philosophy of literary form* (3rd ed.).

Berkeley: University of California Press.

Bush, A., Bush, V., & Harris, S. (1998, March/April). Advertiser perceptions of the Internet as a marketing communications tool. *Journal of Advertising Research, 38(2),* 17–26.

Bush, G. W. (1999). *A charge to keep.* New York: Morrow.

Bystrom, D. G., & Dimitrova, D. V. (2007). Rocking the youth vote: How television covered young voters and issues in a 2004 target state. *American Behavioral Scientist, 50(9),* 1124–1136.

Bystrom, D. G., & Miller, J. L. (1999). Gendered communication styles and strategies in campaign 1996: The videostyles of women and men candidates. In L. L. Kaid, & D. G. Bystrom (Eds.), *The electronic election* (pp. 303–318). Mahwah, NJ: Erlbaum.

Caldeira, G. A., & Patterson, S. C. (1987). Political friendships in the legislature. *Journal of Politics, 49,* 953–975.

Campbell, A. (1966). Interpreting the presidential victory. In M. C. Cummings, Jr. (Ed.), *The national election of 1964.* Washington, DC: Brookings Institution.

Campbell, A., Converse, P. E., Miller, W. E., & Stokes, D. E. (1960). *The American voter.* New York: John Wiley.

Campbell, A., Gurin, G., & Miller, W. E. (1954). *The voter decides.* Evanston, IL: Row, Petersen.

Campbell, A., & Kahn, R. L. (1952). *The people elect a president.* New York: Columbia University Press.

Campbell, K. K., & Jamieson, K. H. (1990). *Deeds done in*

words: *Presidential rhetoric and the genres of governance.* Chicago: University of Chicago Press.

Canary, D. J., & Spitzberg, B. H. (December 1993). Loneliness and media gratifications. *Communication Research, 20,* 800–822.

Cantril, A. H., & Cantril, S. D. (1999). *Reading mixed signals: Ambivalence in American public opinion about government.* Baltimore, MD: John Hopkins University Press.

Capella, J. N., & Jamieson, K. H. (1994). Broadcast adwatch effects: A field experiment. *Communication Research, 21(3),* 342–365.

Capella, J. N., & Jamieson, K. H. (1997). *Spiral of cynicism: The press and the public good.* New York: Oxford University Press.

Caplan, B. (2007). *The myth of the rational voter: Why democracies choose bad policies.* Princeton, NJ: Princeton University Press.

Carey, J. W. (1998). The Internet and the end of the national communication system: Uncertain predictions on an uncertain future. *Journalism & Mass Communication Quarterly, 75(1),* 28–34.

Carl, L. M. (1968). Editorial cartoons fail to reach many readers. *Journalism Quarterly, 45,* 533–535.

Carmines, E. G., & Stimson, J. A. (1989). *Issue evolution: Race and the transformation of American politics.* Princeton, NJ: Princeton University Press.

Carpenter, R. (1999). *Choosing powerful words.* Boston: Allyn and Bacon.

Cass, D. P. (1962). *How to win votes and influence elections: A nonpartisan guide to effective political work.* Chicago: Public Administration Service.

Cassell, C. A., & Luskin, R. (1988). Simple explanations of turnout decline. *American Political Science Review, 82(4),* 1321–1330.

Cassidy, M. (2000). Cyber-citizenship: A consideration of the role of the Internet in American politics. In D. Bystrom, D. B. Carlin, L. L. Kaid, M. Kern, & M. S. McKinney (Eds.), *Communicating politics: Engaging the public in campaign 2000 and beyond* (pp. 57–63). Washington, DC: NCA Summer Conference proceedings.

Cauchon, D. (2008a, January 18). States try to pull plug on 'robocalls'. *USA Today,* p. 1A.

Cauchon, D. (2008b, January 18). Once novel, 'robo-calls' now more of a nuisance. *USA Today,* p. 3A.

Chaffee, S. H. (1978). Presidential debates: Are they helpful to voters? *Communication Monographs, 45,* 330–346.

Chaffee, S. H., & Kanihan, S. F. (1997). Learning about politics from the mass media. *Political Communication, 14(4),* 423–430.

Chaffee, S. H., Ward, S., & Tipton, L. (1970). Mass communication and political socialization. *Journalism Quarterly, 47(4),* 647–659.

Chaffee, S. H., Zhao, X., & Leshner, G. (1994). Political knowledge and the campaign media of 1992. *Communication Research, 21(3),* 305–324.

Chandler, K. (2000, June 14). Bennett questions absentees.

Birmingham News, pp. 1A, 2A.

Chang, M., & Gruner, C. R. (1981). Audience reaction to self-disparaging humor. *Southern Speech Communication Journal, 46(4),* 419–426.

Checkoway, B. (1993). Interest groups and the bureaucracy. *Journal of Applied Behavioral Science, 17(4),* 566–582.

Chia, K., Lu, K. H., & McLeod, D. M. (2004). Sex, lies, and video compact disc: A case study on third-person perception and motivations for media censorship. *Communication Research, 31(1),* 109–130.

Chicksand, L., & Carrigan, M. (2006). Segmenting voters online: The youth vote. *Journal of Public Affairs, 6(3–4),* 269–282.

Choi, J., Yang, M., & Chang, J. J. C. (2009). Elaboration of the hostile media phenomenon: The roles of involvement, media skepticism, congruency of perceived media influence, and perceived opinion climate. *Communication Research, 36(1),* 54–75.

Chong, D. (1993). How people think, reason, and feel about rights and liberties. *American Journal of Political Science, 37(3),* 867–899.

Chong, D. (1999). Creating common frames of reference on political issues. In D. C. Mutz, P. M. Sniderman, & R. A. Brody (Eds.), *Political persuasion and attitude change* (pp. 195–224). Ann Arbor: University of Michigan Press.

Ciglar, A. J., & Loomis, B. A. (2006). *Interest group politics* (7th ed.). Washington, DC: CQ Press.

Citizens United vs. Federal Election Commission, Appeal to the U.S. Supreme Court from the U.S. District Court for D.C, No. 08-205. Decided January 21, 2010.

Cleland, M., & Raines, B. (2009). *Heart of a patriot: How I found the courage to survive Vietnam, Walter Reed and Karl Rove.* New York: Simon and Schuster.

Cloud, Dana L. (1997). *Control and consolation in American culture and politics: Rhetorics of therapy.* Thousand Oaks, CA: Sage.

Clymer, A. (2006, September 4). Warren J. Mitofsky, 71, innovator who devised exit poll. *New York Times,* p. A17.

Coe, K., Tewksbury, D., Bond, B. J., Drogos, K. L., Porter, R. W., Yahn, A., & Zhang, Y. (2008). Hostile news: Partisan use and perceptions of cable news programming. *Journal of Communication, 58(2),* 201–219.

Coffey, S., & Stipp, H. (1999, March/April). The interactions between computer and television usage. *Journal of Advertising Research, 37,* 61–66.

Cohen, A. (2008, January 1). A tale of political dirty tricks makes the case for election reform. *New York Times,* p. A18.

Cohen, A., & Taylor, E. (2000). *American pharaoh: Richard J. Daley—His battle for Chicago and the nation.* New York: Little, Brown.

Cohen, B. (1963). *The press and foreign policy.* Princeton, NJ: Princeton University Press.

Cohen, J., & Tsfati, Y. (2009). The influence of presumed media influence on strategic voting. *Communication Research, 36(3),* 359–378.

Coleman, K. M., & Davis, C. L. (1976). The structural component of politics and dimensions of regime performance: Their importance for the comparative study of political efficacy. *Comparative Political Studies, 9,* 189–206.

Combs, J. E. (1980). *Dimensions of political drama.* Santa Monica, CA: Goodyear.

Companys, Y., DeSantola, A., Rodriguez-Lluesma, C., & Unzueta, M. (2009). *Racist or race-neutral? How the social context of YouTube political speeches affects voter attitudes.* Paper presented at the conference on YouTube and the 2008 Election Cycle in the United States, University of Massachusetts. Amherst, MA.

Comstock, G. (1989). *The evolution of American television.* Newbury Park, CA: Sage.

Connell, R. W. (1972). Political socialization in the American family: The evidence re-examined. *Public Opinion Quarterly, 36(3),* 323–333.

Connelly, M. (2009, March 1). Ailing GOP risks losing a generation. *New York Times,* WK3.

Conover, P. J., & Sigelman, L. (1982). Presidential influence and public opinion: The case of the Iran hostage crisis. *Social Science Quarterly, 63,* 249–264.

Conrad, F. G., & Schroder, M. F. (2000). Clarifying question meaning in a household survey. *Public Opinion Quarterly, 64(1),* 1–28.

Cook, T., & Scioli, F. (1972). Political socialization research in the United States: A review. In D. Nimmo, & C. Bonjean (Eds.), *Political attitudes and public opinion.* New York: McKay.

Corcoran, P. E. (1979). *Political language and rhetoric.* Austin: University of Texas.

Cornfield, M. (2000, June). New media, new coverage rules. *Campaigns & Elections,* p. 55.

Cornog, E., & Whelan, R. (2000). *Hats in the ring.* New York: Random House.

Corrado, A. (1997). Party soft money. In A. Corrado, T. E. Mann, D. R. Ortiz, T. Potter, & F. J. Sorauf (Eds.), *Campaign finance reform: A sourcebook.* Washington, DC: Brookings Institution.

Costello, W. (1960). *The facts about Nixon.* New York: Viking Press.

Cotter, P. R., Perry, D. K., & Stovall, J. G. (1994). Active and passive indicators of public opinion: Assessing the call-in poll. *Journalism Quarterly, 71(1),* 169–175.

Couper, M. P. (2000). Web surveys: A review of issues and approaches. *Public Opinion Quarterly, 64(4),* 464–494.

Couper, M. P., Blair, J., & Triplett, T. (1999). A comparison of mail and e-mail for a survey of employees in federal statistical agencies. *Journal of Official Statistics, 15(1),* 39–56.

Couper, M. P., Conrad, F. G., & Tourangeau, R. (2007). Visual context effects in Web surveys. *Public Opinion Quarterly, 71(4),* 623–634.

Court's Campaign Ruling Threatens the Public Interest. (2010, January 22). *USA Today,* p. 8A.

Craig, R. (2000). Expectations and elections: How television defines campaign news. *Critical Studies in Media Communication, 17(1),* 28–44.

Craig, S. C., Neimi, R. G., & Silver, G. E. (1990). Political efficacy and trust: A report on the NES pilot study items. *Political Behavior, 12(3),* 289–314.

Crouse, T. (1974). *The boys on the bus.* New York: Ballantine Books.

Cundy, D. T. (1986). Political commercials and candidate image: The effect can be substantial. In L. L. Kaid, D. Nimmo, & K. Sanders (Eds.), *New perspectives on political advertising* (pp. 210–235). Carbondale: Southern Illinois University Press.

Cutbirth, C. W., & Rasmussen, C. (1982). *Political direct mail: The state of the art.* Paper presented at the annual meeting of the Central States Speech Association. Milwaukee, WI.

Dabelko, K. L., & Hernson, P. S. (1997). Women's and men's campaigns for the U.S. House of Representatives. *Political Research Quarterly, 50(1),* 121–135.

Dallek, M. (2000). *The right moment: Ronald Reagan's first victory and the decisive turning point in American politics.* New York: Free Press.

Dallek, R. (1999). *Ronald Reagan: The politics of symbolism.* Cambridge, MA: Harvard University Press.

Dalton, A. (2007, April 24). The digital road to the White House. *PC Magazine, 26(9),* 19–20.

Dana L. Cloud (1997). *Control and consolation in American culture and politics: Rhetorics of therapy.* Thousand Oaks, CA: Sage.

Daniel, M. (2011). *Scandal and civility: Journalism and the birth of American democracy.* New York: Oxford University Press.

Daniels, J. (2009). *Cyber racism: White supremacy online and the new attack on civil rights.* Lanham, MD: Rowman & Littlefield.

Dao, J. (1999, November 15). Old-Timers day meets political fund-raiser at bradley garden party. *New York Times,* p. A25.

Dargis, M., & Scott, A. O. (2009, January 19). How the movies made a president. *New York Times,* pp. AR1, AR9.

Daschmann, G. (2000). Vox pop & polls: The impact of poll results and voter statements in the media on the perception of a climate of opinion. *International Journal of Public Opinion, 12,* 160–181.

Daves, R. P., & Newport, F. (2005). Pollsters under attack: 2004 election incivility and its consequence. *Public Opinion Quarterly, 65(5),* 670–681.

Davis, R. (1999). *The web of politics: The Internet's impact on the American political system.* New York: Oxford University Press.

Davis, R., & Owen, D. M. (1998). *New media and American politics.* New York: Oxford University Press.

Davison, W. P. (1983). The third-person effect in communication. *Public Opinion Quarterly, 47(1),* 1–15.

De Zuniga, H. G., Puig-i-abril, E., & Rojas, H. (2009). Weblogs, traditional sources online and political participation: An assessment of how the Internet is changing the political environment. *New Media & Society, 11,* 553–574.

Debro, A. (2010, August 18). Candidate claims Saban endorsement; UA says no. *Birmingham News,* pp. 1A, 5A.

DeFleur, M. H. (1997). *Computer-assisted investigative reporting.* Mahwah, NJ: Erlbaum.

Delli Carpini, M. X. (1989). Age and history: Generations and sociopolitical change. In R. S. Sigel (Ed.), *Political learning in adulthood* (pp. 11–164). Boulder, CO: Lynne Rienner.

DeLuca, T. (1995). *The two faces of political apathy.* Philadelphia: Temple University Press.

Denton, R. E. Jr. (Ed.). (2000). Dangers of "teledemocracy": How the medium of television undermines American democracy. In *Political communication ethics: An oxymoron* (pp. 91–124). Westport, CT: Praeger.

Denton, R. E. Jr. (Ed.). (2010). *Studies of identity in the 2008 presidential campaign.* Lanham, MD: Lexington Books.

Denton, R. E. Jr., & Woodward, G. C. (1985). *Political communication in America.* New York: Praeger.

Denzin, N. K., & Lincoln, Y. S. (Eds.). (2000). *The handbook of qualitative research.* Thousand Oaks, CA: Sage.

Devitt, E. G., Jr. (1997). Framing politicians: The transformation of candidate arguments in presidential campaign news coverage, 1980, 1988, 1992, and 1996. *American Behavioral Scientist, 40,* 1139–1160.

Devlin, L. P. (1973). The McGovern canvass: A study in interpersonal political campaign communication. *Central States Speech Journal, 24(2),* 83–90.

Devlin, P. (1986). An analysis of political television commercials, 1952–1984. In L. L. Kaid, D. Nimmo, & K. Sanders (Eds.), *New Perspectives on political advertising* (p. 22).

Carbondale: Southern Illinois University Press.

DeVries, W. (1975). Taking the voter's pulse. In R. E. Hiebert, R. F. Jones, J. D. Lorenz, & E. A. Lotito (Eds.), *The political image merchants* (pp. 62–81). Washington, DC: Acropolis.

DeVries, W., & Tarrance, V. L. (1972). *The ticket-splitter: A new force in American politics.* Grand Rapids, MI: Eerdmans.

Dexter, L. (1969). *How organizations are represented in Washington.* New York: Bobbs-Merrill.

Diamond, E., & Bates, S. (1988). *The spot: The rise of political advertising.* Cambridge, MA: MIT Press.

Diamond, G. A., & Cobb, M. D. (1999). The candidate as catastrophe: Latitude theory and the problems of political persuasion. In D. C. Mutz, P. M. Sniderman, & R. A. Brody (Eds.), *Political persuasion and attitude change* (pp. 225–248). Ann Arbor: University of Michigan Press.

Diddi, A., & LaRose, R. (2006). Getting hooked on the news: Uses and gratifications and the formation of news habits among college students in an Internet environment. *Journal of Broadcasting & Electronic Media, 50(2),* 193–210.

Didion, J. (2001). *Political fictions.* New York: Knopf.

Dillman, D. A., Tortora, R. D., Conradt, J., & Bowker, D. (1998). *Influence of plain vs. fancy design on response rates for Web surveys.* Paper presented at the meeting of the American Statistical Association. Dallas, TX.

Dionne, E. J., Jr. (1991). *Why Americans hate politics.* New York: Simon and Schuster.

Dobos, J., & Dimmick, J. (1988). Factor analysis and gratifications construct. *Journal of Broadcasting & Electronic Media, 32(3),* 335–350.

Domke, D., McCoy, K., & Torres, M. (1998). News media, racial perceptions, and political cognition. *Communication Research, 26,* 570–607.

Dommeyer, C. J., & Moriarty, E. (2000). *Increasing the response rate on e-mail surveys.* Paper presented at the American Association for Public Opinion Research meeting. Portland, OR.

Donahue, G. A., Tichenor, P. J., & Olien, C. M. (1972). Gatekeeping: Mass media systems and information control. In F. G. Kline & P. J. Tichenor (Eds.), *Communication research.* Beverly Hills, CA: Sage.

Doppelt, J. C., & Shearer, E. (1999). *Nonvoters: America's no-shows.* Thousand Oaks, CA: Sage.

Drew, C. (2007, December 25). Democrats try to rein in fees on consulting. *New York Times,* pp. A1, A18.

Drinkard, J. (2000, February 3). McCain's win nets windfall on Net. *USA Today,* p. 8A.

Drinkard, J. (2000, March 10). Let the fundraising begin— again. *USA Today,* p. 14A.

Drinkard, J., & Pound, E. T. (1999, August 6). GOP donors asked to pay for mailing error; help woman keep job. *USA Today,* p. 4A.

Druckman, J. N., & Jacobs, L. R. (2006). Lumpers and splitters: The public opinion information that politicians collect and use. *Public Opinion Quarterly, 70(4),* 453–476.

Dubriwny, T. (2005). First ladies and feminism: Laura bush as advocate for women's and children's rights. *Women's Studies in Communication, 28(1),* 84–114.

Duffy, M. (1997). High stakes: A fantasy theme analysis of the selling of riverboat gambling in Iowa. *Southern Communication Journal, 62(2),* 117–132.

Duncan, H. D. (1968). *Symbols in society.* New York: Oxford University Press.

Eagly, A. H., Makhijani, M. G., & Klonsky, B. G. (1992). Gender and the evaluation of leaders: A meta-analysis. *Psychological Bulletin, 111(1),* 3–22.

Easton, D. (1965). *A framework for political analysis.* Englewood Cliffs, NJ: Prentice-Hall.

Edelman, M. (1964). *The symbolic uses of politics.* Urbana: University of Illinois Press.

Edwards, J. L. (Ed.) (2009). *Gender and political communication in America: Rhetoric, representation, and display.* Lanham, MD: Lexington Books.

Egeth, J. (1967). Selective attention. *Psychological Bulletin, 67(1),* 41–57.

Ehrenhalt, A. (1991). *The United States of ambition: Politicians, power and the pursuit of office.* New York: Random House.

Ehrenhalt, A. (1996). *The lost city: The forgotten virtues of community in America.* New York: Basic Books.

Einhorn, L. J. (1981). The ghosts unmasked: A review of literature on speechwriting. *Communication Quarterly, 30(1),* 41–47.

Elder, L., & Greene, S. (2003). Political information, gender and the vote: The differential impact of organizations, personal discussion, and the media on the electoral decisions of women and men. *Social Science Journal, 40(3)*, 385–399.

Elliott, W. R., & Sothirajah, J. (1993). Post-debate analysis and media reliance: Influences on candidate image and voting probabilities. *Journalism Quarterly, 70*, 321–335.

Ellul, J. (1965). *Propaganda.* (K. Kellen & J. Lerner, Trans). New York: Knopf. (Original work published 1962.)

Erber, R., & Lau, R. R. (1990). Political cynicism revisited: An information-processing reconciliation of policy-based and incumbency-based interpretations of changes in trust in government. *American Journal of Political Science, 34(1)*, 236–253.

Eveland, W. P. Jr., & Shah, D. V. (2003). The impact of individual and interpersonal factors on perceived news media bias. *Political Psychology, 24*, 101–117.

Fairbanks, A. M. (2008, September 16). Finding her inner palin. *New York Times*, p. 21A.

Falk, E. (2010). *Women for president: Media bias in nine campaigns* (2nd ed.). Champaign: University of Illinois Press.

Farnsworth, S. J., & Lichter, S. R. (2010). *The nightly news nightmare; Media coverage of U.S. presidential elections, 1988–2008.* Lanham, MD: Rowman & Littlefield.

Faulk, K. (2007, June 9). Bishop's not apologizing for punch. *Birmingham News*, p. 1A.

Federal Election Commission (FEC). (1998, November 20). Advisory Opinion #1998–2.

Federal Election Commission (FEC). (1999, June 10). Advisory Opinion #1999–9.

Federal Election Commission (FEC). (1999, November 10). Advisory Opinion #1999–17.

Fenno, R. F. (1978). *Home style: House members in their districts.* Boston: Little, Brown.

Ferber, P., & Pugliese, R. (1999). *Who you talk to and how you vote: Cue-giving in the New York State Legislature.* Paper presented at the Eastern Communication Association. Charleston, WV.

Ferguson, D. A., & Melkote, S. R. (1997). Leisure time and channel repertoire in a multi-channel environment. *Communication Research Reports, 14(2)*, 189–194.

Ferguson, M. A., Hollander, B. A., & Melwani, C. (1989). *The "dampening effect" of post-debate commentary: The Bentsen/Quayle debate.* Paper at the International Communication Association convention, San Francisco, CA.

Ferguson, S. D. (2000). *Researching the public opinion environment: Theories and methods.* Thousand Oaks, CA: Sage.

Files, J. (2000, May 7). For politicians, being funny is a serious business. *New York Times*, p. A24.

Fillippeli, S. (1999, August 29). A buzz about Bush. *Birmingham News*, pp. 1C, 6C.

Fineman, H. (1995, June 5). And now, "the Spiro strategy." *Newsweek, 125(23)*, 28–29.

Finkel, S. E., Guterbock, T. M., & Berg, M. J. (1991). Race-of-interviewer effects in a pre-election poll. *Public Opinion Quarterly, 55(3)*, 313–330.

Fiorina, M. P. (1981). *Retrospective voting in American national elections.* New Haven, CT: Yale University Press.

Fishkin, J. (1995). *The voice of the people: Public opinion and democracy.* New Haven, CT: Yale University Press.

Fishkin, J. S. (2009). *When the people speak: Deliberative democracy and public consultation.* New York: Oxford University Press.

Fleischer, A. (2005). *Taking heat: The president, the press, and my years in the White House.* New York: HarpersCollins.

Fleming, E. D. (1959, August). Ghosts in the closet. *Cosmopolitan, 147*, 68–71.

Flemming, G., & Sonner, M. (1999). *Can Internet polling work: Strategies for conducting public opinion research online.* Paper presented at the American Association for Public Opinion Research meeting. St. Petersburg, FL.

Forbes, S. (1999). *A new birth of freedom.* New York: Regnery.

Frankel, M. R., & Frankel, L. R. (1987). Fifty years of survey sampling in the United States. *Public Opinion Quarterly, 51*, S127–S138.

Franklin, C. H. (1992). Measurement and the dynamics of party identification. *American Political Science Review, 77(2)*, 957–973.

Frankovic, K. A. (2005). Reporting 'the polls' in 2004. *Public Opinion Quarterly, 65(5)*, 682–697.

Frantz, D. (2000, February 21). A beer baron and a powerful publisher put McCain on a political path. *New York Times*, p. A14.

Franzen, J. (1999). Consultants and clients. In D. D. Perlmutter (Ed.), *The Manship school guide to political communication* (pp. 295–302).

Baton Rouge: Louisiana State University Press.

Fraser, N., & Gordon, N. (1994). A genealogy of dependency: Tracing a key word of the U.S. welfare state. *Signs, 19(2)*, 309–336.

Friedenberg, R. V. (1997). *Communication consultants in political campaigns: Ballot box warriors.* Westport, CT: Praeger.

Fritschler, A. L. (2008). *Closed minds? Politics and ideology in American universities.* Washington, DC: Brookings Institution Press.

Fritz, S., & Morris, D. (1992). *The handbook of campaign spending.* Washington, DC: Congressional Quarterly Press.

Gamson, W. A. (1996). Media discourse as a framing resource. In A. N. Crigler (Ed.), *The psychology of political communication* (pp. 111–131). Ann Arbor: University of Michigan Press.

Gans, C. (1999, July 19). Footnotes. *NetPulse, 3(14),* 1.

Gantz, W. (1983). The diffusion of news about the attempted reagan assassination. *Journal of Communication, 33(1),* 56–66.

Gardikiotis, A. (2008). Group distinctiveness, political identification, and the third-person effect: Perceptions of a political campaign in the 2004 Greek national election. *Media Psychology, 11(3),* 331–353.

Garlick, R., & Mongeau, P. A. (1992). Majority/minority size and the evaluations of persuasive arguments. *Communication Research Reports, 9,* 45–53.

Garramore, G. M. (1984). Voter responses to negative political ads. *Journalism Quarterly, 61,* 250–259.

Garramore, G. M. (1985). Effects of negative political advertising: The roles of sponsor and rebuttal. *Journal of Broadcasting and Electronic Media, 29(2),* 147–159.

Garramore, G. M., Atkin, C. K., Pinkleton, B. E., & Cole, R. T. (1990). Effects of negative political advertising on the political process. *Journal of Broadcasting & Electronic Media, 34,* 299–311.

Garrison, B. (1998). *Computer-assisted reporting.* Mahwah, NJ: Erlbaum.

Garver, E. (1994). *Aristotle's rhetoric: An art of character.* Chicago: University of Chicago Press.

Geiger, S. (1993). *Truth in political advertising: The effects of adwatch articles on the evaluation and memory for political candidates.* Paper at the convention of the International Communication Association. Washington, DC.

Gerbner, G., Gross, L., Morgan, M., & Signorielli, N. (1990). Charting the mainstream: Television's contributions to political orientations. In D. A. Graber (Ed.), *Media power in politics.* Washington, DC: Congressional Quarterly Press.

Gerhard, M. E. (1990). A newspaper's 900 telephone poll: Its perceived credibility and accuracy. *Journalism Quarterly, 67,* 508–513.

German, K. M. (1995). Critical theory in public relations inquiry: Future directions for analysis in a public relations context. In W. N. Elwood (Ed.), *Public relations inquiry as rhetorical criticism* (pp. 279–294). Westport, CT: Praeger.

Giglio, E. (2005). *Here's looking at you: Hollywood, film &*

politics (2nd ed.). New York: Peter Lang.

Giridharadas, A. (2009, September 13). 'Athens' on the Net. *New York Times,* WK1, WK5.

Gitlin, T. (1980). *The whole world is watching.* Berkeley: University of California Press.

Glass, J., Bengston, V. L., & Dunham, C. C. (1986). Attitude similarity in three generational families: Socialization, status inheritance, or reciprocal influence? *American Sociological Review, 51(5),* 685–698.

Glenn, R. (2001). *Debating the debates: Assessing the value of televised presidential debates in producing an informed electorate.* Paper presented at the annual meeting of the Southern States Communication Association. Lexington, KY.

Glick, J. A. (1999). Focus groups in political campaigns. In D. D. Perlmutter (Ed.), *The Manship school guide to political communication* (pp. 114–121). Baton Rouge: Louisiana State University Press.

Glynn, C., & McLeod, J. (1984). Public opinion du jour: An examination of the spiral of silence. *Public Opinion Quarterly, 48(4),* 731–740.

Golan, G. (2002). Religiosity and the third-person effect. *Journal of Media & Religion, 1(2),* 105–120.

Golan, G. J., Banning, S. A., & Lundy, L. (2008). Likelihood to vote, candidate choice, and the third-person effect: Behavioral implications of political advertising in the 2004 presidential election. *American Behavioral Scientist, 52(2),* 278–290.

Golan, G. J., & Day, A. G. (2008). The first-person effect

and its behavioral consequences: A new trend in the twenty-five year history of third-person effect research. *Mass Communication & Society, 11,* 539–556.

Gold, E. R. (1978). Political apologia: The ritual of self-defense. *Communication Monographs, 45,* 306–316.

Goldzwig, S. R., & Sullivan, P. A. (2000). Electronic democracy, virtual politics, and local communities. In R. E. Denton, Jr. (Ed.), *Political communication ethics* (pp. 51–74). Westport, CT: Praeger.

Goodman, M., & Gring, M. (1999). *The visual byte: Bill Clinton and the polysemic town hall meeting.* Paper for the Southern Speech Communication Association. St. Louis, MO.

Gore, A. (1993). *Earth in the balance: Ecology and the human spirit.* New York: Plume.

Gormley, K. (2010). *The death of American virtue: Clinton vs. Starr.* New York: Crown Publishers.

Graber, D. (1971). The press as opinion resource during the 1968 presidential campaign. *Public Opinion Quarterly, 35,* 168–182.

Graber, D. (1972). Personal qualities in presidential images: The contribution of the press. *Midwest Journal of Political Science, 16(1),* 46–76.

Graber, D. (2001). Adapting political news to the needs of the twenty-first century. In W. L. Bennett & R. Entman (Eds.), *Mediated politics: Communication in the future of democracy* (pp. 433–452). Cambridge, England: Cambridge University Press.

Graber, D. A. (1976). *Verbal behavior and politics.* Urbana: University of Illinois Press.

Graber, D. A. (1987). Framing election news broadcasts: News context and its impact on the 1984 presidential election. *Social Science Quarterly, 68,* 552–568.

Graff, G. M. (2007). *The first campaign: Globalization, the Web & the race for the White House.* New York: Farrar, Straus and Giroux.

Graham, J. (2005, November 21). Video websites pop up, invite postings. *USA Today,* p. 21.

Green, D. P., & Palmquist, B. (1994). How stable is party identification? *Political Review, 16(4),* 437–466.

Greenberg, B. S. (1964). Diffusion of news of the Kennedy assassination. *Public Opinion Quarterly, 28(2),* 225–232.

Greene County fraud. (1999, June 20). *Birmingham News,* p. 2C.

Greenfield, M. (1999, January 10). A not very good film. *Newsweek,* p. 70.

Greenhouse, S. (2008, August 19). Hitting McCain where he lives. *New York Times,* p. 14A.

Greffenius, S. (2001). *The last Jeffersonian: Ronald Reagan and radical democracy.* Boston: American Book Publishers.

Griffin, E. (2006). *A first look at communication theory* (6th ed.). Boston: McGraw-Hill.

Gronbeck, B. E. (1992). Negative narratives in 1988 presidential campaign ads. *Quarterly Journal of Speech, 78(3),* 333–346.

Gronbeck, B. E. (2000). The ethical performances of candidates in American presidential campaign dramas. In R. E. Denton, Jr. (Ed.), *Political communication ethics: An oxymoron* (pp. 1–22). Westport, CT: Praeger.

Grossman, M. B., & Kumar, M. J. (1981). *Portraying the president: The White House and the news media.* Baltimore, MD: Johns Hopkins University Press.

Gubrium, J. F., & Holstein, J. A. (Eds.). (2001). *Handbook of interview research.* Thousand Oaks, CA: Sage.

Gunderson, R. G. (1960). Political phrasemakers in perspective. *Southern Speech Communication Journal, 26,* 22–26.

Gunter, B. (2000). *Media research methods: Measuring audiences, reactions, impact.* Thousand Oaks, CA: Sage.

Gunther, A. C. (1998). The persuasion press inference. *Communication Research, 25(5),* 486–504.

Gunther, A. C., & Christen, T. C. (Summer 1999). Effects of news slant and base rate information on perceived public opinion. *Journalism and Mass Communication Quarterly, 76,* 277–292.

Gunther, A. C., & Schmitt, K. (2004). Mapping boundaries of the hostile media effect. *Journal of Communication, 54(1),* 55–70.

Gutgold, N. D. (2000). *Living out loud: How Betty Ford expanded the boundaries of the role of the first lady.* Paper presented at the annual meeting of the Eastern Communication Association. Pittsburgh, PA.

Gutgold, N. D. (2009). *Almost Madam President: Why Hillary Clinton 'won' in 2008.* Lanham, MD: Lexington Books.

Haas, A. (1979). Male and female spoken language differences: Stereotypes and evidence. *Psychological Bulletin, 86(3),* 616–626.

Hacker, J. S., & Pierson, Paul (2010). *Winner-take-all politics*. New York: Simon & Schuster.

Hacker, K. L., Howl, L., Scott, M., & Steiner, R. (1996). Uses of computer-mediated political communication in the 1992 presidential campaign: A content analysis of the Bush, Clinton and Perot computer lists. *Communication Research Reports, 13,* 138–146.

Halbfinger, D. M. (2000, February 1). Money attracts money for rich New Jersey Senate contender. *New York Times,* p. A23.

Hale, J. F. (1994). Yes: Campaign commercials should be regulated. In G. I. Rose (Ed.), *Controversial issues in presidential selection* (pp. 130–137). Albany, NY: State University of New York Press.

Hamilton, B., & Beattie, D. (1999). Modern campaign polling. In D. D. Perlmutter (Ed.), *The Manship school guide to political communication* (pp. 93–106). Baton Rouge: Louisiana State University Press.

Hamm, K. (1991). Patterns of influence among committees, agencies, and interest groups. *Legislative Quarterly, 8,* 379–426.

Hansen, A., Cottle, S., Negrine, R. E., & Newbold, C. (1998). *Mass communication research methods*. Washington Square, NY: New York University Press.

Hardy, B. W., & Jamieson, K. H. (2005). Can a poll affect perception of candidate traits? *Public Opinion Quarterly, 65(5),* 725–743.

Harper, M. (2009). *Uploading hope: An inside view of Obama's HQ new media video team*. Paper presented at the conference on YouTube and the 2008 Election Cycle in the United States, University of Massachusetts. Amherst, MA.

Hart, J. (1994, September 3). 'Nattering nabobs of negativism'. *Editor & Publisher, 127(36),* 5.

Hart, R. P. (1987). The sound of leadership: Presidential communication in the modern age. Chicago: University of Chicago Press.

Hart, R. P. (1998). *Seducing America: How television charms the modern voter*. Thousand Oaks, CA: Sage.

Hart, R. P. (2000). *Campaign talk: Why campaigns are good for us*. Oxford: Oxford University Press.

Hartmann, R. (1980). *Palace politics: An inside account of the Ford years*. New York: McGraw-Hill.

Harwood, J. (1998). Viewing age: Lifespan identity and television viewing choice. *Journal of Broadcasting & Electronic Media, 41(2),* 203–213.

Harwood, J. (2009, February 14). Rethinking the Reagan mystique. *New York Times,* WK1, WK6.

Harwood, J., & Seib, G. F. (2009). *Pennsylvania avenue: profiles in backroom power— Making Washington work again*. New York: Random House.

Hastings, C. M. (2000). *A home of her own: Edith Roosevelt's construction of Private White*. Paper presented at the annual meeting of the Eastern Communication Association. Pittsburgh, PA.

Havice, M. J. (1990). Measuring nonresponse and refusals to an electronic telephone survey. *Journalism Quarterly, 67(3),* 521–530.

Havick, J. (1997). Determinants of national media attention. *Journal of Communication, 47(2),* 97–111.

Heerwegh, D., & Loosveldt, G. (2008). Face-to-face versus Web surveying in a high-Internet-coverage population. *Public Opinion Quarterly, 72(5),* 836–846.

Heeter, C. (1988). Gender differences in viewing style. In C. Heeter & B. S. Greenberg (Eds.), *Cableviewing* (pp. 151–166). Norwood, NJ: Ablex.

Heeter, C., & Greenberg, B. S. (1988). *Cableviewing*. Norwood, NJ: Ablex.

Heffernan, V. (2009, April 12). The YouTube presidency. *New York Times Magazine,* p. 12.

Heider, F. (1958). *The psychology of interpersonal relations*. New York: Wiley.

Heilemann, J., & Halperin, M. (2010). *Game Change: Obama and the Clintons, McCain and Palin, and the race of a lifetime*. New York: Harper.

Hellweg, S. A., Pfau, M., & Brydon, S. R. (1992). *Televised presidential debates: Advocacy in America*. New York: Praeger.

Hendricks, J. A., & Denton, R. E. Jr. (Eds.). (2009). *Communicator-in-chief: How Barack Obama used new media technology to win the White House*. Lanham, MD: Lexington Books.

Hendricks, J. A., & Denton, R. E. Jr. (Eds.) (2010). *Communicator-in-chief: How Barack Obama used new media technology to win the White House*. Lanham, MD: Lexington Books.

Herbst, S. (1998). *Reading public opinion: How political actors view the democratic process.* Chicago: University of Chicago Press.

Herrnson, P. S. (2000). Hired guns and House races: Campaign professionals in House elections. In J. A. Thurber & C. J. Nelson (Eds.), *Campaign warriors: Political consultants in elections* (pp. 65–90). Washington, DC: Brookings Institution.

Hershey, M. R. (1974). *The making of campaign strategy.* Lexington, MA: D. C. Heath.

Hertog, J. K., Finnegan, J. R., Jr., & Kahn, E. (1994). Media coverage of AIDS, cancer, and sexually transmitted diseases: A test of the public arenas model. *Journalism Quarterly, 71(2),* 291–304.

Hess, S. (1988). *The presidential campaign.* Washington, DC: Brookings Institution.

Hickson, M. L., & Stacks, D. W. (1992). *NVC: Nonverbal communication studies and applications* (3rd ed.). Dubuque, IA: Brown & Benchmark.

Hill, K. A., & Hughes, J. E. (1998). *Cyberpolitics.* Mahwah, NJ: Rowman & Littlefield.

Hinck, E. A., & Hinck, S. S. (1998). *Audience reactions to Clinton and Dole: Some evidence for explaining audience assessments in terms of political strategies.* Paper for the National Communication Association Convention, New York, NY.

Hinck, E. A., & Hinck, S. S. (2000). Politeness theory and political debates. In D. Bystrom, D. B. Carlin, L. L. Kaid, M. Kern, & M. S. McKinney (Eds.), *Communication Politics:*

Engaging the Public in Campaign 2000 and Beyond (pp. 124–130). Proceedings of the National Communication Association Summer Conference, Washington, DC.

Hitt, J. (1999, July 25). Campaign cash. *New York Times Magazine,* p. 20.

Hochschild, A. R. (1989). *The second shift: Working parents and the evolution at home.* New York: Viking.

Hoffner, C., & Buchanan, M. (2002). Parents' responses to television violence: The third-person perception, parental mediation, and support for censorship. *Media Psychology, 4(3),* 231–252.

Hofstadter, R. (1967). *The paranoid style in American politics and other essays.* New York: Vintage Books.

Hofstetter, C. R., Donovan, M. C., Klauber, M. R., Cole, A., Huie, A. J., & Yuasa, T. (1994). Political talk radio: A stereotype reconsidered. *Political Research Quarterly, 47(2),* 467–479.

Holbert, R. L. (2004). Political talk radio, perceived fairness, and the establishment of President George W. Bush's political legitimacy. *Harvard International Journal of Press/ Politics, 9(3),* 12–27.

Holbert, R. L. (2005). A typology for the study of entertainment television and politics. *American Behavioral Scientist, 49(3),* 436–453.

Holbert, R. L., & Benoit, W. L. (2009). A theory of political media campaign connectedness. *Communication Monographs, 76(3),* 303–332.

Holbert, R. L., & Hansen, G. J. (2006). *Fahrenheit 9/11,* need for closure and the priming

of affective ambivalence: An assessment of intra-affective structures by party identification. *Human Communication Research, 32(2),* 109–129.

Holbert, R. L., & Hansen, G. J. (2008). Stepping beyond message specificity in the study of emotion as mediator and inter-emotion associations across attitude objects: *Fahrenheit 9/11,* anger, and debate superiority. *Media Psychology, 11,* 98–118.

Holbert, R. L., Hansen, G. J., Caplan, S. E., & Mortensen, S. (2007a). Presidential debate viewing and Michael Moore's *Fahrenheit 9/11:* A study of affect-as-transfer and passionate reasoning. *Media Psychology, 9(3),* 673.694.

Holbert, R. L., Kwak, N., & Shah, D. V. (2003). Environmental concern, patterns of television viewing, and pro-environmental behaviors: Integrating models of media consumption and effects. *Journal of Broadcasting & Electronic Media, 47,* 177–196.

Holbert, R. L., Lambe, J. L., Dudo, A. D., & Carlton, K. A. (2007b). Primacy effects of *The Daily Show* and national TV news viewing: Young viewers, political gratifications, and internal political self-efficacy. *Journal of Broadcasting & Electronic Media, 51,* 20–38.

Holbert. R. L., LaMarre, H., & Landreville, K. (2009). Fanning the flames of a partisan divide: The role of debate viewing in the formation of partisan-driven post-election evaluations of personal vote count accuracy. *Communication Research, 36,* 155–177.

Holbert, R. L., Pillion, O., Tschida, D. A., Armfield, G. G., Kinder, K., Cherry, K., & Daulton, A. (2003). *The West Wing* as endorsement of the American presidency: Expanding the domain of priming in political communication. *Journal of Communication, 53(3)*, 427–433.

Holbert, R. L., Shah, D. V., & Kwak, N. (2004). Fear, authority, and justice: The influence of TV news, police reality, and crime drama viewing on endorsements of capital punishment and gun ownership. *Journalism & Mass Communication Quarterly, 81*, 177–196.

Holbert, R. L., Tschida, D. A., Dixon, M., Cherry, K., Steuber, K., & Airne, D. (2005). *The West Wing* and depictions of the American presidency: Expanding the theoretical and empirical domains of framing in political communication. *Communication Quarterly, 53(4)*, 505–522.

Holland, P. (1987). When a woman reads the news. In H. Baehr & G. Dyer (Eds.), *Boxed in: Women in television* (pp. 133–150). New York: Pandora Press.

Holleman, B. (2000). *The forbid/allow asymmetry: On the cognitive mechanisms underlying wording effects in surveys.* Amsterdam: Rodopi.

Hollihan, Thomas A. (2001). *Uncivil wars: Political campaigns in a media age.* Boston: Bedford-St. Martin's.

Hong, C., & Riffe, D. (2008). Attention, perception, and perceived effects: Negative political advertising in a battleground state of the 2004 presidential election. *Mass Communication & Society, 11(2)*, 177–196.

Hovland, C. I., Lumsdaine, A. A., & Sheffield, F. D. (1949). *Experiments in mass communication.* Princeton, NJ: Princeton University Press.

Hu, W. (2000, January 20). Interviewer gets personal with First Lady. *New York Times,* p. C37.

Huang, X., Leong, E., & Stanner, P. (1998, September/October). Comparing the effectiveness of the Web site with traditional media. *Journal of Advertising Research,* pp. 44–49.

Huckfeldt, R. R., & Sprague, J. (1995). *Citizens, politics, and social communication: Information and influence in an election campaign.* New York: Cambridge University Press.

Huffington, A. (1999, September 1). Windom case is bellwether for politics. *Birmingham News,* p. 11A.

Hulse, C. (2010, January 3). The time may be ripe for party-switching, but its risks are apparent. *New York Times,* p. 21A.

Hulse, C. (2010, June 20). Legislative hurdles in an era of conflict, not compromise. *New York Times,* p. A18.

Hutchins, J. M. (1999). Political media buying. In D. D. Perlmutter (Ed.), *The Manship school guide to political communication* (pp. 122–130). Baton Rouge: Louisiana State University Press.

Hwang, H., Pan, Z., & Sun, Y. (2008). Influence of hostile media perception on willingness to engage in discursive activities: An examination of mediating role of media indignation. *Media Psychology, 11(1)*, 76–97.

Impeach this. (2000). *NetPulse, 3(14)*, 2.

Iorio, S. H., & Huxman, S. S. (1996). Media coverage of political issues and the framing of personal concerns. *Journal of Communication, 46(4)*, 97–115.

Ivins, M., & DuBose, L. (2000). *Shrub: The short but happy political life of George W. Bush.* New York: Random House.

Iyengar, S. (1996). Framing responsibility for political issues. *Annals of the American Academy of Political and Social Science, 456*, 59–70.

Iyengar, S., & Kinder, D. R. (1987). *News that matters.* Chicago: University of Chicago Press.

Jackson, D. (2008, December 19). Laura Bush surprised how far voice carried. *USA Today,* p. 10A.

Jackson, J. S. (1977). Review: The management of election campaigns. *Political Communication Review, 2(1)*, 11–12.

Jacobs, L. J., & Shapiro, R. Y. (2005). Polling politics, media, and election campaign. *Public Opinion Quarterly, 69*, 635–641.

Jacobs, L. R., & Shapiro, R. Y. (2000). *Politicians don't pander: Political manipulation and the loss of democratic responsiveness.* Chicago: University of Chicago Press.

Jacoby, J., Troutman, T. R., & Whittler, T. E. (1986). Viewer miscomprehension of the 1980 presidential debate: A research note. *Political Psychology, 7(2)*, 297–308.

Jalonick, M. C. (2000, April). Bringing in the bucks on the Web. *Campaigns & Elections,* pp. 48–49.

James, C. (1999, December 19). We're ready for our close-ups now. *New York Times,* p. Y30.

Jamieson, K. (1984). *Packaging the presidency*. New York: Oxford University Press.

Jamieson, K. H. (1988). *Eloquence in an electronic age: The transformation of political speechmaking*. New York: Oxford University Press.

Jamieson, K. H. (1992). *Dirty politics: Deception, distraction and democracy*. New York: Oxford University Press.

Jamieson, K. H. (1996). *Packaging the presidency*. New York: Oxford University Press.

Jamieson, K. H. (2001). *Everything you think you know about politics… . And why you're wrong*. New York: Basic Books.

Jamieson, K. H., & Birdsell, D. S. (1988). *Presidential debates: The challenge of creating an informed electorate*. New York: Oxford University Press.

Jamieson, K. H., & Campbell, K. K. (1997). *The interplay of influence: News, advertising, politics and the mass media* (4th ed.). Belmont, CA: Wadsworth.

Jasperson, A., & Yun, H. (2007). Political advertising effects and America's racially diverse newest voting generation. *American Behavioral Scientist, 50(9)*, 1112–1123.

Jeffries, L. W. (1986). *Mass media: Process and effects*. Prospect Heights, IL: Waveland.

Jennings, M. K., & Markus, G. B. (1984). Partisan orientations over the long haul: Results from the three-wave political socialization panel study. *American Political Science Review, 78,* 1000–1018.

Jennings, M. K., & Niemi, R. G. (1968). The transmission of political values from parent to child. *American Political Science Review, 62(1),* 169–184.

Jenson, J. R., & Denker, K. J. (2009). Political differences and perceptions of silencing in university classrooms. *Communication Research Reports, 26(3),* 208–214.

Jie, X., & Gonzenbach, W. J. (2008). Does a perceptual discrepancy lead to action? A meta-analysis of the behavioral component of the third-person effect. *International Journal of Public Opinion Research, 20(3),* 375–385.

John, K. E. (1989). The polls: A report. *Public Opinion Quarterly, 53(4),* 590–605.

Johnson, D. W. (2000). The business of political consulting. In J. A. Thurber & C. J. Nelson (Eds.), *Campaign warriors: Political consultants in elections* (pp. 37–52). Washington, DC: Brookings Institution.

Johnson, K. (2010, October 17). In fervor for voting, retirees hold a key. *New York Times,* pp. A17, A21.

Johnson, T. J. (1993). Filling out the racing form: How the media covered the horse race in the 1988 primaries. *Journalism Quarterly, 70(2),* 300–310.

Johnson-Cartee, K. S., & Copeland, G. A. (1991). *Negative political advertising: Coming of age*. Hillsdale, NJ: Erlbaum.

Jones, A. S. (2011). *Losing the news: The future of the news that feeds democracy*. New York: Oxford University Press.

Jones, C. (1988). *How to speak TV*. Tallahassee, FL: Video Consultants.

Jones, C. A. (2000). Soft money and hard choices: The influence of campaign finance rules on campaign communication strategy. In R. E. Denton, Jr. (Ed.), *Political communication ethics* (pp. 179–202). Westport, CT: Praeger.

Jordan, H. (1982). *Crisis: The last year of the Carter presidency*. New York: Putnam.

Joslyn, R. (1986). Political advertising and the meaning of elections. In L. L. Kaid, D. Nimmo, & K. Sanders (Eds.), *New perspectives on political advertising* (pp. 139–184). Carbondale: Southern Illinois University Press.

Jowett, G. S., & O'Donnell, V. (1986). *Propaganda and persuasion*. Beverly Hills, CA: Sage.

Joy, M. (2001). *Listening in politics*. Paper presented at the annual meeting of the Southern States Communication Association. Lexington, KY.

Judis, J. B. (1999, August 8). Race for presidential cash: No way to run democracy, *Birmingham News*, p. 8C.

Just, M., Crigler, A., & Wallace, L. (1990). Thirty seconds or thirty minutes: What viewers learn from spot advertisements and candidate debates. *Journal of Communication, 40(3),* 120–133.

Kahn, K. F. (1993). Gender differences in campaign messages: The political advertisements of men and women candidates for U.S. Senate. *Political Research Quarterly, 46(3),* 481–502.

Kahn, K. F. (1994). Does gender make a difference? An experimental examination of sex stereotypes and press patterns in statewide campaigns. *American Journal of Political Science, 38,* 162–196.

Kaid, L. L. (1996). Technology and political advertising:

The application of ethical standards to the 1992 spots. *Communication Research Reports, 13(2)*, 129–137.

Kaid, L. L. (2000). Ethics and political advertising. In R. E. Denton, Jr. (Ed.), *Political communication ethics: An oxymoron* (pp. 147–178). Westport, CT: Praeger.

Kaid, L. L., & Boydston, J. (1987). An experimental study of the effectiveness of negative political advertisements. *Communication Quarterly, 35*, 193–201.

Kaid, L. L., Gobetz, R. H., Garner, J., & Leland, C. M. (1993). Television news and presidential campaigns: The legitimization of television political advertising. *Social Science Quarterly, 74*, 274–285.

Kaid, L. L., & Johnston, A. (2001). *Videostyle in presidential campaigns: Style and content of televised political advertising*. Westport, CT: Praeger.

Kaid, L. L., Tedesco, J. C., & McKinnon, L. (1993). Presidential ads as nightly news: A content analysis of 1988 and 1992 televised adwatches. *Journal of Broadcasting & Electronic Media, 40*, 279–303.

Kanter, D. L., & Mirvis, P. H. (1989). *The cynical Americans: Living and working in an age of discontent and disillusion*. San Francisco: Jossey-Bass.

Kantrow, B. (1999, August 4). Boastful 1995 ad still posing legal challenge for GOP. *Birmingham News*, p. 5A.

Karpf, D. (2009). *Macaca moments reconsidered: YouTube effects or netroots effects?* Paper presented at the conference on YouTube and the 2008 Election Cycle in the United States, University of Massachusetts. Amherst, MA.

Katz, E., & Lazarsfeld, P. F. (1955). *Personal influence: The part played by people in the flow of mass communication*. Glencoe, IL: Free Press.

Kaye, T. J., & Johnson, B. K. (2002). Webelievability: A path model examining how convenience and reliance predict online credibility. *Journalism & Mass Communication Quarterly, 79(3)*, 619–642.

Keefer, J. D. (1993). The news media's failure to facilitate citizen participation in the congressional policymaking process. *Journalism Quarterly, 70(2)*, 412–424.

Keith, B., Orr, E., Magleby, D., Nelson, C., Wolfinger, R., & Westlye, M. (1988). *The myth of the independent voter*. Berkeley: University of California Press.

Kelley, H. H. (1967). Attribution theory in social psychology. In D. Levine (Ed.), *Nebraska symposium on motivation 15* (pp. 197–238). Lincoln: University of Nebraska Press.

Kelley, S. (1956). *Professional public relations and political power*. Baltimore, MD: Johns Hopkins University Press.

Kelley, S., Jr. (1983). *Interpreting elections*. Princeton, NJ: Princeton University Press.

Kelley, T. (1999, October 19). Candidate on the stump is surely on the Web. *New York Times*. pp. A1, A15.

Kennedy, K. A., & Benoit, W. L. (1997). The Newt Gingrich book deal controversy: Self-defense rhetoric. *Southern Communication Journal, 62(3)*, 197–216.

Kennedy, M. M. (1980). *Office politics: Seizing power, wielding clout*. New York: Warner.

Kenski, H. C. (1996). From agenda-setting to priming and framing. In M. E. Stuckey (Ed.), *The theory and practice of political communication research*. Albany, NY: SUNY Press.

Kenski, K., Hardy, B. W., & Jamieson, K. H. (2010). *The Obama victory: How media, money and message shaped the 2008 election*. New York: Oxford University Press.

Kent, M. L., Harrison, T. R., & Taylor, M. (2006). A critique of Internet polls as symbolic representation and pseudo-events. *Communication Studies, 57(3)*, 299–315.

Kern, M. (1989). *30-second politics: Political advertising in the eighties*. New York: Praeger.

Key, V. O., Jr. (1949). *Southern politics*. New York: Vintage.

Key, V. O., Jr. (1952). *Politics, parties, and pressure groups*. New York: Thomas Crowell.

Key, V. O., Jr. (1961). *Public opinion and American democracy*. New York: Knopf.

Kingdon, J. (1973). *Congressmen's voting decisions* (2nd ed.). New York: Harper & Row.

Kinsley, M. (2007, April 30). The substance gap. *Time, 169(18)*, 34.

Kirkpatrick, D. (2010). *The Facebook effect: The inside story of the company that is connecting the world*. New York: Simon & Schuster.

Kirkpatrick, D. D. (2009, October 11). Lobbyists fight efforts to save on health care. *New York Times*, pp. A1, A20.

Kirkpatrick, D. D. (2010, January 22). Lobbyists get potent

weapon in campaign ruling. *New York Times,* pp. A1, A16.

Kitchens, J. T., & Powell, L. (1975). Discriminant analysis as an instrument for political analysis. *Southern Speech Communication Journal, 40(3),* 313–320.

Kitchens, J. T., & Powell, L. (1986). A critical analysis of NCPAC's strategies in key 1980 races: A third party negative campaign. *Southern Speech Communication Journal, 51,* 208–228.

Kitchens, J. T., & Powell, L. (1994). Ticket splitting: Dead or alive? *Campaigns & Elections,* 34–35.

Kitchens, J. T., & Stiteler, B. (1979). Challenge to the 'Rule of Minimum Effect': A case study of the in man/out man strategy. *Southern Speech Communication Journal, 44,* 176–190.

Kitchens, J. T., Powell, L., & Williams, G. (2003). Information please? Information seeking, mass media, and the undecided voter. *Communication Research Reports, 20,* 73–81.

Klapp, O. E. (1964). *Symbolic leaders: Public drama and public men.* New York: Minerva Press.

Klapper, J. (1960). *The effects of mass communication.* New York: Free Press.

Klein, J. (2006). *Politics lost: From RFK to W: How politicians have become less courageous and more interested in keeping power than in doing what's right for America.* New York: Broadway.

Klein, J. G., & Ahluwalia, R. (2005). Negativity in the evaluation of political candidates. *Journal of Marketing, 69(1),* 131–142.

Kluver, R., Foot, K., Jankowski, N., & Schneider, S. (Eds.) (2007). *The Internet and national elections: A comparative study of Web campaigning.* New York: Routledge.

Kolodny, R. (2000). Electoral partnerships: Political consultants and political parties. In J. A. Thurber & C. J. Nelson (Eds.), *Campaign warriors: Political consultants in elections* (pp. 110–132). Washington, DC: Brookings Institution.

Kraus, S. (1962). *The great debates.* Bloomington: Indiana University Press.

Kraus, S. (2000). *Televised presidential debates and public policy* (2nd ed.). Hillsdale, NJ: Earlbaum.

Kraus, S., & Davis, D. (1976). *The effects of mass communication on political behavior.* University Park: Pennsylvania State University Press.

Kraus, S., Davis, D., Lang, G. E., & Lang, K. (1976). Critical events analysis. In S. H. Chaffee (Ed.), *Political communication: Issues and strategies for research* (pp. 195–216). Beverly Hills, CA: Sage.

Krosnick, J. A., & Kinder, D. R. (1990). Altering the foundations of support for the president through priming. *American Political Science Review, 84(2),* 497–512.

Krueger, R. A., & Casey, M. A. (2000). *Focus groups: A practical guide for applied research.* Thousand Oaks, CA: Sage.

Kurtz, H. (1998). *Spin cycle: Inside the Clinton propaganda machine.* New York: Free Press.

Kushin, M. (2009). *Exploring YouTube: Civic engagement and perceptions about the role of the Internet in civic engagement among college students.* Paper presented at the conference on YouTube and the 2008 Election Cycle in the United States, University of Massachusetts. Amherst, MA.

Kyun, S. K., & Yorgo, P. (2007). Study of partisan news readers reveals hostile media perceptions of balanced stories. *Newspaper Research Journal, 28(2),* 99–106.

Lakoff, G. (2008). The political mind: Why you can't understand 21st-century politics with an 18th-century mind. New York: Viking.

Lane, E. (1964). *Lobbying and the Law.* Cambridge: Cambridge University Press.

Lang, K., & Lang, G. E. (1968). *Politics and television.* Chicago: Quadrangle Books.

Langer, G., & Cohen, J. (2005). Voters and values in the 2004 election. *Public Opinion Quarterly, 69(5),* 744–759.

Larson, C. U. (1995). *Persuasion: Reception and responsibility* (7th ed.). Belmont, CA: Wadsworth.

Larson, E. J. (2008). *A magnificent catastrophe: The tumultuous election of 1800, America's first presidential campaign.* New York: Free Press.

Larson, S., & Psystrup, P. (2000). The Internet gateway: McCain's new realm of politicking. In D. Bystrom, D. B. Carlin, L. L. Kaid, M. Kern, & M. S. McKinney. (Eds.), *Communicating politics: Engaging the public in campaign 2000 and beyond* (pp. 159–172). Washington, DC: NCA Summer Conference proceedings.

Lash, J. P. (1971). *Eleanor and Franklin.* New York: Signet.

Lau, R. (1982). Negativity in political perceptions. *Political Behavior, 4(4)*, 353–378.

Lau, R. R., Smith, R. A., & Fiske, S. T. (1991). Political beliefs, policy interpretations, and political persuasion. *Journal of Politics, 53(3)*, 644–675.

Lawrence, J. (1999, July 1). Bush breaks fund-raising record. *USA Today*, p. 10A.

Lawrence, J. (2000, October 3). Candidates look to previous debates to sharpen strategies. *USA Today*, p. 14A.

Lawrence, J. (2007, June 14). As a campaign tool, Web has its uses and limits. *USA Today*, p. 10A.

Lawson-Borders, G., & Kirk, R. (2005). Blogs in campaign communication. *American Behavioral Scientist, 49(4)*, 548–559.

Lazarsfeld, P. F., Berelson, B. R., & Gaudet, H. (1948). *The people's choice*. New York: Columbia University Press.

Lazarsfeld, P. F., Berelson, B., & Gaudet, H. (1968). *The people's choice* (3rd ed.). New York: Columbia University Press.

Lazarsfeld, P. F., & Morton, R. (1960). Mass communication, popular taste and organized social action. In W. Schramm (Ed.), *Mass communication* (pp. 492–512). Urbana: University of Illinois Press.

Leavitt, P. (2000, January 27). Electionline: Bush TV ads go Spanish for primary in Arizona. *USA Today*, p. 8A.

Lee, F. L. F. (2010). The prevention effect of third-person perception: A study on the perceived and actual influence of polls. *Mass Communication & Society, 13(1)*, 87–110.

Lee, R. (2000). Images, issues, and political structure: A framework for judging the ethics of campaign discourse. In R. E. Denton, Jr. (Ed.), *Political communication ethics: An oxymoron* (pp. 23–50). Westport, CT: Praeger.

Leech, M. (2009, August 21). Womack a no-show for press conference. *Birmingham News*, pp. 1B, 3B.

Leibovich, M. (2008, January 3). Fatigue factor gives equal time to candidates. *New York Times*, pp. A1, A16.

Leibovich, M. (2009, October 11). Another fine mess: Comics whack Obama. *New York Times*, WK1, WK3.

Leshner, G., & McKean, M. L. (1997). Using TV news for political information during an off-year election: Effects on political knowledge and cynicism. *Journalism and Mass Communication Quarterly, 74*, 69–83.

Levine, J. M., & Murphy, G. (1943). The learning and forgetting of controversial statements. *Journal of Abnormal and Social Psychology, 38*, 507–517.

Levy, C. J. (2000, January 20). Giuliani campaign says it brought in $12 million in '99 donations. *New York Times*, p. C37.

Levy, S. (2006, December 11). Smile! You're an unwitting net star. *Newsweek, 148(24)*, 17.

Lewis, C. (Ed.) (1998). *The buying of the Congress*. Washington, DC: Center for Public Integrity.

Lewis, C. (Ed.) (2000). *Our private legislatures: Public service, personal gain*. Washington, DC: Center for Public Integrity.

Lewis, L. K. (1999). Disseminating information and soliciting input during planned organizational change. *Communication Quarterly, 13(1)*, 43–75.

Liebovich, L. W. (2003). *Richard Nixon, Watergate & the press: A historical perspective*. Westport, CT: Praeger.

Lin, C. A. (2009). Selective news exposure, personal values, and support for the Iraq War. *Communication Quarterly, 57(1)*, 18–34.

Lippmann, W. (1922). *Public opinion*. New York: Macmillan.

Lippmann, W. (1955). *Public opinion*. New York: Free Press.

Liptak, A. (2010, January 22). Justices, 5-4, reject corporate spending limits. *New York Times*, p. A1.

Lipton, E., & Urbina, I. (2007, April 12). In 5-year effort, scant evidence of voter fraud. *New York Times*, pp. A1, A15.

Littlejohn, S. W. (1996). *Theories of human communication* (5th ed.). Belmont, CA: Wadsworth.

Loken, B. (1983). *The effects of direct mail appeals on awareness, readership, and cognitive response content in a community heart health campaign*. Paper presented at the Association for Education in Journalism and Mass Communication. Corvallis, OR.

Lowery, D., & Brasher, H. (2004). *Organized interests and American government*. New York: McGraw-Hill.

Lowry, D. T., Bridges, J. A., & Barefield, P. A. (1991). Effects of TV instant analysis and querulous criticism: Following the first Bush–Dukakis debate. *Journalism Quarterly, 67,* 814–825.

Lowy, J. (1999, July 14). Politicians frustrated by critical Web sites. *Birmingham Post-Herald,* p. A2.

Lull, J. (1980). The social uses of television. *Human Communication Research, 6(3),* 197–209.

Lull, J. (1982). How families select television programs: A mass observational approach. *Journal of Broadcasting, 26(4),* 801–811.

Luo, M. (2008, October 20). Obama's September success recasts the campaign fundraising landscape. *New York Times,* p. A21.

MacLin, M. K., & Calder, J. C. (2006). Interviewers' ratings of data quality in household telephone surveys. *North American Journal of Psychology, 8(1),* 163–170.

Magleby, D. B., & Holt, M. (1999). The long shadow of soft money and issue advocacy ads. *Campaign & Elections, 20(4),* 22–27.

Mair, L. (1962). *Primitive government.* New York: Ballantine.

Maltese, J. A. (1994). *Spin control: The White House office of communications and the management of presidential news.* Chapel Hill: University of North Carolina Press.

Mandel, R. B. (1981). *In the running: The new woman candidate.* New York: Ticknor & Fields.

Markus, G. B., & Converse, P. E. (1979). A dynamic simultaneous equation model of electoral change. *American Political Science Review, 73(4),* 1055–1070.

Marsh, B. (2006, November 5). 6 ways to watch the election: The impact of gaffes on the stump. *New York Times,* p. 4A.

Martel, M. (1983). *Political campaign debates: Images, strategies, and tactics.* New York: Longman.

Martin, E., DeMaio, T. J., & Campanelli, P. C. (1990). Context effects for census measures of race and Hispanic origin. *Public Opinion Quarterly, 54(4),* 551–566.

Martinelli, K. A., & Chaffee, S. H. (1995). Measuring new-voter learning via three channels of political information. *Journalism and Mass Communication Quarterly, 72(1),* 18–32.

Matheson, K., & Dursun, S. (2001). Social identity precursors to the hostile media phenomenon: Partisan perceptions of coverage of the Bosnian Conflict. *Group Processes & Intergroup Relations, 4(2),* 116–125.

Matthews, D. R., & Stimson, J. A. (1975). *Yeas and nays: Normal decision-making in the U.S. House.* New York: Wiley.

Mayer, W. G., & Polsby, N. W. (1991). *The divided Democrats: Ideological unity, party reform, and presidential elections.* New York: Westview Press.

Mayhew, D. R. (1974). *Congress: The electoral connection.* New Haven, CT: Yale University Press.

McCaid, K. (1989). The Roundtable: Getting results in Washington. *Harvard Business Review, 59,* 114–123.

McCain, J. (1999). *Faith of our fathers.* New York: Random House.

McCain, J., & Salter, M. (2008). *Hard call: Great decisions and the extraordinary people who made them.* New York: Hachette Book Group.

McClure, R. D., & Patterson, T. E. (1974). Television news and political advertising. *Communication Research, 1(1),* 3–31.

McCombs, M. E. (1976). Agenda-setting research: A bibliographic essay. *Political Communication Review, 1(1),* 1–7.

McCombs, M. E. (1992). Explorers and surveyors: Expanding strategies for agenda-setting research. *Journalism Quarterly, 69(4),* 813–824.

McCombs, M., & Shaw, D. L. (1972). The agenda-setting function of the mass media. *Public Opinion Quarterly, 36(2),* 176–188.

McCombs, M. E., & Shaw, D. L. (1993). The evolution of agenda-setting research: Twenty-five years in the marketplace of ideas. *Public Opinion Quarterly, 36(2),* 176–185.

McCombs, M., & Weaver, D. (1973). *Voters' need for orientation and use of mass media.* Paper for the International Communication Association. Montreal, Canada.

McCroskey, J. C., Jensen, T., & Todd, C. (1972). *The generalizability of source credibility scales for public figures.* Paper for the Speech Communication Association. Chicago, IL.

McCroskey, J. D., Richmond, V. P., & Daly, J. A. (1975). The development of a measure of perceived homophily in interpersonal communication. *Human Communication Research, 1(4),* 322–332.

McFetters, A. (1999, June 21). Keeping beat on campaign trail. *Birmingham News*, p. A6.

McGinniss, J. (2008, April 27). The selling of a president. *Parade*, 12–14.

McGuire, W. J., & Papageorgis, O. (1961). The relative efficacy of various types of prior belief-defense in producing immunity against persuasion. *Journal of Abnormal and Social Psychology*, *62(2)*, 327–37.

McIlwain, C. D. (2007). Racial identity, ideology, and the youth vote: Observations from the 2004 presidential campaign. *American Behavioral*, *50(9)*, 1231–1238.

McKinley, J. (2009, December 13). In California companies, a cottage industry for fighting same-sex marriage. *New York Times*, A29.

McKinney, M., & Banwart, M. (2005). Rocking the youth vote through debate: Examining the effects of a citizen versus journalist controlled debate on civic engagement. *Journalism Studies*, *6(2)*, 153–163.

McLeod, J. M., & Detenber, B. H. (1999). Framing effects of television news coverage of social protest. *Journal of Communication*, *49(3)*, 3–23.

McPeek, R. W., & Edwards, J. D. (1975). Expectancy disconfirmation and attitude change. *Journal of Social Psychology*, *96*, 193–208.

McPherson, B. (1999, July 24). E-mail provides public, leaders with new links. *Pensacola News Journal*, pp. 1C, 3C.

McSweeney, D. (2007). The front-runner falls: The failure of Howard Dean. *Party Politics*, *13(1)*, 109–126.

Medhurst, M. J., & DeSousa, M. A. (1981). Political cartoons as rhetorical form: A taxonomy of graphic discourse. *Communication Monographs*, *48(3)*, 197–236.

Medvic, S. K. (2000). Professionalization in congressional campaigns. In J. A. Thurber & C. J. Nelson (Eds.), *Campaign warriors: Political consultants in elections* (pp. 91–109). Washington, DC: Brookings Institution.

Medvic, S. K. (2001). *Political consultants in U.S. congressional elections*. Columbus: Ohio State University Press.

Mellman, M., & Bloomfield, M. (2008, January 6). Loose lips win elections. *New York Times*, WK12.

Memmott, C. (2007, January 30). Presidential hopefuls write their own ticket. *USA Today*, p. 1D.

Memmott, M. (2009, June 14). McCain, Romney trade barbs over abortion. *USA Today*, p. 11A.

Mendelsohn, H. (1964). Broadcast vs. personal sources of information in emergent public crises: The presidential assassination. *Journal of Broadcasting*, *8(2)*, 147–156.

Meraz, S. (2011). The fight for 'how to think': Traditional media, social networks, and issue interpretation. *Journalism*, *12(1)*, 107–127.

Merton, R. K. (1987). The focussed interview and focus groups: Continuities and discontinuities. *Public Opinion Quarterly*, *51(4)*, 550–566.

Merton, R. K., Lowenthal, M. F., & Kendall, P. L. (1990). *The focus interview: A manual of problems and procedures*. New York: Collier Macmillan.

Michael P. McDonald (2007). The true electorate: A cross-validation of voter registration files and electronic survey demographics. *Public Opinion Quarterly*, *71(4)*, 588–602.

Miller, A., Coleman, R., & Granberg, D. (2007). TV anchors, elections and bias: A longitudinal study of the facial expressions of Brokaw Rather Jenkins. *Visual Communication Quarterly*, *14*, 244–257.

Miller, A. H., & MacKuen, M. (1979). Informing the electorate: A national study. In S. Kraus (Ed.), *The Great Debates: Carter vs. Ford, 1976*. Bloomington: Indiana University Press.

Miller, A. J. (1974). Political issues and trust in government: 1964–1970. *American Political Science Review*, *68(3)*, 951–972.

Miller, J., & Gordon, A. (2005). *When stereotypes collide: Race/ethnicity, gender and videostyle in congressional campaigns*. New York: Peter Lang.

Miller, J. J. (1999). *The campaign theme and an election's controlling frame*. Paper for the Southern Communication Association convention. St. Louis, MO.

Miller, W. E., & Shanks, J. M. (1982). Policy directions and presidential leadership: Alternative interpretations of the 1980 election. *British Journal of Political Science*, *12*, 299–356.

Miller, W. E., & Shanks, J. M. (1996). *The new American voter*. Cambridge, MA: Harvard University Press.

Mitchell, A. (1999, December 12). Underdog McCain develops anti-campaign style. *New York Times*, p. Y26.

Mitchell, F. D. (1998). *Harry S. Truman and the news*

media: Contentious relations, belated respect. Columbia: University of Missouri Press.

Mitchell, G. (1992). *The campaign of the century: Upton Sinclair's race for governor of California and the birth of media politics.* New York: Random House.

Moore, D. W. (1999, June/July). Daily tracking polls: Too much 'noise' or revealed insights? *Public Perspective, 10(4),* 27–31.

Morgan, D. L. (1988). *Focus groups as qualitative research.* Newbury Park, CA: Sage.

Morley, D. (1986). *Family television: Cultural power and domestic leisure.* London: Comedia.

Morley, D. (1988). Domestic relations: The framework of family viewing in Great Britain. In J. Lull (Ed.), *World families watch television* (pp. 22–48). Newbury Park, CA: Sage.

Morozov, E. (2011). *The net delusion: The dark side of Internet freedom.* Public Affairs.

Morris, D. (1999). *The new prince.* Los Angeles: Renaissance Books.

Morris, R. (1993). Visual rhetoric in political cartoons: A structuralist approach. *Metaphor and Symbolic Activity, 8(3),* 195–210.

Moy, P., Domke, D., & Stamm, K. (2001). The spiral of silence and public opinion on affirmative action. *Journalism and Mass Communication Quarterly, 78(1),* 7–25.

Murray, S. K. (2006). Private polls and presidential policymaking: Reagan as a facilitator of change. *Public Opinion Quarterly, 70(4),* 477–498.

Mutz, D. C. (1998). *Interpersonal influence: How perceptions of mass collectives affect political attitudes.* Cambridge: Cambridge University Press.

Mutz, D. C., Sniderman, P. M., & Brody, R. A. (1996). *Political persuasion and attitude change.* Ann Arbor: University of Michigan Press.

Myers, F. (1999). Political argumentation and the composite audience: A case study. *Quarterly Journal of Speech, 85(1),* 55–71.

Myers, R. H. (1999). The inescapability of moral reasons. *Philosophy and Phenomenological Research, 59(2),* 281–307.

Nagourney, A. (2007, August 1). Edwards overhauls his campaign to harness Internet. *New York Times,* p. 12(A).

Napolitan, J. (1972). *The election game and how to win it.* New York: Doubleday.

Nathanson, A. I., Perse, E. M., & Ferguson, D. A. (1997). Gender differences in television use: An exploration of the instrumental-expressive dichotomy. *Communication Research Reports, 14(2),* 176–188.

Neimi, R. G., Craig, S. C., & Mattei, F. (1991). Measuring internal political efficacy in the 1988 National Election Study. *American Political Science Review, 85(4),* 1407–1413.

Nelson, W. D. (1998). *Who speaks for the President? The White House press secretary from Cleveland to Clinton.* Syracuse, NY: Syracuse University Press.

Neuman, W. R. (1986). *The Paradox of Mass Politics: Knowledge and opinion in the American electorate.* Cambridge, MA: Harvard University Press.

Neuman, W. R., Just, M. R., & Crigler, A. N. (1992). *Common knowledge: News and the construction of political meaning.* Chicago: University of Chicago Press.

Newcombe, N., & Arnkoff, D. B. (1976). Effects of speech style and sex of the speaker on person perception. *Journal of Personality and Social Psychology, 37,* 1293–1303.

Newman, B. I. (1999). *The mass marketing of politics: Democracy in an age of manufactured images.* Thousand Oaks, CA: Sage.

Nicholson, J. (2000, April). Informing, mobilizing. *Campaigns & Elections,* p. 23.

Nimmo, D. (1970). *The political persuaders.* Englewood Cliffs, NJ: Prentice-Hall.

Nimmo, D. (1974). *Popular images of politics.* Englewood Cliffs, NJ: Prentice-Hall.

Nimmo, D., & Savage, R. L. (1976). *Candidates and their images.* Pacific Palisades, CA: Goodyear.

Nixon v. Carver. (1996). U.S. District Court, 518 U.S. 1033, Springfield, MO.

Noble, P., & Kennedy, T. (2000, February 15). Online fundraising continues to skyrocket. *Politics online.* Online update.

Noelle-Neumann, E. (1973). Return to the concept of powerful mass media. *Studies of Broadcasting, 9,* 77.

Noelle-Neumann, E. (1977). Turbulences in the climate of opinion: Methodological applications of the spiral of silence theory. *Public Opinion Quarterly, 41,* 139.

Noelle-Neumann, E. (1979). Public opinion and the classical tradition: A re-evaluation. *Public Opinion Quarterly, 43(2),* 143–156.

Noelle-Neumann, E. (1983). The effect of media on media effects research. *Journal of Communication, 33(3),* 157–165.

Noelle-Neumann, E. (1991). The theory of public opinion: The concept of the spiral of silence. In James A. Anderson (Ed.), *Communication Yearbook 14* (p. 256–287), Newberry Park, CA: Sage.

Noelle-Neumann, E. (1993). *The spiral of silence: Public opinion—Our social skin* (2nd ed.). Chicago: University of Chicago Press.

Nolan, M. R. (2005). Orwell meets Nixon: When and why "the press" became "the media." *Harvard International Journal of Press/Politics, 10(2),* 69–84.

Noonan, P. (1997). *What I saw at the revolution.* New York: Ballantine.

Noonan, P. (1998). *On speaking well.* New York: Regan Books.

Noonan, P. (2000). *The case against Hillary Clinton.* New York: HarperCollins.

Noonan, P. (2011, February 26–27). The Internet helps us get serious. *Wall Street Journal,* p. A15.

Norris, P. (Ed.) (1996). *Women, media, and politics.* New York: Oxford University Press.

Norris, P., Curtice, J., Sanders, D., Scammell, M., & Semetko, H. A. (1999). *On message: Communicating the campaign.* London: Sage.

Nossiter, A. (2008, July 10). Officials investigate 3 Alabama counties in voter fraud accusations. *New York Times,* p. A10.

Novak, M. (1974). *Choosing our king: Powerful symbols in presidential politics.* New York: Macmillan.

Obama, B. (2006). *The audacity of hope: Thoughts on reclaiming the American dream.* New York: Random House.

O'Keefe, G. J., & Sulanowski, B. K. (1995). More than just talk: Uses, gratifications, and the telephone. *Journalism & Mass Communication Quarterly, 72(4),* 922–933.

O'Leary, B. S. (2000, April). Direct response. *Campaigns & Elections,* p. 24.

Olson, K., & Peytchev, A. (2007). Effect of interviewer experience on interview pace and interviewer attitudes. *Public Opinion Quarterly, 71(2),* 273–286.

Olson, M. (1971). *The logic of collective action.* Cambridge, MA: Harvard University Press.

Orren, K. (1989). Interest group conflict in the federal courts. *American Political Science Review, 70,* 723–741.

Orwell, G. (1949). *The Orwell reader.* New York: Harcourt Brace.

O'Sullivan, P., & Geiger, S. (1995). Does the watchdog bite? Newspaper ad watch articles and political attack ads. *Journalism and Mass Communication Quarterly, 72(4),* 771–785.

Owen, D., & Cutbirth, J. (2000). The Internet and the youth vote: Possibilities, challenges, and limitations. In D. Bystom, D. B. Carlin, L. L. Kaid, M. Kern, & M. S. McKinney (Eds.), *Communicating politics: Engaging the public in campaign 2000 and beyond* (pp. 212–222). Washington, DC: NCA Summer Conference proceedings.

Page, B. I., & Brody, R. A. (1972). Policy voting and the electoral process: The Vietnam War issue. *American Political Science Review, 66,* 979–995.

Page, B., & Jones, C. (1979). Reciprocal effects of policy preferences, party loyalties, and the vote. *American Political Science Review, 66,* 979–985.

Paletz, D. L. (2002). *The media in American politics.* New York: Longman.

Park, N., Kee, K., & Valenzuela, S. (2009). *Understanding group participation in social networking environment: Motivations for using Facebook groups and social outcomes.* Paper presented at the annual meeting of the National Communication Association.

Parker, A. (2011, January 30). Twitter, as a helpmate, goes to Capitol Hill. *New York Times,* p. A19.

Parry-Giles, T., & Parry-Giles, S. J. (1996). Political socophilia, presidential campaigning and the intimacy of American politics. *Communication Studies, 47(3),* 191–205.

Parry-Giles, T., & Parry-Giles, S. J. (2006). *The prime-time presidency: The West Wing and U.S. nationalism.* Champaign: University of Illinois Press.

Parsons, L. H. (2011). *The birth of modern politics: Andrew Jackson, John Quincy Adams and the election of 1828.* New York: Oxford University Press.

Patrick, B. A. (2002). *The National Rifle Association and the media: The motivating force of negative coverage.* New York: Peter Lang.

Patterson, D. (1999). *Americans are giving up their freedom by not voting.* Birmingham, AL: Policy Exchange Foundation.

Patterson, R. (1999). Bill Bennett and "common culture" politics: Moral and economic fusion in the Reagan presidency. Paper for the Eastern Communication Association. Charleston, WV.

Patterson, S. C. (1959). Patterns of interpersonal relations in a state legislative group: The Wisconsin assembly. *Public Opinion Quarterly, 23(1),* 101–109.

Patterson, T. (1980). *The mass media election.* New York: Praeger.

Patterson, T., & Davis, R. (1985). The media campaign: Struggle for the agenda. In N. Nelson (Ed.), *The elections of 1984.* Washington, DC: Congressional Quarterly Press.

Patterson, T., & McClure, R. (1976). *The unseeing eye.* New York: Putnam.

Patterson, T. E. (1994). *Out of order.* New York: Knopf.

Paul, I. H. (1956). Impressions of personality: Authoritarianism and the fait accompli effect. *Journal of Abnormal and Social Psychology, 53(3),* 338–344.

Pearson, S., & O'Connell, F. (2010, July). Minding your social media. *Campaigns & Elections, 293,* 44–45.

Penner, M., & Penner, S. (1994). Publicizing, politicizing, and neutralizing homelessness: Comic strips. *Communication Research, 21(6),* 766–781.

Perlman, A. M. (1998). *Writing great speeches.* Boston: Allyn & Bacon.

Perlmutter, D. D. (1999). *The Manship school guide to political communication.* Baton Rouge: Louisiana State University Press.

Perlmutter, D. D., & Wu, H. D. (1999). The American political consultant: A profile. In D. D. Perlmutter (Ed.), *The Manship school guide to political communication* (pp. 327–332). Baton Rouge: Louisiana State University Press.

Perloff, R. M. (1989). Ego-involvement and the third person effect of televised news coverage. *Communication Research, 16(2),* 236–262.

Perloff, R. M. (1993). Third-person effect research 1983–1992: A review and synthesis. *International Journal of Public Opinion Research, 5(2),* 167–184.

Perloff, R. M. (1998). *Political communication: Politics, press, and the public in America.* Mahwah, NJ: Erlbaum.

Perse, E. M., & Ferguson, D. A. (1993). Gender differences in remote control use. In J. R. Walker & R. V. Bellamy, Jr. (Eds.), *The remote control in the new age of television* (pp. 169–180). Westport, CT: Praeger.

Persico, J. E. (1972). The Rockefeller rhetoric: Writing speeches for the 1970 campaign. *Today's Speech, 20,* 57–62.

Peters, J. W. (2011, January 30). Political blogs ready to flood campaign trail. *New York Times,* pp. A1, A19.

Pfau, M., & Burgoon, M. (1988). Inoculation in political campaign communication. *Human Communication Research, 15(1),* 91–111.

Pfau, M., Haigh, M., & Gettle, M. (2004). Embedding journalists in military combat units: Impact on newspaper story frames and tone. *Journalism and Mass Communication Quarterly, 81(1),* 74–88.

Pfau, M., Kenski, H. C., Nitz, M., & Sorenson, J. (1990). Efficacy of inoculation strategies in promoting resistance to political attack messages: Application to direct mail. *Communication Monographs, 57(1),* 25–43.

Pfau, M., & Loudon, A. (1994). Effectiveness of adwatch formats in deflecting political attack ads. *Journalism and Mass Communication Quarterly, 21(3),* 324–341.

Pitchell, R. J. (1958). The influence of professional campaign management firms on partisan elections in California. *Western Political Quarterly, 11(2),* 278–300.

Plouffe, D. (2010). *The audacity to win: How Obama won and how we can beat the party of Limbaugh, Beck, and Palin.* New York: Penguin

Pohl, F. (1971). *Practical politics.* New York: Ballantine Books.

Pollard, T. D., Chesebro, J. W., & Studinski, D. P. (2009). The role of the Internet in presidential campaigns. *Communication Studies, 60(5),* 574–588.

Polsby, N. W. (1983). *The consequence of party reform.* Oxford: Oxford University Press.

Polsby, N. W., & Wildavsky, A. B. (1968). *Presidential elections. Strategies of American electoral politics.* New York: Charles Scribner's Sons.

Popkin, S. (1991). *The reasoning voter: Communication and persuasion in presidential campaigns.* Chicago: University of Chicago Press.

Porter, S. R., & Whitcomb, M. E. (2007). Mixed-mode contacts in Web surveys: Paper is not necessarily better. *Public Opinion Quarterly, 71(4),* 649–660.

Powell, J. (1984). *The other side of the story.* New York: William Morrow.

Powell, L. (1974). Strategies in a statewide secondary executive race: A case study. *Georgia Speech Communication Journal, 6,* 18–30.

Powell, L. (1975). The effects of ego-involvement on responses to editorial satire. *Central States Speech Journal, 26(1),* 34–38.

Powell, L. (1977). Voting intention and the complexity of political images. *Psychological Reports, 40(1),* 243–246.

Powell, L. (2010). Obama and Obama Girl: YouTube, viral videos, and the 2008 presidential campaign. In J. A. Hendricks & R. E. Denton, Jr. (Eds.). *Communicator-in-chief: How Barack Obama used new media technology to win the White House* (pp. 83–104). Lanham, MD: Lexington Books.

Powell, L., & Anderson, R. G. (1984). The impact of TV comedy: A test of the friendship theory. *Journal of Communication Studies, 3(1),* 13–19.

Powell, L., & Flick, H. (1982). *Ticket splitting in Mississippi.* Paper for the Southern Speech Communication Association. Hot Springs, AK.

Powell, L., & Kitchens, J. T. (1986). Analyzing campaign strategies: Contingencies, assumptions and techniques. *Southeastern Political Review, 14(2),* 161–179.

Powell, L., & Kitchens, J. T. (1999). Sex and income as factors associated with exposure to jokes about the Clinton–Lewinsky controversy. *Psychological Reports, 84(3),* 1047–1050.

Powell, L., Richmond, V. P., & Williams, G. C. (2011). Social networking and political campaigns: Perceptions of candidates as interpersonal constructs. *North American Journal of Psychology, 13(2),* 331–342.

Powell, L., & Shelby, A. (1981). A strategy of assumed incumbency: A case study. *Southern Speech Communication Journal, 46(2),* 105–123.

Powell, L., & Shelby, A. N. (1985). Para-political opinion leaders as audience: Communicative goals and media usage. *Communication Research Reports, 2,* 135–140.

Powell, M. (2007, November 11). Hey, candidate, I'm all yours, your very own Pied Piper. *New York Times,* WK-1, WK-4.

Preston, J. (2011, February 6). Movement began with outrage and a Facebook page that gave it an outlet. *New York Times,* p. A10.

Price, V. (2006). Public attitudes toward polls: Evidence from the 2000 U.S. presidential election. *International Journal of Public Opinion Research, 18(4),* 393–421.

Price, V., & Li-Ning, H. (1997). Third-person effects of news coverage: Orientations toward media. *Journalism & Mass Communication Quarterly, 74(3),* 525–540.

Price, V., & Stroud, N. J. (2006). Public attitudes toward polls: Evidence from the 2000 U.S. presidential election. *International Journal of Public Opinion Research, 18(4),* 393–421.

Procter, D. E., Aden, R. C., & Japp, P. (1988). Gender/issue interaction in political identity making: Nebraska's woman vs. woman gubernatorial campaign. *Central States Speech Journal, 39(3–4),* 190–203.

Procter, D. E., & Schenck-Hamlin, W. J. (1996). Form and variations in negative political advertising. *Communication Research Reports, 13(2),* 147–156.

Purnick, J. (2000, May 7). Candidates' health has become routine public matter. *New York Times,* p. A24.

Rakow, L. F., & Kranich, K. (1991). Woman as sign in television news. *Journal of Communication, 41,* 20.

Ran, W., & Ven-Hwei, L. (2007). The third-person effects of political attack ads in the 2004 U.S. presidential election. *Media Psychology, 9(2),* 367–388.

Raven, B. H., & Gallo, P. S. (1965). The effects of nominating conventions, elections, and reference group identification upon the perception of political figures. *Human Relations, 18(3),* 217–229.

Ray, D. (1982). The sources of voting cues in three state legislatures. *Journal of Politics, 44(4),* 1074–1087.

Raymond, A. (2008). *How to rig an election: Confessions of a Republican operative.* New York: Simon & Schuster.

Reese, M. (1975). Locating the 'switch-split' vote. In R. E. Hiebert, R. F. Jones, J. Lorenz, & E. A. Lotito (Eds.), *The political image merchants* (pp. 162–164). Washington, DC: Acropolis Books.

Reilly, S. (1999). Outdoor advertising. In D. D. Perlmutter (Ed.), *The Manship school guide to political communication* (pp. 152–155). Baton Rouge: University of Louisiana Press.

Rich, F. (2008a, March 30). Hillary's St. Patrick's Day massacre. *New York Times*, 13WK.

Rich, F. (2008b, May 4). The all-white elephant in the room. *New York Times*, 12WK.

Rich, F. (2009, April 26). The banality of Bush White House evil. *New York Times*, WK-14.

Rich, F. (2009, June 14). The Obama haters' silent enablers. *New York Times*, WK8.

Rich, F. (2009, September 20). Even Glenn Beck is right twice a day. *New York Times*, WK8.

Rich, F. (2010, May 30). Obama's Katrina? Maybe worse. *New York Times*, WK8.

Rich, F. (2010, October 10). Facebook politicians are not your friends. *New York Times*, WK8.

Riegert, K. (Ed.). (2007). *Politicotainment: Television's take on the real*. New York: Peter Lang.

Riffe, D., Sneed, D., & Van Ommeren, R. L. (1985). Behind the editorial page cartoon. *Journalism Quarterly, 62*, 378–383.

Ringer, R. J. (1986). *The language of fund-raising direct mail: Differences between letters for national and local constituencies*. Paper presented at the annual meeting of the International Communication Association. Chicago, IL.

Ritter, K. (1968). Ronald Reagan and "The Speech": The rhetoric of public relations politics. *Western Speech, 32(1)*, 50–58.

Roberts, M. S. (1992). Predicting voter behavior via the agenda-setting tradition. *Journalism Quarterly, 69(4)*, 878–892.

Roberts, M. S., & McCombs, M. (1994). Agenda setting and political advertising: Origins of the news agenda. *Political Communication, 11(3)*, 249–262.

Robertson, T. (2001). *Gender matters: The impact of the media and gender in 1998 mixed-gender senatorial and gubernatorial campaigns*. Paper presented at the annual meeting of the Southern States Communication Association. Lexington, KY.

Robinson, M. J., & Sheehan, M. (1983). *Over the wire and on TV: CBS and UPI in campaign '80*. New York: Russell Sage.

Rogers, E., & Cartano, D. G. (1962). Methods of measuring opinion leadership. *Public Opinion Quarterly, 26(3)*, 435–441.

Rohter, L., & Luo, M. (2008, March 20). Groups respond to Obama's call for national discussion about race. *New York Times*, p. 17A.

Rojas, H., Shah, D. V., & Faber, R. J. (1996). For the good of others: Censorship and the third-person effect. *International Journal of Public Opinion Research, 8(2)*, 163–186.

Rosenthal, A. (1993). *The third house: Lobbyists and lobbying the states*. Washington, DC: Congressional Quarterly Press.

Rosnow, R. C., & Fine, G. A. (1976). *Rumor and gossip: The social psychology of hearsay*. New York: Elsevier.

Rove, K. (2010). *Courage and consequence: My life as a conservative in the fight*. New York: Simon & Schuster.

Rubin, A. M. (1983). Television uses and gratifications: The interactions of viewing patterns and motivations. *Journal of Broadcasting, 27(1)*, 37–51.

Rubin, A. M. (1984). Ritualized and instrumental television viewing. *Journal of Communication, 34(3)*, 67–77.

Rubin, A. M., & Perse, E. M. (1987). Audience activity and television news gratifications. *Communication Research, 14(1)*, 58–84.

Rubin, A. M., & Rubin, R. B. (1982). Older viewers' TV viewing patterns and motivations. *Communication Research, 9(2)*, 287–313.

Rucincki, D., & Salmon, C. T. (1990). The 'other' as the vulnerable voter: A study of the third-person effect in the 1988 U.S. presidential campaign. *International Journal of Public Opinion Research, 2(4)*, 345–368.

Rudd, R. (1986). Issues as image in political campaign commercials. *Western Journal of Speech Communication, 50*, 102–118.

Ruddock, A. (2001). *Understanding audiences: Theory and method*. Thousand Oaks, CA: Sage.

Rutenberg, J. (2007, November 4). Wild cards: When the unexpected changes all expectations. *New York Times*, p. A25.

Rutenberg, J., & Robertson, C. (2010, January 31). From high jinks to handcuffs. *New York Times*, pp. A1, A22.

Ryan, J., & Wentworth, W. M. (1999). *Media and society: The production of culture in the mass media*. Boston: Allyn & Bacon.

Sabato, L. (1981). *The rise of political consultants*. New York: Basic Books.

Sabato, L. J. (1991). *Feeding frenzy: How attack journalism has transformed American politics*. New York: Free Press.

Sabato, L. J. (2000). *Feeding frenzy: Attack journalism and*

American politics. Lanham, MD: Rowman & Littlefield.

Sabato, L. J., Stencel, M., & Lichter, R. (2000). *Peep show: Media and politics in an age of scandal.* Lanham, MD: Rowman & Littlefield.

Safire, W. (1999, July 12). Remembering the speech that never was given. *Birmingham Post-Herald,* p. A7.

Safire, W. (2000, February 14). New 'vast conspiracy.' *New York Times,* p. A27.

Salisbury, R. (1989). An exchange theory of interest groups. *Legislative Studies Quarterly, 8,* 379–577.

Salwen, M. B. (1998). Perceptions of media influence and support for censorship: The third-person effect in the 1996 presidential election. *Communication Research, 25(3),* 259–285.

Sanders, K. R., & Newman, R. P. (1971). John A. Stromer and the Hofstadterm Hypothesis. *Central States Speech Journal, 22,* 218–227.

Santarelli, C. J. (2010, July). Is 'going viral' a golden ticket. *Campaigns & Elections, (293),* 12–13.

Saulny, S. (2007, April 25). Limits sought on 'robo-calls' in campaigns. *New York Times,* pp. A1, A22.

Schaefer, D. R., & Dillman, D. A. (1998). Development of a standard e-mail methodology: Results of an experiment. *Public Opinion Quarterly, 62,* 378–379.

Schatz, A. (2006, October 9). In clips on YouTube, politicians reveal their unscripted side. *Wall Street Journal,* pp. 1A, 14A.

Scheufele, D., & Moy, P. (2000). Twenty-five years of the spiral of silence: A conceptual review and empirical outlook. *International Journal of Public Opinion, 12,* 3–28.

Scheufele, D., Shanahan, J., & Lee, E. (2001). Real talk: Manipulating the dependent variable in spiral of silence research. *Communication Research, 28,* 304–324.

Schill, D. (2009). *Stagecraft and statecraft: Advance and media events in political communication.* Lanham, MD: Lexington Books.

Schlesinger, R. (2008). *White House ghosts: Presidents and the speechwriters.* New York: Simon & Schuster.

Schmidt, M. S., & Schmidt, M. J. (1983). *Applications of direct mail in voter turnout activities.* Paper presented at the annual meeting of the International Communication Association. Dallas, TX.

Schmitt, K. M., Gunther, A. C., & Liebhart, J. L. (2004). Why partisans see mass media as biased. *Communication Research, 31,* 623–641.

Schotland, R. A. (1992). Proposals for campaign finance reform. *Capital University Law Review, 21,* 429–462

Schouten, F., & Biskuic, J. (2010, January 22). It's a new era for Campaign Spending. *USA Today,* p. 1A.

Schram, M. (1976). *Running for president: A journal of the Carter campaign.* New York: Pocket Books.

Schudson, M. (1978). *Discovering the news: A social history of American newspapers.* New York: Basic Books.

Schultz, D. E., Martin, E., & Brown, W. P. (1988). *Strategic advertising campaigns.* Lincolnwood, IL: NTC Business Books.

Scott, M. H., & Lyman, S. M. (1968). Accounts. *American Sociological Review, 33(1),* 46–62.

Seelye, K. Q. (1999, November 23). Flashback, courtesy of the G. O. P. *New York Times,* p. A21.

Seelye, K. Q. (2008, January 1). Huckabee shows negative spot after pulling it from television. *New York Times,* p. 11A.

Seelye, K. Q. (2009, January 18). History as a guide for an inaugural address that frames the moment. *New York Times,* p. A18.

Segal, D. (2009, September 20). Call it Ludacris: The rap-talk kinship. *New York Times,* WK1, WK3.

Seib, P. (1994). *Campaigns and conscience: The ethics of political journalism.* Westport, CT: Praeger.

Seiter, J. S., Weger, Harry, Jr., Kinzer, H. J., & Jensen, A. S. (2009). Impression management in televised debates: The effect of background nonverbal behavior on audience perceptions of debaters' likeability. *Communication Research Reports, 26,* 1–11.

Selby, G. S. (2001). Framing social protest: The exodus narrative in martin luther king's montgomery bus boycott rhetoric. *Journal of Communication and Religion, 24(1),* 68–93.

Seligman, L. (1961). Political recruitment and party structure: A case study. *American Political Science Review, 55(1),* 85.

Selnow, G. W. (1998). *Electronic whistle-stops: The impact of the Internet on American politics.* Westport, CT: Praeger.

Selnow, G. W. (2000). Internet ethics. In R. E. Denton, Jr. (Ed.),

Political communication ethics (pp. 203–240). Westport, CT: Praeger.

Serini, S. A., Powers, A. A., & Johnson, S. (1998). Of horse race and policy issues: A study of gender in coverage of a gubernatorial election by two major metropolitan newspapers. *Journalism & Mass Communication Quarterly, 75(1),* 194–204.

Sethi, S. (1993). Grassroots lobbying and the corporation. *Journal of Politics, 45,* 8–14.

Seymour-Ure, C. (1974). *The political impact of mass media.* Beverly Hills, CA: Sage.

Shadegg, S. (1972). *The new how to win an election.* New York: Taplinger.

Shadow, M., & Peck, G. (1991, May). Politically speaking. *Campaigns and Elections, 12,* p. 54.

Shaver, K. G. (1983). *An introduction to attribution processes.* Hillsdale, NJ: Erlbaum.

Shaw, D. L., & McCombs, M. (1977). *The emergence of American political issues: The agenda-setting function of the press.* St. Paul, MN: West Publishing.

Shaw, D. L., & McCombs, M. L. (1980). The emergence of American political issues: The agenda-setting function of the press. *Journal of Communication, 32,* 100–127.

Sheckels, T. F. (Ed.). (2009). *Cracked but not shattered: Hillary Rodham Clinton's unsuccessful campaign for the presidency.* Lanham, MD: Lexington Books.

Sheehy, G. (1999). *Hillary's choice.* New York: Random House.

Sheppard, S. (2007). *The partisan press: A history of media bias in the United States.* Jefferson, NC: McFarland.

Shogan, R. (2001). *Bad news: Where the press goes wrong in the making of the president.* Chicago: Ivan R. Dees.

Shrum, R. (2007). No excuses: Concessions of a serial campaigner. New York: Simon & Schuster.

Sigal, L. (1986). Who: Sources make the news. In R. K. Manoff & M. Schudson (Eds.), *Reading the News* (pp. 9–37). New York: Pantheon.

Sigel, R. S. (1970). *Learning about politics: A reader in political socialization.* New York: Random House.

Silverberg, C. (2000, April). The secret ingredient for successful PAC fundraising: Discipline. *Campaigns & Elections,* pp. 63–34.

Simon, R. (1987, March 14). Those Sunday interview shows: They're tougher now, but are they better? *TV Guide, 35(11),* 4–7.

Sisk, R. (2009, September 11). With apology accepted, pols cash in on flap. *New York Daily News,* p. 14.

Smith, B. A. (1996). Faulty assumptions and undemocratic consequences of campaign finance reform. *Yale Law Journal, 105(4),* 1049–1091.

Smith, B. A. (1998). Soft money, hard realities: The constitutional prohibition on a soft money ban. *Journal of Legislation, 24,* 179–200.

Smith, C. A. (1977). The Hofstadter Hypothesis revisited: The nature of evidence in politically 'paranoid' discourse. *Southern Speech Communication Journal, 42,* 274–289.

Smith, G. (1999, June 5). *Interview with Larry Powell.* Gulf Shores, AL.

Smith, M. M., Williams, G. C., Powell, L., & Copeland, G. A. (2010). *Campaign finance reform: The political shell game.* Lanham, MD: Lexington Books.

Smith, S. E. (1999). *Dancing in the street: Motown and the cultural politics of Detroit.* Cambridge, MA: Harvard University Press.

Smith, T. W. (1995). Little things matter: A sampler of how differences in questionnaire format can affect survey responses. *Proceedings of the American Statistical Association,* 1046–1051.

Stacks, D. W., & Hocking, J. E. (1998). *Communication Research.* New York: Longman.

Stalder, D. R. (2009). Political orientation, hostile media perceptions, & group-centrism. *North American Journal of Psychology, 11(2),* 383–400.

Staley, S. R. (2001). Ballot-box zoning, transaction cost, and urban growth. *Journal of the American Planning Association, 67,* 13–19.

Stallings-Carpenter, C. (2009). *The Obamachine: Technopolitics 2.0.* Paper presented at the conference on YouTube and the 2008 Election Cycle in the United States, University of Massachusetts. Amherst, MA.

Stanley, A. (2008, June 8). No debate: It's great TV. *New York Times,* pp. 1MT, 6MT.

Steakley, J. D. (1983). Iconology of a scandal: Political cartoons and the Eulenburg affair. *Studies in Visual Communication, 9,* 20–48.

Steen, J. (2000, June 25). Maybe you can buy an election, but not with your own money. *Washington Post,* pp. B1, B5.

Steinberg, A. (1976a). *Political campaign management*. Lexington, MA: D.C. Heath.

Steinberg, A. (1976b). *The political campaign handbook*. Lexington, MA: D.C. Heath.

Steinfatt, T. M., Gantz, W., Siebold, D. R., & Miller, L. D. (1973). News diffusion of the Wallace shooting: The apparent lack of interpersonal communication as an artifact of delayed measurement. *Quarterly Journal of Speech, 59*, 401–412.

Stelter, B. (2008, February 11). Putting candidates under the videoscope. *New York Times*, pp. C1, C4.

Stelter, B. (2008, March 27). Finding political news online, young viewers pass it along. *New York Times*, p. 1A.

Stelter, B. (2010, October 24). Candidates running against, and with, cable news. *New York Times*, p. A20.

Stewart, D. W., & Shamdasani, P. N. (1990). *Focus groups: Theory and practice*. Newbury Park, CA: Sage.

Stone, A. E. W. (1999). Stealth campaigning: Winning 'under the radar.' In D. D. Perlmutter (Ed.), *The Manship school guide to political communication* (pp. 147–151). Baton Rouge: Louisiana State University Press.

Straits, B. C. (1990). The social context of voter turnout. *Public Opinion Quarterly, 54(1)*, 64–73.

Stricker, G. (1964). The operation of cognitive dissonance on pre- and post-election attitudes. *Journal of Social Psychology, 63*, 111–119.

Strother, O. (1999). Television ads. In D. D. Perlmutter (Ed.), *The Manship school guide to political communication* (pp. 186–195). Baton Rouge: Louisiana State University Press.

Strother, R. (1999). Foreword. In D. D. Perlmutter (Ed.), *The Manship school guide to political communication* (pp. viii–xiv). Baton Rouge: Louisiana State University Press.

Sudman, S. (1986). Do exit polls influence voting behavior? *Public Opinion Quarterly, 50(3)*, 331–339.

Suine, K., & Kline, F. G. (1976). Communication, mass political behavior and mass society. In S. Chaffee (Ed.), *Political communication* (pp. 65–84). Beverly Hills, CA: Sage.

Surlin, S. H. (1974). Bigotry on air and in life: The Archie Bunker case. *Public Telecommunication Review, 2*, 34–41.

Surlin, S. H. (1978). *Humor in television entertainment programming: Implications for social relations and social learning*. Paper presented to the Speech Communication Association, Minneapolis, MN.

Sussman, D. (2010, February 28). A question of what to ask. *New York Times*, WK5.

Swain, W. N. (2001). *If my commercial makes fun of my political opponent, do my race and my gender make a difference?* Paper presented at the annual meeting of the Southern States Communication Association, Lexington, KY.

Swanson, D. L. (1976). Information utility: An alternative perspective in political communication. *Central States Speech Journal, 27(2)*, 95–101.

Swanson, L. L., & Swanson, D. L. (1978). The agenda-setting function of the first Ford-Carter debate. *Communication Monographs, 45*, 347–353.

Swarns, R. L. (2009, February 8). 'Mom in Chief' touches on policy, and tongues wags. *New York Times*, p. A16.

Swartz, O. (2005). *In defense of partisan criticism: Communication studies, law, and social analysis*. New York: Peter Lang.

Sweetser-Trammell, K. D. (2007). Candidate campaign blogs: Directly reaching out to the youth vote. *American Behavioral Scientist, 50(9)*, 1255–1263.

Tannen, D. (2000, January 20). Bush's sweet talk. *New York Times*, p. A23.

Tate, E. D., & Surlin, S. H. (1976). Agreement with opinionated TV characters across cultures. *Journalism Quarterly, 53*, 199–203, 210.

Taylor, H. (2000). Does Internet research work? Comparing online survey results with telephone survey. *International Journal of Market Research, 42(1)*, 51–63.

Taylor, P. (1990, June 18–24). In politics, the time for women has arrived. *Washington Post National Weekly*, p. 13.

Taylor, P. (1990a). *See how they run: Electing the president in an age of mediaocracy*. New York: Knopf.

Taylor. S. B. (1990). *Fob: The incredible story of Fob James, Jr*. Mobile, AL: Greenberry.

Tedesco, J. C., McKinnon, L., & Kaid, L. L. (1996). Advertising watchdogs: A content analysis of print and broadcast adwatches from the 1992 presidential campaign. *Harvard International Journal of Press/Politics, 1*, 76–93.

Tedesco, J. C., Miller, J. L., & Spiker, J. A. (1999). Presidential campaigning on the information superhighway: An exploration of content and form. In L. L. Kaid & D. G. Bystrom (Eds.), *The electronic election: Perspectives on the 1996 campaign communication* (pp. 51–63). Mahwah, NJ: Erlbaum.

Teixeira, R. A. (1992). *The disappearing American voter.* Washington, DC: Brookings Institution.

Terhanian, G. (1999). *Understanding online research: Lessons from the Harris Poll Online.* Paper presented at the American Association for Public Opinion Research meeting. St. Petersburg, FL.

Thelan, D. (1996). *Becoming citizens in the age of television: How Americans challenged the media and seized the political initiative during the Iran–Contra debate.* Chicago: University of Chicago Press.

Thomas, R. J. (1999). *How to run for local office: A complete guide for winning a local election.* Westland, MI: R & T Enterprises.

Thurber, J. A., & Nelson, C. J. (Eds.). (2000). *Campaign warriors: Political consultants in elections.* Washington, DC: Brookings Institution.

Tomaszeski, M., Proffitt, J. M., & McClung, S. (2009). Exploring the political blogosphere: Perceptions of political bloggers about their sphere. *Atlantic Journal of Communication, 17(2),* 72–87.

Tomlinson, J. E. (2000). Campaigning in cyberspace: Lessons for political communication in the Net century. In D. Bystrom, D. B. Carlin, L. L. Kaid, M. Kern, & M. S. McKinney (Eds.), *Communicating politics: Engaging the public*

in campaign 2000 and beyond (pp. 333–346). Washington, DC: NCA Summer Conference Proceedings.

Tourangeau, R., Rips, L. J., & Rasinski, K. (2000). *The psychology of survey response.* New York: Cambridge University Press.

Trammell, K. D. (2006). Blog offensive: An exploratory analysis of attacks published on campaign blog posts from a political public relations perspective. *Public Relations Review, 32(4),* 402–406.

Traugott, M. W. (2005). The accuracy of the national preelection polls in the 2004 presidential election. *Public Opinion Quarterly, 69(5),* 642–654.

Trenaman, J., & McQuail, D. (1961). *Television and the political image: A study of the impact of television on the 1959 general election.* London: Methuen.

Trent, J. S. (1978). Presidential surfacing: The ritualistic and crucial first act. *Communication Monographs, 45,* 282.

Trent, J. S., & Friedenberg, R. V. (1995). *Political campaign communication: Principles and practices* (3rd ed.). New York: Praeger.

Trent, J. S., & Friedenberg, R. V. (2000). *Political campaign communication: Principles and practices* (4th ed.). Westport, CT: Praeger.

Trent, J. S., & Sabourin, T. (1993). Sex still counts: Women's use of televised advertising during the decade of the '80s. *Journal of Applied Communication Research, 21,* 21–40.

Tuchman, G. (1982). *Making news.* New York: Free Press.

Tueth, M. V. (2005). *Laughter in the living room: Television*

comedy and the American home audience. New York: Peter Lang.

Turner, K. J. (1977). Comic strips: A rhetorical perspective. *Central States Speech Journal, 28,* 24–35.

Turner, S., O'Connor, P., & Rademacher, E. (2009). Inform, influence, evaluate: The power of state public opinion polls. *Health Affairs, 28(1),* 273–276.

Turow, J. (1992). *Media systems in society: Understanding industries, strategies and power.* New York: Longman.

Turow, J. (1996). *Media today.* Boston: Houghton Mifflin.

Tyson, G. (1990). *An examination of early voting.* Fort Worth, TX: The Tyson Organization.

Tyson, G. S. (1999). GOTV: Get out the vote. In D. D. Perlmutter (Ed.), *The Manship school guide to political communication* (pp. 131–136). Baton Rouge: Louisiana State University Press.

Uslander, E. M., & Weber, R. E. (1979). *Reapportionment, gerrymandering and changes in the partisan balance of power in American states.* Paper presented at the annual meeting of the American Political Science Association. Chicago, IL.

Van Natta, Jr., D. (2000, February 15). Years ago, a Bush adviser helped draft a push poll against a Texas official. *New York Times,* p. A20.

Vancil, D. L., & Pendell, S. D. (1984). Winning presidential debates. *Western Journal of Speech Communication, 48,* 62–74.

Vidmar, N., & Rokeach, M. (1974). Archie Bunker's bigotry: A study in selective perception and exposure. *Journal of Communication, 24, 36–47.*

Viguerie, R. (1975). Direct mail: Campaigning's sleeping giant. In R. E. Hiebert, R. F. Jones, J. Lorenz, & E. A. Lotito (Eds.), *The political image merchants* (pp. 165–167). Washington, DC: Acropolis Books.

Villa, H. E., & Rodgers, R. P. (1999). *Rhetorical clusters of Nazi rhetoric during World War II.* Paper for the Eastern Communication Association. Charleston, WV.

von Drehle, D. (2000, June 25). Awkward oratory as a mark of sincerity. *Washington Post,* pp. A1, A7.

Walker, J. R. (1987). *Exposure to political information during statewide elections: A typology of eligible voters.* Paper presented at the International Communication Association Convention. Montreal, Canada.

Walker, J. R., & Bellamy, R. V. (1991). Gratifications of grazing: An exploratory study of remote control use. *Journalism Quarterly, 68(3),* 422–431.

Walker, J. R., & Bellamy, R. V. (1993). *The remote control in the new age of television.* Westport, CT: Praeger.

Wallsten, K. (2007). Political blogs: Transmission belts, soapboxes, mobilizers, or conversation starters? *Journal of Information Technology & Politics, 4(3),* 19–40.

Wanta, W., & Wu, Y. (1992). Interpersonal communication and the agenda-setting process. *Journalism Quarterly, 69(4),* 847–855.

Ware, B. L., & Linkugel, W. A. (1973). They spoke in defense of themselves. On the generic criticism of apologia. *Quarterly Journal of Speech, 59,* 273–283.

Warner, B. R. (2010). Segmenting the electorate: The effects of exposure to political extremism online. *Communication Studies, 61(4),* 430–444.

Warnick, B. (2007). *Rhetoric online: Persuasion and politics on the World Wide Web.* New York: Peter Lang.

Wayne, L. (2008, October 21). A diminishing till. *New York Times,* p. A21.

Weaver, D. (1980). Audience need for orientation and media effects. *Communication Research, 7,* 361–380.

Weaver, D. H., & Wilhoit, G. C. (1980). News media coverage of U.S. senators in four Congresses, 1953–1974. *Journalism Monographs, 67(1),* 1–34.

Weaver, D. H., Zhu, J., & Willnat, L. (1992). The bridging function of interpersonal communication in agenda setting. *Journalism Quarterly, 69(4),* 856–867.

Webster, J. G. (1998). The audience. *Journal of Broadcasting & Electronic Media, 42(2),* 190–207.

Webster, J. G., & Lichty, L. W. (1991). *Ratings analysis: Theory and practice.* Hillsdale, NJ: Erlbaum.

Webster, J. G., & Wakshlag, J. J. (1982). The impact of group viewing on patterns of television program choice. *Journal of Broadcasting, 26,* 445–455.

Weiss, D. (Ed.). (2010). *What Democrats talk about when they talk about God: Religious communication in Democratic Party politics.* Lanham, MD: Lexington Books.

Wells, S., & Dudash, E. (2007). Wha'd'ya know? *The American Behavioral Scientist, 50(9),* 1280–1290.

Werrett, W. C. (1933). *Motion pictures and youth: A summary.* New York: Macmillan.

Wertheimer, M. M. (2000). *Barbara Bush's refashioning of the White House.* Paper presented at the annual meeting of the Eastern Communication Association. Pittsburgh, PA.

West, D. M. (1993). *Air wars: Television advertising in election campaigns, 1952–1992.* Washington, DC: Congressional Quarterly Press.

Westen, D. (2007). *The political brain: The role of emotion in deciding the fate of the nation.* New York: PublicAffairs.

Wheeler, M. E., & Reed, S. K. (1975). Response to before and after Watergate caricatures. *Journalism Quarterly, 52,* 134–136.

Wheeless, L. R., & Schrodt, P. (2001). An examination of cognitive foundations of informational reception apprehension: Political identification, religious affiliation, and family environment. *Communication Research Reports, 18(1),* 1–10.

Whillock, R. K. (1997). Cyberpolitics. *American Behavioral Scientist, 40(8),* 1208–1225.

Whillock, R. K. (2001). *Federal regulatory oversight in Campaign 2000.* Paper presented at the annual meeting of the Southern States Communication Association. Lexington, KY.

White, B. (2000, June 25). Online innovators showing their stuff in governor's races. *Washington Post,* p. A12.

White, T. H. (1969). *The making of the president 1968.* New York: Atheneum Publishers.

Williamson, J. (1984). *Decoding advertisements: Ideology and meaning in advertising.* New York: Marion Boyars.

Wilson, E. C., & Howard, D. M. (1978). Public perception of media accuracy. *Journalism Quarterly, 55,* 73–76.

Wimmer, R. D., & Dominick, J. R. (1994). *Mass media research.* Belmont, CA: Wadsworth.

Winter, B. (1989). The press & the '88 presidential campaign. *Newspaper Research Journal, 10(3),* 1–10.

Witcover, J. (1999). *No way to pick a president: How money & hired guns have debased American elections.* New York: Farrar, Straus & Giroux.

Wolfe, A. (1998). *One nation, after all: What middle-class Americans really think about.* New York: Penguin Books.

Woodward, G. C. (1997). *Perspectives on American political media.* Boston: Allyn & Bacon.

Worland, G. (1998). Scandals throughout presidential history. *Washington Post,* p. 4A.

Wyatt, E. (2011, March 27). The arsenal of a lobbyist: Hardball and cupcakes. *New York Times,* pp. BU1, BU8.

Wyatt, O., Kim, J., & Katz, E. (2000). How feeling free to talk affects ordinary political conversation, purposeful argumentation, and civic participation. *Journalism and Mass Communication Quarterly, 77,* 99–114.

Xigen, L. (2008). Third-person effect, optimistic bias, and sufficiency resource in Internet use. *Journal of Communication, 58(3),* 568–587.

Yanovitzky, I., & Bennett, C. (1999). Media attention, institutional response, and health behavior change. *Communication Research, 26(4),* 429–453.

Yardley, J. (1999, August 29). Candidates focus on spin, media focus on sensation. *Birmingham News,* pp. 1C, 6C.

Yardley, J. (2000, February 14). Calls to voters at center stage of G. O. P. race. *New York Times,* pp. A1, A16.

Yu, J., & Cooper, H. (1983). A quantitative review of research design effects on response rates to questionnaires. *Journal of Marketing Research, 20,* 36–44.

Zaller, J. (1990). Political awareness, elite opinion leadership, and the mass survey response. *Social Cognition, 8,* 125–153.

Zaller, J. (1992). *The nature and origin of mass opinion.* Cambridge: Cambridge University Press.

Zaller, J. (1996). The myth of massive media impact revived: New support for a discredited idea. In D. C. Mutz, P. M. Sniderman & R. A. Brody (Eds.), *Political persuasion and attitude change* (pp. 17–78). Ann Arbor: University of Michigan Press.

Zaller, J., & Feldman, S. (1992). A simple theory of the survey response: Answering questions versus revealing preferences. *American Journal of Political Science, 36(3),* 579–616.

Zeleny, J. (2008, November 27). Wordsmith in residence. *New York Times,* p. A23.

Zeleny, J. (2008a, April 13). Obama works to limit fallout over remark on 'bitter' working class. *New York Times,* p. 20A.

Zeleny, J. (2008b, October 12). Obama aims for electoral edge, block by block. *New York Times,* pp. A1, A22.

Zeleny, J. (2010, January 21). Political fallout from the Supreme Court ruling. *New York Times,* www.nytimes.com

Zhang, Y., & Buda, R. (1999). Moderating effects of need for cognition on responses to positively versus negatively framed advertising messages. *Journal of Advertising, 28(2),* 1–15.

Zhu, J. (1992). Issue competition and attention distraction: A zero-sum theory of agenda setting. *Journalism Quarterly, 69(4),* 825–836.

INDEX